CRAWFORD'S
ENCYCLOPEDIA OF
COMIC BOOKS

CRAWFORD'S ENCYCLOPEDIA OF COMIC BOOKS

by

HUBERT H. CRAWFORD

JONATHAN DAVID PUBLISHER'S, INC.
MIDDLE VILLAGE, NY 11379

CRAWFORD'S ENCYCLOPEDIA OF COMIC BOOKS

©Copyright 1978

by

Comicade Enterprises

JONATHAN DAVID PUBLISHERS, Inc.
68-22 ELIOT AVENUE
MIDDLE VILLAGE, NEW YORK 11379

Library of Congress Cataloging in Publication Data
Crawford, Hubert H
    Crawford's Encyclopedia of comic books.

    Includes bibliographical references and indexes.
    1. Comic books, strips, etc.—United States—Dictionaries. I. Title. II. Title: Encyclopedia of comic books.
PN6725.C7   741.5'0973   77-24738
ISBN 0-8246-0221-8

Printed in the United States of America

Table of Contents

DEDICATED
TO MY MOTHER
MRS. VERA J.C. PRYOR

Introduction

*The truth is, that delinquency is a
product of the real environment in
which a child lives—and not the
fiction he reads!*

Publisher William M. Gaines made the above statement over twenty years ago during a Senate subcommittee hearing investigating charges that the crime and violence portrayed in comic book literature were the principle causes of juvenile deliquency. But because of loud critical outcries from opponents of comic books, Gaines was ignored. Within six months congressional legislation authorized the creation of the Comics Code Authority—an independent body with censorship powers that soon ripped the comic book industry apart and forced Gaines and many other publishers to suspend their magazines. Supposedly this action was intended to eliminate juvenile delinquency. But for some reason, the problem did not disappear in 1955, nor in the 1960s, nor in the 1970s. Evidently, Gaines' summation seemed correct.

What did disappear, however, was the original art form of the comic book—something that had thrilled millions of youngsters of previous generations. Except for comic books that featured family humor and animal fantasy, the entire genre was discarded as "trash." While there may have been some elements within the contents of certain comic books that justified criticism, the other side of the coin that revealed the positive aspects of this highly creative art form was completely overlooked.

No other media captured and held the juvenile audience as much as the early comics did. Unfortunately, their fascinating history prior to 1955 becomes more obscure with each passing year. Generally speaking, there are two kinds of "comics": the so-called comic book "trash" that was published in magazine form for juvenile consumption and entertainment, and the socially constructive "comics" that appeared as newspaper strips and were published for adult entertainment. This encyclopedia emphasizes the *first* category, and attempts to cover the rise and fall of the comic book industry from the 1930s through the 1950s and explore the relationship of comic books to other forms of American entertainment, including the former movie serials, animated cartoons, radio drama and television, and fiction in the once-popular pulp magazines. The second category, the newspaper comic strip, which has a separate history of its own, is also included here but is generally defined and described as it relates to the history of the comic book.

The information has been compiled from an extensive collection of comic books dating back to the 1930s, and numerous articles about comics that have appeared in a wide assortment of newspapers, magazines and books between 1925 and 1975. Additional research has included personal interviews with parties engaged in different aspects of the industry—publishers, artists and writers, newsstand dealers, bookshop proprietors, wholesale magazine distributors, printers, and newspaper editors of comic strip sections. Not surprisingly, some points of contradiction arose in reconstructing a historical profile of the earlier years.

There is a problem for example in accurately pinpointing the multitude of "names" responsible for the growth of comics. First and foremost there are the names of the fictional stars of the various features, many of which reflected the most imaginative creations applied to any literary fiction. Throughout the years, many have become established as famous trademarks, and are as well known as any other national product. But even here, there have been instances where the same name or very similar names were used for entirely different characters.

Of course these fictional characters were created and named by real people, and this leads to a second area in which there is some confusion. The artists and writers sometimes signed their real names, sometimes their pen names, and sometimes the names of their assistants, or the name of the deceased originator of the feature. Moreover, when comic book features were adapted to movies, television, and radio, characters were portrayed by real people—professional actors who either used their real names or their stage names.

For example, the name Superman provides an almost endless list of names of people who were in some way responsible for the character's popularity. The list would include Jerry Siegel and Joe Shuster, the original creators of "Superman;" Wayne Boring, the second major artist to continue "Superman" during the 1950s; Kirk Alyn, the movie star who portrayed Superman on the screen for two exciting movie serials in the 1940s; George Reeves, who portrayed Superman in the original television series; Bud Collier, the voice of Superman in the original radio series during the 1940s; and Sol Cohen, the promotion manager for D-C Comics who was responsible for getting the character started as a comic book on the newsstands across the country. Of course this list does not include the publishers, editors, directors and others who played major roles behind the scenes in making Superman the phenomenal success he has been over the last four decades.

To simplify matters (hopefully!), this book has been divided into thirteen major sections, each covering the history and output of a major comic book publisher, plus a concluding chapter summarizing the highlights of other publishers who also contributed to the growth of the industry. For the most part, the only names mentioned are those connected with leading and secondary features, and the names of the original creators of these features (most of whom are, at the time of this writing, either retired or deceased). Each section will include an alphabetical listing of the publisher's full line of titles. For cross reference, an index at the end of the book provides an alphabetical listing of the major features covered within the text and the publishers, artists and writers who were connected with their publication.

Basically, it can be said that the comic book gradually evolved as a magazine of pictorial fantasy that combined three essential creative elements.

1. The Cover

The cover served two purposes: first, as a binder for holding the contents together as a titled magazine; secondly, as a sales aid for promoting its purchase when displayed on the newsstand. As a sales aid, comic book cover art quickly evolved into a highly specialized form of magazine illustration. Comic books not only competed against each other for newsstand sales but also competed with other types of magazines, including popular periodicals such as *Life* and *Saturday Evening Post*, plus many dozens of pulp fiction titles, all of which had to rely on cover appeal to attract the public. During the magazine boom of 1938 to 1942, some of the better comic book covers attracted as much buying response as the famous *Saturday Evening Post* covers by Norman Rockwell.

Samples of early comic book cover art as produced by some of the leading illustrators who specialized in this craft and made it into an almost unique art form are included here, many of which are shown in full color.

2. The Story Concept

Unlike paperback publications that utilized text with an occasional photograph or spot illustration to tell its story, the comic book was made up entirely of original hand-drawn art to convey its message. Creating a story for the comic book, whether humorous or adventure, was another area that evolved into a skill of highly specialized creativity.

While it may be true that many good stories often lend themselves to adaptation from one media to another, there are certain types of stories that could only have been told in comic book form. For example, the classic comic book story that depicted the origin of the Spectre (*More Fun Comics No. 52*, February 1940) was so utterly fantastic that it could never be adapted to the screen, or for that matter radio or television. And it would have made rather dull reading if put into words. Thus the origin of the Spectre stands as an example of extraordinary imagination comparable to any other creative concept in fiction literature.

The same can be said for other story concepts that fitted the comic book and nothing else, such as the unforgettable battle between the Human Torch and Sub-Mariner, the superhero versus the anti-super-hero, the clash between fire and water, that held the nation's youth spellbound in 1941. Several of these outstanding creations will be described, often with supporting illustrations reproduced from the original publications in which they appeared.

3. *The Graphic Execution of the Story Concept*

To tell a compelling story by visual means is practiced every day by the movie and television industries. But unlike watching a movie story where real people act out scenes from beginning to end, the reader of the comic book must rely entirely on the artist to serve as producer, cameraman, special effects coordinator, as well as every character in every scene from first to last. The artist accomplishes this monumental task by exercising his imagination and technical skill, knowing that his creative efforts could make or break the story's effectiveness.

During the 1940s, many different approaches to and styles of comic book illustration were introduced and experimented with before it evolved into the polished art form that is familiar to us today. In the early days when art styles leaned heavily toward realism, many comic book stories were unbelievably effective in conveying a three-dimensional illusion of real life. The manner in which the lines and color were executed allowed the reader to grasp at a glance the rage, fear, courage, or sheer ruthlessness of the characters in the story.

The three basic elements of the comic book actually represented three separate skills, and they worked for, as well as against, each other in several ways. Whereas a powerful story concept always shone through a weak graphic execution of the story, a powerful graphic execution of the story seldom helped when the basic concept was a weak one. Similarly, crude cover art never detracted from a comic book whose solid reputation was built on its exceptional story contents. On the other hand, exceptionally executed cover art could never improve a comic book with weak or flat story content.

Owing to the different editorial philosophies that governed the individual publishers, different comic books stressed various levels of importance of the three elements. Usually a publisher would emphasize one element as the one most responsible for sales. But editorial opinion varied widely as to which element was the most important. As a result, the total spectrum of comic books published from the 1930s to the 1950s varies widely in this respect. Whether the three elements taken collectively or separately can, in retrospect, be graded on a scale of exceptional to poor, in practice the pragmatic bottom line that showed whether the magazine was profitable or not was always the final word.

The financial details of the industry during its growth period is a colossal subject of its own, and has been omitted here, except for the mention of one comment that appeared in the *Wall Street Journal* in 1942. The article stated in part: "Popular comic characters as Mickey Mouse, Buck Rogers, and Superman, through licenses for reprints, leasing of rights for radio drama and movies, and for the manufacturing use on numerous toy products, have generated more than $8,000,000,000 of financial activity throughout the U.S. economy during the past three years."

Of course very few creations of the comics can claim such commercial success. In fact most comic books generated only marginal profits and many were financial failures and quickly phased out of publication. These are the comics that remain unknown today and the ones that are brought back and described here, for indeed they formed the foundation of the comic book industry.

In order to conserve space and stress the unknown aspects while covering the entire industry at the same time, many topics, where they are described in detail in other readily available publications, have been condensed to a few paragraphs. References are given to these publications, as well as publications covering more specialized aspects of the comic book industry, such as *Steranko's History of Comics*, for those interested in artists' pay scales and other industry practices, and *Overstreet's Comic Book Price Guide*, for readers interested in the current market values of the few existing copies of comic books that are shown and described throughout this book.

Meanwhile, as yesterday's ten-cent comic book "trash" continued to skyrocket in monetary value as rare literary antiques, the accusing finger of society, still searching for the cause of juvenile delinqency, is now pointing towards a new whipping boy known as "television violence." William Gaines' statement which applied to comic books that have long ceased publication might well apply to other art forms of today that employ violence as a means of reaching and holding an audience, either for reasons of monetary profit, or as an honest expression of artistic integrity, or both. Only time will tell how this matter will finally be resolved.

Acknowledgments

This volume is produced under cooperative arrangement with D-C Comics, Inc., King Features Syndicate, Inc., Fawcett Publications, Inc., Dell Publishing Company, Inc., Walt Disney Productions, E-C Publications, Inc., Edgar Rice Burroughs, Inc., Eastern Color Printing Company, Marvel Comics Group, Ultimate Publishing Company, Inc., and the Comicade Enterprises Library of Rare Books with layout and photography by Comicade Enterprises. Reproduction of contents in any manner is prohibited without written permission from Jonathan David Publishers, Inc.

Credits under pictures Section 2 and Section 4 that are followed by an asterisk (*) indicate that they are being used with permission from D-C Comics, Inc.

D-C COMICS/
NATIONAL PERIODICAL

National Periodical, the publisher of Superman and the complete line of the famous "D-C" Comics, began in 1935 with one title and, within a few short years, introduced the literary concept of superhero fantasy. Whereas up to that time the comic book had generally borrowed its humor from the newspaper funnies and its adventure from the pulp magazines, it was superhero fantasy that established the comic book as a distinct form of literature of its own. And it was the popularity of superhero fantasy that ignited the comic book boom of the early 1940s, attracting scores of other publishers into the field.

National Periodical, or D-C Comics as it was known during the 1940s, refined the comic book by introducing many innovations in character concepts. They produced hundreds of titles in a large variety of categories; some were superhero, others were westerns, science fiction, animal fantasy, romance, nonfiction, screen personality adaptions, humor, religion, war stories, and even reprints of newspaper strips.

During the mid-1950s when the comic book industry toppled, D-C was one of the few publishers to survive even though its long list of titles had dwindled to a mere dozen or so. However, when the ailing D-C Comics became National Periodical Publications, a division of Warner Communications, it made a strong comeback and soon resumed its position as the giant of the industry. Their features now appear regularly on television and as numerous toy products, as well as headlining many comic books. Quite a few of the D-C features that are popular today are actually revivals of features from the past.

Here is a brief review of a few of the original D-C classics from those earlier years.

Action Comics No. 1 (June 1938)
©1938, renewed 1965, DC Comics, Inc.

In June 1938, D-C released the first issue of *Action Comics,* the magazine that introduced Jerry Siegel and Joe Shuster's creation, Superman—and the era of superhero fantasy began! That issue gave a brief one-page synopsis of Superman's background and explained how he, as a newborn infant, had been dispatched to Earth in a small projectile from the doomed planet Krypton.

While the first monthly issues of *Action Comics* carried only one Superman adventure along with several other features, in the following year, D-C, at the suggestion of its promotion manager, Sol Cohen, published a full-length edition of *Superman Comics* which contained reprints of the first four Superman adventures from *Action Comics.* The issue also featured a two-page explanation of Superman's origin plus the first Superman short story in text, an innovation that led to George Lowther's hardcover book adaptation of Superman, published by Random House in 1942.

Shortly afterwards *Superman Comics* went from a quarterly to a bi-monthly publication and has remained a leading title ever since. In 1940, Superman appeared in animated cartoons that were produced by the Max Fleischer Studios. Later he was adapted to radio drama. In 1948, Columbia Pictures introduced the first movie serial adventure of Superman and followed with a second one in 1950. Superman has since become a well-known television series.

More importantly, Superman has since become part of American folklore and, not so incidentally, the American language. Prior to 1938, the word "super" was seldom used to describe an object or person that was well above average; the common equivalent was "superb" or "superior." But, thanks to Superman, the language has now changed. The sports world is populated with "super stars." Stores boast of "super values." A product named Super Suds claimed that it could get clothes cleaner than any other detergent.

And it all stemmed from the origin of Superman that was first explored in George Lowther's hardcover book. Here is the only time we find a detailed account of Superman's home planet, Krypton, and the incredible events leading up to the destruction of that world. It began in the Great Hall of Krypton's Temple of Wisdom where the governing council of One Hundred impatiently awaited the arrival of their chief scientist, Jor-El (Superman's father), to make his report on the strange atmospheric disturbances that were beginning to have dire effects on the planet's environment. Comets of great magnitude whirled dangerously close to Krypton, causing monstrous tidal waves and unbearable heat.

Jor-El arrived. He lifted his drawn, haggard face that reflected days and nights without sleep and solemnly gazed at his fellow council members as he took the floor. "Gentlemen," he said wearily, while unfolding the diagrams and charts in his hand, "Krypton is doomed."

The following scene from Lowther's book depicts the violent eruption of Krypton as Jor-El and his wife sadly bid farewell to their infant son and place him in the experimental spaceship . . .

Adventures of Superman (Random House, 1942)
©1942, renewed 1969, DC Comics, Inc.

The first issue of Superman Comics continued the scene . . .

SUPERMAN by JEROME SIEGEL and JOE SHUSTER

JUST BEFORE THE DOOMED PLANET, KRYPTON, EXPLODED TO FRAGMENTS, A SCIENTIST PLACED HIS INFANT SON WITHIN AN EXPERIMENTAL ROCKET-SHIP, LAUNCHING IT TOWARD EARTH!

WHEN THE VESSEL REACHED OUR PLANET, THE CHILD WAS FOUND BY AN ELDERLY COUPLE, THE KENTS.

LOOK, MARY! --IT'S A CHILD!

THE POOR THING! -- IT'S BEEN ABANDONED!

THE INFANT WAS TURNED OVER TO AN ORPHAN ASYLUM, WHERE IT ASTOUNDED THE ATTENDANTS WITH ITS FEATS OF STRENGTH.

WE -- WE COULDN'T GET THAT SWEET CHILD OUT OF OUR MIND.

WE'VE COME TO ADOPT HIM IF YOU'LL PERMIT US.

I BELIEVE IT CAN BE ARRANGED. (--WHEW! THANK GOODNESS THEY'RE TAKING HIM AWAY BEFORE HE WRECKS THE ASYLUM!)

THE LOVE AND GUIDANCE OF HIS KINDLY FOSTER-PARENTS WAS TO BECOME AN IMPORTANT FACTOR IN THE SHAPING OF THE BOY'S FUTURE.

NOW LISTEN TO ME, CLARK! THIS GREAT STRENGTH OF YOURS --YOU'VE GOT TO HIDE IT FROM PEOPLE OR THEY'LL BE SCARED OF YOU!

BUT WHEN THE PROPER TIME COMES, YOU MUST USE IT TO ASSIST HUMANITY.

As the lad grew older, he learned to his delight that he could hurdle skyscrapers . . .

. . . leap an eighth of a mile . . .

. . . raise tremendous weights . . .

. . . run faster than a streamline train --

. . . and nothing less than a bursting shell could penetrate his skin!

What th' — ? This is the sixth hypodermic needle I've broken on your skin!

Try again, Doc!

The passing away of his foster-parents greatly grieved Clark Kent. But it strengthened a determination that had been growing in his mind.

Clark decided he must turn his titanic strength into channels that would benefit mankind

and so was created--

SUPERMAN

Champion of the oppressed, the physical marvel who had sworn to devote his existence to helping those in need!

Superman No. 1 (1939)
©1939, renewed 1966, DC Comics, Inc.

Superman No. 2 (Summer 1939)
©1939, renewed 1966, DC Comics, Inc.

Superman No. 57 (March-April 1949)
©1949 National Comics Publications, Inc.

Action Comics No. 33 (Feb. 1940)—8
©1945, renewed 1972, DC Comics, Inc.

From the beginning, *Action Comics* was a goose that laid many golden eggs. In addition to Superman there was Mort Weisinger's Vigilante, the Eastern cowboy who sported a motorcycle in place of a horse. The Vigilante made his first appearance in *Action Comics No. 42* (November 1941) as a rodeo showman from the West who turned masked crimefighter in the East in order to carry on the tradition of his father, a sheriff who was killed in the line of duty. Vigilante soon became one of D-C's star attractions and he headlined their new entry, *Leading Comics*, which began as a quarterly publication in January 1942.

In 1946, Columbia Pictures produced the exciting Vigilante movie serial, with veteran movie star Ralph Byrd as the gun-slinging, lariat-twirling cowboy-crimefighter. In the picture, Vigilante thwarts a diabolical scheme to seize the world's richest treasure, a set of giant pearls known as "the tears of blood" that transmitted an evil curse to anyone who possessed them. At the same time, D-C published a special souvenir edition of *Action Comics* featuring Vigilante on the cover for the first time. This was the only issue in which Vigilante took over the lead from Superman.

Action Comics, Special Edition (1945)
©1945, renewed 1968, DC Comics, Inc.

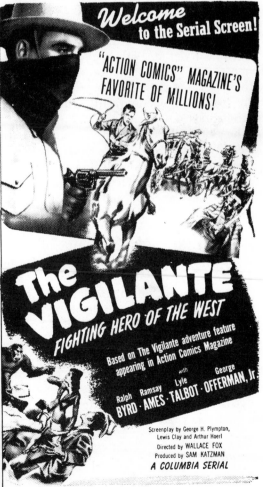

©1946 Columbia Pictures

©1946 Columbia Pictures and DC Comics, Inc.

Similarly, Congo Bill, created by Whitney Ellsworth, first appeared as a minor feature in D-C's *More Fun Comics* for eleven issues, then was dropped. But one month later, *Action Comics No. 37* (May 1940) introduced a new series of Congo Bill in which he suddenly became a star and important enough for Columbia Pictures to adapt to the screen. The Congo Bill movie serial turned out to be one of the better ones of the 1940s.

In the movie serial, the story centered around the Culver Circus Trust Fund that was held in reserve for any surviving heir of Les Culver, founder of the circus, who had mysteriously disappeared in Africa twenty years before while hunting wild game. According to the terms of the trust, the McGraw brothers, who were currently managing the circus, were to inherit the estate if it wasn't claimed by a legitimate heir by the following year. However, the brothers learned of a rumored existence of a white queen who lived somewhere in Icala, Africa. They suspected she was Culver's long lost daughter and the rightful heir to the circus estate. They planned an expedition to Africa to locate her, but during the trip, the older McGraw, Bernie, turned villain and sought to eliminate his younger brother, Tom, by casting him into a cage with a vicious gorilla.

Congo Bill arrived on the scene and tried to save the mangled victim. With his last words, the dying Tom McGraw asked Bill to locate Culver's daughter so that she could claim the estate and prevent Bernie from getting it. Consequently, Bernie McGraw's henchmen set out to stop Congo Bill.

The plot thickened as Bill's search led to the forbidden Valley of Namu where the tribal witch doctor was engaged in gold smuggling. Bernie McGraw teamed up with the witch doctor and together they planned to kill Congo Bill and the white queen whom the witch doctor already hated. However, McGraw had made secret arrangements with other natives to double-cross the witch doctor after the two were disposed of, kill him, and seize the gold for himself.

Meanwhile, Congo Bill had formed an allegiance with a native of the witch doctor's tribe who turned out to be a disguised secret agent of British Intelligence tracking down gold smugglers. In the action-packed events that followed, the heroes were attacked by wild animals, trapped in quicksand, hurled off steep mountains, and pursued by headhunters before they finally defeated their foes. In the end, Congo Bill took Culver's daughter back to America to claim her inheritance and manage the circus.

After the movie serial, Congo Bill was put into his own full-length comic book which ran for seven issues during the mid-1950s.

Action Comics No. 33 (February 1941) marked the debut and origin of Mr. America as comicdom's first patriotic superhero. Created by artist Bernard Bailey who emerged as one of the topflight illustrators on the D-C art staff, Mr. America was a prime example of the kind of feature that permeated the comic book industry in the early years of the war.

Mr. America had actually been introduced in 1938 in *Action Comics No. 1* as a plain, ordinary Midwestern cowboy named Tex Thomson. In the issues that followed, however, Tex underwent a gradual change; he discarded his high hat and boots and became a soldier of fortune seeking adventure around the world.

Tex Thomson's role as Mr. America began with an assignment from the War Relief Commissioner to insure the safe delivery of a cargo shipment of food and critical supplies to a strife-torn country in Europe that had fallen to Nazi invaders. However, a spy ring of enemy agents operating in America sabotaged the ocean liner and it exploded at sea. All aboard were lost—except for Tex Thomson who miraculously survived and was rescued by a Portugese fishing boat.

After adopting a new identity, Tex returned to America and, following up a single clue, tracked down the spy ring responsible for the loss of the ship and destroyed them—as Mr. America! Tex let the world believe he had been lost at sea and continued in his new role as the masked champion of democracy, cracking the whip on enemy spy organizations.

Mr. America ©1940 DC Comics, Inc.

Action Comics No. 23 introduced the swashbuckling adventures of Jon Valor, the Black Pirate, created by Sheldon Moldoff. This short-lived series ran for only nineteen issues and was never regarded as a major feature but it was superbly illustrated. The following scenes from the "Black Pirate" adventure in *Action Comics No. 30* were typical of Moldoff's art. Any re-semblance between Jon Valor, the Black Pirate, and movie star Errol Flynn in his famous swashbuckling role as "Captain Blood" was, in theory at least, purely coincidental.

Here, the sinister Captain Treble's men have captured Jon and threaten to destroy his men if he doesn't surrender.

Black Pirate ©1940 DC Comics, Inc.

Detective Comics No. 27 (May 1939)
©1939, renewed 1966, DC Comics, Inc.

March 1937 marked the entry of D-C's classic title, *Detective Comics*. This was the first comic book to feature all original adventure stories whose heroes were crime sleuths patterned after similar characters in the earlier detective pulp magazines. Concurrently, the concept of the "masked crusader of justice" was rapidly gaining popularity as a literary concept, adding an exciting aura of mystery to adventure heroism. Radio drama had introduced the Lone Ranger, the newspapers were featuring the Phantom, Hollywood had just released its smash hit, *Legend of Zorro*, and the pulps had introduced an avenging masked crime sleuth known as the Black Bat.

Then came *Detective Comics No. 27*, and the first appearance of Batman!

Created by artist Bob Kane, Batman added a novel refinement to the masked crusader concept—a costume with an integrated motif. Previously, there had been no flying crimefighters. But Batman was a skilled trapeze artist and circus acrobat. When he swung down on his linen cord from high rooftops to strike against gangsters, like a bat in the night swooping down on its unsuspecting prey, he represented the closest thing to a man actually flying through the air. And his arched cape blowing behind him gave the visual illusion of the flapping wings of a bat. As the series progressed, the bat motif was expanded to include a batplane, a batmobile, and eventually the underground bat cave that housed a modern laboratory for scientific crime detection.

Then in *Detective Comics No. 38*, Batman adopted young acrobat Dick Grayson who donned a mask and costume to become junior sidekick Robin, the Boy Wonder. More than just a junior sidekick, Robin was an extension of the original motif in that his name and costume represented another bird, the robin redbreast.

The faunal theme also encompassed various villains—the Penguin, another bird, and the Catwoman, another creature of the night. However, the dynamic duo's slam-bang adventures also pitted them against arch-foes, such as the Joker, who had no connection with the motif.

As other costumed characters began to appear undertaking similar feats of derring-do, Batman began to acquire a highly individual tone in which crimefighting was often reduced to a game of sport. The good guys won and the bad guys lost, but no one received serious injury.

Although Bob Kane's art was somewhat crude in the beginning, his style had sharply improved by the time Batman headlined his own quarterly magazine in Spring, 1940. In this issue, the origin of Batman was revealed for the first time—and it is reprinted here.

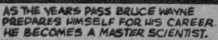

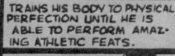

Origin of Batman (1940)
©1940, renewed 1967, DC Comics, Inc.

Batman No. 1 (Spring 1940)
©1940, renewed 1968, DC Comics, Inc.

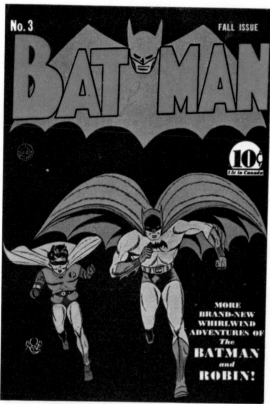

Batman No. 3 (Fall 1940)
©1940, renewed 1968, DC Comics, Inc.

Batman No. 4 (Winter 1940/1941)
©1941, renewed 1968, DC Comics, Inc.

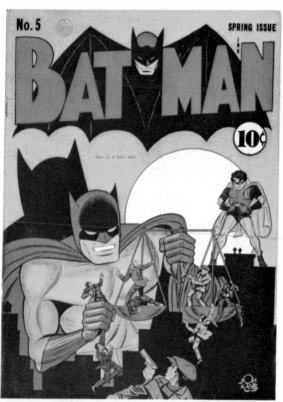

Batman No. 5 (Spring 1941)
©1941, renewed 1968, DC Comics, Inc.

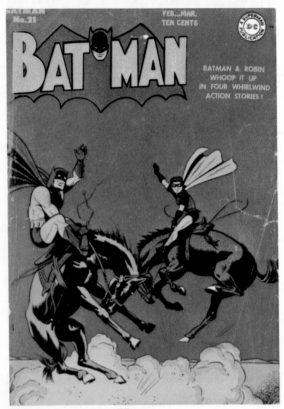

Batman No. 21 (February-March 1944)
©1944, renewed 1971, DC Comics, Inc.

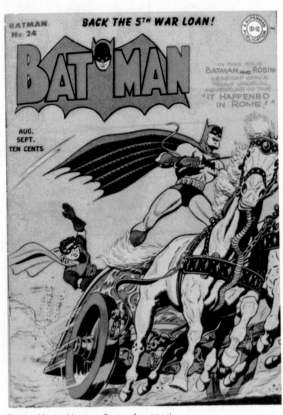

Batman No. 24 (August-September 1944)
©1944, renewed 1971, DC Comics, Inc.

Batman No. 41 (June-July 1947)
©1948 National Comics Publications, Inc.,
renewed 1974, DC Comics, Inc.

Batman No. 47 (June-July 1948)
©1948 National Comics Publications, Inc.
renewed 1975, DC Comics, Inc.

Although Batman started out fighting crime in the streets of Gotham City, he soon emerged as the first truly universal character in comics; he went everywhere and did almost everything as shown in the following scenes from a few of the early adventures.

BATMAN SHOOTS IT OUT IN A BLAZING GUN BATTLE (WINTER 1941).

HE JOURNEYS INTO THE PAST TO ANCIENT ROME AND FIGHTS IN THE GLADIATOR ARENA (AUGUST 1944).

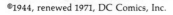

16

BATMAN BECOMES A SHERIFF IN THE WILD WEST (APRIL 1942).

HE SHRINKS INTO A MICROSCOPIC UNIVERSE (SPRING 1941) . . .

. . . VISITS THE ISLE THAT TIME FORGOT (APRIL 1942) . . .

HE BATTLES THE JOKER AND LOSES (SUMMER 1941).

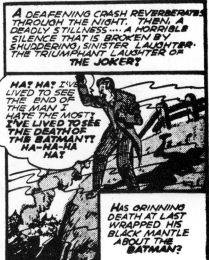

... BATTLES THE JOKER AND WINS (WINTER 1941)...

18

BUT THE DYNAMIC DUO CAN, IN TURN, CONFUSE
THE BAD GUYS—ESPECIALLY WHEN OTHERS ARE
WEARING THEIR COSTUMES (JUNE 1945).

. . . AND TACKLES THE PENGUIN—OR TRIES TO
(AUGUST 1946).

IN THE 21ST CENTURY, BATMAN LEADS EARTH'S LAST OUTPOST TO VICTORY IN THE INTERPLANETARY WAR AGAINST SATURN (DECEMBER 1944).

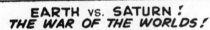

EARTH VS. SATURN! *THE WAR OF THE WORLDS!*

BELIEVE IT OR NOT!

Batman Comics No. 5 **(Spring 1941) Featured the only story in which Batman lost his temper and set out to avenge the murder of Robin! This is what happened...**

HERE IS A PARTIAL RECOUNT OF BATMAN'S
BLOODIEST BATTLE.

BATMAN TRACKS THE CATWOMAN AND FINDS ROMANCE (APRIL 1942) . . .

. . . AND SO DOES ROBIN (JUNE 1945).

HIS IDENTITY WAS EXPOSED IN AUGUST 1948.

©1948, National Comics Publications, Inc.
renewed 1975, DC Comics, Inc.

THIS WAS BATMAN'S MOST TENDER MOMENT (SPRING 1941) . . .

©1941, renewed 1968, DC Comics, Inc.

. . . AND HIS MOST CONTROVERSIAL (FEBRUARY 1944).

©1943, renewed 1970, DC Comics, Inc.

In 1943, Columbia Pictures introduced the action-packed Batman movie serial. Here the Dynamic Duo battled the evil genius Dr. Daka who, as an agent of the Axis powers, had developed a method of transforming people into mindless zombies as part of his plan for conquering America. The accompanying photograph depicts the scene in which Dr. Daka's goons overwhelm Batman during a fierce battle shortly after he had crashed through the skylight rooftop of their hideout. The thugs locked him in their operating chair as Dr. Daka prepared to turn him into a zombie. But in the next chapter, Robin rushed in to the rescue. Needless to say, after a series of cliff-hanging episodes, Batman ultimately smashed the evil plot and saved the country.

Six years later in 1949, Columbia Pictures introduced a second Batman movie serial, with Robert Lowery in the lead role. Here, the Dynamic Duo battled a new arch-foe, the Wizard. This screen adaptation was quite different from the first one that reflected the original concept of Batman's character. By 1949, Batman had become a scientific sleuth who relied more on his laboratory analysis and technical gadgets like his batplane, and less on slam-bang slugfests.

©1944, Columbia Pictures

Life (March 11, 1966) ©1966 *Time*, Inc.

The March 11, 1966 issue of *Life* marked the first time a comic book character appeared on its cover—and the first time a leading international publication of this kind carried a feature article about a comic book character. In this issue, *Life* explored the phenomenal success of the Batman television series that had made its debut on the home screen on January 12, 1966.

At that time, Batman, for the most part, had become almost forgotten. His decline had begun in 1963 when *Batman Comics* was temporarily discontinued. *Detective Comics* had been reduced to just a few issues per year. The comic book industry itself had shrunk to a half-dozen publishers who were concentrating on animal fantasy and family humor titles.

Similarly, the motion picture industry was in a period of crisis. The only studios still in operation were those few who produced special shows for the television networks. Warner Brothers, a former film giant of Hollywood's earlier days, was one of those few. In the 1930s and early 1940s Warner Brothers had maintained an animation department that produced special effects for its major films and, as a sideline, created animated cartoon shorts featuring Bugs Bunny, Porky Pig, Road-Runner, and the rest of the Looney Tunes gang (see Section 7, Dell Publishing Co.).

Years later, in the 1960s, these same cartoons were sold to television and suddenly became popular again as they appeared on the home screen for a new generation of viewers. The continuous reruns of Bugs Bunny and Road-Runner prompted Warner to resume its activity in the comic book field. They acquired the ailing D-C line, which was close to folding, and took one feature to gamble on—Batman!

The experimental show was put together by William Dozier, who had previously produced such television masterpieces as "Studio One," "You Are There," and "Playhouse 90." Batman took the nation by storm and achieved an unbelievably high rating! It held a vast nostalgic appeal for adults who, as youngsters, had grown up with Batman during the 1940s. And for the new generation who had never heard of Batman, the show became an instant favorite.

Of course, the disciples of comicdom's most outspoken critic, child psychiatrist Dr. Frederic Wertham, whose book, *Seduction of the Innocent* described Batman as a dangerous influence on young innocent boys, feared that the television show would have harmful effects on the juvenile audience. They criticized the program, charging that it was un-American to show a masked person running around in long-johns and solving crimes almost in mockery of the police.

Ironically, it was statements like these that promoted the show far more than any paid advertisements could. As it turned out, William Dozier, in anticipation of such attacks, had carefully prepared the series as a slapstick and somewhat satirical portrait of the once-popular superhero fantasy of past comic book literature. Batman was good clean fun for everyone to enjoy.

The show, followed up by a full-length movie of Batman and numerous Batman toys, made Batman an instant national fad and sparked new interest in superhero fantasy. Soon afterwards the comic book industry would boom again.

The success of the Batman television series also opened the door to new avenues in prime time television entertainment. On May 2, 1966, television and motion picture executives held a special luncheon meeting at the Beverly Hills Hotel to discuss the Batman phenomenon. Dozier pointed out that the public liked Batman because he offered the perfect escape from television programs that dramatized familiar situations of everyday life. If television was to grow, he surmised, it needed more escape fantasy. And indeed the Green Hornet, introducing martial arts champion Bruce Lee, followed the very next month.

Sensation Comics No. 1 (January 1942)
©1941 J.R. Publishing Co., renewed 1968, DC Comics, Inc.

Wonder Woman No. 1 (Summer 1942)
©1942 Wonder Woman Publishing Co., ©1968 DC Comics, Inc.

D-C's television smash-hit of the 1970s, "Wonder Woman," was originally created in 1941 by psychiatrist Dr. William Moulton Marston, then a member of the D-C editorial advisory board, and artist H. G. Peters. At the time Wonder Woman made her debut as the leadoff feature in the new title, *Sensation Comics No. 1* (January 1942), comic books were deluged with caped crusaders patterned after Superman or Batman. The introduction of a woman with extraordinary abilities was a highly unique twist in the concept of superhero fantasy.

In Wonder Woman's first adventure she brought the injured Major Steve Trevor of Army Intelligence to medical facilities in Washington and then adopted the secret identity of nurse Diana Prince. But the story did not mention anything about her mysterious background. Who she was, where she came from, and how she achieved her incredible strength and speed was not revealed until her first full-length quarterly magazine, *Wonder Woman Comics No. 1*, which came out in June, 1942.

The origin of Wonder Woman was based on classic mythology, although somewhat loosely. In the Earth's beginnings, mankind was awkwardly evolving under the influences of two opposing forces in the heavens. Pulling mankind in one direction was the god, Ares (also known as Mars, god of war), who held the view that men of strength should conquer the world and shape its destiny, as well as engage in war among themselves to determine who was the strong-

est. Pulling mankind in a different direction, however, was the goddess, Aphrodite. She opposed Ares, embracing the view that women, the weaker sex, should conquer the strongest of men through love, and thus shape the destiny of mankind. Ares and Aphrodite constantly quarreled with each other on these matters as they observed the progress of mortals on Earth.

As men continued to wage war on each other, as Ares declared they must, women, the innocent victims of the losing side, were always taken into slavery as part of the spoils of war. Aphrodite grew to resent the cruel treatment accorded to womankind and took steps to correct the situation. With her own hands, she sculptured a race of new females of strength and called them Amazons. She then selected the fair maiden Hippolyte to serve as their queen, and bestowed upon her a special girdle that endowed its wearer with superhuman strength that was far superior to that of any man. Thus when an army of soldiers invaded the city of the Amazons, they were soundly defeated in battle!

Ares, of course, was furious. He argued with Aphrodite that she had no right to interfere with the mortals by making women stronger than men. Aphrodite merely ignored him. Ares left and devised a plan to bring about the downfall of super women. He discussed the matter with Hercules and persuaded his strong friend to go to Earth in the guise of a mortal and challenge the queen of the Amazons to a duel.

Queen Hippolyte accepted the challenge and armed herself accordingly. The two met in the center of the battlefield that was lined on one side by an army of men and on the other by Amazon warriors. Not surprisingly, the duel resulted in the mighty Hercules succumbing to defeat. Hercules made friends with the beautiful queen and invited her to a banquet as a gesture of friendship between his men and the Amazons. Unfortunately for her subjects, the queen fell in love with Hercules and when he inquired about the source of her strength, she foolishly revealed the secret of her girdle. She even took it off to let him touch it for a brief moment.

Hercules promptly seized the girdle and the queen's power was lost. The men rounded up the Amazons and put them in chains along with their queen. As the prisoners were led away, the queen prayed to Aphrodite for help, pleading for forgiveness of her sin.

Aphrodite answered the prayer and broke Queen Hippolyte's chains, but the divine goddess told her that she must continue to wear the wrist bracelets as a reminder of what could happen to an Amazon when she submitted to a man. With the girdle recovered, the queen regained her super strength, quickly overcame her male captors, and led the Amazons to freedom. The women boarded a ship and, guided by Aphrodite, sailed to a distant island hidden by clouds. And there the Amazons built their paradise to live in peace without men.

Time passed as men continued their wars, but the island of the Amazons remained concealed and undisturbed. The Amazons aged slowly, but as the centuries passed Aphrodite suddenly recognized a serious problem! Without men, there would be no children born for ensuing generations.

To continue the Amazon family, Aphrodite endowed the queen with the ability to precisely recreate the human form in clay. Aphrodite, upon admiring the queen's first sculpture of a baby girl, breathed life into it. The girl, Diana, grew to adulthood as the strongest of the Amazons.

One day when Diana was at the island's beach she discovered the wreckage of a plane that contained the almost lifeless Major Trevor. Diana rescued the unconscious victim and proceeded to nurse him back to health. She also broke the Amazon code by falling in love with her patient! Foreseeing complications, Queen Hippolyte warned Diana that the man must leave the island and return to his own world. The time was the early 1940s and World War II was well underway.

Meanwhile in the heavens, Ares and Aphrodite continued their ageless quarrel about mankind. Ares boasted that his theories were correct for men were again at war. Aphrodite conceded to Ares that his influence was the strongest—but only until America had won the war. And she would see to it that America would win by sending an Amazon to aid that country. Aphrodite appeared to Hippolyte in a dream and instructed her to let the strongest Amazon take the wounded man back to his country.

The following day, the queen held a tournament to select the champion. Diana, of course, won all the events. She was given a new costume to wear, an invisible airplane, and a special lasso that carried the power of Aphrodite. She was also given a pair of the original chain bracelets forged by Hercules to remind her how easily an Amazon can become chained if she developed the mortal weakness of falling in love!

Donning her costume, Diana left the secret island paradise to take the injured patient to America—and the adventures of Wonder Woman began.

However, throughout her exciting career, Diana suffered from a serious inner conflict. She lived by the Amazon code in which love was forbidden, but at the same time, she could not overcome her feelings for Major Steve Trevor. She sought to resolve her problem through her gift of dual identities. As Wonder Woman, she adhered strictly to the Amazon code and remained superior to all men, indeed Wonder Woman had no time to love any male weakling. But in her guise of Diana Prince, she allowed herself to be a woman who wanted the love of only one man—Steve Trevor.

The irony was that Major Trevor did not love the homely and submissive Diana Prince—he loved the beautiful and all-powerful Wonder Woman!

The creator of the series and chief writer of its stories, Dr. Marston, tried to convey to juvenile readership that in the end, love would eventually conquer all. But Marston died in 1947 when the feature had reached its peak. Taken over by other writers, Wonder Woman remained a dynamic action figure in comics until Dr. Wertham, in his book, *Seduction of the Innocent*, criticized the Amazon concept and labeled Wonder Woman as a dangerous influence on young girls. Dr. Wertham's accusations embarrassed D-C. Soon afterwards, the character concept was changed. Wonder Woman lost her Amazonian powers, her magic lasso and costume, and the further adventures of "Diana Prince" acquired a generally romantic theme in the category of confession comic books. But in 1973, Wonder Woman, under the new editorship of Robert Kanigher, returned to her old self as the female supreme.

Further information on D-C's leading super-heroine appears in the book, *Wonder Woman* (New York, Crown Publishers, 1972) with an introduction by Gloria Steinem. The book features color reprints of a selection of "Wonder Woman" adventures from issues of *Sensation Comics* and *Wonder Woman Comics* of the 1940s.

Flash Comics, No. 1 (January 1940)
©1939 All American Comics, Inc., renewed 1966 DC Comics, Inc.

Flash Comics No. 2 (February 1940)
©1940 All American Comics, Inc., renewed 1967, DC Comics, Inc.

Although *Action Comics, Detective Comics,* and *Sensation Comics* carried several different features, each had its own superstar who made the title a success. However, D-C also introduced other comic books that emphasized *two* important stars, not unlike a relay squad of a track team, one to serve as the leadoff feature, and the other to serve as a backup feature. The two stars often alternated on the cover. The other stories in the magazine, for the most part, were of secondary importance.

Flash Comics was an example of a magazine that utilized the "track-team" approach. The first issue, which came out in January 1940, introduced as its leadoff feature the debut of E. E. Hibbard's Flash, the first comic book character to possess lightning speed and one of the earliest fantasy concepts dealing with a specialized superpower. When the Flash whizzed into action, he moved as a blurr of light—the only thing an ordinary mortal could glimpse was the vague shadow of Flash where he had been a moment before. Everything in the world about him seemed to move in slow motion. When armed thugs tried to shoot him where they thought he was, the bullets floated slowly through the air and were easily avoided. And if a lucky shot did strike the Flash while he was moving, the impact of the bullet had less effect than a mosquito bite. However, Flash *was* a vulnerable person. Bullets could very definitely harm him—if he stood still!

The Flash's strange ability resulted from an accident in a laboratory when he, as college student Jay Garrick, was overcome by deadly gas fumes of "hard water" which had been used as part of a research experiment in chemistry. After his recovery in the hospital, Jay discovered that inhaling the gas had affected the molecules in his body in such a way that he was able to move about at fantastic superspeed.

In June 1941, the Flash was elevated to his own quarterly magazine, entitled *All Flash,* which ran as a popular title during the 1940s until its termination at the end of 1948. However, he was revived in 1959 as a slightly different character with a new costume and a new origin.

Flash Comics No. 1 also introduced Gardner Fox's "Hawkman" as the equally exciting backup feature. Hawkman's origin began countless centuries in the past when the world was very young. Prince Khufu, who had been unjustly betrayed by the hawk-god Anubis and slain by the evil priest Hath-Set, was reincarnated in the 20th Century as Carter Hall with full knowledge of the secrets of the ancient sciences. One such secret was the composition of a metal which defied gravity. Hall adopted the guise of the hawk-god he had worshipped in the past as Prince Khufu, and he used the mysterious metal to fashion a pair of artificial wings that gave him the power of flight.

The 20th Century also brought forth the reincarnation of Prince Khufu's sweetheart Shiera, and also his sworn enemy Hath-Set, who returned as the evil scientist Doctor Hastor. During his relentless fight against crime, Hawkman clashed with Dr. Hastor on many occasions. In *Flash Comics No. 24,* Shiera adopted a similar costume with wings to become the Hawkgirl.

Origin of the Flash
©1939 All American Comics, Inc., renewed 1966, DC Comics, Inc.

All American Comics No. 16 (July 1940)
©1940 All American Comics, Inc., renewed 1967, DC Comics, Inc.

©DC Comics, Inc.—

All American Comics, which began in 1939 as a general humor title published by one of the smaller subsidiary companies under the umbrella framework of D-C Comics, gradually adopted the superhero track-team approach with the introduction of various costumed crimefighters in the leadoff and backup positions. These crimefighters replaced the humor features that were actually reprints of newspaper strips from the 1920s. This comic book once carried Bud Fisher's famous "Mutt & Jeff" series and Fontaine Fox's lesser-known, but historically important, "Toonerville Trolley."

Although it has long since been discontinued, "Toonerville Trolley" stands out as one of the most popular humor classics of its period. Its enduring charm lay in the way it reflected the attitudes of a small town community adjusting to the concept of public transportation that was embodied, in this case, by an electric trolley car. Fontaine Fox had lived in Louisville, Kentucky prior to moving to Pelham Manor, New York, and both cities, having public trolley cars at the time, laid claim to being the inspiration of his famous strip. Indeed, both cities named their public transportation "The Toonerville Trolley Line." But as the years passed, the Louisville trolleys were gradually replaced by buses, and the name was ultimately dropped.

However, Pelham Manor's first trolley line leading to the city remained active for many years if only as tribute to the famous comic strip. But in 1937, the trolley finally had to go. The day of its last run became a major event, and over 1,000 saddened residents, fans of the strip as well as regular trolley commuters, turned out to watch "The Toonerville Trolley" make its return run from downtown for the last itme.

"Toonerville Trolley" was about people, and the strip introduced many popular characters. The nation's favorite was Mickey McGuire, a mischievous rascal who was forever playing pranks on the trolley's passengers. In Hollywood, a young child actor of the silent screen, Joe Yule, Jr., decided to change his name to Mickey McGuire. Fox entered lawsuit against Joe Yule for unauthorized use of the name and Yule lost the case. He decided to change his name again, this time to Mickey Rooney.

However, the Mickey McGuire of "Toonerville Trolley" continued to appear in *All American Comics* until the twelfth issue when the magazine underwent a gradual change in format. The eighth issue introduced its new main feature "Ultra-Man," starring a superhero whose adventures took place in the 21st Century.

All American Comics No. 16 (July 1940) marked the debut of Martin Nodell's "Green Lantern" as the new leadoff feature while "Ultra-Man" was shifted to the end of the magazine as its backup feature. Green Lantern represented another novel concept in superhero fantasy. The story of his origin began in ancient China where a crowd watched a meteor plummet through the atmosphere. It crashed nearby and broke open, emitting a fiery, liquid metal. A voice echoed from the liquid, claiming that it would flame green three times: first, to bring death, second, to bring life, and third, to bring power!

Afterwards the liquid cooled. A lampmaker scooped up the soft metal and forged a lamp from it. That night thieves broke into the lampmaker's house—just as the lamp glowed with a green brilliance to fullfill its first prophecy! Everyone in the house, including the unfortunate lampmaker, was fatally affected. Many years later, the lamp turned up as a donation to an insane asylum. One of its patients was toying with the lamp when it began to glow to fullfill its second prophecy. Instantly, the patient was cured of his mental disorder and discharged from the hospital a sane person. The lamp, however, was discarded in the trash and disappeared.

Many years passed and the scene changed to a construction site on a mountainside where a train mysteriously exploded as it crossed a bridge. All the passengers aboard were killed instantly except for young engineer Alan Scott who lay unconscious and near death among the scattered debris, which included twisted remains of the train, fragments of the bridge, bits of rock that had come loose from the mountain—and the lamp!

POWER SHALL BE YOURS, IF YOU HAVE FAITH IN YOURSELF. LOSE THAT FAITH AND YOU LOSE THE ENERGETIC POWER OF THE GREEN LANTERN, FOR WILL POWER IS THE FLAME OF THE GREEN LANTERN!

©1967, DC Comics, Inc.

The lamp began to glow for the final time to fulfill its third prophecy. A voice emanating from the radiating green brilliance penetrated Alan's subconscious and told him to forge a ring from the metal of the lamp and to use its power, together with his own will power, to fight the forces of evil. Once Alan awoke he made the ring, put it on his finger, and discovered he possessed the incredible power to elevate himself at will and fly through the air, to dematerialize and pass through solid walls, and perform other amazing feats that only a god was capable of.

Using his newly acquired power, Alan tracked down the parties responsible for the train explosion and brought them to justice. Then he donned a mask and costume to assume his new role as the Green Lantern!

Green Lantern also headlined his own full-length magazine as a leading D-C title from 1941 to 1949. Although the character was discontinued in 1949 he was later revived in 1962, but under a slightly different concept.

All American Comics No. 19 (October 1940) marked the last appearance of "Ultra-Man" and the first appearance of "The Atom" as the new backup feature. Created by Ben Fenton and Bill O'Connor, the Atom was strictly an action hero with no superpowers. The Atom initially was Al Pratt, a pint-sized weakling who engaged in a rigorous body building program to develop his strength and stamina so that he could better defend himself against the overgrown bullies who constantly threatened him. In his first appearance, we watch Al Pratt develop his frail body into a physique of herculean strength!

In the next issue, Al Pratt adopted a masked identity and vowed to take on all bullies and hoodlums as the mighty Atom. The series ran through Issue 72 and was replaced by the "Black Pirate" feature which had started in *Action Comics*, then moved to *Sensation Comics*, and finally switched to *All American Comics*.

With the exception of the "Mutt & Jeff" reprints, *All American Comics* had dropped its humor content by the twenty-fifth issue and devoted itself almost entirely to superhero fantasy. One of the newer entries—which began with Issue 25—was Dr. Mid-Nite, created by Charles Reizenstein and Stanley Aschmeir. Dr. Mid-Nite served initially as a minor star in the middle position of the comic book. However, the character concept contained a high degree of uniqueness, and in a few years, Dr. Mid-Nite had replaced the Atom as *All American's* important backup star (and had joined the Justice Society in *All Star Comics*). Dr. Mid-Nite, comicdom's only handicapped costumed crimefighter, was in reality *blind* surgeon Dr. Charles McNider who required the aid of special infra-red goggles in order to see. At night and in dark places, these goggles increased his vision to near x-ray capacity which gave him a distinct advantage over the villains he fought. When he went into action, he hurled miniature black-out pellets which exploded into clouds of absolute blackness and blinded his adversaries long enough for him to clobber them unconscious.

In 1947, the entire magazine underwent a major change. The superheroes were replaced by western features and the title became *All American Western Comics*. The cowboys rode through its pages for five years before the magazine underwent yet another change. In 1952, the western features were replaced by war stories and the magazine became *All American Men of War*, a title which continued through the early 1960s.

More Fun Comics No. 52 (February, 1949)
©1939, renewed 1967, DC Comics, Inc.

More Fun Comics, originally titled *New Fun Comics* when it began in February 1935, was the very first D-C comic book. It was the second regular comic book to appear on the newsstands with reprints of humorous newspaper comic strip features that had originated in the 1920s. But *New Fun Comics*, which was changed to *More Fun Comics* at the seventh issue, also introduced for the first time original humor created specifically for the comic book. The magazine's first five issues were published on a bi-monthly basis. Then, starting with the sixth issue in December 1935, the magazine became a monthly publication and the contents underwent certain modifications. The reprint features were gradually phased out and replaced by original humor. Then original detective and other adventure features were added, among which was "Dr. Occult," created by Joe Shuster. And more would follow.

In February 1940, when the era of superhero fantasy was well underway, *More Fun Comics No. 52* introduced the incredible Spectre, a character created by artist Bernard Bailey from an idea of Joe Shuster's.

In the first half of a two-part story that was to run in succeeding issues, a dedicated police detective, Jim Corrigan, upon receiving a tip, broke a date with his fiancee Clarice Frets and rushed to the scene of the crime to stop Gat Benson's gang of hoodlums from robbing a warehouse. After kayoing the thugs with his bare fists and hauling them off to jail, Corrigan joined his sweetheart and took her out for a drive to apologize for standing her up. Unaware they had been followed, the loving couple discussed their marriage plans—until Gat Benson, and a few of his thugs popped into the picture. The hoodlums took the couple at gunpoint to the waterfront. Corrigan tried to make a break for freedom and in the brief scuffle that followed, he was knocked unconscious and unceremoniously dumped into a barrel. The thugs filled the barrel with cement and heaved it into the water. The body of detective Jim Corrigan, ruthlessly murdered in the line of duty, lay encased in cement at the bottom of the river.

As the spirit of Jim Corrigan drifted up through the water and into the sky, a godlike voice spoke and told him that his mission on Earth was not finished, that he was to remain earthbound until he had rid the world of crime. The spirit of Jim Corrigan angrily protested, claiming that he was entitled to eternal peace. But even as he argued he found himself falling back down to Earth. Soon he was sitting on the bottom of the river next to the barrel that no longer contained his body. Physically, Jim Corrigan was dead. But spiritually, he was alive!

After adjusting to the experience of his new existence, the "mirage" of Detective Jim Corrigan arose. He discovered that he did not require to breathe, that he could move easily through water, become invisible, in fact he could do anything he willed—except become the living mortal he once was, or rest in eternal peace as the spiritual soul he had become. Drifting through the air as non-real substance, Jim Corrigan returned to the warehouse where Clarice was held prisoner. Part One concluded when he reached the building and faded through the wall.

In the next issue, *More Fun Comics No. 53*, Part Two continued the story inside the warehouse where the hoods were about to murder a swooning Clarice. Enter the Spectre! The mirage of Jim Corrigan stepped through the wall and confronted the gangsters. The first one to see him screamed in utter disbelief and dropped dead from a heart attack. Jim Corrigan abruptly vanished as the other two thugs turned around—only to reappear on the other side of the room. When the two saw him, they drew their guns and blazed away. The bullets passed harmlessly through Corrigan, and then it was his move. He ordered one thug to shrivel up, die, and go to hell, and that was that! The other mobsters went stark raving mad at the sight.

Clarice, however, presented a different problem. She was beginning to regain consciousness, and to spare her her sanity, Corrigan had to pretend he was still alive, that the mirage that held her so affectionately was the same old Jim. He told her he had swum to safety after being thrown into the river. As he drove her home, he thought about their future relationship and realized that the love and happiness he had once looked forward to with Clarice were human desires that had ended with his death. He broke the silence and told her that their engagement was off. To avoid going into detail to explain his decision, he lied and said he no longer cared about her. He dropped Clarice off at her house and left her in tears, never to see her again.

From then on, Jim Corrigan needed no human companionship whatsoever. The Spectre operated alone! However, to spare those who were once his friends, he adopted an unusual dual identity. First, he made himself a green cloak to drape over his head, and a pair of green trunks, slippers, and gloves. When he put these articles on, the illusion of his human form vanished and he stood in a state that was natural to him—what appeared to be flesh turned pure grey (later pure white), and the pupils of his eyes vanished. He had no eyebrows, and his face reflected only one emotionless expression—the grim visage of death! In this his natural state, the Spectre no longer bore any resemblance to Jim Corrigan or, for that matter, any living human at all.

Without the costume, he materialized as a walking, talking, replica of the person who had once been Detective Jim Corrigan, and he let his associates believe he was still the same old hard-hitting, dedicated cop. Quite often, as the figure of Jim Corrigan walked down the street, nodding here and there to people who passed him or chatting with fellow policemen, the Spectre would leave the mirage and streak invisibly away. Jim Corrigan could be seated at his desk at headquarters and appear as though he were reviewing police files, answering the phone, or handling a routine interrogation, while the Spectre was off in another part of the world—or in another world altogether.

Yet by acting the role of his former self, the Spectre encountered another problem—Detective Corrigan was well known to the underworld and was thus an ideal target for assassins. One time his car exploded as he turned the ignition key. When the police rushed to the scene of the flaming wreckage, they found Corrigan getting up from the ground, claiming he hadn't been inside the car when it blew up. When the mob riddled him with bullets after luring him into a dark alley, he later claimed that the gunfire had missed him.

But as the Spectre in action, there was no pretense! Inasmuch as he sought to rest in eternal peace, he became anxious to rid the world of crime and thus finish his mission. He didn't have time to argue with the bad guys, and he certainly didn't have time to rehabilitate them into useful and productive citizens. To smite them to nothingness with a lightning bolt or his "dead-eye glare" was quicker and much more efficient. And it said something ghastly to the under-

world: "Any time the Spectre is after you, you're as good as dead!"

However, crime was everywhere. And the Spectre, too all-powerful to bother with petty situations that Detective Jim Corrigan could readily handle, devoted his attention to battling and crushing the supernatural forces of evil that threatened mankind. A good example of this appeared in *More Fun Comics No. 66* when the Spectre went after "Black Doom."

The story began when gigantic beasts suddenly appeared from nowhere and invaded the city, wrecking buildings and trains, and creating general havoc. The people fled in panic, but there was no place to go. The beasts were everywhere! Police headquarters was swamped with phone calls from the terrified citizenry pleading for help. Detective Corrigan took one of the calls. As he listened to a screaming woman on the other end, the Spectre streaked off to put an end to the matter. However, the monster's strange mystical power of pure evil that had been killing the police who had already arrived on the scene, hurled the Spectre to the ground. He lay on the pavement dead.

But *no!* The Spectre was dead from the beginning. But as he lay on the street unable to move, Detective Corrigan at police headquarters dropped the telephone and keeled over on the floor. Someone rushed to his aid and felt his pulse. There was none! Jim Corrigan had "died" again.

As the city collapsed in ruins, the awesome beasts suddenly vanished. Only then did the Spectre regain his energy and as he did, Jim Corrigan suddenly sat up. He explained that he had just recovered from a momentary dizzy spell, and he joined the police investigation into the matter. However, whatever the trouble was, it appeared to be over with.

But not quite. The same monstrosities returned the next day, as if they had materialized out of someone's horrifying nightmare. This time the Spectre battled them to a stand-off. The beasts shrank down to human size and ran away. They fled into a museum and vanished again—even out of view of the Spectre's super extrasensory vision! The Spectre searched the building inside and out, from the basement to the roof. The beasts were not to be found anywhere. Yet he was determined to find them. He started his search over again and explored the first floor very carefully, scrutinizing every crack in the wall, every cobweb, anything that appeared to move. An unusual picture of a landscape painting that hung on the wall caught his attention—a dense fog painted on the canvas appeared to be actually blowing across the horizon!

Acting on a hunch, the Spectre reduced himself to the size of a dime and stepped into the two-dimensional scene.

34

More Fun Comics No. 11 (July 1936)
©1936 More Fun Magazine, Inc.

More Fun Comics No. 54 (April 1940)
©1940, renewed 1967, DC Comics, Inc.

More Fun Comics No. 64 (February 1941)
©1940, renewed 1967, DC Comics, Inc.

More Fun Comics No. 65 (March 1941)
©1940, renewed 1967, DC Comics, Inc.

36

More Fun Comics No. 56 introduced a new and equally dynamic backup star. In the deserted Tower of Salem, a strange and mysterious being known as Dr. Fate, whose body was composed of the pure elemental forces of the universe, observed the activities of mankind through a crystal globe. He particularily watched for menaces of evil that could spring forth from ancient wisdom when Earth was young.

The early Dr. Fate adventures, created by Gardner Fox and Howard Sherman, were classics in fantasy. In *More Fun Comics No. 65* for example, Dr. Fate's globe revealed an immortal fish-man of the Nyarl-Amen Dynasty, one of the original amphibian species that dominated Earth before the evolution of man. As he watched the creature emerge from the waves and walk onto the beach of a small Pacific island, Dr. Fate realized that the Nyarl-Amens had succeeded in breaking free of the spell that had imprisoned them for ages on the ocean floor.

The Nyarl-Amens began to appear by the thousands to regain possession of the surface world they had controlled 50,000 years before. The military base on the island took immediate action. The soldiers tried to stop them with ordinary weapons, but the Nyarl-Amens, totally invulnerable to gunfire, quickly disintegrated the troops with flashes of lightning discharged from their spears. Mankind faced absolute obliteration.

Dr. Fate left his tower and sped to the scene . . .

More Fun Comics No.67 revealed the peculiar origin of Dr. Fate. In this episode, young Kent Nelson and his father, an archeologist, embarked on a journey to Egypt to study the pyramids. The senior Nelson professed a theory that the Egyptians had not built these remarkable structures, but a race of people from another planet had come to Earth during an ancient era. As the two investigated the underground temple chambers of one of the pyramids, the young Nelson left his father to explore an adjoining room and discovered a statue of a man encased in a tomb. As Kent Nelson gazed at the stone figure, he heard a voice inside his mind telling him to push a stone lever at the base of the statue. When Kent followed the instructions, a cloud of white gas suddenly filled the room, and the statue came to life. The strangely-garbed being who called himself Nabu, readily admitted he was born on the distant planet Cilia over a million years ago and had come to Earth when the two worlds passed near each other. Then the two went to join Kent's father, only to discover he was dead. Nabu explained he had been overcome by a poison gas which had originally been prepared as a booby trap to prevent strangers from tampering with certain fixtures within the temple rooms that contained Cilian secrets. As a gesture to compensate for the loss of the child's parent, Nabu accepted Kent as his pupil and spent years teaching him Cilian secrets to use against the evil magic of the ancients.

After Kent had grown to adulthood, Nabu spoke to him for the last time . . .

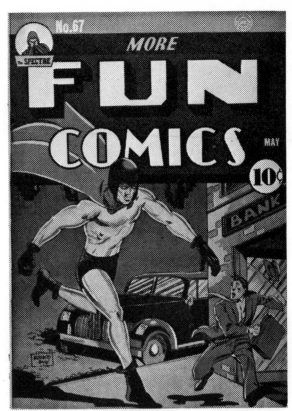

©1941, renewed 1968, DC Comics, Inc.

©1941, renewed 1968, DC Comics, Inc.

It was never explained what happened to Nabu afterwards. Nor was it explained how Kent Nelson, as Dr. Fate, was able to transpose his body into the elemental forces of the universe and discharge cosmic energy from his fingertips, or how Kent Nelson was able to recognize and identify those evils that originated thousands of years in the past. Inasmuch as Dr. Fate never removed the helmet that concealed his entire face, his true identity was open to interpretation.

In later adventures, under a different editorship, the character concept was changed. Dr. Fate became an "ordinary" crimefighter who pursued bank robbers, racketeers, and gangsters, accomplishing routine tasks that did not require the use of his vast superpowers. His abilities grew limited and he began to acquire weaknesses he never had before. The feature lost its exotic appeal, and it was ultimately terminated in *More Fun Comics No. 98*.

In order to smother what might be interpreted as a publishing blunder, *More Fun Comics* began to introduce a score of new superheroes. Aquaman and Green Arrow had already made their debut in Issue 73. Johnny Quick, another superhero of lightning speed, was introduced in Issue 85. *More Fun Comics No. 101* was the last appearance of The Spectre and the first appearance of Superboy whose stories ran for just six issues in that magazine before they were switched to *Adventure Comics*.

With the departure of these main characters, the semi-humorous "Genius Jones" became the new lead-off feature. The episodes started at Issue 108 and ran until *More Fun Comics* was terminated with Issue 129 in March 1946. Yet many of the characters that were first introduced in its pages have been revived in recent years.

All Star Comics No. 3 (Winter 1940)
©1940 All American Comics, Inc.

All Star Comics No. 4 (March-April 1941)
©1941 All American Comics, Inc., renewed 1967, DC Comics, Inc.

As a third alternative to the "track-team" approach and the full-length magazine devoted to a single character, D-C introduced a novel magazine concept that featured an all-star team made up of the leadoff and backup characters from other D-C titles. The first and second quarterly issues of *All Star Comics* debuted in mid-1940 and the featured characters appeared in separate and unrelated stories. It was the third issue that became a revolutionary milestone in comic book literature when the Justice Society of America was formed. The cover shows the original eight members seated at the conference table for their first meeting. They were from left to right:

(1) The Atom, backup star of *All American Comics*.

(2) Sandman, the first costumed crimefighter and the leadoff star of *Adventure Comics* whose series began in Issue 40. At Issue 48, he was shifted to the backup position. Sandman had no superpowers, but he did use a special gas pistol that put antagonists to sleep at critical moments. In order to avoid being affected by the gas himself, he wore a gas mask which also concealed his identity. Later in *Adventure Comics No. 69*, the character was slightly changed. Sandman discarded his gas mask and baggy green suit and donned a colorful purple-and-yellow skintight uniform. He exchanged his gas pistol for a gun that fired a web mesh. And he adopted a junior sidekick, Sandy, who wore a similar costume. The series ran for nine years

before ending in 1948.

(3) The Spectre, leadoff star of *More Fun Comics*.

(4) The Flash, leadoff star of *Flash Comics*.

(5) Hawkman, backup star of *Flash Comics*.

(6) Dr. Fate, backup star of *More Fun Comics*.

(7) Green Lantern, leadoff star of *All American Comics*.

(8) The Hour-Man, created by Bernard Bailey as the first superhero for *Adventure Comics*, and the magazine's leadoff star when he debuted in Issue 48. In the first episode, chemist Rex Tyler accidentally discovered a compound for making a "miracle pill" that gave him super strength for sixty minutes. During this hour of seemingly unlimited energy, the Hour-Man could leap over houses, battle dozens of men, overturn automobiles, and be almost invulnerable to injury. But at the end of the sixty-minute interval, the effect of the pill wore off, and Tyler became an average person again. Tyler had to time his action to the second, otherwise he was in trouble.

During the first meeting of the stars, they became acquainted with each other's abilities by recounting stories of their most exciting adventures. In the next issue, they joined forces as a team and began their first book-length adventure together. The Justice Society of *All Star Comics* was on its way to becoming a classic in its own right. Although its membership changed throughout the years, the crimefighting

All Star Comics No. 6 (August-September 1941)
©1941 All American Comics, Inc., renewed 1967, DC Comics, Inc.

All Star Comics No. 10 (April-May 1942)
©1942 All American Comics, Inc., renewed 1968, DC Comics, Inc.

principles upon which the organization was founded remained the same.

As the various characters were phased out of their own regular magazines, they were dropped from membership in the Justice Society and replaced by others. Some were added as the occasion arose.

All Star Comics No. 5: Hawkgirl appears as an honorary guest of her boyfriend, Hawkman.

All Star Comics No. 7: Superman and Batman appear as honorary guests and congratulate the organization for its splendid work. Superman becomes acquainted with the Spectre. Batman shakes hands with Hawkman and the Atom. However, Hour-Man, who had been terminated from *Adventure Comics*, had to be dropped from membership. Batman temporarily fills the gap. Then Jack Burnley's Starman, the new lead-off star and Hour-Man's replacement in *Adventure Comics* who debuted in Issue 61, joins the Justice Society as the regular replacement for Hour-Man.

All Star Comics No. 8: Wonder Woman makes a brief appearance: Starman and Dr. Mid-Nite join as regular members.

All Star Comics No. 11: Wonder Woman joins the organization as a regular member. In the next issue she is unanimously elected to serve as Secretary of The Justice Society of America.

All Star Comics No. 23: The Spectre realizes he was out of place among a team of living people and resigns his membership.

All Star Comics No. 24: Wildcat of *Sensation Comics* makes a guest appearance and attempts to fill in for the Spectre.

All Star Comics No. 36: The Justice Society needs outside help to tackle an incredible menace that threatens the destruction of mankind. Superman makes a guest appearance and brings Batman along. The particular situation called for the involvement of almost everyone!

In 1949, the Justice Society fell into limbo when *All Star Comics* was momentarily discontinued at Issue 57. A few years later in 1951, the magazine resumed under a western format as *All Star Western Comics*.

In 1960, D-C introduced *Justice League of America*, reviving the team concept of the original Justice Society. Its membership included the new Hawkman, the new Flash, and others. In 1976, *All Star Comics* was revived with the new Issue 58, and the Justice Society of America began again with a membership that generally consisted of the superheroes who left the Justice League. The membership of D-C superheroes was now divided between both organizations. The Justice League team that consisted of Superman, Batman, Wonder Woman, Flash, and Aquaman were the stars of the popular animated Saturday morning television hit *Justice League*. Its reruns are still being shown in many cities.

ALPHABETICAL LISTING OF D-C COMICS
(1935-1977)

Action Comics (1938 - present)
Adventure Comics (1935 - present)
Alan Ladd (1949 - 1951)
All-American (1939 - 1948)
All American (Western) (1948 - 1952)
All American (Men of War) (1952 - 1967)
Angel and the Ape (1968 - 1969)
Anthro (1968 - 1969)
Batman (1940 - present)
Beowulf, Dragon Slayer (1975 - present)
Black Lightning (1977 - present)
Black Magic Comics (1973 - 1975)
Bomba, the Jungle Boy (1967 - 1968)
Boy Commandos (1942 - 1949; and two reprint issues, 1973)
Champion Sports (1973 - 1974)
Claw, the Unconquered (1975 - present)
Comic Cavalcade (1942 - 1954)
Date With Judy (1947 - 1960)
D-C 100 Page Super Spectacular Comics (1971 - 1973)
D-C Special (1968 - 1971, and revived 1975 - present)
Dean Martin and Jerry Lewis (1952 - 1957)
Debbie's Dates (1969 - 1971)
Demon (1972 - 1974)
Detective Comics (1937 - present)
Dodo and the Frog (1954 - 1956)
Eighty Page Giants (1964 - 1971)
Everything Happens to Harvey (1953 - 1954)
Famous First Edition (1974 - 1975)
Feature Films (1950, five issues)
Flash Comics (1940 - 1949)
Flash, The, 2nd Series (1959 - Present)
Forever People (1971 - 1972)
Four Star Battle Tales (1973, five issues)
Four Star Spectacular (1976 - present)
Fox and the Crow (1951 - 1968)
From Beyond the Unknown (1969 - 1973)
Frontier Fighters (1955 - 1956)
Funny Folks (1945 - 1954)
Gang Busters (1947 - 1958)
G.I. Combat (1957 - present)
G.I. War Tales (1973, four issues)
Green Lantern, 1st Series (1941 - 1949)
Green Lantern, 2nd Series (1960 - 1972, and revived 1976 to present)
Here's Howie (1952 - 1955)
Hi-Jinx (1947 - 1949)
Hot Wheels (1970 - 1971)
House of Mystery (1951 - present)
House of Secrets (1956 - 1966)
In The Days of the Mob (1971, one issue)
Jackie Gleason and the Honeymooners (1956 - 1959)

Jerry Lewis (1957 - 1971)
Jimmy Olsen (1954 - 1974)
Jimmy Wakely (1949 - 1952)
Johnny Thunder (1973, three issues)
Joker, Clown Prince of Crime (1975 - present)
Justice, Inc. (1975, four issues)
Justice League of America (1960 - present)
Kong (1975 - 1976)
Korack, Son of Tarzan (1972 - 1975)
Lady Cop (1975 - present)
Laurel and Hardy (1962 - 1967, 1972, one issue)
Leading (1941 - 1948)
Leave It to Binky (1948 - 1958, and revived 1968 - 1970)
Legends of Daniel Boone (1955 - 1956)
Legion of Super-Heroes (1973, four issues. Currently re-titled Superboy and the Legion of Super-Heroes)
Limited Collector's Edition (1972 - present)
Lois Lane (1958 - 1974)
Miss Beverly Hills of Hollywood (1949 - 1950)
Miss Melody Lane of Broadway (1950, four issues)
Mr. District Attorney (1948 - 1959)
Mister Miracle (1971 - 1974)
More Fun Comics (1935 - 1949)
Movie Comics (1939, six issues)
Mutt and Jeff (1940 - 1947, and continued at irregular intervals through 1958, and then resumed as a Dell title through 1959)
My Greatest Adventure (1955 - 1964)
New Book of Comics (1936 - 1938, two issues)
New Gods (1971 - 1972)
New York World's Fair (1939 - 1940, two issues)
Nutsy Squirrel (1954 - 1956)
Omac, the One Man Army (1974 - 1975)
Our Army at War (1952 - 1977)
Our Fighting Forces (1954 - 1977)
Ozzie and Harriet (1949 - 1950, five issues)
Phantom Stranger (1969 - 1976)
Plastic Man, 2nd Series (1966 - 1968; 1st Series by Quality Comics)
Plop (1973 - 1976)
Prez (1973 - 1974)
Raccoon Kids (1955 - 1957)
Real Fact Comics (1946 - 1949)
Real Screen Comics (1945 - 1959)
Rex, the Wonder Dog (1952 - 1959)
Rima, the Jungle Girl (1974 - 1975)
Sandman (1974 - 1976)
Scribbly (1948 - 1950)
Sea Devils (1961 - 1967)
Secret Hearts (1949 - 1974)
Secret Origins (1961 - 1974, seven issues) (1973 - 1974, seven issues)

Sensation (1942 - 1952)
Sensation Mystery (1952 - 1953)
Sgt. Bilko (1957 - 1960)
Sgt. Rock (1977 - present)
Sgt. Rock's Battle Tales (1964, one issue)
Shadow (1973 - 1975)
Shazam (1973 - present)
Showcase (1956 - 1970)
Sinister House of Secret Love (1971 - 1972)
Stalker (1975 - 1976)
Star-Spangled Comics (1941 - 1952)
Star-Spangled War Stories (1952 - 1957)
Strange Adventures (1950 - 1973)
Strange Sports (1973 - 1974)
Sugar and Spike (1956 - 1971)
Superboy and Superboy and the Legion of Super-Heroes (1949 - present)
Supergirl (1972 - 1974)
Superman (1939-present)
Superman Family (1974-present)
  Also the following special issues:
  Superman at the Gilbert Hall of Science (1948)
  Superman Costume Comic (1954, one issue)
  Superman Record Comics (1966)
  Superman Tim (1946-1950)
  Superman 3-D (1953)
  Superman Workbook (1945)
  Superman's Christmas Adventure (1940, 1944)

Superman vs. Spider-Man (1976, one issue published in collaboration with Marvel Comics)
Super D-C Giant Comics (1970-1976)
Swamp Thing (1973-1976)
Tales of Ghost Castle (1975, three issues)
Tales of the Unexpected (1956-1968)
Tarzan (1972-1977)
Tarzan Family (1975-1976)
Teen Beam (1968, one issue)
Teen Beat (1967, one issue)
Teen Titans (1966-present (irregular))
Three Mouseketeers (1970-1971)
Tomahawk (1950-1972)
Tor (1975-1976)
Trigger Twins (1973, one issue)
Tv Screen Cartoons (1959-1961)
Unexpected, The (1968-present)
Warlord (1975-present)
Weird Mystery Tales (1972-1975)
Weird War Tales (1971-1977)
Weird Western Tales (1972-present)
Weird Worlds (1972-1974)
Welcome Back, Kotter (1976-present)
Western Comics (1948-1961)
Witching Hour (1969-1977)
Wonder Woman (1942-present)
World's Finest Comics (1941-present, first issue titled World's Best Comics)

World's Best Comics No. 1 (Spring 1941)
©1941 World's Best Comics Co., renewed 1968, DC Comics, Inc.

World's Finest Comics No. 2 (Summer 1941)
©1941 World's Best Comics Co., renewed 1968, DC Comics, Inc.

QUALITY COMICS GROUP

The Quality Comics Group, which would fold in the mid-1950s and later be absorbed into the D-C line, was the outgrowth of Everett M. Arnold's short-lived Centaur comic book titles of the 1930 era. The Centaur comic books were among the first to introduce original story content in such titles as *Amazing Mystery Funnies*, *Detective Picture Stories*, and *Keen Detective Comics*. The stories generally followed the standard pulp formula that featured an avenging masked sleuth.

In one of the many variations within the formula, the masked sleuth was a dedicated law enforcement officer whose crime smashing assignments were always snarled by a maze of legal red tape that prevented his making an arrest. But by assuming a masked identity, he was freed from legal restrictions and, acting as an independent and unknown agent of justice, better able to track down and do battle with the hoodlums on their own ruthless and brutal terms. Arresting the bad guys was not the masked avenger's objective—he simply did away with them for fear that legal loopholes might set them free again.

In line with this formula, *Keen Detective Comics* featured such masked avengers as the Clock and the Masked Marvel, as well as other straight detectives who did not adopt a masked identity. Other Centaur titles injected variations on the masked avenger motif that bordered on superhero fantasy.

In addition to the Centaur titles, Arnold had also formed a separate firm called Comic Favorites, Inc. which published *Feature Funnies*, a comic book that began in October 1937. *Feature Funnies* continued to reprint several newspaper serials that had expired with Eastern's *Famous Funnies*, until then the major title on the newsstands. It also carried such all-time favorites as "Joe Palooka," "Dixie Dugan," "Jane Arden," and "Ned Brant," all of which had formerly contributed to *Famous Funnies'* success. These features appar-

ently proved to be more successful than those in the other Centaur titles and Everett Arnold decided to phase out the latter. He would gamble on his sure winner, *Feature Funnies*, even though the Masked Marvel had been bought by Republic Pictures for an exciting movie serial adaptation in 1942. A similar masked sleuth, the Clock, created by George Brenner, was transferred to *Feature Funnies* as the major attraction of the magazine.

During this time, the comic book industry was beginning to grow in several different directions. Reprinting serialized newspaper strips represented one direction. D-C's *Action Comics* with Superman and *Detective Comics* with Batman was another. A third direction was taken by publishers already well established in pulp fiction. They opened up art departments to create new comic book material from already extant plots. In the early stages, many of these publishers depended upon firms representing independent artists to produce original comic book material and cover art. But for professional artists steady employment with a publisher was a desirable alternative, thus by 1942 most of the publishers had expanded their own art departments to such a degree that the small independent art studios were beginning to wither away.

Everett Arnold proved to be the exception among his publishing peers. He continued to maintain an informal arrangement with many outside studios which, as they began to lose their clients, decided to pool the best of their free-lance talent and form a single group to produce art for Arnold's new titles. This was done and the magazines carried the group's new name, The Quality Comics Group, and the trademark "Quality Comics." *Feature Funnies* was included in the Quality group.

Feature Comics No. 77 (April 1944)*
©1944 Comic Favorites, Inc.

Doll Man Quarterly No. 1 (Autumn 1941)*
©1941 Comic Favorites, Inc.

Although the new Quality Comics would emphasize well-illustrated superhero fantasy, Arnold was perhaps the only publisher to encourage the avenging masked sleuth genre. Following "The Clock" came Jack Cole's "Midnight" series which debuted in *Smash Comics No. 18* and Will Eisner's "Spirit" series which was introduced in *Police Comics No. 11* and subsequently became one of Quality's outstanding attractions. *Feature Funnies No. 13* introduced Will Eisner's Black X, a hero who specialized in the espionage game.

Throughout the 1940s, the Quality Comics Group underwent several generations of varying character concepts in the tug-of-war between superhero fantasy and the avenging masked sleuth who did not rely on super powers. The superhero side was led by Jack Cole's Plastic Man, one of the most ingenious creations in comic books, and Lou Fine's Doll Man; whereas the straight action side was led by The Spirit and Blackhawk.

With Issue 21, *Feature Funnies* became *Feature Comics* and was scheduled to offer original content in place of the reprint series that had expired and would be resumed by Columbia Features Syndicate who owned the newspaper strips and was planning to enter the comic book field. The first to appear in *Feature Comics* was Lou Fine's Doll Man, a novel feature of superhero fantasy that would branch out into its own full-length quarterly title in mid-1941.

The Doll Man, who stood at six inches in height,

was in reality a miniaturized version of private detective Darrel Dane whose normal strength turned to compact super strength when he became his diminutive self. The changeabout came when Darrel's future father-in-law and eminent scientist, Dr. Roberts, discovered a formula for making a pill that could compress living tissue and increase its physical density. Of course, the effect was only temporary for the tissue under compression would soon expand and return to its normal size. Darrel Dane felt that the pill could be used as an effective tool to combat crime!

In the first few stories, Darrel relied on the pill to become the dynamic Doll Man. But the pill had an unexpected side effect: his system had adjusted to the change in such a manner that Darrel found he could compress himself at will by sheer concentration.

©1940 Comic Favorites, Inc.*

The Doll Man used his miniature size to maximum advantage. He could slip under locked doors, conceal himself behind wastebaskets or inside the villain's suit pocket, and sting like a bee when he went into action.

Being only six inches in height, he became an elusive and difficult target to shoot. But his Lilliputian dimensions had its disadvantages. The Doll Man was often threatened by hungry alley cats and other small but hostile animals. Ordinary stairsteps became a rigorous exercise in "mountain climbing." An ordinary rainfall could sweep him into the sewer, and crossing the street in heavy traffic, difficult enough at normal size, became an extremely hazardous undertaking.

Feature Comics No. 77 (August 1944) marked the first appearance of Darrel's girl friend Martha Roberts in a new role as "Midge," the Doll Girl. Her changeabout came one day when she happened to be wondering how she could aid her boy friend's war against crime as an active partner. At the same moment, Darrel, in another part of the city, was wondering how the Doll Man might acquire a partner. Through a strange phenomenon apparently resulting from two wills concentrating on a single thought, Martha found herself shrinking to the same dynamic size as her fiance. (Although the story did not say so, there were those who believed that Martha, being the daughter of Dr. Roberts, had somehow taken a compression pill by mistake when she needed an aspirin.) At any rate, the two shared their first adventure as the Doll Team, but for some reason Doll Girl did not appear again until seven years later in 1951.

Feature Comics No. 32 introduced Ted Cain's Samar, a strapping, bucolic aerialist of the wilds who un-doubtedly rated as comicdom's chief contender for the title "Lord of The Jungle."

©1940 Comic Favorites, Inc.*

In answer to the girl's question, Samar replied that he came from a tribe of nomads who had adopted him as a child. He did not remember his real parents, just his teacher, an elderly nomad who had been unjustly banished from the tribe a few months before. Samar left the tribe and joined his teacher to explore the jungles and find another tribe to join. But the old man was stricken with malaria and soon died. Samar decided to seek a new life in the unexplored regions on his own. It was here that he saw a herd of elephants stampeding toward a helpless village—he took to the trees and rushed ahead to warn the unsuspecting people.

The same issue also introduced Paul Gustavson's Rusty Ryan, a junior adventurer who would later form the Boyville Brigadiers as a patriotic fighting team. Gustavson had created a variety of short-lived superhero features, all of which were well-illustrated but lacking in conceptual uniqueness. While several of his characters appeared in different titles throughout the Quality line, his best known and most popular was a costumed crimefighter called the Angel who appeared in Timely Publications' *Marvel Mystery Comics* and *Sub-Mariner Comics.*

Feature Comics No. 32 (May 1940)
©1940 Comic Favorites, Inc.

Smash Comics, another title of the Quality Comics Group, began in August 1939 and ran for ten years, during which time a wide assortment of characters and character concepts were introduced. The first generation of features included "Hugh Hazard and his Iron Man, Bozo, the Robot." When space was limited, the title was often shortened to "Bozo, the Robot" (especially when Bozo was featured on the cover), or "Hugh Hazard," or "Hugh Hazard's Iron Man." When Bozo, created by George Brenner, made his debut in *Smash Comics No. 1*, robots were already firmly established in pulp science fiction and veritable near-indestructible armies of them already marched through comic book literature. The difference here was that Bozo was the first robot crimefighter.

Originally, a villainous scientist named Dr. Van Thorp had built Bozo as part of a plot to conquer the world. But Hugh Hazard intervened and thwarted the diabolical scheme before the super robot had been fully perfected. Dr. Van Thorp was sent to jail while Hazard took charge of the robot. He made certain alterations in its control panel and converted Van Thorp's creation into an instrument of justice to fight the forces of evil. In the early stories, Bozo was a complex machine which Hugh Hazard controlled by vocal instructions. Bozo could streak through the air, crash through brick walls, hurl automobiles great distances, overturn speeding trains, walk on ocean floors, break submarines in half, relax in flaming infernos, and wipe out entire gangs of armed hoodlums with a single blow of his iron fist.

One of Bozo's unique traits was the manner in which he derived his flying ability. A small disc mounted on top of his head housed a miniature propellor that was capable of lifting him off the ground. When he activated the elevation control switch on his chest panel he could roar through the sky like an airplane.

However, as the series progressed it underwent a slight change. Hugh Hazard discovered that Bozo's interior was practically hollow and provided sufficient space for a man to fit into. So Hugh Hazard climbed inside the machine and began operating it from within.

Smash Comics No. 14 introduced Lou Fine's golden superhero, the Ray, who, as reporter Happy Terrill, had been caught in a violent electrical storm and struck by lightning in such an uncanny manner that he absorbed its energy instead of burning to a crisp. As a fusion of a human being and a lightwave, he was able to streak through the sky like a ray of light. The Ray also had the power to discharge light energy from his fingertips.

Of course the Ray used his awesome power to combat crime. But he soon discovered that when in a

Smash Comics No. 14 (Sept. 1940)*
©1940 by E.M. Arnold

dark or nighttime environment, his powers were nullified and he became an ordinary human until sunlight restored his energy. The exciting series ran in *Smash Comics* for several years, with a few of the later adventures illustrated by artist Reed Crandall.

Just prior to the Ray's debut, *Smash Comics No. 13* introduced Paul Gustavson's Magno, a superhero whose body was charged and recharged with electricity. Magno's power lay in his hands which became two powerful magnets when he was fully charged. When someone shot at Magno, the bullets were drawn to his hands which he easily caught and melted. He did the same to knives and other metal weapons. A blow from his fist carried the impact of an electric shock. But his powers often ran out and he constantly had to recharge himself by poking a finger into a handy lightbulb socket and pulling the switch, or gripping exposed electrical wires while the current was on.

In the other genre, *Smash Comics No. 18* introduced Jack Cole's avenging masked sleuth Midnight, who in reality was radio announcer Dave Clark. At the stroke of midnight, Dave would put on a face mask and go on a crimefighting spree. The "Midnight" series acquired a semi-humorous slant and became popular enough to take over the cover slot.

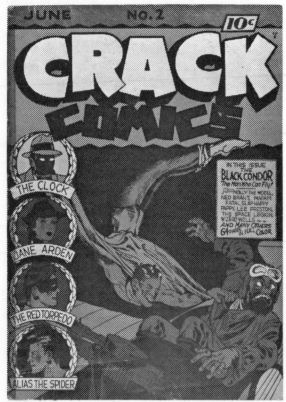

Crack Comics No. 2 (June 1940)
©1940 Comic Magazines, Inc.

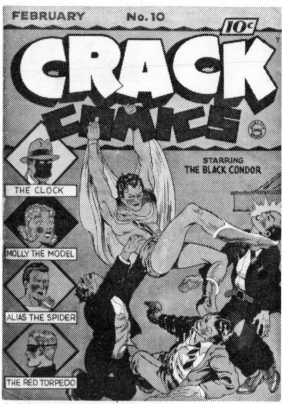

Crack Comics No. 10 (Feb. 1941)*
©1941 Comic Magazines, Inc.

Crack Comics, which began in May 1940 and ran for nine years also underwent changes in format. The first generation of features, basically those of the superhero genre, introduced Lou Fine's classic "Black Condor" series which debuted in the first issue and ended at the twenty-fifth issue. As an infant the Black Condor had been seized by a giant condor and raised in a nest as the condor's offspring. In essence he thought he was a bird and he was indeed able to communicate quite fluently with the species. His "mother" even taught him how to fly. But upon reaching adulthood, he realized that his human characteristics prevailed and he flew away from his condor family to live among those of his own kind. However, he discovered that the human race was infested with crime and evil and he resolutely set out to destroy those factions with the aid of his only true friends—vultures!

The Black Condor holstered a special gun that shot a deadly paralyzing ray of black light. The ray immobilized the enemy while Black Condor's winged assistants finished the job. In later adventures, the character concept was slightly altered. The Black Condor's close relationship with vultures and other birds was dropped and he assumed different alter-identities, first as an undercover policeman and then as an impersonation of a murdered senator. Even-

tually he even discarded his ray gun.

In a typical early adventure, the Black Condor, while sailing over the lonely Indian desert wastelands with a flock of vultures searching for carrion to feed upon, came across what appeared to be a lifeless human body on the ground. The group swooped down to examine the condition of the body's flesh. The human bird discovered that the victim was still alive and 'learned that desert bandits of the evil Ali Kan had attacked him and kidnapped his fiance, Andrea Kent, while the two were enroute to the Province of Raj to take over their legally inherited kingdom estate. The Black Condor set out to free Andrea and bring an end to Ali Kan's bandit regime. However, during a brief battle with Ali Kan's guards, the Black Condor was overwhelmed, taken prisoner, and thrown into a cage. Ali Kan decided to use the prisoner for a spectacular sporting event. The cage would be dragged into an open arena, raised on top of a high post and opened so that his army of expert archers could slay the prisoner as he attempted to flee to the skies.

In the meantime, one of the vultures to whom the prisoner had whispered secret instructions, flew off to a family of condors. The giant birds returned to aid their brother and when the cage was opened, the Black Condor did not flee as expected . . .

DEFTLY DODGING THE HAIL OF ARROWS, HE IS FURTHER PROTECTED BY A FLIGHT OF CONDORS.

THEN, SUDDENLY SWOOPING DOWN TO THE SQUARE, HE SEIZES A BOW AND QUIVER FROM A STARTLED ARCHER AND ZOOMS SKY-WARD AGAIN......

NOW, ALI KAN, I'LL GIVE YOU A TASTE OF YOUR OWN MEDICINE!

RUN FOR YOUR LIVES! HE'LL KILL US ALL!

JUST A MOMENT, ALI KAN.... WE'VE A SCORE TO SETTLE!

YOU LEFT ME AS SPORT FOR YOUR FRIENDS—THEREFORE, I SHALL RETURN THE COMPLIMENT!

LEAVING ALI SUSPENDED BY HIS PANTS ON THE VERY POST HE HAD SET UP, THE BLACK CONDOR FLIES OFF TO RESCUE ANDREA.

SHE'S LOCKED IN THIS TOWER!

ANDREA, COME WITH ME!

THIS MUST BE A DREAM! NO MAN CAN FLY LIKE A BIRD! WHO ARE YOU? WHERE ARE YOU TAKING ME?

WE'RE GOING TO RAJ PROVINCE.

I'VE A SURPRISE FOR YOU!

DON'T BE FRIGHTENED BY THE HEIGHT... YOU'RE PERFECTLY SAFE WITH ME.

AMAZING! THIS IS LIKE RIDING ON A MAGIC CARPET!

AS THE TWO SOAR OVER RAJ, THEY SEE THE TROOPS OF ALI KAN, SENT AHEAD TO INVADE THE CAPITAL.

I'LL TEND TO THEM! BUT FIRST—

Crack Comics also started off with several characters that were transferred from *Feature Comics*. These included Ned Brant, a college athlete, Molly, the Model, and Jane Arden, female criminal investigator. One of the elements that made Jane Arden popular among young girls was the paper doll cutout section that always accompanied the story. The paper doll cutouts often reflected the latest fashion designs of the era.

Another transfer from *Feature Comics* was "The Clock" series. In reality, the Clock was Brian O'Brien, a polished socialite who at one time had served as a district attorney. Although he was no longer associated with the state law enforcement agency, Brian still continued his never-ending fight against the underworld as the Clock. In tracking down a group of crime lords who operated a legitimate business as a front for their otherwise illegal activities, the Clock would administer justice in this typical, if somewhat arbitrary, fashion . . .

©1940 Comic Magazines, Inc.*

Crack Comics also introduced the ultimate twist in the genre of the avenging masked sleuth with Art Pinajan's "Madam Fatal", a short-lived series that featured the only known transvestite crimefighter in the history of literature.

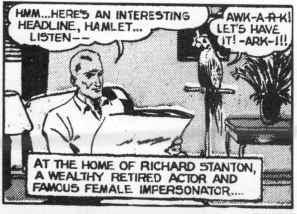

©1940 Comic Magazines, Inc.*

Madam Fatal did not care to bruise her knuckles in the course of a fist fight. When it came to a showdown with hoodlums she used her trusty walking stick as an efficient weapon of defense. A sharp poke in the forehead or throat would knock the naughty man right off his feet.

©1940 Comic Magazines, Inc.*

Within a few years the original characters of the first generation were phased out and replaced by others. The most notable replacement came in *Crack Comics No. 27* with the introduction of Captain Triumph, a superhero who came into being from a physical-spiritual fusion of two identical twin brothers—Michael Gallant, who was killed in an explosion, and Lance, his surviving brother. They both had identical "T" birthmarks on their wrists. Although Michael was dead, his spirit remained in mental communication with Lance. When Lance pressed the birthmark on his wrist, Michael's spirit merged with his. The result was the super two-persons-in-one,

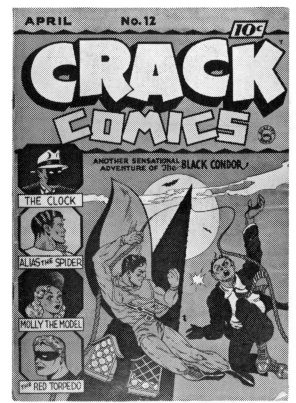

Crack Comics No. 12 (April 1941)*
©1941 Comic Magazines, Inc.

Captain Triumph, who could fly through the air and perform feats of incredible strength. After Captain Triumph had solved the problem at hand and matters were under control, he would press his birthmark and split into his two selves again, the spiritual Michael Gallant and the living Lance Gallant.

©1944 Comic Magazines, Inc.*

In 1949, *Crack Comics* underwent a major change and converted to a western format. The title became *Crack Western Comics* and ran as a moderately popular title for four years. It was terminated in 1953.

*Hit Comics No. 12 (June 1941)**
©1941 Comic Magazines, Inc.

*Hit Comics No. 16 (Oct. 1941)**
©1941 Comic Magazines, Inc.

Hit Comics, another title that underwent several changes, started in May 1940 and featured Hercules as the super superhero of the Quality Comics Group. Although Hercules was originally an average person who worked in a circus strong-man act, he ac-quired incredible, although unexplained, super strength when he left the circus. Nevertheless the series was well illustrated and jam-packed with action that displayed the power of the story's hero.

©1941 Comic Magazines, Inc.*

Neon was a superhero who also made his debut in the first issue of *Hit Comics*. The story of his origin began when a French Foreign Legion platoon made an unsuccessful attempt to cross the arid deserts of Africa. One by one, they were felled by the heat. The only survivor, Legionnaire Tom Corbett, dragged himself over the burning sands toward what appeared to be an oasis in the distance. When he finally reached it, he found a pool with strange phosphorescent vapors rising from its depths. As he drank the water, he began to glow and while renewed to life he was also transformed into a being of "neonic" power. He discovered he could control electrical energy, firing it from his fingertips, or flash through the sky by discharging a spiralling lightwave at his feet. Neon never returned to his other identity of Tom Corbett.

WITH STRANGE NEONIC POWERS, NEON STOPS THE BULLETS..

©1941 Comic Magazines, Inc.*

One of the less convincing *Hit* features was a costumed crimefighter called the Red Bee and his partner, Michael, a trained pet bee who accompanied him on his adventures and stung the villains into submission whenever the occasion warranted. The series represented a clever attempt to be unusual and different, but Michael just didn't fit in with the serious adventure theme—the Red Bee often read like animal fantasy. By contrast, one of the more convincing *Hit* features was Betty Bates, lady attorney-at-law, who investigated cases scheduled for court trial.

In addition, the early issues of *Hit Comics* carried H. C. Kiefer's "Blaze Barton," a futuristic adventure series with an interesting science fiction concept. In the distant future, scientists discovered that Earth was slowly moving closer to the sun and calculated that within three years all life on the surface would

perish from the extreme heat. Plans were drawn to build heat-proof cities deep underground as man's new world. However, as the excavating team, led by Blaze Barton, bored through to the hollow core of Earth, they encountered a strange race of monstrous creatures who had dwelled there since the beginning of time. Earth's hollow core representing man's last chance to survive was occupied by indestructible creatures who wanted to drive the humans away! Needless to say, war erupted.

Unfortunately, Kiefer left the series after the first few exciting adventures of man versus subterranean-man. It was taken over by other artists who changed the concept and patterned the series after Flash Gordon.

Within a year, new features began to replace the original ones. The next major character was Kid Eternity who made his debut in *Hit Comics No. 25* (December 1942) and took over the magazine as the embodiment of a highly innovative concept in surrealistic fantasy. It began at sea when a Nazi submarine torpedoed a merchant vessel and all hands aboard were lost. As the spirits of the deceased moved toward heaven, the keeper of the records that listed each man's predetermined lifespan discovered that the spirit of one young lad among those awaiting admission to the empyreal domain was there in error—the boy was not scheduled to die for another seventy-five years! In order to correct the unbelievable mistake, the young lad was allowed to return to Earth as an ethereal spirit to fight crime and evil, with the powers to summon anyone in history or mythology who was best suited to handle a particularly difficult situation. Upon speaking the magic word "Eternity" the boy, as he willed, could become a ghost, or a living person, or call anyone from the past to appear in the real world. In the beginning, Mr. Keeper accompanied him as a special tutor for his new powers. Kid Eternity seldom called on the same person twice, one situation may have required the services of Attila, the Hun, another Benjamin Franklin, another Samson, and so on.

As a result, the series exposed its readers to a rundown of famous figures in world history. In 1946, Kid Eternity moved to his own full-length magazine which ran quarterly through 1949. His last appearance was in *Hit Comics No. 60*, a few issues before the magazine ceased publication.

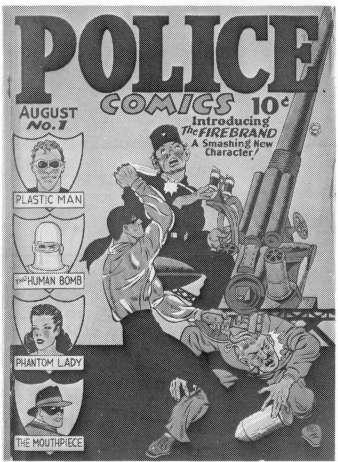

Police Comics No. 1 (Aug. 1941)*
©1941 Comic Magazines, Inc.

Another Quality title was *Police Comics*. The first issue, August 1941, marked the debut of Reed Crandall's Firebrand, a colorfully costumed crimefighter who initially served as the magazine's leadoff feature. In reality, Firebrand was millionaire playboy Rod Reilly whose butler Slugger, an ex-prizefighter, aided him in his relentless battle against the underworld. Although the series was exceptionally well illustrated with story lines of fast paced action, the character concept lacked a sufficient degree of originality to set it apart from the rising tide of other costumed crimefighters who were also emerging on the scene. Firebrand survived for a year and then was terminated in the thirteenth issue.

Police Comics No. 1 also marked the debut and origin of Jack Cole's Plastic Man, who quickly emerged as not only the leading star of *Police Comics* but also one of the most ingenious creations in the history of comics. Plastic Man could stretch himself like a rubberband, twist his body into a 1001 different shapes, bounce fifty feet in the air like a rubber ball, slip through keyholes or flatten himself as thin as a sheet of paper when speeding cars ran over him and then quickly spring back into human shape again. He acquired his fantastic ability through a strange quirk of fate when as Eel O'Brian, a notorious criminal at large, he was engaged in robbing a chemical factory. As Eel and his gang of hoodlums opened the safe they were discovered by a guard who attempted to stop them. A blazing shootout followed and the crooks fled with the cash. But during their escape, Eel was wounded and accidentally overturned a vat of acid, some of which spilled on him. His companions jumped into their getaway car and roared away, leaving Eel behind to take the rap.

However, Eel managed to escape on his own, and though seriously wounded he managed to find a hiding place in the nearby countryside where he finally collapsed. Later, he awoke and found himself the honored guest of a monk who ran a monastic retreat. After a brief philosophical discussion with the monk, Eel acquired a new slant on life and decided to abandon his criminal ways. Meanwhile, the acid which had spilled on him had penetrated the bullet wound, seeped into his bloodstream, and produced an incredible effect on his body. Eel found he had been transformed into a being of flexible plastic that could stretch and retract like rubber!

©1941 Comic Magazines, Inc.*

A new person, morally as well as physically, Eel decided that his peculiar abilities could be used as a powerful weapon against crime, and also as a means of atoning for his past evils. He assumed a dual identity. Under one guise, he wore dark glasses and a costume of rubber as Plastic Man. But he also resumed the role of Eel O'Brian, a known thief and criminal, in order to keep close contact with the underworld and thwart criminal activities from within. Unknown to anyone, the person of Eel O'Brian was just a fabricated rubber disguise, one of many that Plastic Man was capable of.

In *Police Comics No. 13*, Plastic Man met Woozy Winks, a lovable stumblebum of a petty criminal who decided to go straight and join Plastic Man's fight against crime which, from this point on, acquired a highly stylized and often humorous tone. The bad guys were thwarted by some of the most unorthodox methods ever depicted in comic books and the results were often hilarious. Woozy and "Plas," as he was often referred to, became an inseparable team. In *Police Comics No. 19*, Plastic Man played his role as Eel O'Brian for the last time and from then on he remained "Plas" all the time.

Beginning in 1943, Plastic Man was also featured in his own full-length comic book, an exceptionally popular title that ran until 1956, six years after Jack Cole retired from the series. The later adventures were handled by other artists who, unfortunately, were unable to maintain Cole's zany and humorous style. Plastic Man began to lose his appeal and was soon terminated. In 1966, Plastic Man was revived for a brief period as a D-C title. But previous to D-C's revival, Marvel Comics took Plastic Man's stretchable talents and gave them to Reed Richards of the Fantastic Four.

Police Comics' superheroine entry was Arthur Peddy's Phantom Lady. Although Phantom Lady did not possess super powers, she did nevertheless wear a colorful cape and costume, and carried a unique "black ray" flashlight that emitted a cone of absolute darkness. The ray momentarily blinded her adversaries, and during this dark moment she moved around like a silent cat, pummelling her enemies at will while remaining unseen. After rendering the evildoers helpless and calling the police, she vanished from view and assumed her true identity of Sandra Knight, the daughter of Senator Knight.

Police Comics was not all superhero fantasy. Representing the other department of law and order was an avenging masked sleuth called the Mouthpiece, created by Fred Gardineer. The Mouthpiece, who was garbed in a conservative blue suit and hat, was in reality District Attorney Bill Perkins. Again, when legal restrictions prevented him from performing his job as district attorney to his satisfaction, he simply put on a mask and settled the matter as the Mouthpiece. For example, the introductory episode of the series concerned the district attorney's efforts to break up a racket that involved the smuggling of alien refugees into the country. Perkin's preliminary investigation indicated that the operator of a fishing schooner was behind the scheme, but he lacked sufficient evidence to make an arrest. Every time he obtained a legal search warrant to inspect the schooner as it pulled into the harbor, the crew members, forewarned by the sight of the approaching police ship, would tie up the refugees and throw them overboard. And Perkins had no legal jurisdiction to inspect the schooner on the high seas. But as the Mouthpiece, he stowed away aboard the vessel and waited for its next trip. When he was discovered by the crew he whipped out his pistol and blasted away at the bad guys. And after he had fired the last bullet, he seized a harpoon and drove it cleanly through the schooner's captain. Upon taking off his mask, District Attorney Bill Perkins advised the shaken refugees that the immigration authorities would grant them every consideration for legal entry into the country.

Reed Crandall's Chic Carter of *Police Comics* straddled the fence between costumed superhero and avenging masked sleuth. Chic Carter was actually a crime reporter but his normal investigative assignments were sometimes restricted by law. To maneuver around these restrictions, Carter would adopt a disguise. But he went a step beyond the simple face mask and blue suit and hat. Chic Carter went into action wearing a colorful skintight yellow-and-red costume under the guise of the Sword. In keeping with his costumed identity, he discarded the conventional hand gun and armed himself with a sword which he used with all the deftness of a highly skilled fencer. Ironically, the story situations did not always require Chic Carter to change into his other identity. More often than not, he handled matters in his role as a crime reporter.

Police Comics No. 1 also introduced Steele Kerrigan, a clever variation of the avenging masked sleuth. Kerrigan was a tough prison convict who earned his parole by saving the warden's life during a violent riot that erupted within the prison walls. Upon his release, Steele Kerrigan decided to go straight and aid the police as an undercover agent in their fight against underworld racketeers who still accepted Kerrigan as a fellow gangster.

"711" was a similar feature. Here a criminal named Jacob Horn was sentenced to life imprisonment and assigned the convict number 711. But in reality Jacob Horn was District Attorney Daniel Dyce! The peculiar mix-up occurred when Dyce apprehended his life-long friend, Jacob Horn, a wanted criminal and three-time loser. By strange coincidence, the two men resembled each other so much that they could pass for identical twins. Horn had no regrets for the life he had led, but he did have one request: his wife was pregnant and due to have the baby in a few days and he wanted to be with her to offer his comfort. He asked Dyce to exchange places with him until the baby was born, promising he would surrender as soon as he saw his child. Dyce granted the favor and thus became Jacob Horn.

The "district attorney" then took the "prisoner" Jacob Horn into custody, and Horn is sent to trial, convicted, and sentenced to prison. However, while in prison and waiting for the real Jacob Horn to keep his end of the bargain, Dyce learns that his look-alike was accidentally killed by a hit-and-run motorist. Now he is permanently trapped with no identity other than Convict 711. Dyce digs a secret tunnel, escapes from prison, and adopts a cloak and costume to resume his fight against crime as the mysterious masked avenger known only as 711. But after seeing that justice is done, he slips back into prison to assume the role of a convict again. Of course no one is aware that one of the convicts is actually responsible for catching the criminals who ultimately end up in the same prison.

This was a feature whose theme, although quite different from anything else, did contain certain literary flaws and proved awkward to sustain over an extended period. "711" was terminated at *Police Comics No. 15*, the same issue that the creator of the series, artist George Brenner, introduced another character called Destiny. Destiny broke the tradition of the avenging masked sleuth. He exchanged the typical blue suit and hat for a *brown* suit and hat! And he dispensed with wearing a mask. Destiny also possessed limited occult powers that enabled him to foresee death and disaster whenever he slipped into a trance. Instead of personally participating in bringing the evildoers to justice, he directed events in such a manner that the bad guys often ended up killing themselves.

However, the ultimate concept of the avenging masked sleuth emerged in Will Eisner's "Spirit" series which began as a newspaper comic strip in June 1940, and ran for four years as a feature of the Register and Tribune Syndicate. The first few episodes were adapted into a comic book format and reprinted in *Police Comics*, beginning with Issue 13. As the Spirit's popularity increased, the other avenging masked sleuths were quickly phased out. Yet, in many ways, the Spirit resembled his competition. He wore the typical blue suit and hat, face mask, gloves, and he carried a pistol. His origin, however, was something quite unique.

It all began when Denny Colt, a criminologist and private detective, was tracking down the notorious Dr. Cobra who had recently escaped from jail. In the final showdown between the two men a vat of experimental chemicals was smashed and the contents spilled over, drowning Denny Colt. The detective sank to the floor, apparently dead from the effects of the volatile liquid. Dr. Cobra fled as the police rushed in and found Colt's body. He was declared dead and was buried. But that night, Colt climbed out of the grave, adopted a masked identity, and visited Police Commissioner Dolan to inquire about Dr. Cobra.

During the conversation, Dolan recognized Denny Colt, and Colt explained that the chemical had only put him in a temporary coma, and that he had broken out of the grave as soon as he had awakened. After bringing a swift and violent end to Dr. Cobra, Colt confided his plans for the future to the commissioner—he wanted to let the world believe that Denny Colt was dead so that in his guise as the Spirit, he could continue his war against those criminals who, for one reason or another, remained beyond the reach of the police. Dolan agreed, but issued a warning: if Colt stepped outside of the law, he would be arrested!

"If you can catch me," quipped the Spirit.

Thus, the stage was set for the continuing theme. The feature was rounded off with the introduction of Ellen Dolan, the commissioner's attractive daughter who developed a romantic interest in the Spirit. Up to this point, counterparts of the feature's three main characters could be found in many other police-detective thrillers. Then one day, the Spirit hailed a taxi and met its driver, Ebony White, a young black youth who became his junior sidekick and chauffeur. Ebony, who had no counterpart anywhere in comics, added an element of unique humor to a theme which otherwise would have fallen into the standard mold of non-stop violent action that was so typical of the other avenging masked sleuths.

Ebony had a speech handicap that made him a readily identifiable character—he lisped, stuttered, and spoke with the pronounced Southern drawl of a poor kid from the ghetto. But he was adorable and quick-witted. Hardly twelve years old, the little tyke wheeled his taxi at 100-miles-an-hour speeds through the busiest traffic, up and down back alleys, and across rough country roads, on a never-ending mission to meet the Spirit who would usually be racing toward him with bullets whizzing by in all directions. Ebony would screech on the brakes and slow down just long enough for the Spirit to leap on the running board, open the door and jump inside. Then Ebony would negotiate a nervy two-wheeled U-turn and roar away with his foot pressing the gas pedal to the floor. The bewildered hoodlums would be left scratching their heads.

"Atta boy, Ebony, you're right on the job," the Spirit would say while glancing out through the rear window.

"Yes, Mist' Spirit Boss!"—*Zoom!*

Between 1944 and 1950, the Spirit also appeared in his own full-length comic book as a leading Quality title. (The feature was later taken over by other publishers and is currently produced as a black-and-white magazine by Warren Publishing Company.)

Plastic Man and the Spirit were the star attractions of *Police Comics,* and the two virtually dominated the magazine, often forcing the other features into obscurity. One that was lost somewhere in the middle pages was the Human Bomb, a unique superhero whose origin was revealed in *Police Comics No. 1.*

When Roy Lincoln was assisting his father, a research chemist who was developing a secret explosive for the government, a group of enemy agents burst into the laboratory to seize the formula. During the struggle that followed, Roy's father was killed. Roy battled courageously to avenge his father and to save the precious capsule containing the formula, but he was heavily outnumbered. Sensing defeat, he swallowed the capsule to prevent the enemy from getting it. As the strange chemical surged through his veins, his entire body began to glow, and slowly the glow began to settle in his hands. The startled henchmen drew their guns and fired away at Roy, but the bullets exploded harmlessly upon striking his flesh which had been transformed into a super-hard substance.

The fight continued and during the vicious struggle, Roy landed a crushing punch that not only knocked out one enemy agent but also burst a wall apart, causing the laboratory to explode. Again, Roy Lincoln was not affected as the falling debris glanced harmlessly off him. He quickly realized that his fist had caused the blast, that he could blow up anything he touched, and that in reality he had become a "Human Bomb"!

He also realized that he was a dangerous hazard because anything he touched might explode. Remembering that the capsule he swallowed was made of a special "fibro-wax" that prevented the chemical from activating, Roy fashioned a pair of asbestos gloves and a complete asbestos suit and helmet, all of which he lined with the special wax.

Roy Lincoln's new attire was perhaps the most functional costume of any superhero in comics; he wore it as a protective measure to restrain his naked power and to protect those around him. Of course when he went into action he simply took off his gloves and delivered the final blow!

REMOVING HIS PROTECTING GLOVE, ROY LINCOLN, THE HUMAN BOMB, GRASPS THE MASONRY...THERE IS A SHATTERING BLAST...

©1941 Comic Magazines, Inc.*

In later issues the character concept underwent a gradual transition from superhero to crime sleuth. First, Roy Lincoln abandoned his protective asbestos suit for a green business suit and hat, and then he exchanged his asbestos gloves for ordinary leather gloves which he removed only when he had to punch through locked doors.

Military Comics No. 1 (Aug. 1941)*
©1941 Comic Magazines, Inc.

Military Comics No. 3 (Oct. 1941)*
©1941 Comic Magazines, Inc.

Military Comics, which began in August 1941, was Quality's answer to the patriotic trend that many comic books were turning to during the early 1940s. A complete departure from superhero fantasy and the avenging masked sleuth themes that dominated the other Quality titles, *Military Comics* was introduced as a single-theme magazine devoted to war fiction about the army and navy. The first half of the magazine's contents centered on army-oriented features and included "Blackhawk," created by Charles Cuidera, and "Blue Tracer," created by Fred Gardineer. The second half centered on navy-oriented features, including "Yankee Eagle," created by John Stewart, "Death Patrol," created by Jack Cole, and "Q-Boat," created by H. C. Kiefer. Of the lot, "Blackhawk" became *Military Comics'* star attraction and one of the leading creations in the Quality Comics Group.

The adventures of Blackhawk began in the 1930s when Poland was under attack by a Nazi air force squadron led by Captain von Tepp. During one of the invasions that crushed the last resistance of Poland's freedom fighters, one survivor angrily swears vengeance for the ruthless murder of his family. He reorganizes a new group of freedom fighters and sets out to bring about the downfall of Captain von Tepp.

In succeeding adventures, it is learned that Blackhawk's legion of mercenaries consists of freedom fighters from different countries in Europe who banded together under a common cause to oppose Nazi tyranny. Of the international makeup of the Blackhawks, Hendrickson of Germany was perhaps the most striking personality, and whose membership on the team of good guys carried a powerful message to the juvenile readers who might have been inclined to regard all Germans as villains during the war years. Hendrickson pointed out there was a vast difference between the common people of Germany and Adolf Hitler's dictatorial government. Hendrickson, a native of Germany who fled persecution from the Nazis, was violently opposed to Hitler's regime, and the distinction that was drawn between the German people and Hitler's Nazis was almost unique in comic book literature.

The theme of the feature was democratic freedom versus Nazism on a global scale, and the stories often included a heavy infusion of violent deeds by both sides. Quite often, the stories would show Blackhawk shooting his adversaries to bits or blowing them up with hand grenades or bombs as the only course of action necessary for meting out justice in the fight for freedom. Violent action was the feature's trademark and one of the elements responsible for its popularity. But violent action was not the only element!

The mascot of the Blackhawk team was Chop-Chop, a jolly Chinese cook who wielded a mean meat cleaver and who would also give his life for the cause if necessary. Chop-Chop added an important touch of light-hearted humor to the series and helped prevent it from falling into the monotonous doldrums of continuous shoot-em-up sequences. Although Chop-

Blackhawk Comics No. 22 (Dec. 1948)
©1948 Comic Magazines, Inc.

©1952 Columbia Pictures

Chop was not a full-fledged uniformed member of the team, he nevertheless remained Blackhawk's close buddy and sidekick whenever the group had to split up in pairs to attack the enemy from different positions. Chop-Chop emerged as the major co-star of the series and was soon elevated into his own semi-humorous feature in the full-length *Blackhawk* comic book that began as a quarterly title in 1944.

Another fascinating element about the "Blackhawk" series was the high degree of realism with which the stories were illustrated. Top artists, such as Reed Crandall, who handled most of the graphic execution, were chiefly responsible for maintaining the high level of artistic excellence the feature was known for, especially in the rendering of the use of military hardware as well as the background settings of European cities and countryside.

In 1952, Columbia Pictures produced an exciting movie serial adaptation of Blackhawk that featured Kirk Alyn in the lead role, and Weaver Levy as Chop-Chop. In a typical Blackhawk story that embraced spies, espionage, double agents, secret inventions, and political dictators plotting world conquest, the movie serial adventure centered around the attempts of the Blackhawks to thwart a gang of international criminals who sought to secure a new invention for the world's most powerful weapon, a deadly electronic ray.

Curiously enough, Blackhawk was the only feature from the Quality Comics Group that was adapted to the screen, and the Blackhawk movie serial turned out to be Hollywood's last serial production that featured a character from the comics. When Quality Comics folded and its titles were absorbed by the D-C line of comic books, Blackhawk was continued as a leading D-C character whose new adventures included guest appearances of Batman, the new Green Lantern, the new Flash, and even Superman.

The other unique features in *Military Comics*, such as "Blue Tracer," were phased out prior to the forty-third issue in 1945 when the magazine dropped its patriotic theme and changed its title to *Modern Comics*. While the names of most comic book features usually reflected the name of the leading hero, a few of the early *Military* features introduced exceptions to the rule. For example, the title of "Blue Tracer," which ran as an exciting series in the first sixteen issues, referred to a German tank that American engineer Bill Dunn had confiscated and converted into an indestructible war vehicle that could fly like an airplane, submerge to the bottom of the ocean like a submarine, crash through mountains, burrow tunnels in the ground, and roll unimpeded across swamp marsh, snow, dense jungle foliage, and sandy deserts. It could also streak along paved highways like a supercharged locomotive.

Similarly, "The Yankee Eagle," another short-lived *Military Comics* feature, was not a costumed superhero as the name might imply. The Yankee Eagle referred to Sam, a trained pet eagle owned by Jerry Noble, the flamboyant son of a distinguished senator who cleverly directed the bird to aid him in his patriotic struggle to serve the country's war efforts. The theme of the series generally centered around naval and air action on the sea where Sam often delivered critical messages, clawed and bit enemy sailors into submission, and glided down to the water where the periscope of an enemy submarine was protruding, and where it spread its wings to cover the view, thus saving an allied ship from torpedo fire. Jerry's pet also flew aboard enemy ships and chewed away the ropes that bound American prisoners. The Yankee Eagle was also known to aid helpless survivors downed at sea by flying to their defense and fighting off threatening sharks.

Military Comics No. 1 also featured the unique origin of the heroes of the "Death Patrol," created by Jack Cole who applied the reformed criminal theme in a manner similar to that which was used in "Plastic Man." The story of the Death Patrol began when Del Van Dyne, a commercial pilot, was fired from the airlines for apparent loafing on the job. Realizing he was blacklisted from working for another airline, Van Dyne decided to go to England to find employment, and he warmed up his personal "stratoliner" for its last takeoff from U. S. soil.

Meanwhile, in another part of the city, five convicts successfully scale the prison wall and make a break for freedom. With the police authorities hot on their heels, the escapees steal a car and speed away toward the airport where they abandon the vehicle and hijack the first airplane they see—which happens to be Van Dyne's stratoliner. At gunpoint, they force Van Dyne to take off before the police are able to stop them.

While in the air, Van Dyne persuades the convicts to join him in starting a new life by lending support to Britain's war against the Axis powers. After crossing the Atlantic, they eventually approach an R.A.F. base that is under attack by Nazi airplanes. After driving the enemy away, the group lands and is greeted by the commanding officer of the base who enlists their services for a special assignment. The job calls for someone to penetrate the enemy base at nearby Ostend and seize critical military papers that outline Hitler's plans for conquering England.

Van Dyne and his men take off for Ostend. After a series of dramatic clashes with the enemy in the air and on the ground, they succeed in penetrating the base and seize the plans. But in the course of their escape, the Nazis shoot and kill Pee Wee, one of the convicts. Upon returning to the R.A.F. headquarters, Van Dyne and his men decide to call themselves the Death Patrol in memory of Pee Wee.

H. C. Kiefer's "Q-Boat," another short-lived *Military Comics* feature, was about a super battleship that sailed the seas disguised as an antiquated fishing schooner of the 18th century. The ship was manned by Captain Foghorn and three teenaged sailors who guarded the shorelines of allied countries from enemy ships and submarines.

However, the one feature that was perhaps out of place in this particular magazine was "Miss America," a series about a fanciful superheroine who had been granted magic powers by the spirit of the Statue of Liberty. Miss America, who in reality was newspaper reporter Joan Dale, used her magic to thwart enemy acts of sabotage on the home front.

Beginning with the second issue, *Military Comics* introduced "Secret War News," a short semi-fictional feature about new military weapons and airplanes that was illustrated by A. C. McWilliams. When *Military Comics* was changed to *Modern Comics* and the patriotic theme was dropped, the magazine included several other features that had no connection with the war. The new format was set off by the romantic miscapades of Torchy, one of Comicdom's glamour queens of the early 1950s, who is best described as an eighteen-year-old version of Marilyn Monroe.

In addition to the titles described here, the Quality Comics Group also included many others that were published during the 1940s.

ALPHABETICAL LISTING OF QUALITY COMICS' COMIC BOOKS

All Humor Comics (1946 - 1949)

Amazing Man Comics (1939 - 1942, Centaur Publications)

Amazing Mystery Funnies (1938 - 1940, Centaur Publications)

Arrow (1940 - 1941, Centaur Publications)

Barker Comics (1946 - 1949)

Blackhawk Comics (1944 - 1949, succeeded *Uncle Sam Quarterly*)

Broadway Romances (1949 - 1951)

Buccaneers (1950 - 1951)

Buster Bear (1953 - 1955)

Candy Comics (1947 - 1956)

Comics Funny Pages (1936, five issues, Centaur Publications)

Cowboy Comics (1937 - 1938, Centaur Publications)

Crack Comics (1940 - 1949, changed to *Crack Western* at Issue 63)

Crack Western Comics (1949 - 1953)

Detective Eye Comics (1940, two issues, Centaur Publications)

Detective Picture Stories (1936 - 1937, Centaur Publications)

Diary Loves (1949 - 1953)

Exotic Romances (1955 - 1956)

Feature Comics (1937 - 1950, formerly *Feature Funnies*)

Funny Pages (1936 - 1942, Centaur Publications)

Girls in Love (1950 - 1956)

Hickory Comics (1949 - 1950)

Hit Comics (1940 - 1950)

Hollywood Secrets (1949 - 1950)

Intrigue (1955, one issue)

Keen Detective Funnies (1937 - 1940, Centaur Publications)

Little Giant Comics (1938, two issues, Centaur Publications)

Little Giant Detective Funnies (1938 - 1939, Centaur Publications)

Love Confessions (1949 - 1956)

Love Scandals (1950, four issues)

Love Secrets (1949 - 1956)

Man of War (1941, two issues, Centaur Publications)

Marmaduke Mouse (1946 - 1956)

Military Comics (1941 - 1945, changed to *Modern Comics* at Issue 43)

Modern Comics (1945 - 1950, formerly *Military Comics*)

National Comics (1940 - 1949)

Police Comics (1941 - 1953)

Range Romances (1949 - 1950)

Star Ranger (1937 - 1938, Centaur Publications)

Star Ranger Funnies (1938 - 1939, Centaur Publications)

Stars and Stripes Comics (1941, six issues, Centaur Publications)

Super Spy (1940, two issues)

Uncle Joe's Funnies (1938, one issue)

Uncle Sam Quarterly (1941 - 1943, changed to *Blackhawk Comics* at Issue 9)

Wham Comics (1940, two issues, Centaur Publications)

Yanks in Battle (1956, four issues)

For further information on the biographies of many of the artists for the Quality Comics Group, see James Steranko's *History of Comics, Vol. 2,* (published by Supergraphics, 1972).

KING FEATURES SYNDICATE

The late 1800s marked a growth period in the newspaper publishing industry as an ever increasing number of publications made the transition from weekly to daily circulation. Because of the transition, news coverage was expanded to include articles of interest that occurred outside the immediate locality of individual papers. Expanded news coverage was greatly enhanced by centralized syndication bureaus that came into being to receive stories and articles from one locality and circulate them to other newspapers across the country. By 1900, newspapers, largely through the efforts of these news bureaus, emerged as the nation's most influential mass communication media.

In addition to providing news pieces, the bureaus began to introduce a wide range of fillers, such as short stories, poems, jokes, historical facts, crossword puzzles, and cartoon features. King Features Syndicate was one of the first news bureaus to introduce cartoons and as cartoons grew in popularity it soon became common practice among the daily newspapers to devote a full page to the "funnies" from King Features and from other news bureaus.

In 1926, King Features published *All the Funny Folks*, the first hardcover book of any kind devoted to comics. Far from a collection of comic strip reprints, the book told a rather clever story about a party that "all the funny folks" from the newspaper attended. Among the famous celebrities present were Jiggs and Maggie, The Katzenjammer Kids, Felix the Cat, and Popeye's girl friend, Olive Oyl, as well as many other characters that were well known during the 1920s but faded into obscurity shortly after the book was published. Many of these characters who are unfamiliar to us today were the first efforts of such artists as Chic Young who would later create "Blondie," and Chester Gould who would turn from humor to crime detection with his sensational "Dick Tracy."

At the time *All the Funny Folks* came out, newspaper comics were published in black and white. But the 112-page book was lavishly published in full color as King Features' way of presenting a new look to its syndicated comic strips. However, the color printing process had not yet been perfected to the point where it was economically feasible for this kind of use, and the book had to be placed on sale for the then incredibly high price of four dollars. Although these funny folks were popular features in the two-cent newspapers of the day, they were not popular enough to make the book a commercial success. Moreover, *All the Funny Folks* was not recognized as a serious book publication. It never received widespread distribution, and very few copies were sold.

A full decade passed before King Features attempted another publication of comics in color (although by then, color comics for Sunday newspapers had become commonplace, and the color comic book was coming into its own). In association with David McKay publishing company, they entered the infant comic book field with the first edition of *King Comics*. The book offered a reprint series of the syndicate's most popular features, many of which had been added to their family of funny folks over the intervening years.

The immediate and widespread success of the book generated a full line of King Features' comic books that ran monthly until the early 1950s. As a group, these publications were one of the few real links that joined the newspaper comic strip to the entirely separate field of the comic book. Although King Features discontinued its activity in comic books more than twenty years ago, many of its features have acquired worldwide fame and continue to appear in hundreds of newspapers today. These include such funny folks as Popeye, Jiggs and Maggie, Henry, and the ones that aren't so funny—Flash Gordon, Mandrake, the Phantom, and Prince Valiant.

All the Funny Folks (1926)
©1926 King Features Syndicate, Inc.

King Comics No. 22 (Jan. 1938)
©1938 King Features Syndicate, Inc.

"Popeye," one of the early classics of stylized cartoon humor, was created by E.C. Segar. The offbeat "sailorman" was introduced on January 17, 1929 as part of the cast of characters of the popular "Thimble Theater" feature which had started ten years earlier. Prior to Popeye's appearance, the zany heroine Olive Oyl had been the star character of the feature that stressed the kind of elaborate slapstick comedy that was typical of the humor strips of the early 1900s. Popeye, as the bumbling, super strong sailor, added a unique touch to Thimble Theater, and with his appearance the routine slapstick comedy changed to "knock-down-drag-out" comedy in which the punches were thrown a bit harder and with more pronounced results.

At the same time, the motion picture industry was creating its own equivalent offspring of the comics—the animated film cartoon short. Although Walt Disney made the medium famous, there were several other studios that also specialized in the animated film short, one of which was the Max Fleischer Studio. And it was the Max Fleischer Studio that brought Popeye to screen life complete with the gravelly voice that truly defined him as a rugged "sailor man" whose lungs were filled with the fresh salty air of the ocean. Indeed, Popeye's voice was as readily identifiable as the exaggerated anatomy of his forearms.

Popeye's trademark was, of course, his regular diet of spinach from which he derived an abundance of zest and power. And the trademark was taken seriously. In 1938, Crystal City, Texas, the spinach raising center of the country, erected a twenty-foot statue of Popeye in memoriam to E.C. Segar.

Segar died in 1938, but his famous character was continued by other artists. While the newspapers carried the "new" Popeye, *King Comics*, on the other hand, reprinted Segar's original series from the early 1930s. In addition, several full-length Popeye comic books of Segar reprints were published in the King Features/David McKay Feature Book Series. Samples of the reprints are shown here . . .

©1938 King Features Syndicate, Inc.

The other humor favorite was O. Soglow's "Little King," the silent comic strip known for its utter simplicity in gag lines as well as in art style. Soglow's characters are drawn without ears, and they wear clothes that refuse to wrinkle! In addition, these characters, including the Little King himself, seldom have anything to say. Yet, this unusual technique in simplified cartoon art has proved quite effective, and has been used in almost every strip since the Little King made his debut in September 1934. Here is a sample of a typical episode from the earlier years that was reprinted in *King Comics No. 19*:

The Little King

The Little King

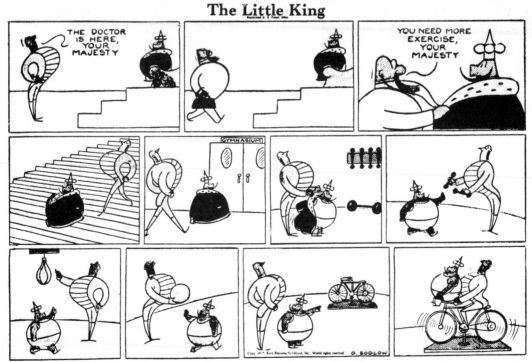

Bringing Up Father

BY
GEO. McMANUS

Registered U. S. Patent Office.

The feature "Bringing Up Father," created by George McManus, first appeared as an occasional cartoon spot in the newspapers as early as 1913 and then became a regular strip in 1916. It featured Jiggs and Maggie, two of the earliest "Funny Folks." Twenty years later the feature was reprinted in *King Comics,* even though its adult-oriented humor was miles above the level of comic book literature that was mostly intended as juvenile entertainment. In fact, it was miles above comic strip entertainment for adults even though it appeared innocent enough fun on the surface.

In reality, Jiggs was carefully studied by a chosen few, not for its surface humor, but for what was said *beneath the surface.* They knew that between the words and pictures lay a secret code that predicted in advance a substantial number of transactions on the New York Stock Exchange!

The truth came out September 15, 1948 when the legal staff of the New York State Attorney General's office, then headed by L. Goldstein, finally broke the code after a ten-year investigation of a suspected link between "Bringing Up Father," often referred to as "the Wall Street comic strip," and the stock market. Action was taken against F. N. Goldsmith Financial Service, then the nation's largest stock broker, who had used the strip to manipulate various securities transactions in favor of its investment clients. It was found that the code within the comic strip was based on 800 key words, phrases and pictographs which, according to their arrangement in the comic strip panels, dictated price fluctuations of various stocks.

For example, on June 15, 1948, "Bringing Up Father" centered on an episode in which Jiggs complained about a stage play Maggie had forced him to attend. The disgruntled Jiggs remarked, "The intermissions are the only good thing about this show."

As far as the general public was concerned, the remark was ingenuously humorous. But when decoded, Jiggs actually said, "Mission Oil Stock is the only good thing to invest in tomorrow."

The following day, Goldsmith's customers, well aware of what Jiggs really said, bought up Mission Oil Stock at the market price. In three days, the value of Mission Oil Stock tripled!

A few weeks later the strip depicted *almost* the same episode. This time, Jiggs complained that the intermissions were too long, a signal to the investors that they had held Mission Oil Stock long enough and it was time to sell. The investors took the cue and sold the stock at a tidy profit. A few days later, Mission Oil Stock took a tremendous drop.

Goldsmith's customers reaped the reward while other investors lost a fortune during the transactions. When the story of the stock market code leaked out as a result of the court proceedings, untold thousands of investors who had previously ignored the comic page suddenly became its most avid fans. Many realized windfall profits during the two-week trial, when much of the daily rise and fall of the nation's stock market depended on our hero, Jiggs!

(No charges were entered against the strip's creator, George McManus, after he claimed he had no connection with the investment firm.)

Here is a typical page of the "Bringing Up Father" comic strip that originally appeared in the newspapers during 1937 and was reprinted in *King Comics No. 32* (November 1938). When decoded, its innocent humor was, during 1937, a signal to Goldsmith's clients to buy up a stock in the growing motion picture industry with particular emphasis, as Jiggs' closing punch line specified, on the studio that was then "shooting" the western extravaganza "Stagecoach," starring John Wayne.

Needless to say, almost every newspaper in the country started carrying the "Wall Street comic strip" in a featured position on the funny pages. When McManus died a millionaire in 1954, his exceptionally popular feature was continued by other artists but its humor acquired a different slant.

King Comics also featured reprints of "King of The Royal Mounted," a strip created by the foremost author of western fiction, Zane Grey. His feature about Sergeant King of the Canadian Royal Mounted Police was the first "western" comic strip to hit the newspapers during the early 1930s, a time when adventure was gradually being added to the funny pages.

Actually, Sergeant King was not a western character in the usual sense of the word. His adventures encompassed the contemporary Northwest along the Canadian border and involved tracking down international racketeers and smugglers rather than horse thieves and cattle rustlers. While he usually rode a horse or travelled the snow regions on dog sled, he occasionally travelled the skies in light aircraft or the waters by motorboat or canoe. The actual time period in which the series occurred was never clearly defined although it was assumed to be in the early 1900s.

In 1940, Republic Pictures introduced a movie serial adaption of "King of The Royal Mounted." The action was set in 1940, and reflected the coming world crisis. In the movie, Sergeant King battled a gang of enemy agents who were engaged in extracting a secret mineral compound from a government-owned mine that could be used as a war weapon against England. (At the time the movie serial was produced, the growing war in Europe had not extended far enough to involve the North American continent and the movie never specified the enemy agents' actual homeland.)

King Comics started as a sixty-four page magazine but it was reduced to fifty-two pages during 1941. As a result of the cutback, "King of The Royal Mounted" was dropped. However, it would appear later in *Red Ryder Comics*, a Hawley publication which was made up of discontinued features from several syndicates, and gradually acquired an all-western format.

The strip was first illustrated by Allen Dean, but it was soon taken over by Charles Flanders, the same artist who was illustrating "The Lone Ranger" series. Flanders illustrated both features for more than a decade. Here is a sample of his work on "King of The Royal Mounted" in a typical adventure that truly captures the wintery feeling of the Yukon.

UNSCRUPULOUS FOREIGN AGENTS..
Desperate in their quest for an all-powerful, secret element that threatens the might of the British Navy

ZANE GREY'S
KING
OF
THE
ROYAL
MOUNTED

Based on the newspaper cartoon sensation

ALLAN ROBERT
LANE · STRANGE
ROBERT LITA
ELLARD · CONWAY
HERBERT
RAWLINSON

A *Republic* SERIAL IN 12 CHAPTERS

©1940 Republic Pictures

KING COMICS ALSO MEANT FLASH GORDON!

Created by artist Alex Raymond, "Flash Gordon" was introduced in the Sunday newspapers on January 7, 1934 as one of the new continuous adventure strips of King Features Syndicate. The grand epic began when a strange planetary body was sighted rushing through space on a collision course with Earth. There were atmospheric disturbances. Flaming meteors fell through the atmosphere, one of which struck a small aircraft carrying two passengers—Flash Gordon, a Yale University graduate and world renowned polo player, and the lovely Dale Arden. The two parachuted to safety and landed near the estate of Dr. Hanz Zarkov, an eccentric scientist who had devised the means to stop the impending disaster. He had built a rocketship that would shoot through space toward the oncoming planet and explode upon striking its surface, thus deviating the path of the planet away from Earth. The only problem was that the ship required manual operation. At gunpoint, Dr. Zarkov forced Flash and Dale to accompany him on a suicide mission that would save Earth.

The ship departed for its destination and eventually did crash on the wayward planet, that by now had acquired the name Mongo. Somehow the trio managed to survive. And from this point on, fantasy flowed from Alex Raymond's pen with the force of a tidal wave. In ensuing episodes Flash Gordon battled all forms of grotesque beasts and monsters in the treacherous jungles of Mongo, beneath the seas of Mongo, and in the skies of Mongo. But his chief antagonist, of course, was the ruthless dictator Ming the Merciless, whose government possessed scientific technologies far beyond anything known on Earth.

In the beginning, Alex Raymond was given a full newspaper page in which to develop the strip. Instead, Raymond used the page to develop *two* dynamic features—"Flash Gordon", which occupied three-fourths of the page, and "Jungle Jim" which occupied the rest. As a result, the early issues of *King Comics* carried reprints of pages containing part "Flash Gordon" and part "Jungle Jim." Later, the comic book dropped "Jungle Jim" and devoted the full page to "Flash Gordon" reprints.

Alex Raymond was among the early craftsmen of the pen-and-ink technique who expressed "cartoon art" in a highly realistic style which (together with Hal Foster) set the artistic standards for adventure comics and was emulated by many illustrators who entered the field after 1934. In addition, Raymond's style in handling "Flash Gordon" started a school of action-fantasy that made comics more exciting than ever.

For example, in one typical incident, Flash, Dale, and Dr. Zarkov, having left the dangerous depths of the water world of Mongo, took to the skies in an airship and were immediately blasted down by Ming's patrol fleet. Flash's vessel spun out of control and crashed in the dense swamps of the jungle. After swimming safely through a lake infested with monsterous creatures and reaching land, the trio was suddenly attacked by a flock of deadly flying squirlons whose bite caused instant madness. Although they courageously fought off the hideous beasts, Dr. Zarkov was bitten during the course of the battle. Burning with fever and raving with insanity, Zarkov ran blindly off only to fall into a whole nest of squirlons. Giving their companion up for dead, Flash and Dale sought a way out of the marshes which was alive with danger at every turn. Shortly after they had successfully extracted themselves from a pit of deadly quicksand . . .

FLASH GORDON

BY ALEX RAYMOND

FLASH AND DALE, HOPELESSLY LOST IN THE JUNGLE, CONTINUE THEIR SEARCH FOR BARIN'S FOREST PEOPLE·····

A HEAVY CRASHING NOISE REACHES THEIR EARS··· SUDDENLY, A GIANT MAGNOPED LUMBERS INTO VIEW!···

SEEKING REFUGE, FLASH AND DALE SCRAMBLE INTO A TREE····

HE'S COMING TOWARD THIS TREE!

UGH··· WHAT A HORRIBLE CREATURE!

THE HUGE BEAST SEIZES A VINE WHICH HANGS FROM THE LIMB ON WHICH FLASH AND DALE ARE PERCHED··· HE SHAKES THE LIMB UNTIL DALE TOPPLES TO THE GROUND!···

IN A MAD ATTEMPT TO SAVE DALE, FLASH SWINGS DOWNWARD, FIRING HIS GUN··· HIS SHOTS HAVE NO EFFECT ON THE MONSTER'S THICK HIDE!

STUNG TO FURY, THE MAGNOPED SNATCHES FLASH FROM HIS VINE AND RAISES A MIGHTY FOOT!···

The Movie Advertisement that made headlines in July, 1936
©1936 Universal Pictures

In 1936, Universal Pictures produced the classic movie serial adaptation of Flash Gordon. The serial began much like the comic strip did—a strange planetary body was sighted approaching Earth, and the team of Flash Gordon, Dale Arden, and Dr. Zarkov crash-landed in the barren swamplands of the mysterious world of Mongo. They miraculously crawled out of the flaming wreckage a few moments before it exploded. But before they could catch their breath the ground began to tremble. Ferocious roars echoed through the air, and trees crashed to the ground as gigantic creatures resembling prehistoric dinosaurs charged toward the startled trio.

They jumped to their feet and fled for their lives, frantically splashing through muddy swamps and marshes. Of course Dale couldn't keep up, and moments later she tripped and sprained her ankle. As Flash stopped to pick her up, she screamed at the sight of a huge monster that was lunging toward them. Its two bulging eyes were looking straight at Dale and its gaping jaws were clearly large enough to swallow her whole! *And those teeth!* Dale fainted in Flash's arms and he, in turn, froze in fear as the massive jaws snapped shut and then gaped widely open again. Flash dropped Dale and fell back.

Dr. Zarkov turned around. He clasped his mouth and his eyes widened as he cried out at the incredible sight, "Oh, no! Flash! Dale! How *horrible!*"

It seemed obvious that the monster had gobbled them both when the screen suddenly went blank and one of the world's most irritating phrases popped into view:

"TO BE CONTINUED NEXT WEEK."

Juvenile audiences across the country sprang from their seats. "No fair! No *fair!*" Boos and hisses followed. Popcorn was flung at the screen. But there wasn't anything they could do about it, except be at that same theater the following week!

Chapter two revealed that Flash and Dale were saved by one of Emperor Ming's patrol cruisers that had sailed out to investigate the explosion and subsequently blasted the beast with heat rays in the nick of time. The Earth trio was taken to Ming's palace headquarters where even more hazardous perils awaited them. They were seized as spies of Prince Thun's rebel forces who opposed Ming's oppressive rule. In order to prove his innocence, Flash had to step into the Arena of Death to face the great horned ape .

©1936 Universal Pictures

It was one incredible peril after the other, and included such formidable adversaries as the sharkmen who dwelled beneath the sea, the lion-men who dominated the jungle, and the flying hawkmen who controlled a floating city in the sky. The celebrated last chapter came three months later when Flash Gordon finally conquered the forces of evil. He bid farewell to Prince Thun and his people, and headed back to Earth, vowing to Dale that he would never let her out of his sight. *Yay-y-y-y!!*

©1936 Universal Pictures

©1936 Universal Pictures

King Comics, only featured reprints of the Flash Gordon adventures that appeared in color on the Sunday comic pages. But Flash Gordon also appeared in separate adventures in the daily newspapers. Here, artist Austin Briggs assisted Alex Raymond and was generally responsible for illustrating Raymond's sto-ry line for the daily feature. Briggs achieved results that were almost equal to the master. Although the original daily comic strip adventure never appeared in *King Comics*, it was reprinted in *Feature Book No. 25* (1940) as the first full-length comic book of Flash Gordon stories.

Flash Gordon on the Planet Mongo
Feature Book No. 25 (1940)
©1940 King Features Syndicate, Inc.

©1940 King Features Syndicate, Inc.

The humor side of King Comics also included reprints of Carl Anderson's mouthless "Henry," which began newspaper syndication as a daily strip in December 1934 and then expanded into a full-color Sunday feature in March 1935. However, prior to newspaper syndication, "Henry" first appeared as a series of single-panel gag cartoons in the *Saturday* *Evening Post,* beginning with the March 19, 1932 issue. "Henry" is one of the very few comic strips to have survived without change through the years; indeed, this lovable character looks exactly the same as he did forty years ago even though the feature has been drawn by other artists since Anderson's retirement in 1942.

©1937 King Features, Inc. and Carl Anderson

King Comics also reprinted the "Brick Bradford" series, created by William Ritt and Clarence Gray, which began as a daily strip in August 1933 and later became a Sunday feature in November 1934. The strip still runs in some newspapers today but under the hand of artist Paul Norris. In the early years, Bradford was noted for the "Time Top," a unique vehicle which he frequently used to travel into the past and the future in both the comic strip and Columbia Features' movie serial adaption that premiered in 1947.

©1938 King Features Syndicate, Inc.

©1947 Columbia Pictures

©1947 King Features Syndicate, Inc. and Columbia Pictures

Brick Bradford, overshadowed by the popularity of Flash Gordon, never attained major status even though the series did include several novel ingredients within its fantasy concept. In addition to being a regular commuter in time travel, Brick spent a considerable amount of his adventurous career among a secret civilization at the middle of the Earth. He also shrank into the molecular universe of the atoms within a copper penny. The movie serial adaptation of "Brick Bradford," which starred Kane Richmond in the lead role, featured the Time Top almost exactly as it appeared in the comic strip. It also featured the "Crystal Door," a teleportation system which, when opened from the side in Professor Salisbury's laboratory on Earth, enabled Brick to materialize on the surface of the moon, which lay on the other side of the door.

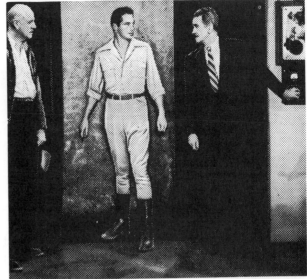

©1947 Columbia Pictures

©1947 King Features Syndicate, Inc. and Columbia Pictures

A quick wave of the hand, a hypnotic gesture, and the stars in the heavens would seem to vanish as Mandrake the Magician, another major figure of *King Comics*, delved into the unknown to combat the mysterious elements of surrealistic worlds. Mandrake was created by the team of writer Lee Falk and artist Phil Davis and began as a daily newspaper comic strip feature in June 1934, and then as a Sunday strip in February 1935. The Sunday strips were later reprinted in *King Comics*, starting with the first issue.

Mandrake was a master of creating hypnotic illusions which at times did appear as if he possessed pure magical powers even though he actually did not. And he was accompanied by his strong-arm African bodyguard, Lothar, whose herculean strength often prevented disaster when hypnotic illusion failed. Together, they formed a dynamic team and shared many fascinating adventures that were truly out of the ordinary. Typical of these was the episode that ran in *King Comics* in 1937 when Mandrake and Lothar crossed over into the Land-of-X, somewhere in another dimension.

It began when Mandrake and Lothar happened to save a certain Professor Theobold from accidentally falling to his death. They learned that Theobold had, to his regret, invented a device capable of transporting a person through the time-space barrier. His daughter Fran had tested the machine and had mysteriously disappeared. Mandrake decided to try and locate the girl and bring her back to her father. With Theobold's invention set for operation, Mandrake and Lothar stepped inside and faded away, materializing moments later in a totally alien environment. Mandrake was greeted by one of its inhabitants—a metal wheel-man.

Having rendered Mandrake helpless in the wirey mesh, the wheel-man rolled toward Lothar, but . . .

But when Lothar tried to disentangle Mandrake from the sticky mesh he also found himself entrapped by it. Other wheel-men rolled onto the scene, quickly observed what had transpired, and carted the two prisoners away on a moving sidewalk. While Lothar was sent to the acid chamber, Mandrake was dropped down a chute that emptied into a mine far beneath the surface. He finds the missing girl, Fran, and several human inhabitants of that world whom the wheel-men had enslaved to dig for their vital food-mineral, coal. Mandrake conceived a daring plan of escape and led Fran and one of the other prisoners, Tolac, to freedom. Meanwhile, in another part of the city, Lothar faced execution for destroying a wheel-man.

However, Mandrake and Tolac, armed with acid spray guns, blasted past the executioners and saved Lothar. Then the action really began!

At the sudden appearance of the awesome fire bird whose radiating heat waves melted metal as though it were butter, the wheel-men momentarily forgot about their human prisoners to take up arms against their most dreaded enemy. As Mandrake and party burst out of the acid chamber, they suddenly faced what appeared to be certain death as the flaming horror swooped toward them.

Of course they escaped. And while the wheel-men battled the fire bird, Mandrake and party seized cartmobiles and fled to the outskirts. But then, having reached the edge of the jungle, they encountered new problems. First, it was the flesh-eating plants that snatched Fran . . .

Then the seed traps . . .

Fortunately, the peaceful plant people, whom Tolac was on friendly terms with, came upon the scene and calmed the living vines that were beginning to strangle the Earth trio. But their presence was observed by the ruthless crystal men . . .

MEANWHILE, IN A FAR-OFF GLITTERING CRYSTAL CITY ATOP A HIGH PEAK, MANDRAKE IS BEING WATCHED!

THERE ARE FLESHMEN DOWN THERE AMONG THE PLANT PEOPLE! REAL FLESH MEN!

THE CRYSTAL MEN! TRANSPARENT, COLD, CRUEL, RELENTLESS--ONE OF THE DOMINANT RACES OF "X"!

THE FLESH MEN HAVE BECOME WARY AND HARD TO CATCH! AND WE NEED SKINS! WE MUST CAPTURE THEM AT ONCE!

A patrol of crystal men leaped on their glider sleds, sailed silently through the air towards the unsuspecting group and captured them with little effort.

--AND THE CRYSTAL FLEET "TAKES OFF" FROM THE MOUNTAIN CITY. . . .

--AND TRAVELS IN CLOSE FORMATION, TRANSPARENT -- INVISIBLE FROM THE GROUND BELOW!

THE ATTACK OF THE CRYSTAL MEN! SUNLIGHT, PASSING THROUGH THEIR TRANSPARENT BODIES, IS FOCUSED INTO BURNING RAYS!

THE FLESH PEOPLE ARE TO BE TAKEN ALIVE AND MANDRAKE AND FRAN FALL BEFORE SUFFOCATING WAVES OF HEAT THAT STREAM FROM THE GLITTERING CRYSTAL ATTACKERS!

When they regained consciousness, they found themselves prisoners in the Emperial Tower of the Crystal Men. Tolac explained that the crystal men used human skin to polish their glass bodies and enhance the absorption of sunlight. Lothar and Fran were led away and tied to the racks as the first victims to be skinned. As the crystal executioner approached Fran and raised his razor-sharp, disc-like hand to her face, Mandrake rushed into the chamber. With a quick gesture, an illusion of a pile of rocks appeared and he began hurling them at the executioner and the other crystal men. Lothar finally broke his bonds and joined Mandrake.

The crystal men retaliated by flashing their deadly rays of concentrated sunlight energy that could burn the humans to a crisp. Again, Mandrake gestured! He engulfed the glass beings in a cloud of smoke that caused blinding confusion. It was only for a moment, but that was enough time to untie Fran and escape. The crystal men quickly sliced through the illusionary smoke cloud by flashing reflections of sunlight through their polished glass hands. Having no defense against them, Mandrake and his party fled for their lives. With the crystal men hard on their heels, they frantically raced through the Emperial Tower up to a balcony overlooking the river almost a mile below. They had no alternative except to dive! Lothar held the rear guard as Mandrake and Fran hit the water . . .

Mandrake saved Fran from the serpent's clutches by ramming a log into its mouth, but the monster's tail instantly seized him in a crushing grip. Mandrake was dragged to the bottom.

Fortunately, Lothar was observing . . .

86

Inspired by Mandrake, the humans prepared for war! They made protective suits of asbestos and armed themselves with catapults. Then they marched toward the city of the crystal men for all-out battle.

Having defeated the crystal men, the humans reorganized their army and marched toward the city of the wheel-men to engage in another incredible battle. The wheel-men met them half way . . .

As the war drew to an end, the three races arrived at terms for everlasting peace. Tolac was proclaimed the new emperor.

Fran decided to stay with Tolac, the man she loved, and Mandrake and Lothar bid them farewell.

©1937 King Features Syndicate, Inc.

©1937 King Features Syndicate, Inc.

In 1939, Columbia Pictures introduced an exciting movie serial adaptation of *Mandrake the Magician*. Warren Hull starred as Mandrake and Al Kikume starred as Lothar. Here Mandrake and Lothar battled a notorious crime lord known as the Wasp.

The popularity of the movie serial prompted King Features to introduce a new comic book, *Magic Comics*, which began in August 1939 and featured Mandrake as the main attraction. In addition to the "Mandrake" reprint series which was transferred from *King Comics*, *Magic Comics* also ran "Secret Agent X-9," "Barney Baxter," "Henry," "Lone Ranger," "Blondie," and reprints of the new Popeye series. (King Comics continued to carry the original "Popeye.")

Blondie, an outgrowth of one of "the funny folks," made her debut in the newspapers in September, 1930. In the beginning, she was a pretty socialite who was relentlessly pursued and wooed by Dagwood Bumstead. They finally became engaged. Then on February 17, 1933, the funny pages depicted their marriage ceremony, marking the first such event to have occurred in the history of comics. After their marriage, the Bumsteads emerged as a reflection of the typical American family. Between 1938 and 1951, the feature inspired a series of more than two dozen movies. Movie star Penny Singleton as Blondie brought the charm of the comic strip character to screen life.

This is an early sample of Chic Young's famous comic strip "Blondie," which originally appeared in newspapers during 1942 and was reprinted in *Magic Comics No. 51*, October 1943.

Magic Comics No. 51 (Oct. 1943)
©1943 King Features Syndicate, Inc.

©1942 King Features Syndicate, Inc.

Ace Comics, which began in April, 1937, was another King Features reprint comic book. It carried Alex Raymond's "Jungle Jim," after the series had been dropped from *King Comics* and in Issue No. 11 (February 1937) *Ace Comics* introduced the reprint series of "The Phantom," created by Lee Falk and Ray Moore, which had started newspaper syndication in 1936.

The origin of the Phantom was a highly imaginative concept in superhero fantasy. It began in the 16th Century when a British trading vessel was attacked by a pirate ship. A fierce battle erupted and the British crewmen were slaughtered almost to a man. The ship went down in flames and all hands were lost—except for the captain's son Kit, who was eventually washed ashore on a remote island. A friendly tribe of pygmies found the half-dead Kit and nursed him back to health. Several days later, Kit, while exploring the beach, came across a swarm of vultures feeding on the dead body of a pirate. Kit recognized the clothing—it was the same pirate who had killed his father!

After the vultures had stripped the body clean, Kit lifted the pirate's skull in his hands and swore an oath.

©1936 King Features Syndicate, Inc.

The legend was effectively dramatized for the first time in a scene from "The Sky Band Adventure" which originally ran in the newspapers from November 1936 to April 1937. It was reprinted in monthly episodes in *Ace Comics*, and reprinted again as a complete story in *Feature Book No. 57*. In this story, a band of female sky pirates, led by a ruthless baroness, was engaged in hijacking small aircraft. During the course of one of these villainies, they captured the Phantom when he unwittingly parachuted into their secret island headquarters. The baroness held him prisoner as the band set out for another raid. But this time the sky pirates had been led into a clever trap. An armed military squadron was waiting for them high in the clouds. The baroness knew that the Phantom was somehow responsible for upsetting her ambitious scheme to control the airline insurance system. Pistol in hand, she angrily spun around and fired at him point blank! But the Phantom just stood there, staring silently at her . . .

©1937 King Features Syndicate, Inc.

Rather than face imprisonment, the baroness quickly swallowed poison and committed suicide. As her plane plunged into a nose dive, the Phantom, who was in fact seriously wounded and bleeding internally, parachuted to safety and landed in his jungle territory where the natives nursed him back to health. He continued his relentless fight against the forces of evil until it was time for his son to resume the role of "The Ghost Who Walks."

©1943 King Features Syndicate and Columbia Pictures

©1943 Columbia Pictures

In 1943, Columbia Pictures introduced the movie serial adaptation of "The Phantom" that starred Tom Tyler in the lead role. The serial story centered around a missing ivory key, the seventh centerpiece of an ancient puzzle-map that pointed the way to the legendary lost city of Zoloz where untold treasures were to be found. Professor Davidson, an archeologist, who had three of the ivory keys, organized an expedition and set out to try to locate the city that lay somewhere in the darkest jungles of Africa. His niece, Diana Palmer, accompanied him. While at the trading post stocking up on supplies, Davidson met Singapore Smith, a villainous outlaw who owned three additional ivory keys to the puzzle-map but was totally unaware of their value. As the two men talked and matched their keys to form the peculiar puzzle arrangement, they found that the seventh, the key centerpiece, was missing.

During the night, Smith stole Davidson's three keys and made a deal with Dr. Bremmer, an international renegade who was engaged in smuggling guns and ammunition. However, a closer inspection of the partial map revealed a serious problem—the route passed through Tonga Village, the forbidden district ruled by the Phantom. With the use of poison, Bremmer carefully planned the Phantom's death and, surprisingly, accomplished his mission successfully!

The tom-toms spread the word that the "Ghost

©1943 Columbia Pictures

Who Walks" was seriously stricken. Bremmer, of course, was quite happy at the news. However, unknown to anyone, two faithful native servants, Soobu and Muku, sent an urgent message to the Phantom's son, Geoffery Scott, who immediately left his home in England and went to Africa to secretly resume his father's role. When the Phantom appeared to have risen from his grave, the tom-toms echoed once more throughout the night. This time the message said: "The Ghost Who Walks, walks again!" And the startled Bremmer shuddered in fear.

Aided by the two natives, the Phantom, along with his four-legged pal Devil, who was part wolf and part German shepherd, set out to track down Bremmer's henchmen, and this soon brought him into contact with Davidson's expedition, and Diana.

During the following course of events, the Phantom was lured into an alligator-infested swamp. As he sank into the quicksand the ferocious beasts moved in to devour him. But in the next chapter, Devil rushed to the rescue. His loud barking and growling frightened off the alligators long enough for the Phantom to seize hold of a vine and pull himself out of the quicksand. When he set out to block Bremmer's ship-

ment of munitions, two henchmen attacked him on a narrow rope bridge overhanging a deep chasm. During the ensuing battle, the unstable bridge suddenly collapsed. Of course the next chapter revealed that the Phantom had landed safely in the branches of a convenient tree while the two thugs plunged to their death.

A series of other gruesome battles led the Phantom into a flaming pit where he was almost burned to a crisp. He was then thrown into an execution chamber to face a starving lion. Successfully cheating death both times, the "Ghost Who Walks" leaped into a pit to battle a ferocious gorilla that wore the seventh ivory key around its neck! After killing the gorilla with his bare hands, the Phantom seized the key and raced to free Diana and her uncle who were hopelessly trapped in the underground catacombs—just as Brenner set off an explosion that nearly buried them under an avalanche of rock. Again the heroes managed to escape. Finally, the Phantom had had enough. He rounded up the natives and had them wipe out the bad guys once and for all. Peace returned to the jungle as the Phantom led Davidson's expedition to the Lost City.

Ace Comics No. 26 (May 1939) reprinted the origin of Hal Foster's famous "Prince Valiant," which began in the newspapers on February 13, 1937.

This adventure classic started with Val as a child. His father was the dethroned King of Thule, and a few of his followers had been forced to leave the country and settle on a small island. Hoping to regain his throne one day, the king saw that his men trained constantly in the arts of combat, exercises that young Val cheerfully participated in. Val often ventured out alone. Once he had to use his newly acquired skills in a battle for his life against a grotesque being called Thorg.

He defeated Thorg, then helped the creature home where he met Thorg's mother, Horrit, a sorceress who possessed the power to foretell the future. She created a vision that held the prophecy of Val's future, and Val saw himself as he would be several years later—a warrior in knight's armor fighting in the service of King Arthur of England.

When Val returned home, he found that his mother was dying and that his father had lost interest in the throne of Thule. When his mother passed away, the embittered Val returned to England, the country that had driven his father away, to find out if Horrit's prophecy was true.

The artwork of "Prince Valiant" emerged as a rare exception in the world of comics and cartoons. Not only was it a fine example of realistic illustration, but the feature itself represented an authentic reconstruction of medieval history during King Arthur's reign. The clothing of the characters and their hair styles, the cities, the castles and ships, all were based on years of tedious and meticulous research. Even the individual stories were based on situations that very probably could have existed during that period. Peo-

ple believed in witchcraft and sorcery in those days, and these elements often provided the background for many of Val's adventures.

©1937 King Features Syndicate, Inc.

In 1946, Eagle Lion Pictures produced a full-length movie of Prince Valiant, starring Robert Wagner. Interestingly, the picture came out at the same time Universal-International released *Knights of the Round Table*, starring Douglas Fairbanks Jr. Of the two films, *Prince Valiant* became the bigger hit!

©1937 King Features Syndicate, Inc.

On the light hearted humor side, *Ace Comics* featured a reprint series of those two mischievous rascals known as "The Katzenjammer Kids."

Prince Valiant

IN THE DAYS OF KING ARTHUR   BY HAROLD R FOSTER

Registered U. S. Patent Office

SYNOPSIS: THE MIGHTY TRISTRAM AT LAST TUMBLES VAL FROM HIS HORSE. AS HE LIMPS FROM THE FIELD GREAT CHEERS RING OUT FOR HIS GALLANT EFFORT, BUT VAL HEARS THE JEERS OF THE ENVIOUS SQUIRES AND THINKS THE WHOLE CROWD MOCKS HIM. QUIETLY HE RETURNS TO CAMELOT.

HE LEAVES CAMELOT WITH THE SINGING SWORD

AND TURNS HIS STEPS TOWARD THE PEACE AND QUIET OF HIS OLD HOME IN THE MYSTERIOUS FENS

BY THE EDGE OF THE GREAT MARSH HE MEETS AGAIN HIS BOYHOOD FRIEND

THE YOUNG SHEPHERD AGREES TO TAKE CARE OF VAL'S MOUNTS

TO HIS GREAT JOY VAL FINDS HIS OLD DUGOUT STILL IN ITS HIDING-PLACE

WITH MELTED RESIN AND CHARCOAL HE REPAIRS THE CRACKS

ONCE AGAIN HE DRIVES HIS CANOE THRU THE MAZE OF CHANNELS

AFTER TWO YEARS OF WANDERING VAL APPROACHES THE ISLAND WHERE HIS KINGLY FATHER LIVES IN EXILE

WHILE AT COURT THE KING COMMANDS—"BRING ME PRINCE VALIANT THAT HE MAY BE KNIGHTED—THERE ARE NONE SO BRAVE OR SKILLFUL!"

Origin of Prince Valiant ©1937 King Features Syndicate, Inc.

ALPHABETICAL LISTING OF COMIC BOOKS OF KING FEATURES

Ace Comics (1937 - 1949)

Blondie Comics (published as assorted issues in the "Feature Book" series between 1937 and 1947, then continued as a monthly title to present in association with different publishers. *Blondie Comics* is currently published as a Charlton title.)

Dagwood Splits the Atom (1949, one issue as a special science edition)

Dagwood Comics (published as a monthly title in association with Harvey Publications during 1950 through 1965)

Dick Tracy Comics (published as three issues in the "Feature Book" series during 1937 to 1938, and continued as assorted issues in Dell's "4-Color" series through 1949, and then as a monthly title by Harvey Publications during 1950 through 1961)

Feature Book Comics (1937 - 1947, assorted issues of single features published in association with David McKay Publications)

Future Comics (1940, four issues)

Gang Busters (published for one issue in the "Feature Book" series in 1938, and continued as assorted issues in Dell's "4-Color" series through 1943, and then revived as a monthly title of D-C Comics during 1948 through 1958)

Giant Comic Album (one issue as a special reprint edition of comic strips from the 1940s and 1950s)

Henry (1935, one issue published by David McKay Publications, then continued as assorted issues in Dell's "4-Color" series and eventually a monthly title through 1961. *Henry* was also continued as assorted issues in K.K.'s "March of Comics" series published in association with Dell and King Features)

Katzenjammer Kids (published as assorted issues in the "Feature Book" series during 1944 through 1946, and continued as a monthly title in association with David McKay Publications and other publishers through 1954 (also see "Captain and The Kids", Section 12, United Feature's *Tip Top Comics.*)

King Comics (1936 - 1952)

Little Orphan Annie (1937, one issue in the "Feature Book" series, and continued as assorted issues in Dell's "4-Color" series through 1949.)

Mandrake the Magician (published as assorted issues in the "Feature Book" series during 1940 through 1947, and continued as assorted issues in Dell's "4-Color" series)

Phantom (published as assorted issues in the "Feature Book" series during 1940 through 1947, and continued by Dell and other publishers through present and is currently a title of Charlton Comics)

Popeye (1935, two black-and-white issues published in irregular format by David McKay Publications, then continued as assorted issues in the "Feature Book" series during 1937 through 1939, and continued by Dell and other publishers through 1973.)

Throughout the years, King Features had produced comic books in association with other publishers, and quite often the comic strips might have appeared in other publishers' magazines under original titles as *Junior Funnies* produced by Harvey Publications during the early 1950s. *Junior Funnies,* formerly Harvey's *Tiny Tot Funnies,* actually included reprints of such features as "Blondie," "Popeye," "Felix," "Katzenjammer Kids," and "Flash Gordon." However, during the early 1960s, King Features did introduce its own comic book line that included original story material based on their famous characters, but within three years King Features terminated its comic book line which, for the most part, was taken over by Charlton Comics and continued up through the present. In addition, King Features in association with Nostalgic Press, Inc. has introduced a current series of large-size hardcover and paperback publications that include reprints of the Golden Age comic strip adventures of such features as "Flash Gordon," "Mandrake," "Prince Valiant," and "The Phantom." Each of the Nostalgic Press editions, which is devoted to one feature, also provides a detailed biography on the strip's creator.

FAWCETT PUBLICATIONS

Fawcett Publications, currently one of the major publishers of mass market paperback books, at one time put out a major line of comic books. During the 1940s, Fawcett experimented with various ideas for improving the standard comic book format. One innovation, published in the midst of competing comics that contained sixty-four pages and sold for ten cents, was the one and only *Nickel Comics,* a half of a comic book with thirty-two pages that sold for just five cents. *Nickel Comics,* featuring Bulletman, ran bi-weekly for eight issues before it was terminated. Bulletman was moved to *Master Comics,* a monthly publication that Fawcett had originally introduced as an oversized magazine, measuring almost 11" × 14". *Master Comics* was later converted to the smaller standard size.

Fawcett also brought out a few hefty giant-sized comic books that contained a whopping 300 and more pages, such as *Xmas Comics* and *Gift Comics.* Yet, in direct contrast, they also introduced a two-color miniature pocket comic book whose size was 4" × 5", and which contained only sixteen pages. The pocket miniatures were usually inserted within the regular comic books as an extra feature. Fawcett's experiments proved that a comic book was an extremely flexible type of publication that had little if any physical restrictions. Although the experiments were discontinued in the early 1940s, the 32-page comic book was destined to make a comeback in later years.

In addition, Fawcett had perfected a color lithography printing process that was beginning to be widely used on covers of slick magazines. Fawcett (along with Dell Publishing Company) was among the first to adapt that process successfully to certain comic book titles that were based on real-life stars of the screen. The covers of *Hopalong Cassidy Comics,* for example, utilized photos of the screen star instead of the normal hand-drawn art. During the 1950s, photographic covers had become somewhat of a fad as other publishers began using them to give the illusion that their comics were actually a "better magazine."

Besides pioneering these mechanical innovations, Fawcett also published books that dealt with the exploits of famous characters which were equally well-known for their radio and movie serial adventures. But Fawcett's real explosion in the comic book field stemmed from artist C. C. Beck's invention of one little six-letter word—SHAZAM!

1939 was the year in which many publishers of paperback and pulp fiction books made a mad rush into the comic book field as a sideline. But inasmuch as the stiff competition forced many to withdraw and drop out of sight after a brief spurt of a few issues, Fawcett approached the arena with caution. In early

96

January 1940, Fawcett released a few sample copies of *Thrill Comics No. 1* to its newsstand dealers for a general opinion of the contents. The lead-off feature told the story of a mysteriously cloaked stranger who led a young newspaper boy down into an abandoned subway where they boarded a single-car train that glided silently through a labyrinth of tunnels until it came to a stop at the end of the line. The youth was led off the train and introduced to a strangely garbed old man seated upon what appeared to be a stone throne.

"And now, Billy Batson," said the old man, "speak my name."

The startled boy looked up at the old man and called out, "SHAZAM!" BOOM!—a mighty roar of thunder ripped through the air as a bolt of lightning appeared from nowhere and struck the youth, who was instantly transformed into an entirely different person. In Billy Batson's place now stood the crimson-clad figure of Captain Thunder, the World's Mightiest Mortal! Endowed with the wisdom of Solomon, the strength of Hercules, the stamina of Atlas, the power of Zeus, the courage of Achilles, and the speed of Mercury, Captain Thunder sprang into being! He was informed that his mission was to carry on the elderly man's fight against evil throughout the world.

"And now, Captain Thunder," said the old man, "it is written that I must pass. Speak my name, my son."

Captain Thunder nodded understandingly and called the old man's name, "SHAZAM!" BOOM! Again a mighty roar of thunder filled the air as lightning struck for a second time. Captain Thunder was transformed back to young Billy Batson but, at the same time, the ancient wizard had vanished!

Captain Thunder's first adventure pitted him against the crafty mad scientist Sivanna, who would return again and again as his number one arch villain.

Fawcett received a highly favorable response from the dealers, who applauded the story as the greatest thing that happened to comics since the appearance of Superman. But Fawcett was also advised to abandon the idea. Another publisher had already introduced a character named "Captain Thunder,"[1] while yet another competitor had just released a title called *Thrill-*

ing Comics,[2] not to mention the publisher of the pulp magazine, *Thrill*, who strongly objected to Fawcett's comic book entry of the same title.

Instead of abandoning the idea, Fawcett made a few hasty revisions, and in late January 1940, reissued the comic book for general release under a different title, *Whiz Comics No. 2*. The lead-off story remained generally the same, except that the hero's name, Captain Thunder, was changed to Captain Marvel.

However, Fawcett's clever escape from one set of legal complications led to a new and different problem. In effect, Fawcett had registered copyright for the same magazine twice, but under two different titles, and the validity of copyright protection became questionable. There was disagreement even within the Copyright Office as to whether *Whiz Comics No. 2* (featuring the birth of Captain Marvel) was the second edition of *Thrill Comics* (that featured the similar birth of Captain Thunder), or the first edition of *Whiz Comics*. In order to resolve the matter and straighten out the numbering sequence to the satisfaction of the Copyright Office, Fawcett, after it had published four monthly issues of *Whiz Comics*, decided to omit the May issue, substituting instead a book with the unusual title *Special Edition Comics*. The *Special Edition* featured four Captain Thunder adventures (with the character's name changed to Captain Marvel). It was intended to serve as the legal answer for the fifth issue of the *Thrill-Whiz* mixup so that *Whiz Comics No. 5* could resume the following month, June 1940.

However, the unexpected sellout of the *Special Edition* prompted Fawcett to start a separate full-length series of *Captain Marvel Adventures*, initially on a quarterly basis, then on a monthly basis. The title would later become the only bi-weekly comic book in the industry.

Of course the captivating element was the unique transformation of Billy Batson to Captain Marvel, all through the use of one magic word. Needless to say, the most spellbinding experiences Billy encountered were those that prevented him from shouting the magic word just when Captain Marvel was needed

1. See Section 5, Fiction House.
2. See Section 14, Better Publications.

Whiz Comics No. 2 (Feb. 1940)*
©1940 Fawcett Publications, Inc.

Special Edition Comics (Summer 1940)*
©1940 Fawcett Publications, Inc.

the most. He often found himself tied up and gagged at the most inappropriate moments, and sometimes even hypnotized. In one adventure he fell victim to amnesia thus forgetting the magic word, and in another he suffered from a sore throat and was unable to speak loudly enough for the magic word to produce the hoped for results. Billy was left to solve his vocal problems the best way he could and, in time, to save the day. Any number of strange things occurred to the young hero and they all combined to make C. C. Beck's magic word concept one of the most ingenious creations in fantasy literature.

In *Captain Marvel Comics No. 4*, three lads whose name coincidentally just happened to be Billy Batson were visiting *the* Billy at the radio station just when arch villain Sivanna sent his thugs to kidnap his young foe. Because of the name confusion, the thugs returned with the wrong Billy Batsons. Enraged at his henchmen for bringing in three strange boys instead of the correct one, Sivanna decided to do away with the three prisoners, just as *the* Billy Batson appeared. The four Billy Batsons shouted the magic word in unison. The result: Captain Marvel appeared, and so did the three Lieutenant Marvels who were equally endowed with super powers!

The Lieutenant Marvels, however, made only three guest appearances within the series and were never considered as major characters. The magic word only worked for the other three Billy Batsons when they shouted it together with the real Billy Batson.

In *Captain Marvel Comics No. 8*, the magic word concept was utilized in the clever origin of Ibac, a super villain and another of "Cap's" arch enemies. It began when a petty criminal, Stinky Printwhistle, attempted to blow up a train but was foiled by Captain Marvel. Captured in the act on top of a 50-foot bridge, Stinky accidently dropped out of Captain Marvel's hands and plunged to what appeared to be his certain death. But the Devil popped into view and saved his life, for a price. Stinky made a pact with the Devil and was given the powers of the four most evil men in history: Ivan the Terrible, Borgia, Attila the Hun, and Caligula, Rome's most fiendish emperor. Upon speaking a magic word that was made up of the first letter of each name, Stinky was transformed into the powerful Ibac to carry on a vicious campaign of evil across the world. Naturally, Ibac clashed with Captain Marvel in a titanic battle to the finish. Supposedly, Iban was killed in the end . . . but he would return again in *Captain Marvel Comics No. 22*.

And it was this issue, *Captain Marvel Comics No. 22*, (March 1943) that "Cap" faced the toughest challenge of his career . . .

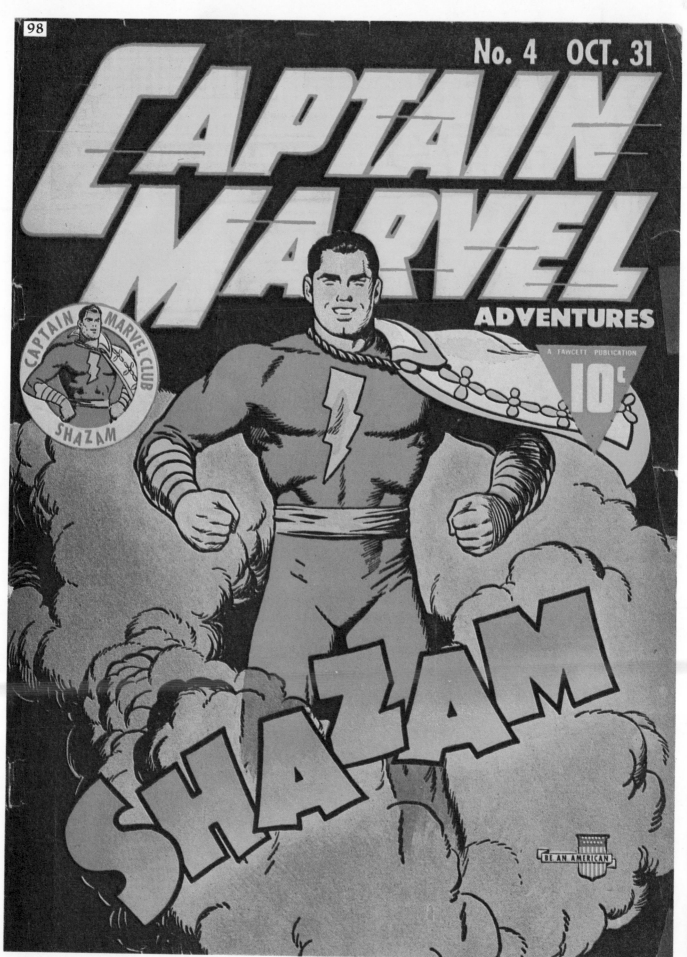

Captain Marvel Adventures No. 4 (Oct. 1941)*
©1941 Fawcett Publications, Inc.

Captain Marvel Adventures No. 1 (1941)*
©1941 Fawcett Publications, Inc.

Captain Marvel Adventures No. 2 (Summer 1941)*
©1941 Fawcett Publications, Inc.

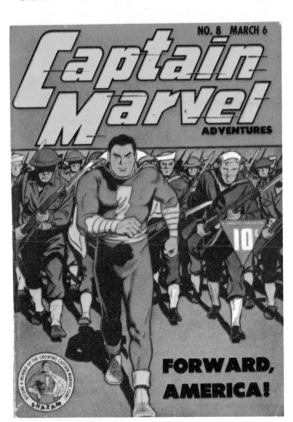

Captain Marvel Adventures No. 8 (March 1942)*
©1942 Fawcett Publications, Inc.

Captain Marvel Adventures No. 22 (March 1943)*
©1943 Fawcett Publications, Inc.

This was the opening scene of Captain Marvel's fantastic war against the newly formed Monster Society of Evil whose membership included Ibac and Sivanna, to name only a few. It was serialized over twenty-five issues and became one of comicdom's ultra-classics in fantasy.

The first exciting episode began when Billy, in his role as a news broadcaster, covered the arrival of Princess Rajabuti, who brought with her a gift of two mystical pearls as her country's contribution to America's war effort. In the meantime, the enemies of mankind had joined together for the first time to form a new and sinister organization with visions of worldwide conquest. Their leader was an unseen voice heard over a radio loudspeaker who identified himself only as Mr. Mind. His first order of the day was the theft of the two mystical pearls. Of course when the organization attacked the unsuspecting princess they ran smack into Captain Marvel, and a predictable battle royal erupted. First Ibac was slammed to the ground, then Nippo, the champion of Japan, and then Captain Nazi, the pride of Germany, all of whom Captain Marvel had clashed with before but on separate occasions. Ibac quickly recovered and fled with the pearls while Captain Nazi sent a gigantic stone idol tumbling down on Captain Marvel and the princess.

Naturally "Cap" saved the princess and took off after Ibac. But Ibac had passed the pearls on to Nippo. "Cap" caught up with Nippo and demolished him just in time enough to prevent a second Pearl Harbor disaster. He also retrieved the pearls and while trying to untap their mystic power as Nippo had done,

Captain Marvel accidently found he could see Sivanna who, halfway across the world, was building an incredible apparatus that would switch Earth's magnetic poles thus turning America into a frozen wasteland. Again, "Cap" acted in time to crush the diabolical plot, but too late to catch Sivanna who had fled to parts unknown.

Captain Marvel then used the pearls to discover the location of Mr. Mind's headquarters which turned out to be a small undetected planetoid near the moon. Here "Cap" battled the other members of the organization, which included all manner of alien monsters that served Mr. Mind. One was the fiendish Octopoid, Oliver . . .

©1943 Fawcett Publications, Inc.*

In an awesome test of super-strength, Captain Marvel managed to wrest himself free from the deadly clutches of Oliver and defeat him. But other monsters rushed in and ganged up on "Cap" who relentlessly proceeded to clobber them one by one until he was on the edge of exhaustion. Then the voice of Mr. Mind spoke, threatening to destroy the crimson-clad hero and continue the war on civilization from a new location directly on Earth. The enraged Captain Marvel tore the castle apart in a futile search for the owner of the voice. But Mr. Mind spoke on! And the World's Mightiest Mortal was truly baffled, for the voice seemed to come from thin air.

In Chapter VI, Mr. Mind's shocking identity became known. He was revealed as an intelligent, bispectacled worm from outerspace who broadcasted his thought waves through a tiny amplifer that was strung around his body. Mr. Mind and his ghouls left for Earth via spaceship. Of course Captain Marvel was not far behind. The battle continued on earth

where Mr. Mind resumed his fiendish schemes of destruction, which "Cap" managed to foil every time. But "Cap" often made the mistake of underestimating his little opponent . . .

©1943 Fawcett Publications, Inc.*

Billy escaped the bullets and changed to Captain Marvel, but only just in time. In the course of the battle that followed, Mr. Mind fled into a patch of weeds. After demolishing the evildoer's goons, "Cap" set out to track down "the worm." As he searched through the weeds, Mr. Mind hurriedly tossed his spectacles to an ordinary earthworm. When Captain Marvel found the worm wearing the spectacles, he assumed it was Mr. Mind and crushed it in his hand. Assuming he had destroyed his foe, he changed back to Billy Batson, an assumption that nearly turned into a fatal disaster . . .

©1943 Fawcett Publications, Inc.*

In the end, however, Mr, Mind was electrocuted and the world was safe at last.

Captain Marvel Adventures No. 61 (May 1946)*
©1946 Fawcett Publications, Inc., and
renewed ©1976 Fawcett Publications, Inc.

Although it was explained in every issue that Captain Marvel's powers were derived from the six gods which comprised the wizard's name, the full and complete background of "Cap's" origin was withheld until *Captain Marvel Comics No. 61* (May 1946). Here it was revealed for the first time that the wizard's name was originally Shazamo, comprised of *seven* letters. The letter "O" represented Oggar, the powerful god of magic!

The story took place in ancient times on the heavenly mountain top of Mt. Olympus where Oggar had grown evil and rebellious. He challenged Shazamo for the throne. Shazamo accepted the challenge and thus the strange test of power began. Oggar, seeking to end the match quickly with one fatal blow, rammed into the wizard with the full brunt of his seemingly invincible force. Actually, Oggar would have been better off ramming into the mountain itself for the wizard didn't budge! Oggar bounced off in a complete daze for such a blow would have easily felled Hercules, Zeus, or Achilles who were spectators to the awesome event. Then the wizard-ruler of Mt. Olympus made his move. He turned to the throne on which his named was engraved, raised his hand, and then with the force of a sledgehammer, he chopped away the corner that held the letter "O." The mountain shook violently as Oggar melted away to nothing-

ness. But in his parting words before vanishing completely, Oggar angrily swore that he would return one day and seek vengeance against the wizard and the rest of the gods. Then he was no more.

From that moment on, the wizard-ruler referred to himself as Shazam, and completely ignored the absence of Oggar. However, Shazam realized that Oggar was an immortal god whose strength would eventually renew itself and that one day he would break out of his temporary state of nonexistence and return to carry out his threat. During council with the other gods, Shazam set up an elaborate plan to prepare for the day when Oggar would appear again. Under this plan, it was decided that each of the gods would pass their individual powers into one mortal of a distant era, a champion capable of opposing the evil god of magic.

It was the 20th Century when Oggar finally returned to life. It was an entirely new world to him. Mt. Olympus was gone! The wizard-ruler was gone! And so were Solomon, Hercules, Atlas, Zeus, Achilles, and Mercury! To satisfy his burning quest for vengeance, Oggar decided to set out against mankind and rule the world—only to collide head-on with Captain Marvel in a no-holds-barred, knockdown, drag-out battle that was serialized in no less than six action-packed issues.

They fought each other over and over again, and they fought to a standstill. In one dramatic collision, Oggar lured "Cap" to a remote island in the South Pacific which happened to be occupied by Circe, an evil sorceress to whom Oggar had given the curse of immortality during the ancient days when she had been a beautiful princess of Greece. Throughout the centuries of her loneliness, Circe had mastered the arts of black magic which she used against any man that dared venture to her island.

While exploring the island in search of Oggar, "Cap" accidently ran into Circe. Before he could utter a word, she changed him into a goat! As the transformation was taking affect, however, "Cap" invoked the magic word and changed into Billy Batson thus breaking Circe's spell. However, Circe retaliated by changing Billy into a goat, and Billy was trapped!

Oggar had observed the scene from a hiding place and arming himself with a rifle, he set out after the goat to kill it. Billy, unable to speak his magic word, fled for his life. As a goat, he was able to scale the mountains with ease, galloping up one hill and down the other. Oggar sprinted after him, firing a few warning rounds in an effort to tease Billy before the final kill.

But it wasn't long before Oggar grew tired of the game. The next time the goat came into view, Oggar fired for a direct hit. The goat yelped and collapsed as the bullet struck its heart!

Was this the end of Captain Marvel?

As it turned out, there was another goat grazing on the hillside where Billy was hiding. Billy had nudged his four-legged companion out into the clearing, and Oggar had shot *it*. Billy was temporarily safe as Oggar, confident of his triumphant victory over the last surviving son of the wizard Shazam, streaked back to the mainland to resume his plans for enslaving the world. Meanwhile, Billy galloped back to Circe and tricked her into lifting the magic spell. Upon shouting the magic word, Captain Marvel pulled away from Circe, who was momentarily blinded by the lightning flash, and streaked after Oggar for the final decisive battle.

This time it was "Cap" who lured Oggar back to the same island. And ironically, it was through the help of Circe that Oggar was ultimately killed. The adventure concluded with Circe's immortality rapidly wearing away. She thanked "Cap" as she died and at last found eternal peace.

Master Comics No. 21 (Dec. 1941)*
©1941 Fawcett Publications, Inc.

Whiz Comics No. 25 (Dec. 1941)*
©1941 Fawcett Publications, Inc.

Captain Marvel met and defeated all types of opponents, but none were as vicious nor as ruthless as the super villain known as Captain Nazi. The two had clashed in several different stories in the Fawcett comic book line, including *Whiz Comics, Master Comics,* and in the first thrilling serialization of Captain Marvel's battle against the Monster Society of Evil of which Captain Nazi was a member. However, Captain Nazi made his first appearance in a Bulletman story in *Master Comics No. 21* (December 1941—which coincided wth America's entry into World War II). In this issue, "Cap" guest-starred with Bulletman in a spectacular epic that would earmark a major change for *Master Comics,* which had already experienced several changes in its earlier issues.

Master Comics started off with Masterman as the star attraction, but he was terminated after appearing in eight adventures. At the same time, two other Fawcett titles, *Slam Bang Comics* and *Nickel Comics* were discontinued, but the best from both were combined into *Master Comics* starting with the ninth issue. Bulletman, the former star attraction of *Nickel Comics* became the leading feature of the new *Master Comics.* Bulletman, who in reality was police laboratory chemist Jim Barr, derived his flying ability from a unique antigravity, bulletproof helmet he had invented that was shaped like a bullet. The helmet was made of a special magnetic alloy that would attract any bullets fired in Bulletman's direction. The slugs would then bounce away harmlessly even though Bulletman himself was vulnerable to injury. Later in the series, his girl friend, Suzan Kent, became his partner as Bulletgirl and, wearing an identical helmet, she joined his crusade against crime. Suzan was the daughter of the unsuspecting police commissioner whom Jim worked for, thus the two were able to keep abreast of the latest criminal activities. Bulletman also moved into his own full-length magazine, fighting racketeers and other run-of-the-mill bad guys, but lacking super strength, he ran into complications when he encountered Captain Nazi in *Master Comics No. 21.* Fortunately, Captain Marvel happened to show up.

The story began in a secluded mountain retreat in Germany where Hitler unveiled to members of his senior staff the successful results of a laboratory experiment that had converted their top athlete into a being imbued with superhuman strength. Captain Nazi, clad in a colorful skintight version of the uniform of the Third Reich, gave a brief demonstration of his newly acquired abilities, punching and kicking through brick walls and soaring through the air like a bird. His flying ability was derived from inhaling a gas mixture from a small vial that he kept in his belt. Hitler informed his staff that Captain Nazi would serve on special assignment in America where he would eliminate Bulletman and Captain Marvel and disrupt the country from within by sabotaging important wartime installations.

Captain Nazi departed on his assignment and, upon his arrival in America, began to create general havoc wherever he set foot. But Bulletman intervened to stop him. The two clashed in midair in a gruesome battle to the finish. Bulletman, more or less on the losing end, was forced to retreat in order to save the life of a young boy whom Captain Nazi had flung over a nearby hillside. Vowing his return, Captain Nazi streaked off to the waterfront to dynamite a shipyard where munitions were being loaded. But this time, he ran into Captain Marvel. Instead of blowing up the ships, Captain Nazi hurled the dynamite at Captain Marvel who absorbed the explosion without blinking an eye. The noise attracted Bulletman to the scene.

Both Captain Marvel and Bulletman had assumed that Captain Nazi had been killed in the violent explosion. Instead they found a note in the wreckage stating that Captain Nazi was coming over into *Whiz Comics* to beat the brains out of Captain Marvel there.

The sequel was continued in *Whiz Comics No. 25* (also December 1941). Captain Nazi was no doubt the most irritating villain ever depicted in comic books. Readership outrage reached a fever pitch as Captain Nazi cursed, ridiculed, and spat on American ideals. His unmerciful style included slugging helpless old ladies and butchering young children—and he got away with it! Nothing could stop Captain Nazi, for he was almost invulnerable. Yet any story he appeared in promised to be one of fantastic action and excitement—especially the shocking sequel in *Whiz Comics No. 25* in which Captain Nazi carved a path of destruction and senseless murder right around Captain Marvel.

The World's Mightiest Mortal arrived just in time to save a young child whom Captain Nazi had hurled toward the ground from atop the high antenna.

Captain Nazi fled from the scene while his crimson-clad antagonist repaired the antenna, reappearing at the new power dam project. He realigned the giant turbin-powered generators so that they would explode the moment the electrical current was fully turned on. As the generators whined faster and faster toward the danger point Captain Marvel sped to the rescue! With sheer brute strength, he braced his shoulder against the gigantic spinning rotors forcing them to screech to a halt, as vividly shown on the *Whiz* cover.

But Captain Nazi slipped away again! He turned up next inside an airplane where he strangled the pilot, seized the controls, and steered the craft into a nose-dive toward a screaming crowd below. Again

The story continued with a power failure at the radio station while Billy Batson was broadcasting the news about the maniac, Captain Nazi. He changed to Captain Marvel and went to investigate the problem only to discover that Captain Nazi was the culprit who had wrecked the radio transmitting antenna.

Captain Marvel sped to the rescue. He pulled the plunging plane safely out of its dive and caught Captain Nazi before he could escape, yanking him bodily through the wall of the cockpit. Captain Marvel's fist struck Captain Nazi's jaw with incredible force, sending his foe whizzing through the air for miles . . .

Some distance away, Captain Nazi's limp form fell into a lake near two fishermen, a young boy and his grandfather. The unsuspecting pair pulled the unconscious form out of the water and revived him.

When Captain Nazi recovered, he displayed his gratitude by throwing the old man into the water. Then he seized an oar and savagely beat the boy across the back and knocked him overboard.

Captain Nazi sped off with the boat as the helpless victims sank beneath the surface of the lake.

Meanwhile, Captain Marvel had decided to find Captain Nazi's body and deliver it to Hitler. He arrived at the lake in time to see the boy's hand going under, and he pulled him safely out. However, he was not aware of the boy's grandfather, who by then had drowned. Captain Marvel took the seriously injured lad to a hospital, where it was discovered the boy's back was broken and that he would not survive the night.

In a last-ditch effort to save the boy's life "Cap" took him to the abandoned subway station to summon the wizard Shazam. Shazam explained that the only chance the boy might have would be for Captain Marvel to transfer some of his strength to the dying youth. Captain Marvel agreed, and as Shazam vanished, the youth, Freddy Freeman, slowly opened his eyes to find the World's Mightiest Mortal standing in front of him . . .

THE WRAITH OF SHAZAM VANISHES AND IN HIS PLACE STANDS THE FAMILIAR RED-CLAD FIGURE, CAPT. MARVEL.

WHY IT-IT'S CAPTAIN MARVEL!

AS THE WONDERING BOY MURMURS CAPTAIN MARVEL'S NAME THERE IS A FLASH OF LIGHTNING!

I'M ALL WELL AGAIN! I'M STRONG, - I-I'M LIKE YOU!

THAT'S RIGHT! YOU'RE CAPTAIN MARVEL JUNIOR!

NOW YOU HAVE ALL THE POWERS I HAVE. USE THEM TO FIGHT THE FORCES OF EVIL WHEREVER THEY APPEAR.

AND DO I CHANGE BACK TO MY OWN SHAPE TOO, LIKE YOU DO TO BILLY BATSON?

YES, YOU WILL HAVE TO GO THROUGH LIFE IN YOUR OWN FORM, BUT WHENEVER YOU NEED ME, SPEAK MY NAME AND AS CAPT. MARVEL JR. YOU WILL BE ABLE TO DO THE THINGS I DO. NOW GO BACK IN THERE AND GET WELL. AND THEN I'M GOING TO SEND YOU INTO MASTER COMICS TO TAKE CARE OF CAPT. NAZI.

GOODBYE, CAPT. MARVEL.

BOOM

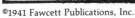

The vicious battles between Captain Marvel Jr. and Captain Nazi began in *Master Comics No. 22* (January 1942) when Captain Nazi returned to finish off Bulletman. Bulletman and Captain Nazi clashed again and just as Bulletman was going down in defeat, a new figure burst onto the scene. The enraged Captain Marvel Jr. would now avenge his grandfather's death! This was *his* fight! He pushed Bulletman aside and slammed into the bewildered Captain Nazi like a volcano that had just erupted! But Captain Nazi managed to flee as Captain Marvel Jr. turned to aid the injured Bulletman.

In *Master Comics No. 23*, Captain Marvel Jr. began as the new star attraction above Bulletman who stepped down to second billing. Captain Marvel Jr. was also elevated to his own book. And between the two titles, it was Captain Marvel Jr. versus Captain Nazi almost once a month!

A unique superhero concept, Captain Marvel Jr. was developed into a streamlined bolt of lightning-fast action through the polished style of artist Emanuel MacRaboy as shown here in typical scenes from *Master Comics* . . .

Master Comics No. 27 (June 1942)*
©1942 Fawcett Publications, Inc.

MacRaboy also worked on other stories besides those featuring Captain Marvel Jr. and executed many outstanding covers for the various titles within the Fawcett line. However, MacRaboy's first popular feature, "Dr. Voodoo," which appeared in the early issues of *Whiz Comics* was somehow lost in the middle pages behind Captain Marvel and was finally terminated in *Whiz Comics No. 25* with the introduction of Captain Marvel Jr.

MacRaboy's "Dr. Voodoo," although not in the same category with other superhero features, was nevertheless an exciting series concept for the short duration it ran. The story featured Dr. Hal Carey, an American physician who turned adventurer during a South American expedition, and began as straight jungle action—until Carey and a native guide, Nero

were accidentally catapulted many centuries backwards into the past. Carey's only hope of returning to the 20th Century rested in recovering a legendary golden flask hidden somewhere on a distant island inhabited by giants. But the flask also represented a highly prized treasure that notorious Viking pirates of that era were also seeking. During a brief clash with the pirates at sea, Dr. Voodoo seized their map to the island and he and Nero escaped. With the pirate ship pursuing them, the daring twosome from the 20th Century reached the island and scrambled up the cliff. They soon reached a point where they could go no further and realized they would have to turn back to search for another path.

Here is an example of MacRaboy's execution of the sequence that occurred when Dr. Voodoo and Nero turned around . . .

110

AND THE KEEN EDGED SWORD
IS DRIVEN DEEPLY IN. UP
REARS THE BEAST IN A
BLINDING RAGE, STRIVING
FURIOUSLY TO UNSADDLE
THIS PUNY HUMAN FOE....
AT THE SAME TIME, LOOSEN-
ING ITS CLUTCH ON NERO.

THE DRAGONS ROARS
ARE DEAFENING, AND
ITS HOT BREATH MELTS
THE JAGGED STONES.
..BUT DR. VOODOO
AVOIDS THIS AND LITHE-
LY LEAPS TO THE GROUND

"HES GOT TO FALL SOON,"
SPEAKS VOODOO,"I DROVE
THE SWORD CLEAR THROUGH
HIS BRAIN!" BUT THE MORTALLY
WOUNDED DRAGON STILL
COMES FORWARD, INTENT ON
DESTROYING ITS ENEMIES.

*Captain Marvel Adventures No. 18 (Dec. 1942)**
©1942 Fawcett Publications, Inc.

Mary Marvel Comics No. 1 (Dec. 1945)
©1945, renewed 1973, Fawcett Publications, Inc.

The feature story in *Captain Marvel Comics No. 18* (December 1942) that described the origin of Mary Marvel introduced still another aspect of the magic word concept. It all began when Billy Batson's radio station W-H-I-Z sponsored a quiz show for the area's youth. Among the contestants was Mary Bromfield, a young girl from a wealthy family who was chosen to represent the girls. The contestant chosen to repre-

sent the poor children was none other than a crippled newspaper boy named Freddy Freeman.

This was the first time that Billy, acting as master of ceremonies of the quiz program, had met Mary Bromfield—and it was also the first time he had met Freddy Freeman even though the two were well-acquainted with each other in their roles of Captain Marvel and Captain Marvel Jr.

As the program got under way, Billy received an urgent telegram from a retired nurse Sarah Primm who lay on her deathbed. She confessed to Billy that he had a twin sister, a story that she had concealed as a lifelong secret. She had been the hospital nurse who attended Billy and his twin sister Mary as babies upon the unexpected death of their parents. Nurse Primm was supposed to surrender the two to an orphanage. But she had also been the attending nurse for a wealthy woman's infant daughter who had suddenly died during the night. She exchanged Billy's sister for the dead child, who was then put to rest as Mary Batson, while the real Mary Batson was raised as the wealthy woman's daughter. Sarah Primm gave Billy a broken half of a locket, stating that his sister wore the other half and that she could be identified by it. But the aged nurse passed away in Billy's arms before she had a chance to reveal the name of the family who had raised his unknown sister.

When Billy returned to the station, he made the startling discovery that Mary Bromfield wore a broken locket that appeared to match his own. However, a gang of hoodlums also had their eyes on the young heiress and attempted to kidnap her for ransom. Of course Captain Marvel and Captain Marvel Jr. rushed to the rescue and quickly foiled the plot with one blow each. As the hoods lay dazed on the floor, the Marvels changed back to Billy and Freddy right in front of Mary to continue their discussion of the locket. Upon comparing the two halves, it was found that they matched. Just then, the crooks revived and jumped Billy and Freddy before either could shout their magic word. And this is what happened. . .

©1942 Fawcett Publications, Inc.*

114

Of course Billy and Freddy were dumbfounded by Mary's change. The trio flew to the abandoned subway station to summon the spirit of the Great One for the answer. . .

MARY DERIVES HER POWERS FROM A *DIFFERENT* GROUP OF MY OLD FRIENDS THAN YOU, BILLY... AS YOU SEE! BUT IT STILL ADDS UP TO MY NAME — SHAZAM...

SELENA ——— GRACE
HIPPOLYTA ——— STRENGTH
ARIADNE ——— SKILL
ZEPHYRUS ——— FLEETNESS
AURORA ——— BEAUTY
MINERVA ——— WISDOM

©1942 Fawcett Publications, Inc.

Mary, being Billy's twin sister, had actually acquired the power of the magic word the same moment Shazam first granted Billy the power to become Captain Marvel, but she was never aware of it. Mary Marvel became the new star attraction of Fawcett's *Wow Comics* which featured the costumed crimefighting duo, Mr. Scarlet and his young partner Pinky. *Wow Comics,* which began as a quarterly title in spring 1941, had just introduced two separate patriotic action features, Commando Yank and Phantom Eagle, when Mary Marvel made her debut in the ninth issue. She was also put into her own magazine and, in addition, made occasional guest appearances with Captain Marvel in *Whiz Comics* and with Captain Marvel Jr. in *Master Comics.*

In effect, the three were a family—the Marvel Family!

The Marvel Family became a separate title of its own in December 1945. It was during the middle 1940s that Otto Binder, a noted science fiction writer whose popular "Adam Link" series appeared in many issues of the early *Amazing Stories,* took over writing the bulk of the story material for Captain Marvel and the Marvel Family titles. Through Binder's creative skill, both features acquired a level of highly sophisticated fantasy that featured popular science fiction themes told with fairy tale simplicity.

For example, the book-length adventure in *The Marvel Family No. 36* (June 1949) concerned fireball invaders from a distant galaxy who threatened to destroy all life in the solar system. The inhabitants of

an outpost on the distant planet of Pluto were the first victims. But before they had been destroyed they managed to send off a warning signal to a station of Planet Neptune who in turn relayed the message to the World Security Council on Earth, whereupon the Marvel Family was called in.

Upon hearing the news, the mighty trio, who could journey through interplanetary space effortlessly without the aid of spaceship, left for Neptune to survey the situation, but by the time they arrived, it was too late! All life on Neptune had been obliterated by the invaders. It was a dead world, its thriving civilization was no more.

The Marvel Family journeyed to the neighboring world Jupiter which was now under attack. The Jovian defense fleet set out to engage the oncoming hordes of living spheres of fire in an incredible battle that took place in the outer atmosphere of Jupiter. The trio from Earth joined in with the Jovians but it was a useless cause. The invaders were invincible. All the Marvel Family could do was assist the Jovians in evacuating their world before all was lost. The Jovians headed towards Mars but by then, the invaders had split their forces and began attacking the helpless Martians. Captain Marvel told the Jovians to bypass Mars and take their fleet directly to Earth while he, Captain Marvel Jr. and Mary Marvel rushed to offer what aid they could to the Martians. But the Martians had surrendered their world and by the time the Marvels arrived, Mars was under control of the invaders.

The Marvel Family No. 36 (June 1949)*
©1949, renewed 1976, Fawcett Publications, Inc.

The invaders split their forces again and prepared to attack Earth. The Marvel Family rushed back home to Earth where they tried to stop the enemy from entering the atmosphere in one of the most fantastic struggles of their career. The following page is a sample scene from the epic. . .

Of course the fireballs eventually burned themselves out and the Marvels cleaned up their ashes.

The Jovians returned home and it was a happy ending for all.

The original "Captain Marvel" movie serial advertisement
©1941 Fawcett Publications, Inc. and Republic Pictures*

The plot of Republic Studio's exciting movie serial adaptation, *Adventures of Captain Marvel*, centered around "Cap's" herculean attempt to smash the Scorpion organization who possessed a set of mystical lenses that could focus unlimited energy and were thus capable of destroying the world. It began when the Malcom Scientific Expedition set out for a remote island near Siam to seek knowledge about a legendary Scorpion Dynasty that was believed to have had, in the misty past, incredible sciences that far surpassed 20th Century technology. A young radio assistant, Billy Batson, was among the ship's passengers.

When the group reached their destination, they uncovered the remains of a forbidden tomb held sacred by the local natives who warned that a curse of death would befall anyone who dared to enter it. Ignoring the warning, the scientists entered the tomb and followed a series of passages that led to a hidden stone chamber in which the strange lenses were encased. Upon translating the inscription, the scientists learned that the lenses could unleash incredible power, enough for anyone unscrupulous enough to control or destroy the world. They divided the lenses among themselves so that each member of the party would be dependent on the safe return of the others.

In the meantime, Billy, who didn't follow the crowd and was unaware of what had transpired inside the tomb, explored other parts of the island with a native who led him toward a strange cave, in a manner quite similar to the original story in the comic book where a cloaked stranger led Billy to an abandoned subway station. In the movie version, a storm was building up. Lightning and thunder flashed as Billy sought shelter inside the cave. His escort mysteriously vanished just as a rock slide closed off the entrance. Billy searched the cave for another exit. As he lit a match, he discovered a strange throne. Then the spirit of Shazam suddenly appeared on the throne and, just as in the original comic book story, Billy was awarded the power of the magic word to become Captain Marvel.

©1941 Republic Pictures

Shortly afterwards, the members of the expedition along with Billy boarded their ship and returned home. Everything appeared normal, until the Sign of The Scorpion appeared and claimed its first victim, one of the scientists who possessed a mystical lens. The scientists realized they were in grave danger as freak accidents began to occur with unusual frequency. Sudden explosions! Poison darts thrown in the dark! Runaway automobiles! Planes falling out of control!

But each attempt to kill one of the scientists was blocked by the mighty Captain Marvel. Although a lens always disappeared with each "accident" which everyone assumed was caused by the curse, "Cap" soon learned otherwise. A ruthless gang of hoodlums was responsible and "Cap" set out to bring them to justice. Through a hail of gunfire, grenades, dynamite, poison darts, and runaway vehicles, Captain Marvel mopped up the villains in a series of brutalizing slugfests that ultimately led to the masked gang-leader, the Scorpion. And the Scorpion turned out to be none other than Dr. Malcom, the scientist who had organized the expedition in the first place!

In the end, "Cap" collected the lenses and returned them to the tomb on the island where they were found. Then he sealed the tomb so that no one would ever be able to open it again.

One of the elements that made this serial stand out as a motion picture classic was the incredible flying sequences that depicted Captain Marvel soaring through the air.

Spy Smasher No. 1 (1941)
©1941 Fawcett Publications, Inc.

Thrill/Whiz Comics also introduced Spy Smasher, another leading character of Fawcett Publications who was to headline his own full-length magazine shortly afterwards. The first episode introduced the basic elements of what would become a unique, patriotic drama that emphasized military undercover operations on the home front during the war years.

The opening episode described how a mysterious fire had destroyed a naval aircraft carrier. Then a naval cruiser suddenly exploded when it struck a submerged mine! An experimental submarine met with disaster on its trial run! Then a new navy dirigible disappeared without a trace! Admiral Corby, commanding officer of Naval Intelligence, discussed the incidents with his daughter Eve Corby and her trusted fiance Alan Armstrong, and they agreed that enemy acts of sabotage were responsible. But unknown to the admiral and his daughter, Alan would look into the matter on his own, as Spy Smasher!

Meanwhile, in another part of the city, a second meeting was taking place. An unidentified figure whose face was concealed behind a white mask ordered his henchman to pay a visit to Admiral Corby's home, kill him, and seize certain top secret documents from the safe. The henchmen left to carry out their assignment—but their plans were thwarted by Spy Smasher who had been guarding the admiral's home.

As the thugs fled, Spy Smasher followed them in his gyroplane. The trail ultimately led to the missing dirigible which hovered in the upper atmosphere far above the clouds. Spy Smasher landed his gyroplane on top of the massive blimp and lowered himself inside for the grand-slam slugfest. Although he routed the gang, their masked leader escaped. The story concluded without revealing anything about the gang's leader—he was simply referred to as the Mask.

The stage was now set for a continuing theme. As the series developed, it was learned that the Mask headed an elaborate spy organization that spread across North America. Its membership included gangsters of the underworld, Nazi agents who had infiltrated into responsible government positions under the pretext of being loyal American citizens, and honest Americans who were blackmailed into serving the organization. Acting on direct assignment from Hitler, the Mask was actively engaged in crippling America's defenses by sabotaging strategic military installations, weapons factories, power supply sources, research laboratories, and air transportation facilities—all to clear the way for Nazi invasion of North America!

Spy Smasher had his hands full trying to crush the Mask's extensive spy network. His secret identity as Alan Armstrong was soon shared with Admiral Corby and Eve, and through Admiral Corby, Spy Smasher had the unofficial cooperation of Naval Intelligence. Weapons, radio equipment, transportation, and manpower support were at his disposal whenever he needed them in his undercover war against the Mask. While the Mask did not appear in every story, almost all of the villains that Spy Smasher fought, were directly or indirectly linked to the Mask's organization.

In 1942, Republic Pictures translated the theme into an exciting twelve-episode movie serial. With the exception of giving Armstrong a twin brother, the serial followed the comic book feature fairly closely. Spy Smasher, acting on a lead from Admiral Corby, went to France to seek information about the Mask's operations in America only to be captured by German

©1942 Republic Pictures

occupation forces and sentenced to death before a firing squad. However, a guerilla team of underground Free French led by Pierre Durand intervened and saved Spy Smasher. In the midst of the rip-roaring battle that followed, Pierre helped Spy Smasher escape back to America where he continued his search for the Mask. He uncovered the Mask's scheme to flood the country with counterfeit money and learned that the bogus bills were being made on the French Island of Martinidad whose government had been taken over by the Nazis. Spy Smasher arranged to meet his friend Pierre on the island, and after a series of breath-taking battles with Nazi agents, they succeeded in destroying the enemy base, putting an end to the counterfeit operations. But the Mask was still at large. His next diabolical plan concerned the theft of the government's new secret weapon—a machine that was capable of freezing, then melting aircraft engines on planes while in flight. The Mask aimed the awesome raybeam at Spy Smasher's gyroplane as he flew in for a landing. Of course Spy Smasher escaped! The final battle took place aboard the Mask's submarine. Overcoming seemingly insurmountable odds, Spy Smasher blew up the U-boat, thus destroying the enemy once and for all.

During the 1940s, the major theaters that featured first-run movies rarely showed movie serials, and their distribution was generally restricted to smaller neighborhood movie houses. But the strong patriotic theme of Spy Smasher prompted many of the major theaters to break their policy for the first and only time to show *this* movie serial as a regular weekly feature. The neighborhood theaters that carried the serial in 1942 when it was first released, offered a repeat showing in 1944. Spy Smasher's unexpected popularity in the movies was a major reason for *Whiz Comics* becoming the number one comic book title from 1942 to 1944.

Spy Smasher's trademark was his custom-made gyroplane—a small, versatile, single-passenger vehicle that could soar through the sky, scoot along the highways, and skim across the ocean waves. It was small enough to hide almost anywhere—on a skyscraper rooftop, behind shrubbery, in a dark alleyway, or inside a truck trailer. In the comic book, the gyroplane was constantly restyled as the series progressed. The version that was used in the movie serial resembled a delta-wing design. (In 1951, Republic Pictures used the gyroplane in another movie serial, *Flying Disc Man From Mars*, where it served as a vehicle that could make right-angled turns in midair and outrace the fastest aircraft.)

As World War II came to an end in 1945, Spy Smasher found himself in a predicament that he shared with a host of other patriotic protagonists—a superhero without a cause. The Fawcett titles carried similar characters such as Minuteman in *Master Comics* and Commando Yank in *Wow Comics*, both of whom had seen their heyday and were soon terminated. However, an attempt was made to save Spy Smasher.

In *Whiz Comics No. 76*, Alan Armstrong discarded his famous green costume, colorful red cape and famous gyroplane to don a business suit and hat so that he could join the fight against the underworld in a new feature called "Crime Smasher." Although Eve Corby still remained his girl friend, her father Admiral Corby faded out of the series. Unfortunately the transition did not work well. Without the highly identifiable costume, the gyroplane, Admiral Corby and Naval Intelligence, and the Mask's spy organization as the ever challenging opposition, Alan Armstrong as Crime Smasher became just another run-of-the-mill private detective. The feature was dropped in 1948.

Ibis Comics No. 1 (1942)
©1942 Fawcett Publications, Inc.

Ibis, a novel character concept based on Egyptian mythology which also appeared in *Whiz Comics*, was the third reason this magazine was the leading comic book during the early 1940s. While the first issue of *Thrill/Whiz* had briefly touched upon his origin (showing only that he awoke inside a modern museum after a 4,000-year-sleep to seek his mate and to perform magic feats with the assistance of a strange wand called the "Ibistick"), it wasn't until Ibis had expanded into his own book in 1942 that his background was more fully explained.

The startling story began in ancient Egypt when a Prince Amentep was among those being considered as the new ruler of strife-torn Egypt. The prince, however, was young and would first have to prove himself worthy of handling a crisis before he was eligible to hold the Ibistick, a sacred instrument which contained the awesome powers of Osiris, god of light and life. At the same time, another prince known as the Black Pharaoh sought to rule Egypt and through worshipping Set, the god of darkness and death who violently opposed Osiris, he was given an army of demons to help him conquer the people of Egypt.

During the ultimate confrontation between the supernatural forces of Set led by the Black Pharaoh and the Egyptian people led by Prince Amentep, the helpless mortals fought a losing battle and the prince was taken prisoner. Although defeated, the prince had nevertheless proven himself a worthy heir to the sacred Ibistick. It was secretly given to him during his imprisonment whereupon the prince discovered that at his command the Ibistick could wield the power of Osiris. With the sacred instrument clutched in his hand, the prince set himself free and armed with the sword and shield of Osiris made ready to battle the demon hordes of Set. The prince fought courageously, slashing the demons to bits. Afterwards, he set out to rescue his beloved Princess Taia from the clutches of the Black Pharaoh only to discover that she had been accidentally slain by an arrow during the peak of the fight.

The story of the origin of Ibis is a simplified version of the Egyptian legend of the battle between the gods, Osiris and Set. To prevent Set, god of death, from claiming the soul of a slain princess, Osiris immediately placed her in a state of suspended animation. Hovering between life and death, the princess remained in a permanent sleep for many centuries until Osiris was able to overcome Set and return her to life. Accordingly, the arrow that struck Princess Taia was enchanted, and instead of taking her life it put her into a mystical coma that would last 4,000 years. Prince Amentep, unable to break the magic spell even with the power of the Ibistick, placed himself under a similar trance so that he would awake at the same time his beloved returned to life. Both bodies were entombed as mummies.

Some 4,000 years later, Prince Amentep awoke inside a 20th Century museum. Still clutching the Ibistick, he donned a black dress suit and red turban and set off for Egypt to find the tomb of his princess. When she awoke, the two were finally united again. As holder of the sacred instrument, Prince Amentep became known simply as Ibis and using the Ibistick's magical powers he fought all forms of evil and supernatural forces that threatened mankind, including Set who frequently returned to Earth in various disguises.

©1941 Fawcett Publications, Inc.

Captain Midnight No. 1 (Sept. 1942)
©Fawcett Publications, Inc.

©Columbia Pictures

Captain Midnight was originally created for radio drama in 1940 by Wilfred Moore and Robert Burit who, as a team, specialized in writing aviation fiction for the pulp magazines. The name "Midnight" was adopted in the introductory episode in which Air Corps pilot Captain Albright successfully completed a vital mission by the stroke of midnight—just in time to save an allied regiment from defeat during the war. Shortly thereafter Dell Publications adapted Captain Midnight as a comic book feature, first for a brief series that ran in *The Funnies,* then in *Popular Comics* where it ran until that magazine's contents were converted to humor and animal fantasy.

In 1942, Columbia Pictures featured the popular aviation ace in a movie serial which coincided by a few months with Fawcett's revival of Captain Midnight as a comic book feature. While the movie serial generally followed the radio format which stressed the Secret Squadron, Fawcett introduced several innovations to tailor the character concept to the trend of superhero fantasy. In the comic book version, Captain Midnight was equipped with an arsenal of scientific devices, including a unique stretch cape that enabled him to glide through the air. His alter ego of Captain Albright, which no longer served a purpose in the radio series after the first episode, had been given the role in the comic book as that of a scientific inventor with a modern laboratory. In his guise of Captain Albright—or better, Doctor Albright—he was constantly de-

veloping new products for the War Department. Thus, in his spare time, Albright was also able to invent such items as the "Swing Spring," the "Doom-Beam Torch," a watch-sized radio transmitter and receiver, black cloud pellets, and heel knives, all for his personal use as Captain Midnight.

The first issue of Fawcett's *Captain Midnight Comics* made its debut in September 1942. The lead-off story began in Albright's laboratory where he and his assistants were testing a new electrical system for a radio-controlled dive bomber, a strategic military weapon that was the pride and joy of the War Department. Enemy agents, however, were also aware of Albright's work and set out to seize the blueprints when Albright took them to Washington, a plan that was successfully executed. While Albright was imprisoned and awaiting execution at the enemy hideout, he removed his outer garments to reveal his colorful crimson costume which could only mean one thing to the world—*Captain Midnight was back!*

Needless to say, Captain Midnight wiped out the spy ring and retrieved the vital blueprints. His further adventures would place him in confrontation with Axis powers both on the home front and on the battlefield. He emerged as a leading patriotic hero, often teaming up with Spy Smasher. But unlike Spy Smasher, Captain Midnight was able to convert to a straight aviation ace when the war had ended.

In 1946, *Master Comics No. 50* introduced "Nyoka, the Jungle Girl," as a candidate to replace "Minuteman," a war theme feature. Attractive Nyoka Gordon was a star athlete who left college to find her long lost father who had mysteriously disappeared in the jungles of darkest Africa. During her hazardous search, she experienced one peril after the other— wild animals, head hunters, quicksand, earthquakes, brush fires, avalanches, mysterious beings who inhabited hidden cities, and so on.

This dynamic heroine, who constantly faced danger at every turn starred in a movie serial as well as her own magazine which utilized photo covers of movie star Kay Aldridge as Nyoka. The movie serial was originally billed *Jungle Girl* which led to a legal conflict with Edgar Rice Burroughs, Inc. who had previously created a feature of the same name that had also been adapted to the screen. As a result, the Fawcett *Jungle Girl* was changed to *Perils of Nyoka*.

The movie serial centered around an ancient scroll whose translation, it was thought, would reveal the location of long lost treasures of Greece as well as the tablets of Hippocrates which recorded the medical knowledge of the ancient Greeks. Professor Campbell, an American archeologist, and his young assistant Dr. Larry Grayson, led an expedition to the Arabian deserts to locate Nyoka Gordon, the only person who could translate the directions on the scroll. Nyoka was living with a friendly tribe of Bed-

ouins who were helping her trace her lost father, Henry Gordon. However, Vultura, Queen ruler of a renegade band of Arabian outlaws, learned of the expedition and launched a surprise attack against them to seize the scroll. But the attack took place within the territorial boundaries of the Bedouin tribe, sworn enemies of Vultura's renegades, and they quickly rushed to the rescue. During the battle that followed, the renegades were driven off—but they escaped with the scroll! Nyoka and Larry teamed up to follow them back to Queen Vultura's temple where they expected to slip past the guards, ease inside, and recover the ancient scroll without being noticed. Instead, they ran into Satan, Vultura's powerful gorilla bodyguard, who angrily tore away the supporting pillars of the temple and brought the stone roof crashing down on the startled twosome!

In Episode Two, Larry and Nyoka miraculously escaped through a narrow opening in the broken walls a split second before the roof collapsed. But Vultura, in possession of the scroll, realized she needed Nyoka to translate it and made plans to lure her into a clever trap. Nyoka was captured but as she was tied to the torture rack, Larry and the Bedouins stormed into the renegade camp to rescue her. Nyoka broke free, walloped Vultura, seized the scroll, and attempted to escape in Vultura's chariot, but in the ensuing confusion, she was knocked unconscious and the chariot broke away from the speeding horses and

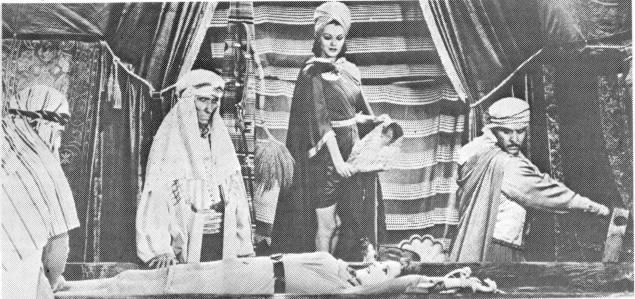

rolled off a steep mountain ledge—a sheer drop of 1,000 feet to the jagged rocks below! *Crash!* Was this the end of Nyoka?

In Episode Three Nyoka had regained consciousness at the last minute, quickly diving off the chariot just as it began to plunge down toward the rocks. She landed safely on the mountain's edge, but in the meantime the scroll was temporarily lost. However, Nyoka had glanced at it long enough to read directions pointing to the dreaded Valley of the Tuaregs where another inscription awaited with further instructions. Nyoka organized a group of Bedouin warriors to accompany the archeological expedition to the Tuareg Valley. As the party set out, Queen Vultura learned of the plan through a spy who had infiltrated the expedition. She prepared to ambush Nyoka's team as they crossed a narrow suspension bridge overhanging a river infested with alligators. The renegades attacked and a fierce battle broke out on the wobbily bridge. Nyoka lost her footing when the supporting ropes were cut—but she managed to catch hold of a loose end of one of the ropes and swing safely to a lower ledge. Many had fallen to their death while some were still clinging desparately to the mountainside, struggling to climb to safety. Larry was dangling from a limb of a rotting tree that jutted out from the mountain, and Nyoka alertly threw a rope to him so he could climb to the ledge where she was. The tree limb broke just as he caught the rope.

Separated from the others, the two found an opening to a cave that led into a treacherous volcanic tunnel. They reluctantly decided to follow the tunnel and try to enter the valley by a different route. However, a few of Vultura's henchman had also discovered the tunnel through a by-pass that led from the surface above and they tried to head off Larry and Nyoka. Another battle broke out along the narrow

ledges that stood high above pits of flaming lava. Suddenly a club applied to the back of Nyoka's head sent her plunging downward toward the white-hot bubbling pools!

Episode Four: Nyoka deftly tumbled through the air onto a lower embankment and with steaming lava nibbling at her feet, she waited there until Larry had fought off the renegades and lowered a rope down to pull her up. It was one peril after the other.

In the next episode, after Larry and Nyoka finally reached the valley, Nyoka unknowingly pried open a booby-trapped vault that exploded in her face, bringing a landslide of rock crashing down around her. Miraculously escaping *this* incident, she was then captured by the vicious Tuareg tribesmen who tied her up and hurled her into the sacrificial flames of death—which she escaped from, only to come to grips once again with the awesome gorilla, Satan, who was intent upon tearing her apart if he could catch the record-breaking track star! Nyoka ran for her life with the giant beast sprinting after her. Having escaped Satan by outrunning him across an open field and diving off a plateau into a river fifty feet below, she then outswam a host of alligators that hungrily pursued her until she reached land. But there she was very nearly trampled by the thundering hoofs of Vultura's stampeding horses . . . and so on.

But twelve episodes later Nyoka emerged victorious! When Satan cornered her again and caught her in a death grip, she seized a gun and fired bullet after bullet at point blank range until he released her and keeled over. Having killed the gorilla, Nyoka brought the evil doers to justice, and located her father as well as the ancient tablets for the archeologists.

Nyoka's full-length comic book series, which followed later, reflected that fascinating movie serial.

Although Fawcett produced a variety of comic book titles ranging from superhero to romance, to animal fantasy and westerns, Captain Marvel still remained the most popular feature. In fact, he was as popular as D-C's Superman, and as a superhuman, just as strong. Both Captain Marvel and Superman were invulnerable, and both could fly, all of which led to the inevitable debate among comic book fans across the country: which one *was* the strongest?

This seemingly trivial question carried serious legal implications. In 1951, D-C Publications entered a lawsuit against Fawcett Publications, alleging that "Captain Marvel" was a copyright infringement on "Superman." While the rest of the comic book industry was being battered by critics objecting to the portrayal of crime and violence, D-C and Fawcett waged their own private battle against each other in what turned into one of the most complex court trials in the history of copyright law.

Was the Captain Marvel character imitating the Superman character? In trying to define the thin line that separated originality from imitation, attorneys for D-C pointed out that:

1. Captain Marvel imitated Superman's flying ability and super strength.

2. Captain Marvel's other identity as news broadcaster Billy Batson imitated Superman's alter ego, newspaper reporter Clark Kent.

3. The supporting character of Mr. Morris, manager of Billy Batson's radio station, imitated the supporting character of Perry White, managing editor of Clark Kent's newspaper.

4. Captain Marvel's arch villain Sivanna was a baldheaded scientist that imitated Superman's arch villain Lothor, who was also a baldheaded scientist.

5. The covers of *Whiz Comics* often depicted Captain Marvel imitating some of the same feats that Superman accomplished on the covers of *Action Comics*.

In trying to define the same thin line, attorneys for Fawcett pointed out the following:

1. Captain Marvel's powers were based on Greek mythology, whereas Superman's powers were based on the advanced sciences of another planet, a vastly different concept.

2. When Billy Batson changed to Captain Marvel, he underwent a complete physical transformation, whereas Clark Kent merely discarded his outer clothing to change to Superman.

3. Captain Marvel answered to the Wizard, Shazam, whereas Superman answered to no one.

4. Captain Marvel's other identity, Billy Batson was known to many, including his enemies, whereas Superman's alter ego, Clark Kent, was a closely guarded secret shared with no one.

5. Captain Marvel had no supporting female star, whereas Superman as Clark Kent, had to play hide-and-seek constantly with Lois Lane. Captain Marvel had a twin sister with comparable powers, whereas Superman had no relatives.

The court case dragged on for two years. It finally came to an end in 1953 when Fawcett settled the matter with its decision to discontinue publishing comic books altogether. Several factors led to Fawcett's decision: the general state of the comic book industry which was under attack as "literary trash"; the growth of television that was wooing the public away from buying magazines for leisure reading, thus cutting sharply into newsstand sales; and the loss of radio drama and movie serial production studios as potential licensing outlets for comic book features.

Captain Marvel made his last appearance in November, 1953.

Meanwhile, D-C Publications continued to expand as the leader of comic books. Some twenty years later, as interest in superhero fantasy was renewed, D-C decided to revive some of the classic characters from the past. And one of the first to be revived was Captain Marvel!

Shazam! (No. 1, Feb. 1973)
©1972 D.C. Comics, Inc.

Captain Marvel had returned!

1950 marked the coming of home television, a new era of entertainment that would begin to replace radio drama, movie serials, pulp magazines, and continuous adventure strips in the newspaper comic pages, as well as the already overly criticized comic book industry. But the trend toward television also brought forth a fantastic new character that reflected the change—Captain Video!

This feature took place in the late 20th Century when Captain Video and the Video Rangers observed world activities through an elaborate television surveillance system at the Solar Observatory Station of mountaintop headquarters. The V.R. (Video Rangers) remained on the alert for any potential evil that would threaten civilization. They crushed diabolical schemes of would-be dictators who sought to rule the world through the use of robots, death rays, and weather controlling devices, and they battled interplanetary invaders from around the galaxy. Captain Video was becoming a smash hit as a daily television series when Fawcett Publications introduced the comic book adaptation in February 1951.

However, it was Columbia Pictures who actually created Captain Video as a character for an original movie serial that was made at a time when, ironically, the impact of television was gradually forcing the film studios out of business.

Captain Video No. 1 (Feb. 1951)
©1950 Fawcett Publications, Inc.

ALPHABETICAL LISTING OF FAWCETT COMIC BOOKS

All Hero Comics (1943, one issue)
America's Greatest Comics (1941 - 1943)
Andy Devine Western (1950 - 1952)
Animal Fair (1946 - 1947)
Baseball Heroes (1952, one issue)
Battle Stories (1952 - 1953)
Beware Terror Tales (1952 - 1953)
Big Book Romances (1950, one issue)
Bill Battle, the One Man Army (1952 - 1953)
Bill Boyd Western (1950 - 1952)
Billy the Kid and Oscar (1945, three issues)
Bob Colt Western (1950 - 1952)
Bob Steele Western (1950 - 1952)
Bob Swift Comics (1951 - 1952)
Bulletman Comics (1941 - 1946)
Captain Marvel Adventures (1941 - 1953)
Captain Marvel and the Good Humor Man (1950, one issue)
Captain Marvel and the Lieutenants of Safety (1950 - 1951)
Captain Marvel Storybook (1946 - 1948)
Captain Marvel Thrill Book (1941, one issue)
Captain Marvel Well Known Comics (1944, one issue)
Captain Marvel Jr. Comics (1942 - 1953)
Captain Marvel Jr. Well Known Comics (1944, one issue)
Captain Midnight Comics (1942 - 1948)

Captain Video (1951, six issues)
Comic Comics (1946 - 1947)
Comics Novel (1947, one issue)
Cowboy Love Comics (1949 - 1955)
Cowboy Western Comics (1948 - 1949)
Crime Smasher (1948, one issue)
Daisy Handbook (1946 - 1948, pocket book format)
Dennis the Menace[1]
Don Newcombe Comics (1950, one issue)
Don Winslow of the Navy (1943 - 1955)
Down With Crime (1952 - 1953)
Eddie Stanky Comics (1951, one issue)
Exciting Romances (1949 - 1953)
Fawcett's Funny Animals (1942 - 1953)
Fawcett's Miniature Comics (1946, three issues)
Fawcett's Movie Comics (1949 - 1952)
Gene Autry Comics (1941 - 1944, and continued in Dell's "4-Color" series)
Gift Comics (1941 - 1949, four issues)
Holiday Comics (1942, one issue)
Hopalong Cassidy Comics (1943 - 1954)
Hoppy, the Marvel Bunny (1945 - 1947)
Hot Rod Comics (1951 - 1953)
I Love You Comics (1950, one issue)

Ibis, the Invincible (1942 - 1948)
Jackie Robinson Comics (1950 - 1952)
Joe Louis Comics (1950, two issues)
Ken Maynard Western (1950 - 1952)
Lance O'Casey (1946, three issues)
Lash LaRue Western (1949 - 1953)
Life Story (1949 - 1952)
Love Memories (1950, four issues)
Love Mystery Comics (1950, two issues)
Marvel Family (1945 - 1953)
Mary Marvel Comics (1945 - 1948)
Mike Barnett, Man Against Crime (1952, six issues)
Motion Picture Comics (1950 - 1953)
Negro Romance (1950, three issues)
New York Giants (1952, one issue)
Nickel Comics (1952, eight issues)
Nyoka, the Jungle Girl (1945 - 1953, and continued by Charlton Comics through 1957)
Ozzie and Babs (1947 - 1949)
Pinhead and Foodini (1951, three issues)
Puppetoons (1945 - 1947)
Real Western Hero (1948 - 1949)
Rocky Lane Western (1949 - 1953, and continued by Charlton Comics through 1959)
Rod Cameron Western (1950 - 1953)
Romantic Secrets (1949 - 1951)
Six-Gun Heroes (1950 - 1953, and continued by Charlton Comics through 1965)

Slam Bang Comics (1940, seven issues)
Smiley Burnette Western (1950, four issues)
Special Edition Comics (1940, one issue)
Strange Stories from Another World (1952 - 1953)
Sunset Carson Western (1951, one issue)
Suspense Detective (1952, five issues)
Sweetheart Diary (1949 - 1951)
Tex Ritter Western (1950 - 1953, and continued by Charlton Comics through 1959)
This Magazine is Haunted (1951 - 1953, and continued by Charlton Comics through 1958)
Thrill Comics (1940, one issue published for limited circulation and revised for reprinting as *Whiz Comics No. 2*)
Tom Mix Western (1948 - 1953)
True Confessions (1949, one issue)
True Confidences (1949 - 1950)
True Sweetheart Secrets (1950 - 1952)
Undercover Crime (1952, six issues)
Unknown World (1952, one issue, and title changed to *Strange Stories from Another World* beginning at second issue).
Western Hero (1949 - 1952)
Whiz Comics (1940 - 1953)
World's Beyond (1951, one issue)
Wow Comics (1941 - 1948)
X-Mas Comics (1941 - 1949, published annually)
Yogi Bera Comics (1951, one issue)

1. Publishers-Hall Syndicate, which handles the newspaper syndication for Hank Ketcham's "Dennis the Menace" comic strip series since it began in March 1951, has recently become the Hallden Division of Fawcett Publications which currently produces a complete line of comic books about Dennis the Menace. The various titles include *Dennis the Menace, Dennis the Menace and His Friends, Dennis the Menace and His Dog, Ruff, Dennis the Menace and His Pal, Joey, Dennis the Menace Bonus Magazine, Dennis the Menace Pocket Full of Fun, Dennis the Menace Television Special,* and *Dennis the Menace Triple Feature.* In addition to comic books, Fawcett also publishes several paperback pocket book editions about Dennis the Menace.

5

FICTION HOUSE

During the 1920s, Fiction House reigned supreme as the leading publisher of pulp fiction. Their line included such monthly titles as *Aces, Action Stories, Action Novels, Air Stories, Detective Book, Detective Classics, Fight Stories, Jungle Stories, Love Romances,* and *Wings.* In 1929, Fiction House acquired Doubleday's *Frontier Magazine,* then the top ranking dime western. But due to the adverse business conditions that arose within the publishing industry during the early 1930s, Fiction House was forced to terminate most of its titles in 1932—thus closing the door to many aspiring writers and illustrators. *Jungle Stories,* however was one of the few titles the house retained and it continued as a leading pulp in strong competition with *Argosy Magazine* and *Blue Book Magazine* (both of which featured the adventures of another denizen of the sweltering forest—*Tarzan*).

In 1939, having survived the effects of the Depression and with eyes toward the burgeoning field of comic books, Fiction House issued a black-and-white edition of *Jumbo Comics* featuring the swashbuckling adventures of the Hawk, created by Will Eisner. *Jumbo Comics* also included a host of minor features one of which was about a lost girl in the jungle named Sheena.

However, 1939, was also the year of *Action Comics* featuring Superman, *Detective Comics* with Batman, *King Comics* starring Flash Gordon, *Famous Funnies* with Buck Rogers, *Super Comics* with Dick Tracy, and *Marvel Mystery Comics* with Human Torch and Sub-mariner. And 1940 was the year that the mighty roar of "Shazam!" echoed throughout comicdom and Captain Marvel appeared for the first time. The overwhelming competition virtually smothered whatever the first eight black-and-white issues of *Jumbo Comics* had to offer.

Under the circumstances it would appear that *Jumbo Comics* would have folded within the year. But the fact that it was published by Fiction House made a difference. The former leader of pulp fiction was equally determined to become the leader of comic books.

First some changes had to be made in *Jumbo Comics.* Beginning with the ninth issue, *Jumbo* converted to full color in line with the trend set by its competitors. The ninth issue also introduced "Stuart Taylor" created by Curt Davis and illustrated by Lou Fine. Although "Stuart Taylor" was subtitled "Weird Stories of the Supernatural," the hero was basically just another student of the Flash Gordon school whose adventures in the supernatural took him into the fourth dimension, other worlds, and even through time. His girlfriend, Laura, and scientist Dr. Hayward accompanied him throughout his episodes.

Unfortunately for Fiction House, the introduction of Stuart Taylor was not unique enough to make *Jumbo* stand out as a major title. The big change came in the next issue, *Jumbo Comics No. 10* (October-November 1939). Up to this point, heroic adventure in comics, as well as in the pulps, had been assigned exclusively to male characters with the woman's role limited to that of the helpless damsel-in-distress. And such had been Sheena's role until this issue. In *Jumbo No. 10* Sheena encountered her first true challenge to become a star in her own right. With eyes narrowed and nostrils twitching, she gripped her knife tightly and slowly advanced toward the jaw-dripping charge of a ferocious killer lion. Actually, Sheena's historic battle was more than just a story about a fight with a lion—it also represented Fiction House's battle to survive in the comic book arena dominated by male superstars. Here is the now-famous turning point.

Jumbo Comics No. 10 (Oct. Nov. 1939)
©1939 Real Adventures Publishing Co., Inc.

NAMU, OBTAINING THE SCENT OF TAMUR, THE ZEBRA, CROUCHES FOR A SPRING...TEEKA SCREAMS IN TERROR FROM ALOFT.....

QUICKLY REACHING THE SCENE OF THE TENSE JUNGLE DRAMA, SHEENA LEAPS TO A BOUGH....

LISTEN! TEEKA WARNS OF A LION---IT MAY BE NAMU!

SNARLING FURIOUSLY, THE LION TWISTS AND TURNS, FINALLY UNSEATING THE FEARLESS GIRL.

SPINNING ABOUT, NAMU MAKES A SAVAGE LUNGE AT SHEENA....

NIMBLY, SHE DARTS FROM UNDER THE BRUTE'S FIERCE SWIPE...

EYES NARROWED NOSTRILS TWITCHING, SHEENA SLOWLY ADVANCES...

SURPRISED AT HIS OPPONENT'S COURAGE, NAMU STANDS AND GLARES. SUDDENLY, WITH A LOUD ROAR....

HE BREAKS INTO A BOUNDING RUN, HIS JAWS DRIPPING AND EYES ABLAZE.

FINALLY THE ANIMAL SINKS TO THE GROUND AND ROLLS OVER... DEAD!

Sheena survived with flying colors. And with the change into a new leopard skin costume, she stood as Queen of the Jungle!

From this issue on, Sheena (created by W. Morgan Thomas) became Fiction House's star attraction and one of the most dynamic figures in comics. With the ferocity and litheness of the jungle beast after her first kill, Sheena burst into action with an entirely new wave of explosive adventure.

She battled white men . . .

... black men ...

ALL THIS TIME, SHEENA WATCHES FOR ANY POSSIBLE NEW DANGER...

HER HAIR FLOWING IN THE WIND, HER BODY TAUT, SHEENA DIVES FROM HER TREE PERCH......

AND LANDS IN THE MIDST OF THE STARTLED MOB.

UGH!

... other females ...

YOU'LL REGRET THIS! WHEN I WANT SOMETHING I GET IT!

NOT HERE.. IN AFRICA OUR JUNGLE LAW IS SUPREME..NOT YOURS!

IRENE PALES IN FURY.

MALAIS! SHOOT HER! SHE CAN'T DEFY ME?

NO, IRENE, THAT WOULD ONLY BRING THE NATIVES UPON US!

GET OUT OF HERE AT ONCE OR..

BLIND WITH ANGER, THE GIRL LUNGES AT SHEENA.

THEN I'LL KILL HER MYSELF!

BUT THE JUNGLE QUEEN, FALLING FLAT ON HER BACK, SENDS IRENE SPRAWLING WITH A CLEVER FOOT ACTION.

. . . and ferocious beast.

She was sometimes violent.

WITH MURDER IN ITS GLITTERING EYES AND ITS HORNS LOWERED MENACINGLY THE BEAST CHARGES SHEENA.

BUT THE GIRL LEAPS NIMBLY TO ITS BACK.

SUDDENLY A WHITE MAN HURTLES DOWN . . . BORIS RADCHEK, WHOSE OWN GREEDY AMBITIONS CAUSED HIS DEATH.

A HUGE BLACK FIGURE DRAGS SHEENA UNDER WATER. FIGHTING LIKE A SLIPPERY EEL, SHE DODGES THE FATAL STRANGLE HOLD.

She gave no quarters and expected none.

QUICKLY, SHEENA DUCKS BEHIND THE HUGE CAGE . . BUT BY NOW THE VOODOO DANCERS HAVE SEEN HER.

WHITE QUEEN! KILL!

FURIOUSLY RADCHEK'S VOODOO DANCERS PURSUE THE COUPLE.

QUICK! TO THE PASSAGE OF SIGHS!

THEY REACH THE NARROW TUNNEL, BUT . . .

QUICKSAND!

The Hawk and Stuart Taylor took a back seat in *Jumbo Comics* and were eventually dropped. It was Sheena alone who carried *Jumbo* to the top. And it came as no surprise when she also headlined her own magazine.

Jumbo Comics No. 18 (Aug. 1940)
©1940 Real Adventures Publishing Co., Inc.

Jumbo Comics No. 19 (Sept. 1940)
©1940 Real Adventures Publishing Co., Inc.

Jumbo Comics No. 31 (Sept. 1941)
©1941 Real Adventures Publishing Co., Inc.

Sheena Comics No. 1 (Spring 1942)
©1942 Real Adventures Publishing Co., Inc.

Jungle Comics No. 1 (Jan. 1940)
©1939 Glen Kel Publishing Co., Inc.

Wambi No. 1 (Spring 1942)
©1942 Glen Kel Publishing Co., Inc.

To break away from the standard mold of the typical variety-type comic book that offered a main feature, a detective feature, a wild west feature, a humor feature, and often a little of everything else, Fiction House brought their expertise in pulp literature into the comic book arena and introduced a series of single theme magazines that began in December 1939 (but were dated January 1940). One such title was *Jungle Comics*, patterned after their popular pulp *Jungle Stories*.

The pulp often featured the adventures of Ki-Gor, Jungle Lord, and the character concept was carried over into the comic book but under the name of Ka'anga. As with Ki-Gor, Ka'anga was a house character whose stories were written by different writers on the Fiction House Staff and were illustrated by different artists, all of whom used the pen name "Red Bradey." The fact that Ka'anga was a crude imitation of Tarzan did not matter for a single-theme comic book. The character made a dynamic cover attraction, a secret ingredient used by the pulp publishers for assuring newsstand sales, and a device that Fiction House adapted to its comic book line. The *Jungle Comics'* covers that artistically depicted the muscular Ka'anga in action always commanded immediate attention even though the Ka'anga stories themselves represented only six to eight pages of the book's total sixty-four pages.

Jungle Comics carried several different features of the jungle theme—the Red Panther (superhero), Tabu, Wizard of the Jungle, Captain Terry Thunder, Roy Lance, and others. However, the truly unique star of this comic book was a young lad named Wambi who, since infancy, had been raised by the animals. In a broad sense, Wambi could be viewed as a spin-off of Rudyard Kipling's *The Jungle Book*, the classic tale also about a young lad raised by the animals in the jungle. But *The Jungle Book* did not become well known to the general public until Hollywood produced the popular movie version—some ten years after Wambi first appeared in *Jungle Comics*. One of Wambi's novel traits was that he was *not* a strongarm fighter. He did, however, possess a great deal of courage, a sound moral instinct, and the rare ability to communicate with the animals.

"Wambi" was originally created by Roy L. Smith and illustrated mostly by artist H. C. Kiefer whose uncanny style in realistically depicting animals in action added an unusual depth to the feature. (H. C. Kiefer emerged as one of the foremost pen-and-ink artists of animal anatomy whose work appeared in numerous other publications during the 1940s.)

With the greatest of ease, Wambi speaks to the animals.

While he was sympathetic to the problems of animals. . .

. . . he had no sympathy at all for those who would harm his animal brothers.

And as the animals depended on him, he also depended on them.

A sample of Wambi's philosophy during a rescue of a wounded lion trapped in a brush fire.

Wambi's unique role in the jungle was best summed up in his eighth adventure which appeared in *Jungle Comics No. 8* (August 1940). Here, Wambi hears news from the birds that the friendly natives of the Inga village were stricken with a serious plague that reached epidemic proportions. While on the way to the village to offer his assistance, Wambi discovers the bodies of two messengers who were sent to deliver a handwritten note to the British outpost but were struck down by the hostile Kurga tribesmen. Wambi retrieves the note—a letter from Dr. Downs, a British mercenary physician, who had been treating the natives and was now requesting an additonal supply of serum.

When the tom-toms spoke of Wambi's brave deeds, native tribesmen everywhere watched over him during his travels and safeguarded him from danger.

©1941 Glen Kel Publishing Co., Inc.

Wambi was also the key link that bonded the natives and the animals together during their fierce battles against the European oppressors.

©1941 Glen Kel Publishing Co., Inc.

Wambi became Fiction House's second star attraction and though he never appeared on the cover of *Jungle Comics*, he was soon elevated to his own quarterly magazine that began with the Spring 1942 issue, and continued for fifty-three more issues until the series was terminated in 1953.

150

The next unique *Jungle Comics'* feature was Camilla, Queen of the Lost City. During the first six issues, the lost city, although buried deep in the unexplored jungles, resembled a culture of ancient Rome where the people worshipped the gods of Greek mythology. Camilla herself had the power to call upon the gods in times of distress. However, the feature switched hands and was taken over by Ted Carter who introduced some major changes. He eliminated the mythological background, changed the "Lost City" to the "Lost Empire," and made the Queen an entirely different character. The new Camilla discovered that by bathing in the fountain of eternal youth, she not only retained her youth and beauty but also acquired Amazonian strength making her capable of almost super-human feats.

During 1942, Carter left the series and it was taken over by another artist who incorporated other changes—the fountain had somehow "disappeared" and Camilla's strength faded away. Yet none of her later adventures compared to those of the Ted Carter years. A typical Carter story concerned an invading army from Mongolia that laid siege to Camilla's empire. Surrounded on every side and heavily outnumbered by superior fighting forces, Camilla sought to penetrate the enemy lines and seek help from an unusual ally.

A sample of this adventure from *Jungle Comics No. 8* (August 1940) is shown here.

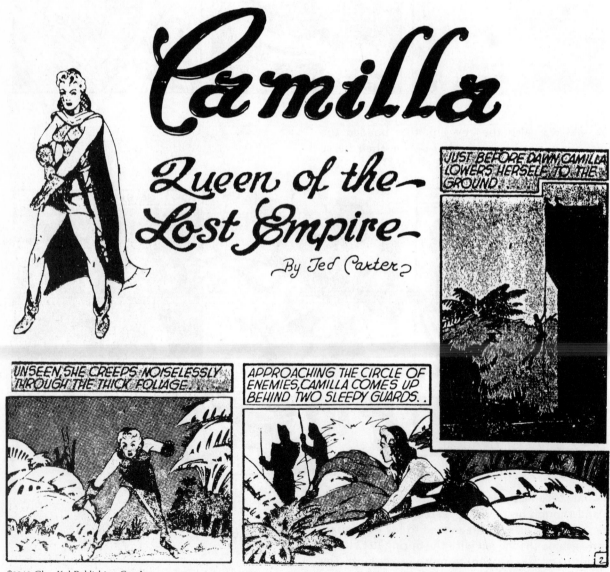

Camilla
Queen of the Lost Empire
By Ted Carter

JUST BEFORE DAWN CAMILLA LOWERS HERSELF TO THE GROUND.

UNSEEN, SHE CREEPS NOISELESSLY THROUGH THE THICK FOLIAGE.

APPROACHING THE CIRCLE OF ENEMIES, CAMILLA COMES UP BEHIND TWO SLEEPY GUARDS..

Of course Camilla and the powerful ape tribe drove the enemy away in a gruesome battle.

Following the pulp formula for holding the attention of their readership, *Jungle Comics* was loaded with violent action as shown in the above scenes from "Camilla," or in the following scenes from "Roy Lance World Traveller" (*Jungle Comics No. 4*).

©1940 Glen Kel Publishing Co., Inc.

Violence also played an important role in "Captain Terry Thunder." Here is a typical scene as it appeared in *Jungle Comics No. 4.*

TERRY RETREATS SLOWLY BEFORE THE OVERWHELMING ODDS.

LIFTING ONE OF THE BRUTES..

HE HURLS HIM INTO THE MIDST OF HIS TRIBESMEN!

THIS SLIDING PANEL WILL FOOL THOSE BIRDS!

A BATTERING RAM BREAKS DOWN THE HEAVY DOOR...

TUN!

ENTERING, THEY ARE STARTLED TO FIND CAPTAIN THUNDER GONE.

Although Captain Terry Thunder never became a major character, his debut in the first issue of *Jungle Comics* had a powerful impact on the legal aspects of the industry. In 1940, Fiction House blocked Fawcett Publications from using the name Captain Thunder for their new character (later changed to CAPTAIN MARVEL) which had just come out in Fawcett's *Thrill Comics No. 1* a few weeks after *Jungle Comics No. 1* had been on the newsstand.

Fiction House's single-theme innovation proved to be highly successful and *Jungle Comics* ran monthly until 1954. Ironically, the violence content which contributed to the magazine's success was the very element that drew sharp criticism during the mid-1950s and ultimately forced Fiction House to terminate its comic book line.

Planet Comics No. 1 (Jan. 1940)
©1939 Love Romances Publishing Co., Inc.

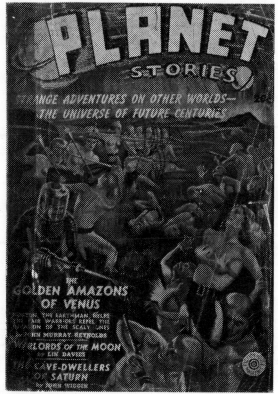

Planet Stories No. 1 (Nov. 1939)
©1939 Fiction House, Inc.

Planet Comics was another single-theme title that Fiction House initiated in January, 1940. This one featured all-interplanetary adventure. Again, the action-packed "pulpish" cover art helped shove *Planet Comics* into a top ranking slot. But unlike *Jungle Comics* which fell into a category of its own, *Planet Comics* was bucking stiff competition in all directions—"Buck Rogers" and "Flash Gordon" on one end, and the upcoming wave of science fiction pulps at the other.

To meet this challenge, Fiction House placed their pulp line under the heading "Love Romance Publications," and then introduced their own science fiction pulp, *Planet Stories*. In many instances the same story was used in both the pulp and the comic book. However, while *Planet Stories* stood its own ground as the third most popular science fiction pulp (with stories from such high ranking authors as Ray Bradbury), *Planet Comics* underwent many changes during its fourteen-year publishing life in an attempt to produce one solid science fiction feature equivalent to "Sheena." New characters were introduced in almost every issue, all of which were well illustrated. Indeed, some were quite unique.

Planet Comics No. 21, for example, introduced the first episode of "Lost World" which remained as the lead feature. Basically, the series was set in the distant future after an atomic holocaust had destroyed most of the world. What was left of human civilization was thrown back to the prehistoric era—but with a novel twist.

Voltamen from Mars (green skinned ape-like creatures who wore Nazi-styled uniforms) came to Earth and decided to take over the uncivilized world and set it up as a colony of Mars. Of course they met unexpected resistance from the remaining tribe of Earthmen led by hero Hunt Bowman. The Earthmen were at a serious disadvantage being armed with only bows and arrows while the Voltamen possessed ray guns, disintegrator bombs, spaceships and an arsenal of other highly sophisticated weapons. The series developed around Hunt Bowman's never-ending struggle to drive the enemy away from Earth. Later on, his relentless efforts were joined by amphibious super beings from Venus, also enemies of the Voltamen.

Another equally exciting feature was "Star Pirate," created by topnotch artist Murphy Anderson. Star Pirate's adventures took him throughout the nearby star systems where he constantly fought all forms of alien life. . .

Auro, Lord of Jupiter appeared in *Planet Comics No. 1*. It was terminated after a few episodes, but was later revived in *Planet Comics No. 42* (March 1946) with a different theme based on an interesting reincarnation concept created by Dick Charles. Auro was an inhabitant of Jupiter but, unknown to him, his ethereal spirit was Earthman Chester Edson whose physical body lay in a near-lifeless coma as the result of a peculiar medical experiment. Auro constantly faced danger in his quest to maintain peace among the various warring factions who sought control of his government. If he were killed, Edson too would die. The series centered around the spirit of Chester Edson struggling to protect Auro from harm even though communication between the two was impossible.

Planet Comics No. 43 introduced "Futura," magnificently created by artist John Douglas. Here, secretary Marcia Reynolds who was destined to play the title role of the strip, and a few of her girl friends are accidently caught in a time wave and teleported to Venus which was in a state of war. The sinister being known as Mentor and his men had captured the Earthgirls for an incredible medical operation. Marcia managed to escape and sought help from Mentor's enemies, as shown here in Part II.

Futura

by JOHN DOUGLAS

TOO WELL HAD SPECIMEN NINE FROM TERRA BELT GREEN SURVIVED THE CYMRAD TESTS... FOR IT WAS FUTURA, THE CAPTURED EARTH GIRL, WHO HAD SLIPPED FROM MENTOR'S CLUTCHES, HAD PIERCED THE PURPLE MISTS TO REACH SARGAZZO, LAND OF THE ABOROTES, WHERE EVEN NOW SHE DWELT, AS LEADER... AND IN CYMRAD CITY...

"AH YES, BUT WHICH CYMRADIAN BRAIN SHALL I USE?" PONDERS MENTOR... "INCAPABLE OF DYING, WE OF THE PAN COSMOS, YET INCAPABLE OF LIVING WITHOUT A FRAME... A BODY."

IN THE DUNGEON OF THE OTHER-WORLD CAPTIVES, MENTOR RANTS AND RAVES... "WE MUST FIND A BODY CAPABLE OF HOLDING OUR BRAINS, WE MUST... OR PERISH! THIS ONE, SYNTHOS, BRING HER TO CHAMBER THREE FOR TEST FIVE OF PROJECT SURVIVAL!"

THEN THE GREATEST OF THE GREAT-BRAINS GESTURES... "THERE, SYNTHOPOID, LET US TRY THE BRAIN OF IONTRA. BRING HIM AND THE SUBJECT TO CHAMBER THREE!"

A SHAVEN HEAD... A MASS OF MATTER... A LAST TESTING OF ELECTRODES... THEN TEST FIVE IS READY TO BEGIN. "HA!" MENTOR GLOATS. "FUTURA ESCAPED US, BUT THIS ONE MAY YET SOLVE OUR PROBLEM!"

WHILE IN ABOROTE LAND, A FORMER EARTH SECRETARY NOW FINDS HERSELF THRUST INTO A STRANGE, AND SOMETIMES FRIGHTENING, LEADERSHIP "HERE," COMMANDS FUTURA. "BRING THE SWAMP-DRAGON TO A HALT, FOR AHEAD LIES A THING WE MUST CONQUER, IF YOU WOULD RETURN TO CYMRADA."

"FAR DISTANT, THE GUARDING TOWER OF MENTOR _ AND BEFORE US THE GEYSER OF OIL," SAYS FUTURA... "AND WITH IT WE SHALL CAPTURE THAT TOWER. YOU WILL FOLLOW MY PLAN?"

MANY ARE THE GRUMBLINGS... WHO IS THIS EARTH GIRL WHO DARES ORDER US? FOR TENSE SECONDS, INDECISION_INCIPIENT REBELLION THREATENS...

THEN THE STRENGTH OF FUTURA'S VOICE, AND THE GREATER STRENGTH OF JARL NORD'S RING TAKES COMMAND. "QUICKLY," SHE ORDERS. "GIVE ME THE TOOLS I NEED!"

TOOLS INDEED! FOR AHEAD LIES A TOWER WITH RAYS, VISOS, ERG-GUNS_WITH BLASTERS, SYNTHOS, AND FISS-RODS.

WITH POUNDING HEART, FUTURA DONS HER BIRD GUISE... "HOW ELSE TO NEAR THE TOWER UNNOTICED?" SHE WONDERS.. "YET, IF I FAIL___"

2

WHILE ON CYMRADA, TEST FIVE CONTINUES. "TAKE CARE," WARNS MENTOR.. "THE MEDULLA OBLONGATA IS DELICATE.. AND TIME GROWS SHORT."

A RIGOROUS CHECK.. CHARTS, GRAPHS, TESTING OF NEURO-SPINOS... THEN, FOR THE FIRST TIME, MENTOR SMILES. "HA, SO FAR SO GOOD, WE MAY YET FIND THE TYPE STRONG ENOUGH TO HOLD OUR BRAIN-CITADELS OF KNOWLEDGE!"

AS IN THE SWAMPLANDS THE ABOROTES SEIZE A MAMMOTH BYSOP-BIRD.. THEIR TASK IS SIMPLE COMPARED TO THAT OF FUTURA, WHO EVEN NOW CREEPS CLOSER TO THE PILLAR OF POWER.

IN THE TOWER, A TRANS-VENUSIAN, THE LIVING OUTCOME OF A NEARLY SUCCESSFUL PROJECT SURVIVAL, BARKS A GRIM COMMAND.. "A SHADOW SPOTTED IN THE RADA-SCOPE.. QUICKLY, SYNTHOS, TRAIN YOUR GUNS!"

THE OBJECT OF THEIR TRACKING FINDS DISGUISE NO LONGER NEEDED.. NOW UNFOLDS HER PLAN.. "THEIR ATTENTION TURNED THIS WAY.. AND IF THE GODS BE WITH ME, THEY'LL NOT SEE THE BYSOP-BIRD, UNTIL.. TOO LATE!"

AND AS THE PARA-RAYS DART THROUGH THE DARKNESS OF THE PURPLE SWAMPS, FUTURA DANCES, DODGES.. ELUSIVE AS A SHADOW! BUT, FOR HOW LONG?

FEVERISHLY THE ABOROTES WORK, FOR THE PRICE OF FAILURE IS THE LIFE OF THEIR LEADER.... NOW, THE BYSOP-BIRD, UP AND AWAY!

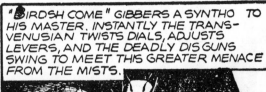

"BIRDSH COME" GIBBERS A SYNTHO TO HIS MASTER. INSTANTLY THE TRANS-VENUSIAN TWISTS DIALS, ADJUSTS LEVERS, AND THE DEADLY DIS GUNS SWING TO MEET THIS GREATER MENACE FROM THE MISTS.

BUT DOWN, LANCING THROUGH THE SWIRLING FOG, PLUNGES THE WINGED CREATURE.. DOWN TOWARDS THE TOWER..

A CLASH OF GIANTS... A SICKENING THUD OF BEAST AGAINST METAL.. AN ABOROTE LEAPING FREE....

AND INSIDE, THE TRANS-VENUSIAN SCREAMS, "QUICKLY, SUBMERGE TO THREE DEPTHOS, FOR THERE THE FOOLS CANNOT BOTHER US.. AND OUR ERG-RAYS CAN BLAST THEM DOWN!"

NOW, ON SHORE, FUTURA WORKS WITH A SPEED BORNE OF DESPERATE URGENCY. "HURRY, HURRY," SHE ORDERS. "BRING THE HOLLOW LOG AND DO AS I SAY!"

160

"HEAVY, YES... BUT HEAVIER YET YOUR TASK IF WE FAIL!" WARNS FUTURA. "RAISE THE LOG, PLACE IT OVER THE STREAM OF OIL!"

AND NOW NEAR-VICTORY FILLS FUTURA'S VOICE. "WELL DONE. WELL DONE! BUT HIGHER... HIGHER... IT MUST COAT THE WATERS OF THE SWAMP!"

SLIME OVER THE SWAMP LANDS, AND BENEATH IT THE SUBMERGED TOWER IN SAFETY... ON SHORE FUTURA, DETERMINED TO SHATTER THAT SAFETY!

THEN A FIRE-BRAND CAST UPON OILY WATERS, AND IN IT CENTERED THE HOPES AND PRAYERS OF A NEAR-LOST RACE.

AND AS RAGING FLAMES SPEAR SKYWARD, FUTURA EXULTS, "WATCH NOW, FOR SOON THEY WILL RISE, AND THEN___"

WHILE, IN CYMRAD CITY, MENTOR GLOATS, "ENOUGH FOR NOW, LET US NOT EXHAUST THIS MOST EXCELLENT SUBJECT..." BUT HE IS VERY ABRUPTLY INTERRUPTED BY A SHRILL WARNING, "LORD MENTOR, A DANGER SIGNAL FROM OUTPOST TOWER 7!"

DANGER... DEADLY DANGER ON OUTPOST 7! CLUTCHING, CLAWING, OXYGEN-EXHAUSTING HEAT!

"WHERE COMES THIS HEAT, I KNOW NOT," THE TRANS-VENUSIAN SCREAMS. "BUT RISE WE MUST... OR DIE... THE SURFACE, PERHAPS THERE LIES SAFETY!"

BUT INSTEAD, UP INTO A HORROR OF HEAT, A FURY OF FLAME, A RAGING INFERNO! SCREAMS, ANGUISHED CRIES ECHO THE SWAMPLANDS... YET LOUDER STILL THE CRIES OF FUTURA AND THE ABOROTES... FOR THEIRS IS THE VOICE OF VICTORY!

AND IN CYMRADA, A GRUMBLING MENTOR FACES THE VISIRAD: TROUBLE ON OUTPOST 7, EH? THOSE INFERNAL ABOROTES... WHAT ARE THEY UP TO NOW? WAIT, THAT FACE, FUTURA... AND HER VOICE COMING THROUGH...

"FUTURA BY YOUR NAMING, MENTOR... AND BY THAT NAME I'LL CONQUER YOU... TAKE WARNING, BIG HEAD... THIS TOWER IS OURS AND NOT UNTIL I LEAD MY ABOROTES TO CYMRADA WILL I RETURN TO EARTH AS MARCIA REYNOLDS."

WAR! EARTH GIRL FUTURA PITTED AGAINST THE MAD GENIUS OF LORD MENTOR. ANOTHER STIRRING ADVENTURE IN THE NEXT ISSUE OF PLANET COMICS!

LIFE ON OTHER WORLDS

NEPTUNE

MURPHY ANDERSON

NEPTUNE, ANOTHER OF THE MYSTERY PLANETS. ITS DISCOVERY STARTLED THE SCIENTIFIC WORLD BECAUSE IT OCCUPIES A POSITION FURTHERMOST FROM THE SUN, AND TRAVELS IN AN ORBIT WHOSE CIRCUMFERENCE IS NEARLY SEVENTEEN BILLION MILES! THE THIRD LARGEST PLANET, 33,000 MILES IN DIAMETER, NEPTUNE IS ALWAYS SHROUDED IN DENSE VEILS OF HEAVY ATMOSPHERE, WHICH PREVIOUSLY HAD MADE IT IMPREGNABLE TO EARTH'S FAR-REACHING TELESCOPES. WHAT LIFE, IF ANY, DWELLS THERE?

WILL THE GIANT, 200 INCH TELESCOPE OF MT. PALOMAR SOLVE THIS RIDDLE OF THE UNIVERSE?

Planet Comics No. 4 (April 1940)
©1940 Love Romances Publishing Co., Inc.

Planet Comics No. 5 (May 1940)
©1940 Love Romances Publishing Co., Inc.

Planet Comics No. 8 (Sept. 1940)
©1940 Love Romances Publishing Co., Inc.

Planet Stories, Vol. IV, No. 2 (Spring 1949)
©1948 Love Romances Publishing Co., Inc.

Wings Comics No. 1 (Spet. 1940)
©1940 Wings Publishing Co.

Wings Magazine, Vol. VIII, No. 3 (Winter 1936)
©1940 Wings Publishing Co.

Wings Comics, another single-theme comic book, was a direct spin-off from Fiction House's discontinued pulp magazine *Wings*, which had been extremely popular during the 1920s when aviation was just beginning to attract worldwide interest. It was not unusual to pick up a *Wings* pulp and see a hero climb out of the open cockpit of one airplane, drop down onto the wing of another plane that was flying directly below him, and then deftly climb aboard without falling off. However, aviation fiction in literature had difficulty keeping pace with true-life aviation progress. Such dramatic air stunts of the 1920 era appeared ridiculous in the 1940 era when pilots were flying speedy fighter planes and high-altitude bombers. In fact, *Wing Comics* was already obsolete before the first issue came out in September 1940.

To overcome this particular dilemma, Fiction House injected heroic fantasy into the book with a string of imitations of Captain Midnight, Blackhawk, and Spy Smasher. With no more than change of names and costumes, *Wings Comics* introduced Skull Squad, Ghost Patrol, Phantom Falcon, and Captain Wings, none of which created much excitement in the comic book arena. But there was more to *Wings Comics* than its fantasy content.

Later issues included more serious aviation fiction with war stories about Red Cross air rescue missions and air-sea engagements between the famous Flying Tigers and Japanese battle cruisers. In addition, *Wings Comics* also carried a series on true-life aviation history as well as helpful articles on model airplane building, then one of the nation's most popular hobbies for boys. Although *Wings Comics* never became a top selling comic book, it did maintain for fourteen years a steady readership of young enthusiasts. And within this specialized field of airplane literature, which included a host of other publications besides comic books, *Wings Comics* clearly stood out as the leader.

Rangers of Freedom which Fiction House introduced in October 1941, was quite similar to *Wings Comics* in the sense that it also stressed war adventure with such characters as Commando Ranger. As the war drew towards an end, *Rangers of Freedom* dropped the military slant and converted to adventure fantasy with a new star, Firehair—a Wild West version of the ever popular Sheena.

Fight Comics No. 5 (May 1940)
©1940 Fight Stories, Inc.

Fight Comics No. 14 (Oct. 1941)
©1940 Fight Stories, Inc.

Fight Comics was not a single-theme title in the same sense that *Jungle Comics* and *Planet Comics* were, but, its contents did cover he-man adventure exclusively. The early issues also included a series on the history of prize fighters with illustrated story adaptations of some of the more famous ring fights of the 1920s and 1930s. It was here that Fiction House introduced various new concepts in superhero fantasy with such costumed characters as Saber and Shark Brodie. Issue No. 3 marked the debut of Rip Reagan, the Powerman. This was a fairly unique character that might have made the top grade if it hadn't been for Superman and Captain Marvel.

Powerman wore a special crimson jacket which imbued him with superhuman strength and also made him weightless enough for long-distance leaps through the air. Of course when he took off his jacket he was just an ordinary person. The oddity here was that Powerman had no secrets. Everyone, including the villains he constantly kayoed, knew about his jacket, which he wore as much of the time as he could. But for some unknown reason, the series ran for only twelve issues before it was abruptly terminated in *Fight Comics No. 14.*

This was the same issue in which Super American made his dramatic first appearance. Super American had travelled backward in time from the 23rd Cen-

tury, materializing in the mid-20th Century during the war years. Endowed with the amazing powers that everyone possessed in the 23rd Century, Super American leaped to aid the country in the war against Nazi Germany as Fiction House's contribution to comicdom's growing team of patriotic superheroes.

During 1943, *Fight Comics* gradually shifted away from superhero fantasy and began to rely heavily on war adventures with true-to-life characters such as Rip Carson, Paratrooper. After the end of World War II, *Fight Comics* underwent another change with the introduction of a third generation of new characters. Undoubtedly with the success of "Sheena" in mind, Fiction House introduced "Tiger Girl" as a main attraction of *Fight Comics*. Realizing that "Tiger Girl" lacked a certain spark of originality, the feature was strengthened by giving Tiger Girl a male companion—Tiger Man. Another new feature was "Captain Fight."

Fiction House also published other titles not covered within this section.

Fight Comics No. 17 (Feb. 1942)

Wings Comics No. 6 (Feb. 1942)

Rangers of Freedom No. 3 (Feb. 1942)

ALPHABETICAL LISTING OF FICTION HOUSE COMIC BOOKS

Apache Comics (1951, one issue)
Fight Comics (1940 - 1954)
Firehair Comics (1949 - 1950)
First Christmas (1953, one issue)
Ghost Comics (1951 - 1954)
Indians (1950-1953)
Jumbo Comics (1938 - 1953)
Jungle Comics (1940 - 1954)
Ka'anga Comics (1949 - 1954)
Knockout Adventures (1954, one issue)
Long Bow, Indian Boy (1951 - 1953)
Man O'Mars (1953 - 1954)
Monster Comics (1953, two issues)
Pioneer West Romances (1949, three issues)
Planet Comics (1940 - 1954)
Rangers of Freedom (1941 - 1953)
*Sheena (1942 - 1953)
Toyland (1947, one issue)
Wambi (1942 - 1953)
Wings Comics (1940 - 1954)

*In addition to headlining Fiction House's most popular comic book, Sheena also headlined her own pulp magazine published by Fiction House during the 1940s.

6

DELL PUBLICATIONS

Dell Publishing Company, a major publisher of hardcover and paperback books, was at one time a leader in the comic book field. In 1929, Dell introduced *The Funnies*, a tabloid-type magazine that included black-and-white reprints of daily newspaper comic strips as well as reprints of Sunday strips that were reproduced in black and either red or blue. *The Funnies* also contained reprints of short stories, crossword puzzles, humorous articles, and various word games, all of which had previously appeared in newspapers. It ran for fifteen issues at irregular intervals between 1929 and 1931. *The Funnies,*which varied between sixteen pages and thirty-two pages per issue, might well be regarded as the first color comic book even though the strips were not printed in full color. (Comic book publishers would employ this process a few years later.)

In October, 1936, Dell introduced the second series of *The Funnies* which did include full color reprints of Sunday strips that featured both humor and adventure. 1940 saw the introduction of original superhero features that gradually supplanted the reprint material. In 1942, the magazine became *New Funnies*, a comic book of animal fantasy that headlined such characters as Andy Panda, Felix the Cat, and Raggedy Ann.

There were many other titles as well. In fact, Dell produced the most diversified line of comic books ever undertaken by a single publisher. The list included original superhero features, reprints of newspaper comic strips, illustrated adaptations of movies and literary classics, special comic book adaptations of animated films and cartoon shorts, and various radio and (later) television programs. In fact, Dell published comic books in almost every subject category except for crime. The Dell line became famous for its association with Walt Disney Studios, out of which emerged *Walt Disney Comics, Mickey Mouse Comics,* and *Donald Duck Comics.* In 1953, Dell Publishing Company produced an all time record high of more than 2-½ billion comic books between January and March 1953. This accounted for one-third of the combined total of all comic books published during that three-month period.

In 1955, the Thomás Alva Edison Foundation was established for the purpose of granting awards and honors for publications and movies of literary excellence for children. Among the five comic books selected as winners were three Dell titles: *Dell 4-Color Comics No. 755,* "The Littlest Snowman," also reprinted as *Dell 4-Color Comics No. 864; Dell 4-Color Comics No. 716,* "Man In Space" (Walt Disney), also reprinted as *Dell 4-Color Comics No. 954;* and *Dell Giant Comics No. 1,* "A Treasury of Dogs." The "Man In Space" issue was also adapted to *Dell 4-Color Comics No. 1148,* "I Aim At The Stars—The Wernher von Braun Story." (The other two awards were granted to Gilberton Company.)

In the late 1950s, Dell Publications began to phase out its comic book line due to its unyielding refusal to submit to the censorship demands of the Comics Code Authority, and also because of its rapid growth in the mass market paperback field. Western Publishing Company, noted producer of children's hardcover picture books under the Big Golden Series, Little Golden Series, Golden Play and Learn Series, and Tell-A-Tale Series, was making plans to enter the comic book field and took over the Dell line, now known as *Gold Key Comics.* Most of the animal fantasy features that appear in Gold Key Comics also appear in hardcover form in the Little Golden Series. In recent years, Gold Key Comics has introduced original titles that were not carried over from the Dell line.

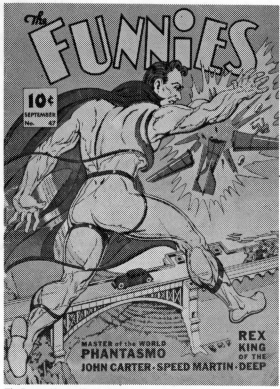

The Funnies No. 47 (Sept. 1940)—234
©1940 Dell Publishing Co., Inc.

Phantasmo No. 1 (Dell B/W No. 18, 1940)
©1940 R. S. Callender

The second series of *The Funnies*, which began in October 1936, introduced the reprints of V. T. Hamlin's Alley Oop, Bud Fisher's "Mutt and Jeff," and several other newspaper features. Issue No. 30 offered the first comic book adaptation of Edgar Rice Burroughs' famous "John Carter of Mars" epics that first appeared in *All Story Magazine*, September 1912 and continued in *Blue Book Magazine* during the 1920s. The Dell series ran continuously for twenty-six issues.

The Funnies No. 45 (July 1940) introduced Dell's first original superhero feature, "Phantasmo," created by E. L. Stoner. Phantasmo, it was revealed, had spent twenty-five years in Tibet where Grand High Lamas taught him the mysteries of the body and mind which he mastered well. Through sheer will power and concentration, Phantasmo was able to separate his ethereal spirit from his physical body. In his spiritual form he could float through walls, fly through the sky, expand in size, become invisible or partially invisible, or materialize as a force capable of moving mountains. Phantasmo returned to his homeland, America, to use his powers to benefit mankind.

Upon arriving in New York, he adopted the identity of Phil Anson and met a young bellhop, Whizzer McGee, who would become his junior assistant and "bodyguard."

Phantasmo had one peculiar weakness. When he

willed himself into a deep trance to free his spiritual self, his physical body lay in a lifeless state and should anything happen to the body it meant instant disaster for Phantasmo. During the trance state he had to rely on young Whizzer to watch over his body and guard it from harm until he returned from solving various crucial problems that threatened the world.

Whizzer's job was not an easy one, for Phil Anson, whose extrasensory vision could observe trouble spots anywhere in the world, often went into a sudden trance in full public view. From all outward signs, it appeared that Whizzer had a corpse on his hands.

©1940 Dell Publishing Co., Inc.

Between 1939 and 1941, Dell also published a series of twenty-four black-and-white full length comic book editions each devoted to a single feature. No. 18 was the only edition to feature Phantasmo (which included reprints from *The Funnies*). The black-and-white series, although short lived, was the forerunner to the "Dell 4-Color Comics" series which ran for more than 1,300 issues.

The Funnies No. 46 introduced the first comic book adaptation of Philip H. Lord's "Mr. District Attorney," then a famous radio program.

Another feature that began in this issue was the first part of a two-part story that dealt with the origin of the Black Knight, a character concept in the "Prince Valiant" category, except that the Black Knight wore a mask.

The Funnies also carried "Rex, King of the Deep," the first feature created by noted artist A. C. Mc-Williams who, during the 1940s, had produced several features for other different comic books. Although the McWilliams' features never achieved major fame, they nevertheless stand out as classic examples of realistic illustration in the mode of Hal Foster and Alex Raymond. McWilliams left the comic book field during the mid-1940s, but twenty years later he returned to create a popular science fiction comic strip entitled "Twin Earths" which ran in many newspapers throughout the country.

Super Comics No. 36 (May 1941)
©1941 K.K. Publications, Inc.

Super Comics No. 36 (May 1941)
©1941 K.K. Publications, Inc.

In May 1938, Dell introduced the first edition of *Super Comics* featuring reprints of such famous newspaper strips as "Dick Tracy," "Little Orphan Annie," "Terry and the Pirates," "Smilin' Jack," and others.

Chester Gould's "Dick Tracy," which began as a regular feature in Sunday newspapers in October 1931 reflected, on the comic page, the headlines of the front page that detailed the crime and violence that was so prevalent during Prohibition. Dick Tracy was the dedicated cop who tracked down ruthless hoodlums and he meant business, even if he had to blast a hole through the gangster's head to prove it!

When Dick Tracy went into action, crashing through doors with Tommy gun blazing, blood was splattered in liberal quantities over the appropiate panels. And after the smoke had cleared and the agonizing moans and groans fell silent, the case was irrefutably closed forever!

Dick Tracy pitted brain and brawn against such notorious killers as Pruneface, Flattop, and the Mole—and his wanted list was almost endless. But with a little clue here and there, he relentlessly tracked down the crooks and gave them their due.

King Features had originally introduced "Dick Tracy" as a daily strip for newspaper syndication in 1929 under a two-year contract, but did not renew it when it expired. The Chicago Tribune Syndicate quickly picked up the series and kept it going for more than forty-five years.

In 1937, Republic Pictures introduced the first movie serial adaptation of "The Dick Tracy" strip, starring Ralph Byrd. The serial proved so popular, that the next year Republic produced a second serial, *Dick Tracy Returns*. In 1938, the studio produced a series of full-length (and for those days quite violent) Dick Tracy films (also still starring Ralph Byrd) that started a whole trend of detective films in an entertainment area that until then had been almost the exclusive domain of westerns. In 1939, Republic made a third movie serial, *Dick Tracy's G-Men*, and in 1941 the fourth and last, *Dick Tracy vs. Crime Inc.*

Dick Tracy made *Super Comics* a leading title during the era when superhero fantasy dominated the scene; he stood out as one of the few crimefighters who did not rely on any super powers or technical gadgets. Dell also published several full-length editions of *Dick Tracy Comics* within the "4-Color" series, and the title was continued by Harvey Publications through 1961. (In 1976, Dick Tracy was revived once again in comic book format as a special oversize D-C title.)

When Western took over the Dell line to concentrate on animal fantasy, the "Dick Tracy" comic book series exchanged hands and was continued by Harvey Publications up through 1961. In recent years, National Periodical revived "Dick Tracy" as a D-C title.

Further information of Chester Gould's famous creation appears in *The Celebrated Cases of Dick Tracy* (New York, Chelsea House) an anthology of reprints of comic strip adventures throughout the years.

Milton Caniff's famous "Terry and the Pirates," also reprinted in *Super Comics,* started in the newspapers on October 19, 1934. It was among the first of the adventure comic strips to employ extensive use of black shadows as a means of giving three-dimensional depth to the art form. In 1940, Columbia Pictures produced a movie serial adaptation of "Terry." Shortly afterward, the feature was adapted to radio drama.

In December 1946, Milton Caniff left the strip to begin another one, "Steve Canyon." Artist George Wunder took over the "Terry and the Pirates" series and kept it going until February 25, 1973 when it was finally terminated from newspaper syndication. During its thirty-eight year run, "Terry and the Pirates" enjoyed worldwide fame as a leading adventure feature. This is a sample of what the strip was like when it started out in 1934.

©1935 Chicago Tribune Syndicate

Popular Comics No. 59 (Jan. 1941)
©1940 Dell Publishing Co., Inc.

Popular Comics No. 60 (Feb. 1941)
©1941 Dell Publishing Co., Inc.

Popular Comics, which began in February 1936, was another Dell title that also, in its early stages, reprinted an assortment of newspaper strips. However, the reprint series were gradually transferred to *Super Comics* and other Dell titles as *Popular Comics* began to stress original features, mostly of the superhero variety.

For example, *Popular Comics No. 46* introduced "Martan, the Marvel Man," created by G. Ellerbrock. Martan, a telepath from the distant planet Antaclea, journeyed to Earth with his wife Vana to spend their honeymoon among the intelligent life which their scientists had detected there. But upon arriving on Earth and disguising themselves as a human couple, they discovered that sinister alien beings, acting under directions of the Supreme Three of the Universe who had failed to conquer the couple's home planet Antaclea, were now invading Earth. The invaders, however, did not count on the visitor from Antaclea who leaped to Earth's defense. The Earth people called him the Marvel Man, but to the invaders, he was known as "Martan, the Antaclean Super Warrior!"

Martan and his wife were superbeings, both physically and mentally, and were able to use their telepathic powers to full advantage.

Popular Comics also carried the first comic book adaptation of Philip H. Lord's other famous radio program "Gang Busters." (This feature also appeared as a full-length edition in the black-and-white series.) After Dell had discontinued "Gang Busters" and its companion feature "Mr. District Attorney," both were later revived for a second go around as leading D-C titles during the late 1940s.

In the superhero category, *Popular Comics No. 51* introduced an invisible sleuth in the feature "The Voice." Created by Jim Chambers, the Voice, in reality, was private detective Jim Brant who became invisible when wearing a suit of transparent cellulose material that permitted lightwaves to pass through it. The suit was invented by his colleague Professor Bert Wilson. What made this feature an interesting adaptation of the invisibility concept was that Professor Wilson made enough of the material to use for other purposes, such as draping over an automobile to make it "disappear."

In later issues, *Popular Comics* introduced "Smilin' Jack", "Captain Midnight," and "The Owl." But the best constructed superhero feature to appear in the magazine was "Professor Supermind and Son," a unique crimefighting team created by Maurice Kashuba. *Popular Comics No. 60* (February 1941) published their first appearance.

PROFESSOR **Supermind** and **Son**

COPR., 1941, BY R. S. CALLENDER

MAURICE KASHUBA

ON HIS FAMOUS MOUNTAIN-TOP LABORATORY, PROFESSOR WARREN, KNOWN TO THE WORLD AS SUPERMIND, AND HIS EQUALLY FAMOUS SON, DAN, ARE IN A STATE OF GREAT EXCITEMENT.

THE TELEVISOSCOPE...THE FIRST TELEVISION MACHINE ABLE TO RECEIVE LIGHT REFLECTIONS OUT OF THE AIR FROM ANYWHERE OR ANY DISTANCE.

JUST LIKE THE RADIO.

DAD, IF OUR MACHINE WORKS, DO YOU KNOW WHAT IT WILL MEAN TO THE REST OF THE WORLD.

I DO, SON, AND I ALSO KNOW WHAT IT WILL MEAN TO AMERICA!

SOMEWHAT, BUT IN RADIO THEY MUST SEND THE SOUND FIRST. WHILE, FOR OUR MACHINE, THE WHOLE GLOBE BECOMES A CONSTANT SENDING STATION, OPERATING TWENTY-FOUR HOURS A DAY!

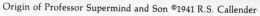

Origin of Professor Supermind and Son ©1941 R.S. Callender·

WITH THE TERRIFIC SPEED OF A LIGHTNING FLASH, DAN HURTLES INTO THE SKY.

HIS DESTINATION A SMALL ISLAND IN THE WIDE PACIFIC OCEAN.

WHILE ON THE ISLAND.... THERE IS GREAT ACTIVITY..... PREPARATION FOR A SUDDEN ATTACK ON THIS FAR PEACEFUL SHIPPING LANES.

SOLDIERS ARE BUSY TRANSFERRING HIGH EXPLOSIVES TO SECRET MUNITION DUMPS.

CAMOUFLAGED TO HIDE THEIR EXISTENCE FROM PASSING SHIPS OR PLANES.

DAN'S DYNAMIC POWER SENDS THE ORIENTALS FLYING IN ALL DIRECTIONS....... SQUEALING WITH TERROR.

CALL OFF YOUR MISERABLE SOLDIERY BEFORE I LOSE MY TEMPER!....

LET GO HONORABLE STRANGER, ALL VELLY BIG MISTAKE!.... TS—TS....

I'VE ONLY GIVEN YOU A SMALL SAMPLE OF WHAT I CAN DO!.... NOW HERE ARE MY ORDERS.... LEAVE THIS ISLAND IMMEDIATELY AND RETURN TO YOUR OWN COUNTRY!

I GIVE YOU EXACTLY TWENTY MINUTES FOR YOUR SUBMARINES TO CLEAR THE INLET.

AS DAN WATCHES THE MINUTE HAND ON HIS WATCH, THE INVADERS ARE HASTILY BOARDING THEIR SHIPS....

.WELL....THERE THEY GO!.... THIS WAS TOO EASY, I WOULD HAVE ENJOYED A GOOD SCRAP.

DAN DOES NOT REALIZE THAT HE IS STANDING ON THE SECRET MUNITION DUMP.

SHELL SCREAMS TOWARD THE ISLAND AIMED TO EXPLODE THE DEADLY STORE OF HIGH EXPLOSIVES.

BANG!

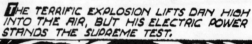

THE TERRIFIC EXPLOSION LIFTS DAN HIGH INTO THE AIR, BUT HIS ELECTRIC POWER STANDS THE SUPREME TEST.

SO THAT WAS YOUR TRICK, YOU TREACHEROUS DOGS. WELL, YOU PLAYED YOUR CARD, NOW I'LL PLAY MINE!........

HUMAN LIGHTNING STREAKS AT THE SUBMARINES.

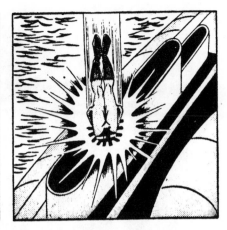

AND SMASHES STRAIGHT THRU THE STEEL PLATES WHICH TURN WHITE HOT UPON CONTACT WITH DAN'S POWERFUL ELECTRIC CHARGE!

DAN'S FURY IS AT ITS PEAK WHEN.... SUDDENLY ....

STOP....STOP.... DO NOT DESTROY NEEDLESSLY! .....RETURN..... YOUR DEED IS DONE........ RETURN.......THIS IS SUPERMIND.....DO YOU HEAR MY THOUGHT VOICE!

SUPERMIND'S DEMAND TRAVELING THOUSANDS OF MILES THRU THE ETHER HAS REACHED DAN.

..I..... HEAR..... ...YOU..... I.....AM COMING!

DAN FLASHES THRU THE SKY.....

I AM BACK, DAD, I AM SORRY I LOST CONTROL OVER MY TEMPER!

SO I SAW.....BE CAREFUL IN THE FUTURE, DO NOT MISUSE YOUR GREAT POWER.

SON, THE POWER OF OUR INVENTION IS BREATH TAKING. WE MUST USE IT TO SERVE HUMANITY AND THRU US OUR COUNTRY WILL LEAD THE WORLD TO A HAPPIER FUTURE.

"Felix, the Cat" ©1917 Pat Sullivan

Felix, the Cat Comics No. 10 (Aug. Sept. 1949)
©1949 King Features Syndicate, Inc.

During 1945, *Popular Comics* underwent a change in content and format when its superhero and adventure features were replaced by animal fantasy and humor features. "Felix, the Cat" became its new star feature. The classic creation of Pat Sullivan, Felix dates back to the early 1900s, long before the comic book industry began, and came into being when the camera was still a new invention called "the magic box." Even though single photographs were a novelty, various experimenters tried different techniques to produce a sequence of photographs that could be shown as a "moving picture."

As live film making slowly evolved into a separate art, it was Emile Cohl of France who, in 1904, originated the process of drawing stick figures in different dancing positions, then photographing each sketch separately. When they were projected by revolving lantern slide apparatus, they became the world's first animated cartoon.

In 1917, Pat Sullivan took Cohl's process one step further. Instead of using stick figures, Sullivan drew distorted sketches of his pet cat Felix, which when photographed separately and shown together as successive movements on film, became an art form that was then called "animated exaggeration." From this point on, the animated cartoon film slowly came into being. Of course the first efforts in animated cartoons were black-and-white silent films. Felix reigned su-

preme in this category—he was the only movie star in the world who could take off his tail, use it as a handle or lasso, and then stick it back on again.

During the early 1920s, Pat Sullivan's "Felix" cartoons became the guideline for all animation in the motion picture industry, and was not improved upon until Walt Disney, ten years later, added sound and color to the art.

In August 1923, "Felix the Cat" made his debut in the newspapers as a Sunday comic strip of King Features Syndicate. The comic strip was reprinted in *Popular Comics* and was published in several full-length editions of *Felix, the Cat Comics* in the "Dell 4-Color Comics" series. Starting in 1948, Dell published "Felix the Cat" as a monthly comic book. In later years, after Dell had phased out its comic book line, Felix continued for a while as a Gold Key title. And Toby Press as well as Harvey Publications also put out a series of *Felix, the Cat Comics*, with the last issue appearing in 1965.

Although Pat Sullivan died in 1933, the newspaper comic strip series has been continued by other artists throughout the years and is currently being handled by Oriolo Productions. The strip, which appears in relatively few newspapers in this country, is widely distributed throughout Europe where Felix still reigns supreme.

Dell's *Crackajack Funnies* began in June 1938 with reprints of such newspaper comic strips as "Dan Dunn," "Wash Tubbs" and several others. The magazine also introduced the first comic book adaptations of the wild west adventures of such Hollywood stars as Tom Mix and Buck Jones. A similar feature was the adaptation of the fictional adventures of Clyde Beatty, then a famous movie star of several jungle films and movie serials, and a world-renowned wild animal trainer.

Crackajack Funnies carried a variety of subject matter, including some original material. Issue 25 marked the debut of Dell's costumed crimefighter, the Owl, created by Frank Thomas. The character concept was one of the first based on a specific motif and theme, in this case, an owl as a creature of the night and a bird of prey. In line with the theme, the Owl operated strictly at night, stalking criminals in dark streets and alleys. By day, he was private investigator Nick Perry, and he did not don his mask and costume until after normal business hours. In Issue 32, Nick's girl friend joined his crimefighting crusade and wore a similar costume as the Owl Girl.

Crackajack Funnies also carried an A.L. McWilliams feature entitled "Stratosphere Jim and His Flying Fortress." The Flying Fortress was the most advanced design of an aircraft ever depicted in fiction anywhere. This is what it looked like.

Crackajack Funnies No. 39 (Sept. 1941)
©1941 K.K. Publications, Inc.

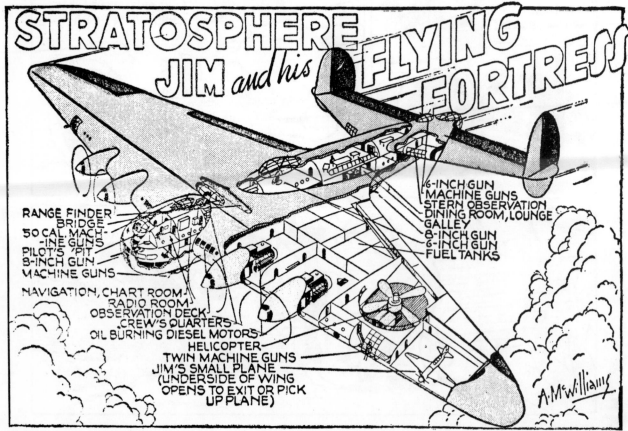

Crackajack Funnies No. 39 (Sept. 1941)
©1941 K.K. Publications, Inc.

Crackajack Funnies No. 15 was one of the first comic books to utilize original short stories on its center page. At one time, over a twenty issue span, the center page of this magazine featured short episodes of Edgar Rice Burroughs' Tarzan that never appeared anywhere else. Unlike the Tarzan novels which have seen several reprintings in hardcover and paperback editions, the short episodes, like the one reproduced here from *Crackajack Funnies*, were written especially for the comic book.

TARZAN
By EDGAR RICE BURROUGHS
COPR., 1941, BY EDGAR RICE BURROUGHS, INC.

Into the camp of the shiftas, Tarzan of the Apes had stolen silently to rescue a captive white man. Killing the lone sentry with a powerful thrust, Tarzan had quickly cut the captive's bonds and the two were about to make away in the night.

At that moment, however, Tarzan's faithful lion, Numa, chose to let forth a mighty roar of triumph. So close was the lion that the sudden shattering of the deep silence of the night startled every sleeper into wakefulness. A dozen men seized their matchlocks and leaped from their shelters. In the waning light of the fire they saw no lion; but they did see their liberated captive and they saw Tarzan of the Apes standing beside him.

One of the shiftas, who had encountered Tarzan earlier that day, recognized him at once. "It is he!" he shouted loudly to his companions. "It is the white demon who killed our friends today."

"Kill them both!" cried the leader of the shiftas.

Completely surrounding the two white men, the shiftas advanced upon them; but they dared not fire because of fear that they might wound one of their own comrades. Nor could Tarzan loose an arrow or cast a spear because he had left all his weapons except his knife and his rope hidden in a tree above the camp.

One of the bandits rushed to close quarters with his musket clubbed. It was his undoing. The ape-man crouched and as the other was almost upon him, charged. The musket butt, hurtling through the air to strike him down, was seized and wrenched from the shifta's grasp as though it had been a toy in a child's hands.

Tossing the matchlock at the feet of his companion, Tarzan laid hold upon the rash shifta and and held him as a shield against the weapons of his fellows. Two of the other shiftas rushed in behind the ape-man. But Tarzan's companion had grabbed the musket and holding it by the muzzle was using it as a club. The musket butt struck the foremost of the bandits on the side of the head and the second bandit leaped back just in time to avoid a similar fate.

Meanwhile, Tarzan, using the man in his grasp as a flail, sought to mow down those standing between him and liberty but there were many of them and presently they succeeded in dragging their comrade from the clutches of the ape-man. The shiftas were now in a transport of rage and several of them had withdrawn to one side where they might have free use of their weapons. One of them in particular was well placed and he now raised his matchlock and took careful aim at Tarzan.

As the man raised his weapon, a scream of warning burst from the lips of one of his comrades to be drowned by the throaty roar of Numa, the lion, as the swift rush of his charge carried him over the brush and into the midst of the camp.

The man who would have killed Tarzan cast a quick backward glance as the warning cry apprised him of his danger; and when he saw the lion he cast away his rifle in his excitement and terror. In his anxiety to escape the fangs of the man-eater he rushed into the arms of the ape-man.

In that brief instant, as the lion paused, crouching, Tarzan seized the fleeing shifta, lifted him high over his head and hurled him into the face of Numa. Then, as the lion seized its prey and its great jaws closed on the head and shoulder of the hapless bandit, Tarzan motioned to his companion to follow him and, running directly past the lion, leaped the brush. Before the bandits had recovered from the shock and the surprise of the lion's unexpected charge, the two white men had disappeared into the shadows of the night.

Crackajack Funnies No. 32 (Feb. 1941)
©1941 K.K. Publications, Inc.

By sharp contrast, Issue 30 introduced Walter Lantz's "Andy Panda." Here's how it began in September, 1941.

WALTER LANTZ Presents ANDY PANDA

COPR., 1941, BY WALTER LANTZ

Andy Panda was the first original character created by the Walter Lantz Studios who until then had been producing *Oswald the Rabbit* animated silent films for Universal Pictures. In 1927, Universal contracted with Walt Disney Studios to further develop "Oswald" for animation. The Disney Studios had just opened at the time and, after producing the first few "Oswald" films, lost its contract back to the Walter Lantz Studios who continued the series. But when sound was added to the animation, Universal Pictures quickly phased out "Oswald." Walter Lantz's art drafts for films that were never produced, were converted into a comic strip and proposed for newspaper syndication. Although "Oswald the Rabbit" was turned down by the syndicates, Dell agreed to schedule the feature for a few issues within its comic book line, and invited Lantz to create additional characters for the comic book.

At this point Lantz developed Andy Panda as a new character for *Crackajack Funnies* and began to introduce several of Andy's friends within the feature, one of whom happened to be Woody Woodpecker. In late 1941, Lantz produced the first animated cartoon about Andy's friend which was distributed by Universal Pictures. Needless to say, Woody Woodpecker (whose unforgettable voice was characterized by Lantz's wife, Grace Stafford) became a smash hit in the animated film world.

Woody Woodpecker also became a smash hit in Dell's line of comic books. In 1942, Dell converted its first comic book title *The Funnies* into *New Funnies,* a comic book of animal fantasy featuring the Walter Lantz characters. *New Funnies,* starting with Issue 62, included the new adventures of Woody Woodpecker, Andy Panda, Oswald the Rabbit, Raggedy Ann, Homer Pidgeon, and Li'l Eight Ball.

Lantz's two main stars, Woody Woodpecker and Andy Panda, also headlined their own magazines within the "Dell 4-Color Comics" series and as monthly titles which have been continued through the years up to their present appearances in Gold Key comics. Oswald the Rabbit also appeared in his own magazine, but that was eventually terminated in 1962.

The two ragdoll characters Raggedy Ann and her brother, Raggedy Andy were originally created as a fairy tale by Johnny Gruell, and were adapted to the comic strip by the Walter Lantz Studios. The two were featured in their own full length comic book, *Raggedy Ann and Raggedy Andy Comics* for several issues within the "Dell 4-Color Comics" series and eventually became a monthly publication, which was continued as a Gold Key title up to 1971. While the feature was discontinued as a comic book, it is still published as a hardcover children's book in the Little Golden Series. In addition, Raggedy Ann was produced as the original world-famous ragdoll and after thirty years, she still remains a popular item in toy stores today.

During the early 1950s, Andy Panda met a mute penguin called Chilly Willy who invadvertently became a star in the animated film world and began appearing in his own comic book in the "Dell 4-Color Comics" series.

Although the Walter Lantz Studios ceased operation in 1973, its famous characters are still popular.

New Funnies No. 113 (July 1946)
©1946 Walter Lantz Productions.

Andy Panda Comics No. 31 (Aug. Oct. 1955)
©1955 Walter Lantz Productions

Red Ryder Comics No. 37 (Aug. 1946)
©1946 K.K. Publications, Inc.

©1940 Republic Pictures

Crackajack Funnies No. 9 introduced the reprint series of the first episodes of Fred Harman's western classic "Red Ryder", which began as a Sunday newspaper comic strip in November 1938. The adventures of Red Ryder ran in *Crackajack Funnies* for twenty-four issues. However, the magazine was terminated with Issue 43 (January 1942). While some of the features were dropped altogether, others were transferred to other Dell titles. "The Owl" moved to *Popular Comics* while "Andy Panda" moved to *New Funnies* as part of the new animal fantasy format.

In the meantime, "Red Ryder" started as a full-length magazine for Hawley Publications in association with Dell and several newspaper syndicates. Many of the *Crackajack Funnies* features that were not transferred to other Dell titles were continued in the newly-formed *Red Ryder Comics*. *Red Ryder Comics* started off with "Captain Easy" (formerly "Wash Tubbs"), "Alley Oop," "Terry and the Pirates," and introduced the continuation of the reprint series of "King of the Royal Mounted" which was dropped from *King Comics*.

Except for "King of the Royal Mounted," the other non-western features were eventually phased out during the mid-1940s and replaced by original western stories created for the comic book. During this time, "Red Ryder," the hard-hitting, crack-shot cowboy who fought for law and order on the range during the early days of the Wild West, was adapted to three different movie serials. One of the elements that

set Red Ryder apart from other quick-drawing gunslingers was his young adopted Indian son, Little Beaver, who struggled to adjust to a lawless adult environment. As *Red Ryder Comics* converted to an all western format, Little Beaver, in addition to appearing in the adventures with Red Ryder, was placed in a separate semi-humorous series as an added attraction to the magazine. Little Beaver in his solo series introduced a fresh new form of western humor that was never seen before—and it prompted Dell to begin full-length editions of *Little Beaver Comics* in the "Dell 4-Color Comics" series.

Artist-rancher Fred Harman retired in 1957 and the "Red Ryder" series was discontinued soon afterwards. However, Little Beaver still continues to appear as a favorite in children's coloring books.

One aspect of Red Ryder that was often overlooked was the character's use in the successful promotion of the Daisy Air Rifle, commonly called the "Red Ryder B-B Gun" and the pride and joy of many a ten-year-old. The "Red Ryder B-B Gun" was the standard back cover advertisement for almost every comic book published during the early 1940s, especially the D-C titles.

This advertisement was the one that helped establish the comic book as an extremely effective advertising media.

Of course there were more Wild West thrills from Dell. A hearty "Hi-Ho, Silver!" and . . .

©1939 Republic Pictures and Lone Ranger, Inc.

The Lone Ranger Comics, Dell 4-Color No. 118
©1939 Lone Ranger, Inc.

©1939 Republic Pictures

Originally created for radio drama by Fran Striker, "The Lone Ranger" first went on the air on January 30, 1932. Soon after, the feature was adapted to a newspaper comic strip of King Features Syndicate and made its debut on the funny pages on September 10, 1938. The comic strip, which was first illustrated by Ed Kressy for a few months and then taken over by Charles Flanders in 1939, was reprinted in two issues of Dell's black-and-white series during 1938 and 1939. It was also reprinted as a regular, continuing series in King Features' *Magic Comics*. When *Magic Comics* was terminated in 1949, Dell resumed rights to the feature and published a series of full-length "Lone Ranger" comic books within the "Dell 4-Color" series, and then made *The Lone Ranger Comics* a monthly title— which was continued as a Gold Key entry.

During this time, the "Lone Ranger" was adapted to several movie serials produced by Republic Pictures, and later a famous television series, all of which is covered in great detail in David Rothel's book, *Who Was That Masked Man?*

"The Lone Ranger" illustrated by Ed Kressey (last adventure)
©1939 Lone Ranger, Inc.

A *Mickey Mouse Storybook*
©1936 Walt Disney Productions

A *Mickey Mouse Alphabet Book*
©1936 Walt Disney Productions

1927 was the year Hollywood started its transition from silent to sound films—it was also the year that Mickey Mouse was born! Walt Disney created the first Mickey Mouse cartoon as a silent film to be shown as a supplementary attraction with *Steamboat Willie*, Disney's first cartoon in sound. Within a few short years, Mickey Mouse had become a world-famous superstar of the screen.

On January 13, 1930, "Mickey Mouse" began as a daily newspaper comic strip, distributed by King Features Syndicate. During the first year, the comic strip was written by Walt Disney and illustrated by Ub Iwerks and then Win Smith, both of whom had served as regular full-time animation artists for the Disney Studios. Approximately six months later, the strip was assigned to Floyd Gottfredson who managed the story lines as well as the artwork and turned Mickey Mouse into an adventurous hero. Gottfredson's series was later reprinted as a continuation feature in *Walt Disney Comics* which began in October 1940 and became one of Dell's leading titles. The comic book, which featured stories about the Disney characters, including Mickey Mouse, Donald Duck, Pluto, Li'l Bad Wolf, and Bucky Bug, was an outgrowth of the earlier *Mickey Mouse Magazine*, a softcover publication of stories, rhymes and jingles as well as cartoon art. The two series of *Mickey Mouse Magazine* ran quarterly from 1933 to 1940.

Yet the magazine was an outgrowth of Disney's

Mickey Mouse Storybook, published by David McKay Company in 1931. This book carried the printed versions of the first four Mickey Mouse animated cartoons and included the original cast of Disney characters—Mickey Mouse, Minnie Mouse, Pluto, Dr. Pep (whose name was later changed to Pegleg Pete), Horsecollar Horace, Clarabelle Cow, and Minnie's two little brothers who appeared on the storybook cover. The brothers were never given names and were dropped after appearing briefly in one animated cartoon segment. The original cast also included a cat named Tabby, but Tabby was soon dropped because of his resemblance to the already famous Felix.

On July 16, 1937, *Mickey Mouse Magazine* was put on the recommended reading list for elementary schools throughout New York State and was adopted for classroom use in the following September. In response to the honor, Walt Disney Productions prepared a special hardcover edition of *A Mickey Mouse Alphabet Book*, the only one of its kind for use in kindergarten. The book explained the letters of the alphabet in the form of a delightful story about Mickey and his friends. The alphabet book was probably the only Disney product that was never distributed commercially in book stores or on newsstands.

On March 30, 1954, Mickey Mouse moved into television—and he has remained there ever since!

Once upon a time in a far off land there was a lovely young princess named Snow White whose wicked step-mother, the Queen of the land, forced her to dress in rags and work as a scullery maid around the castle. Often Snow White would sing to herself beside the wishing well, dreaming that a handsome prince would some day come for her. And the Queen, who was extremely jealous of the child's beauty, would go to her magic mirror every day and ask, "Mirror, mirror on the wall, who is the fairest one of all?" As long as the mirror answered that the Queen was the fairest, Snow White was safe. But one day, when the queen asked the question, the magic mirror replied that Snow White was the fairest one of all—and the Queen fell into a rage! She summoned her huntsman to take Snow White into the forest and slay her. . . .

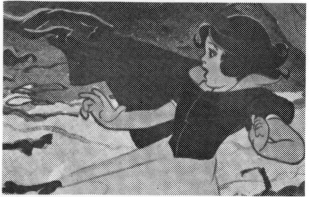

"Snow White and the Seven Dwarfs" ©1937 Walt Disney Productions

Once upon a time in Hollywood, feature-length movies were the exclusive domain of live actors. Then on December 21, 1937, the premiere of Walt Disney's classic masterpiece, *Snow White and the Seven Dwarfs,* set a revolutionary milestone in the motion picture industry by becoming the world's first feature-length animated movie. The eighty-three minute film, which took the Disney Studios more than three painstaking years to produce, introduced an entirely new direction in "movie magic" which captured the imaginations of young and old alike. Throughout the ensuing years, *Snow White and the Seven Dwarfs* has been brought back periodically for each upcoming generation of young theater-goers—and still carries the impact of freshness and vitality of an award-winning movie today as it did in 1937.

The film was also adapted into comic book format which Dell published as 4-Color No. 382. Perhaps not so curiously enough, the comic book version was almost identical to the original film. Here are comparative scenes of that dramatic highlight in the story when the Queen, disguised as the infamous witch, tries to persuade the innocent Snow White to take a bite of the poisoned apple . . .

Snow White Comics, 4-Color Comics No. 186
©1944 Walt Disney Productions

The Movie:

The Comic Book:

©1937 Walt Disney Productions

©1944 Walt Disney Productions

Pinocchio Comics, 4-Color No. 92 (1945)
©1945 Walt Disney Productions

Donald Duck Comics, 4-Color No. 318 (1951)
©1951 Walt Disney Productions

Pinocchio the famous fairy tale about the adventures of a wooden puppet brought to life by a blue fairy, was Walt Disney's second feature-length animated film production which premiered in January 1940. As with *Snow White and the Seven Dwarfs, Pinocchio* was brought back periodically through the years and also appeared in comic book format. Walt Disney's *Pinocchio* was published four times within the "Dell 4-Color" series, issues 92, 252, 545, and 1203.

Although Pinocchio was never associated with Donald Duck, the above cover of 4-Color 92 depicts the two together. Their unusual relationship goes back to the making of *Pinocchio* when the writers and the animators were first planning an approach to the film scenario. The original concept called for Donald Duck to appear as Pinocchio's pal, but in the final story draft, Donald was replaced by little Jiminy Cricket whom the blue fairy appointed to serve as Pinocchio's guiding conscience.

Donald Duck, however, had previously made his first screen appearance in a bit role in the cartoon short *The Wise Little Hen* which the Disney Studios produced in 1934. He then appeared in similar bit roles in three other animated cartoons, including one epi-sode with Mickey Mouse. In 1937, the time when the Disney Studios was engaged in the feature-length *Snow White* film, Donald Duck was cast as the star in a semi-educational cartoon short entitled *Modern Inventions.* Because of the extra work involved in producing the feature-length film, the cartoon shorts were temporarily halted and *Modern Inventions,* even though it was finished, never received wide theatrical distribution. Donald Duck began to slip into oblivion. The studio intended to revive Donald by casting him as a major co-star in *Pinocchio,* but as noted before, that idea was subsequently abandoned.

When *Pinocchio* was adapted into comic book format, the first edition, Dell 4-Color No. 92, included two versions of the story. The first version was based directly on the film. But the second version featured Donald Duck reading the Pinocchio fairy tale to his three nephews. When Donald retired to bed afterwards, he immediately fell asleep and dreamed he was a wooden puppet. In his dream sequences, which were similar to the film, Donald—or "Donocchio" as he was referred to—meets Jiminy Cricket as shown here in a scene reproduced from the comic book . . .

Meanwhile, Donald Duck had been cast to make occasional guest appearances in Walt Disney's second newspaper comic strip feature, "Silly Symphonies," which began on January 10, 1932 as the lower half of the "Mickey Mouse" Sunday page. "Silly Symphonies" consisted of short humorous episodes about different characters which were generally spin-offs from Disney's animated cartoons. The "Silly Symphonies" episode on September 16, 1934 featured the Little Red Hen, a spin-off from the animated cartoon short *The Wise Little Hen* in which Donald had made his screen debut, and it was here that he made his debut in the newspaper comic strip. He appeared in the strip several times after that and soon became its favorite star. On August 30, 1936, the title was changed to "Silly Symphony Featuring Donald Duck" with an all new gag series illustrated by Al Taliaferro, one of the animation artists of the Disney Studios. During the following year, the strip's title was shortened to "Donald Duck."

The "Donald Duck" cartoon narratives were later reprinted in *Walt Disney's Comics*. Beginning with Issue 31, the reprints were supplemented with original Donald Duck story material created by Disney animator Carl Barks who was soon afterwards given the full-time assignment of handling the comic feature. Under the talented hand of Carl Barks, Donald Duck expanded from limited gag situations to more elaborate adventures that soon warranted a full-length *Donald Duck* comic book as a separate title.

In addition to appearing in comics and animated cartoon shorts, Donald Duck, during the 1940s, was featured in a host of government art posters used for promoting U. S. Bonds and the national paper drive.

Donald's primary supporting co-stars, his girl friend, Daisy Duck, his three mischievous nephews, Hewey, Dewey, and Louie, plus the penny-pinching miser, Uncle Scrooge McDuck, were introduced in the feature under completely different circumstances. Daisy Duck made her debut in the 1940 animated cartoon short *Mr. Duck Steps Out* where she and Donald met each other on the dance floor. Later in the same year she appeared with Donald in a Mickey Mouse animated cartoon where Donald and Daisy joined Mickey and Minnie on a double date.

However, Hewey, Dewey, and Louie made their debut in the daily "Donald Duck" comic strip on October 17, 1937 when their mother, Della Duck, a cousin of Donald's, sent them over to visit their uncle for the weekend. And to the delight of millions of readers, the trio decided to stay.

By contrast, Uncle Scrooge McDuck made his debut in the full-length *Donald Duck Comics*, Dell 4-Color No. 178 (1947), in the adventure, "Christmas on Bear Mountain" which was created by Carl Barks as a special Christmas holiday issue. The story itself was a clever adaptation of Charles Dickens' classic "A Christmas Carol." Afterwards, Uncle Scrooge McDuck began appearing in other stories with Donald and was eventually elevated to his own full-length comic book, *Uncle Scrooge Comics*, which began in March 1952 as a monthly Dell title and has been continued up to the present as a Gold Key title.

The Walt Disney characters, cartoon shorts, and feature-length films encompass many, many others which are not mentioned here but are described in more detail in other books devoted exclusively to the art and films of Walt Disney.

Looney Tunes and Merrie Melodies No. 30
(April 1944) ©1944 Leon Schlesinger Productions

Bugs Bunny's Great Adventure, 4-Color No. 88
©1945 by Warner Bros. Cartoons, Inc.

Dell's *Looney Tunes and Merry Melodies*, which began in 1941, was another leading title of animal fantasy which featured the family of Warner Brothers' characters: Bugs Bunny, Porky Pig, Elmer Fudd, Henry Hawk, and Sniffles and Mary Jane. The Warner characters, which had previously appeared in animated cartoon films, were developed by the Leon Schlesinger Studios, originally an independent animation studio under contract with Warner Brothers from 1935 until 1944 and then became Warner Brothers Cartoon Division.

Porky Pig, the first of the Warner characters, made his debut in the animated cartoon short *Haven't Got a Hat* which the Schlesinger Studios produced in 1935. Porky was also the first character to utilize the famous voice characterization of Mel Blanc who perfected the highly distinctive stutter that Porky Pig is known for. The Porky Pig stories that appeared in *Looney Tunes and Merry Melodies* were largely written by such animation humorists as Roger Armstrong and Chase Craig. In 1943, Porky Pig was featured in his own full-length comic book, Dell 4-Color No. 25, which eventually became a regular series that ran until 1952, and was then resumed in 1965 as a major Gold Key title.

However, it was Bugs Bunny that emerged as the superstar of the Warner family, and he made his debut in 1938 in a Porky Pig cartoon short *Porky's Hare Hunt*. Actually, the hare in this film served as the

prototype for the character of Bugs Bunny which developed gradually in appearances in three other animated cartoon shorts, *Prest-O, Change-O, Hare-Um, Scare-Um,* and *Elmer's Candid Camera,* all produced during 1939. In 1940, the Schlesinger Studios produced a cartoon short entitled *A Wild Hare* with the rabbit as its star. It was this film, directed by Tex Avery, in which Bugs Bunny acquired his name and the famous voice that was created by Mel Blanc.

This is how Bugs Bunny looked in 1938 . . .

©1938 Leon Schlesinger Productions

Beginning in 1942, Bugs Bunny was adapted as a newspaper comic strip feature for the N.E.A. Syndicate. Although the strip was written and illustrated by several different members of the Schlesinger Studios, it was the art style of Ralph Heimdahl that greatly influenced the graphic execution of the feature. Many of the comic strip episodes were reprinted in the early issues of *Looney Tunes and Merry Melodies*, but the later issues utilized original stories. Bugs Bunny also appeared in his own full-length comic book series, the first issue of which was published as Dell 4-Color No. 33 (1943).

For the most part, comic books of the animal fantasy category were slanted toward the eight-to-ten-year-olds, and the other comic books were slanted toward older children. However, the third full-length Bugs Bunny comic book, Dell 4-Color No. 88 (1945), made a dramatic departure from animal fantasy stories and brought the more serious science fiction theme of space travel down to a simplified level for the very young readers. In this issue, Bugs and Porky Pig set out in a spaceship on a journey to Saturn to search for evidence of alien life that might exist there. Together, Bugs Bunny and Porky Pig dared to venture someplace much farther than anyone else had in the history of fairy tale literature. Needless to say, the daring twosome did run into alien life on Saturn—a sinister species of talking rabbits!

As far as the eight-year-olds who were too young to be familiar with Buck Rogers and Flash Gordon were concerned, Bugs Bunny's historic flight to Saturn made him one of the greatest comic book heroes of all time. Here are a few scenes . . .

©1945 by Warner Bros. Cartoons, Inc.

Of course Bugs Bunny and the Looney Tunes gang, which in recent years has extended its membership to include superstar "Beep-Beep," the Roadrunner, were among the favorites in the 4-Color series, and they have been continued up to the present as leading Gold Key titles—as well as emerging as popular stars of television.

However, Dell's 4-Color series which began in 1941 contained throughout the years more than 1,000 issues on a wide variety of features which encompassed many that were not in the animal fantasy category. The subject matter also included Westerns, adaptations of movie versions of literary classics, and comic books based on popular television programs; and many of these were later resumed as Gold Key titles. The following is an alphabetical listing of major features and special issues that comprised the series.

DELL 4-COLOR SERIES

Andy Panda (Walter Lantz)
    4-Color No. 25, 54, 85, 130, 154, 198, 216, 240, 258, 280, 297, 326, 345, 358, 383, 409, and continued as a current Gold Key title.
Alley Oop (V. T. Hamlin)
    4-Color No. 3.
Bambi (Walt Disney)
    4-Color No. 12, 30, and 186.
Beetle Bailey (Mort Walker)
    4-Color No. 469, 521, 552, 622, and continued as a Gold Key title.
Bugs Bunny (Warner Brothers)
    4-Color No. 33, 51, 88, 123, 142, 164, 187, 200, 217, 233, 250, 266, 274, 281, 289, 298, 307, 311, 338, 347, 355, 366, 376, 393, 407, 420, 432, 498, 585, 646, 724, 838, 1064, and continued as a current Gold Key title.
Chilly Willy (Walter Lantz)
    4-Color No. 740, 852, 967, 1017, 1074, 1177, 1212 and 1281.
Chip and Dale (Walt Disney)
    4-Color No. 517, 581, 636, and continued as a current Gold Key title.
Dick Tracy (Chester Gould)
    4-Color No. 21, 34, 56, 96, 133, 163, 215 (*Sparkle Plenty*), and continued as a new series by Harvey Publications.
Donald Duck (Walt Disney)
    4-Color No. 9, 62, 108, 147, 159, 178, 189, 199, 203, 223, 256, 263, 275, 282, 291, 299, 308, 318, 328, 339, 348, 353, 356, 367, 379, 394, 408, 422, 450, 492, 531, 586, 600 (*Daisy Duck*), 649, 659 (*Daisy Duck*), 726, 743 (*Daisy Duck*), 763 (*Grandma Duck*), 873 (*Grandma Duck*), 948 (*Daisy Duck*), 965 (*Grandma Duck*), 995, 1010 (*Grandma Duck*), 1051, 1055 (*Daisy Duck*), 1073 (*Grandma Duck*), 1099, 1140, 1150 (*Daisy Duck*), 1182, 1190, 1198, 1239, 1247 (*Daisy Duck*), 1279 (*Grandma Duck*), and continued as a Gold Key title.
Elmer Fudd (Warner Brothers)
    4-Color 470, 558, 689, 725, 783, 841, 888, 938, 977, 1032, 1081, 1131, 1171, 1222, 1293.
Felix, the Cat (Pat Sullivan)
    4-Color No. 15, 46, 77, 119, 135, 162.
Flash Gordon (Alex Raymond)
    4-Color No. 10 (reprints of Alex Raymond art), 84 (reprints of Alex Raymond art), 173, 190, 204, 247, 424, 512, and continued as a new series by Harvey Publications (also see Section 3, King Features' *King Comics*).
Goofy (Walt Disney)
    4-Color No. 468, 562, 627, 658, 747, 899, 952, 987, 1053, 1094, 1149, and 1201.
Helen of Troy
    4-Color No. 684, based on movie adaptation of "The Iliad" by Homer (also see Section 7, *Classics Illustrated*).
Henry (Carl Anderson)
    4-Color No. 122, 155 (also see Section 3, King Features' *King Comics*).
Howdy Doody (Buffalo Bob)
    4-Color No. 761, 811.
John Carter of Mars (Edgar Rice Burroughs)
    4-Color No. 375, 437, 388, with later reprints as Gold Key titles.
Jungle Jim (Alex Raymond)
    4-Color No. 490, 565, 1020, and continued as a title of Charlton Comics (also see Section 3, King Features' *King Comics*).
King of the Royal Mounted (Zane Grey)
    4-Color No. 207, 265, 283, 310, 340, 363, 384, 935 (also see Section 3, King Features' *King Comics*).
Li'l Bad Wolf (Walt Disney)
    4-Color No. 386, 456, 495.
Little Beaver (Fred Harman)
    4-Color No. 211, 267, 294, 332, 483, 529, 660, 695, 744, 817, 880, and continued as a monthly title for five issues.
Little King (O. Soglow)
    4-Color No. 490, 597, 677 (also see Section 3, King Features' *King Comics*).
Little Lulu (Margarie Buell)
    4-Color No. 74, 97, 110, 115, 120, 131, 139, 146, 158, 165, 430 (*Tubby*), 444 (*Tubby*), 461 (*Tubby*), and continued as a Gold Key title.
Little Orphan Annie (Harold Grey)
    4-Color No. 18, 52, 76, 107, 152, 206.
Littlest Snowman
    4-Color No. 755, 864 [Winner of the Thomas Alva Edison Award for Best Comic Book] and reprinted as a Gold Key title.

Lone Ranger (Fran Striker)
    4-Color No. 82, 98, 118, 125, 136, 151, 167, 369 (*Silver*), 392 (*Silver*) and continued as a monthly issue and as a Gold Key title.

Mandrake, the Magician (Lee Falk and Phil Davis)
    4-Color No. 752 (also see Section 3, King Features' *King Comics*).

Man In Space (Walt Disney)
    4-Color No. 716, 954 [Winner of the Thomas Alva Edison Award for Best Comic Book].

Mickey Mouse (Walt Disney)
    4-Color No. 27, 79, 116, 141, 157, 170, 181, 194, 214, 231, 248, 261, 268, 279, 286, 296, 304, 313, 325, 334, 343, 352, 362, 371, 387, 401, 411, 427, 819, 1057, 1151, 1246, and continued as a current Gold Key title.

Napoleon (Clifford McBride)
    4-Color No. 526 (also see Section 13, *Famous Funnies*).

Oswald, the Rabbit (Walter Lantz)
    4-Color No. 21, 39, 67, 102, 143, 183, 225, 273, 315, 388, 458, 507, 549, 593, 623, 697, 792, 894, 979, 1268.

Peanuts (Charles Shultz)
    4-Color No. 878, 969, 1015 and continued as a Gold Key title.

Pinocchio (Walt Disney)
    4-Color No. 92, 252, 545, 701 (*Jiminy Cricket*), 795 (*Jiminy Cricket*), 897 (*Jiminy Cricket*), 989 (*Jiminy Cricket*), 1203.

Pluto (Walt Disney)
    4-Color No. 429, 509, 595, 654, 736, 1039, 1143, 1248.

Pogo (Walt Kelly)
    4-Color No. 105, 148, and continued as a monthly title for sixteen issues.

Popeye (E. Segar)
    4-Color No. 17, 26, 43, 70, 113, 127, 145, 168, and continued as a Gold Key title for a few issues and then continued again as a title of Charlton Comics (also see Section 3, King Features' *King Comics*).

Porky Pig (Warner Brothers)
    4-Color No. 16, 48, 78, 112, 156, 182, 191, 226, 241, 249, 260, 271, 277, 284, 295, 303, 311, 322, 330, 342, 351, 360, 370, 385, 399, 410, 426, 463 (*Petunia Pig*), and continued as a monthly title, then resumed as a Gold Key title).

Prince Valiant (Hal Foster)
    4-Color No. 567 (adaptation of *Prince Valiant* feature-length movie), 699, 719, 788, 849, 900, and continued as a title of Charlton Comics.

Raggedy Ann and Andy (Walter Lantz)
    4-Color No. 45, 72, 262, 306, 354, 380, 452, 533, and continued as a Gold Key title through 1973.

Roadrunner (Warner Brothers)
    4-Color No. 918, 1008, 1046, and continued as a current Gold Key title.

Ruff and Ready (Hanna-Barbera)
    4-Color No. 937 (September 1958, first comic book adaptation of Hanna-Barbera's family of animated television characters), 981, 1038, and continued as a Gold Key title through 1962.

Snow White and the Seven Dwarfs (Walt Disney)
    4-Color No. 49, 227, 382, and reprinted periodically as special comic book premiums.

Tarzan (Edgar Rice Burroughs)
    4-Color No. 134, 161, and continued as a Gold Key title through 1972 and then continued again as a D-C title through 1977, and is currently a title of Marvel Comics (also see Section 12, United Feature's *Tip Top Comics* and *Sparkler Comics*).

Terry and the Pirates (Milton Caniff)
    4-Color No. 28, and continued as a monthly title by Harvey Publications through 1956, and then resumed for two issues by Charlton Comics.

Tom and Jerry (MGM Studios, created by William Hanna and Joseph Barbera)
    4-Color No. 193, and then published as a monthly issue and continued as a current Gold Key title.

Tweety and Sylvester (Warner Brothers)
    4-Color No. 406, 489, 524, and then published as a monthly issue and continued as a current Gold Key title.

Uncle Scrooge (Walt Disney)
    4-Color No. 386, 456, 495, and continued as a monthly issue up to the present as a Gold Key title.

Wash Tubbs (Roy Crane)
    4-Color No. 11, 24 (*Captain Easy*), 28, 53, 111 (*Captain Easy*), and with issues reprinted by Standard Publications from 1947 to 1949.

Western Stories by Zane Grey
    4-Color No. 222 ("West of the Pecos"), 246 ("Thunder Mountain"), 255 ("The Ranger"), 270 ("Drift Fence"), 314 ("Ambush"), 333 ("Wilderness Trek"), 346 ("Hideout"), 357 ("Comeback"), 412 ("Nevada"), 433 ("Wildfire"), 467 ("Desert Gold"), 484 ("River Feud"), 511 ("Outlaw Trail"), 532 ("The Rustlers"), 555 ("Range War"), 616 ("To the Last Man"). Also see *King of the Royal Mounted*.

Woody Woodpecker (Walter Lantz)
    4-Color No. 169, 188, 202, 232, 249, 264, 288, 305, 336, 350, 364, 374, 390, 405, 416, 431, and continued as a Gold Key title with several issues published in the Golden Comics Digest series.

Yogi Bear (Hanna-Barbera)
    4-Color No. 1067, 1104, 1162, 1271, 1310 (*Huck and Yogi*), 1349, and continued as a Gold Key title through 1970, then continued as a new series as a title of Charlton Comics (who is currently producing comic books about the Hanna-Barbera family of characters).

In addition to the 4-Color Series, Dell also published other comic books and illustrated magazines. The complete listing of Dell comic books published prior to 1960 are listed here.

ALPHABETICAL LISTING OF DELL COMIC BOOKS

Abraham Lincoln (1958, one issue)
Animal Comics (1942 - 1947)
Black-and-White Comic Book Series (1939 - 1941, twenty-four issues of assorted features as the predecessor to the "4-Color" Series)
Bug Movies (1931, one issue of irregular format)
Camp Comics (1942, three issues)
Charlie Chan (1955 - 1956)
Christmas In Disneyland (1957, one issue)
Color Comic Book Series (1939 - 1941, eighteen issues of assorted features as the predecessor to the "4-Color" Series)
Comic Album (1952 - 1962, eighteen issues of assorted features)
Comics, The (1937 - 1938)
Crackajack Funnies (1938 - 1942)
Dell Giant Comics (1959 - 1961)
Dell Junior Treasury (1955 - 1957)
Donald and Mickey in Disneyland (1958, one issue)
Fairy Tale Parade (1942 - 1946)
Famous Stories (1942, two issues)
Ferdinand, the Bull (1938, one issue)
Flying A's Range Rider (1953 - 1959)
Four Color Comics ("4-Color" series) (1941 - 1962)
Funnies, The (1929 - 1930, first series)
Funnies, The (1936 - 1942, title changed to *New Funnies* at Issue 65)
Gerald McBoing-Boing (1952 - 1953, five issues)
Golden West Rodeo Treasury (1957, one issue)
Henry Aldrich Comics (1950 - 1954)

Huey, Dewey, and Louie Back to School (1958, one issue)
Key Ring Comics (1941, two issues)
Large Feature Comics (1941 - 1943)
Lassie (1950 - 1960)
Life Stories of American Presidents (1957, one issue)
Looney Tunes and Merry Melodies (1941 - 1960, continued to present as *Looney Tunes* as a Gold Key title)
Moses and the Ten Commandments (1957, one issue)
Movie Classics (1953 - 1969 with later issues in magazine format)
New Funnies (1942 - 1960, and continued as a Gold Key title with some issues called *New TV Funnies*)
100 Pages of Comics (1937, one issue in hardcover book format)
Our Gang Comics (1942 - 1949; title changed to *Tom & Jerry Comics* beginning at Issue 60)
Picnic Party (1955 - 1957)
Pogo Parade (1953, one issue)
Popular Comics (1936 - 1948)
Silly Symphonies (1952 - 1959)
Super Book of Comics (1943 - 1946)
Super Comics (1938 - 1949)
Three-D Ell (1953, three issues)
Tiny Tots Comics (1943, one issue)
Tonto (1952 - 1958)
Treasury of Dogs (1956, one issue [Winner of the Thomas Alva Edison Award for Best Comic Book])
Vacation Parade (1950 - 1954)
Walt Disney's Comics (1940 - 1961, and continued to present as a Gold Key title)

The above listings of Dell titles do not include magazines, pocket books, paperback fiction and non-fiction, and hardcover books published by Dell and its affiliate companies. During the 1940s, K.K. Publications produced a few comic books in association with Dell. One of the most popular K.K. titles was *March of Comics* which ran for 423 issues and utilized many of the features that appeared in Dell's "4-Color" series.

As Dell began to phase out its comic book line during the late 1950s, the animal fantasy features and several others were taken over by Western Publishing Company who continued the comic book series as Gold Key titles. But owing to legal problems, there were many instances where a few years had lapsed before the feature resumed as a Gold Key comic book. In addition, many of these features were also adapted into children's hardcover picture books as part of Western's "Little Golden Book" series which often included famous fairy tales. And the Gold Key comic book line itself was expanded with several original titles. This is a listing of the Gold Key titles with special indication being made of those features that have been adapted to the "Little Golden Book" series as well.

ALPHABETICAL LISTING OF GOLD KEY COMIC BOOKS

Adam-12 (1973 - 1976)

Adams Family (1974 - 1975)

Adventures of Robin Hood (1974 - 1975, Walt Disney version)

Aliens, The (1967, one issue and 1972, one issue)

Amazing Chan (1973 - 1974)

Andy Panda (continued from Dell to present)

Astro Boy (1965, one issue)

Atom Ant (1966, one issue)

Augie Doggie (1963, one issue)

Avengers, The (1968, one issue)

Baby Snoots (continued from *March of Comics*, 1970 - 1975)

Baloo and Little Britches (1968, one issue)

Bamm Bamm and Pebbles (1964, one issue)

Beagle Boys (1964 - present)

Beetle Bailey (continued from Dell, 1962 - 1966)

Best of Donald Duck (1965, one issue)

Best of Donald Duck and Uncle Scrooge (1964, one issue and 1967, one issue)

Best of Walt Disney Comics (1974, four issues in hardcover format)

Boris Karloff Tales of Mystery (1963 - present)

Bozo, the Clown (continued from Dell and adapted to "Little Golden Book" series)

Buck Rogers (1964, one issue [also see Section 13, *Famous Funnies*])

Bugs Bunny (continued from Dell to present and adapted to "Little Golden Book" series)

Bugs Bunny and Porky Pig (1965, one issue)

Captain Nice (1967, one issue)

Captain Venture (1968 - 1969)

Chip and Dale (continued from Dell to present)

Christmas Parade, Walt Disney's (continued from Dell, 1963 - 1972, nine annual issues)

Close Shaves of Pauline Peril (1970 - 1971)

Cowboy in Africa (1968, one issue)

Daffy Duck (continued from Dell to 1976)

Dagar, the Invincible (1972 - 1976)

Daisy and Donald (continued from Dell as a spin-off from *Walt Disney's Comics*, 1973 - present)

Dark Shadows (1969 - 1976)

Davy Crockett (continued from Dell, 1963, one issue and 1969, one issue)

Dear Nancy Parker (1963, two issues)

Dinky Duck (1965, one issue)

Doc Savage (1966, one issue, and continued in 1972 through present by Marvel Comics [also see Section 14, Street & Smith])

Donald Duck (continued from Dell to present and adapted to "Little Golden Book" series)

Dr. Solar (1962 - 1969)

Duke of the K-9 Patrol (1963, one issue)

Dumbo (continued from Dell and adapted to "Little Golden Book" series)

Family Affair (1970, four issues)

Fat Albert (1974 - present)

Flash Gordon (1965, one issue reprinted from the 4-Color series)

Flintstones (continued from Dell to 1970 and adapted to "Little Golden Book" series; also continued by Charlton Comics)

Flipper (1966 - 1967, three issues)

Fractured Fairy Tales (1962, one issue)

Frankenstein Jr. and the Impossibles (1967, one issue)

Freedom Agent (1963, one issue)

Gallant Men (1963, one issue)

Garrison's Gorillas (1968 - 1969, five issues)

G-8 and his Battle Aces (1966, one issue revived from pulp fiction)

George of the Jungle (1969, two issues)

Golden Comics Digest (assorted features continued from Dell, 1969 - 1976)

Gold Key Spotlight (1976 - present)

Gomer Pyle (1966 - 1967, three issues)

Governor and J.J. (1970, three issues)

Green Hornet (1967, one issue)

Hanna-Barbera Band Wagon (1962 - 1963)

Hanna-Barbera Hi-Adventure Heroes (1969, two issues)

Hanna-Barbera Super Tv Heroes (1968 - 1969)

Hardy Boys (1970 - 1971)

Harlem Globetrotters (1972 - 1975)

Heckle and Jeckle (1962 - 1963, four issues)

Honey West (1966, one issue)

Huckleberry Hound (continued from Dell through 1970 and adapted to "Little Golden Book" series; and continued by Charlton Comics from 1970 to 1972)

Huey, Dewey, and Louie Junior Woodchucks (1966 - present)

Inspector, The (1974 - present)

Invaders (1967 - 1968, four issues)

I, Spy (1966 - 1968)

It's About Time (1967, one issue)

Jet Dream (1968, one issue)

Jetsons, The (1963 - 1970 and adapted to "Little Golden Book" series; also continued by Charlton Comics)

John Carter of Mars (1964, two issues reprinted from Dell's 4-Color Series)

John Steele, Secret Agent (1964, one issue)

Jonny Quest (1964, one issue)

King Louie and Mowgli (1968, one issue)

Korak, Son of Tarzan (1964 - 1972)

Lancelot Link, Secret Chimp (1971 - 1973)

Lancer (1969, three issues)

Land of the Giants (1968 - 1969)

Laredo (1966, one issue)

Lassie (continued from Dell through 1969 and adapted to "Little Golden Book" series)

Laurel and Hardy (1967, two issues)

Legend of Jesse James (1966, one issue)

Legend of Young Dick Turpline (1966, one issue)

Little Lulu (continued from Dell to present)

Little Monsters (1964 - present)

Littlest Snowman (1964, one issue reprinted from Dell's 4-Color No. 755 [Winner of the Thomas Alva Edison Award for Best Comic Book])

Lone Ranger (continued from Dell to present)

Looney Tunes (continued from Dell to present)

Lucy Show, The (continued from Dell, 1963 - 1964)

Magilla Gorilla (1964 - 1968)

Magnus, Robot Fighter (1963 - 1977)

Man from U.N.C.L.E. (1965 - 1969)

M.A.R.S. Patrol (1966 - 1969, ten issues)

Mickey Mouse (continued from Dell to present and adapted to "Little Golden Book" series)

Mighty Hercules (1963, two issues)

Mighty Mouse (1966 - 1968)

Mighty Samson (1964 - 1976)

Milton, the Monster and Fearless Fly (1966, one issue)

Mr. Ed, the Talking Horse (continued from Dell to 1964 and adapted to "Little Golden Book" series)

Mr. & Mrs. J. Evil Scientist (1963 - 1966)

Moby Duck, Walt Disney's (1967 - present)

Modnicks, The (1967 - 1970)

Mod Wheels (1971 - 1975)

Munsters, The (1965 - 1968)

My Favorite Martian (1964 - 1968)

Mystery Comics Digest (1972 - 1975)

New Adventures of Huck Finn (1968, one issue)

Occult Files of Doctor Specktor (1973 - 1977)

O. G. Whiz (1971 - 1972)

O'Malley and the Alley Cats (1967 - 1974)

Owl, The (continued from Dell (*Crackajack Funnies*), 1967 - 1968)

Peanuts (continued from Dell, 1963 - 1964)

Pink Panther (1971 - present)

Porky Pig (continued from Dell to present)

Raggedy Ann and Andy (continued from Dell through 1973)

Robinhood, Walt Disney's (1973, one issue in hardcover book format)

Roman Holidays (1973, four issues)

Roy Rogers Comics (continued from Dell through 1967)

Roadrunner (continued from Dell to present)

Ruff and Ready (continued from Dell through 1962 and adapted to "Little Golden Book" series)

Run, Buddy, Run (1967, one issue)

Scamp, Walt Disney's (continued from Dell to present and adapted to "Little Golden Book" series)

Scarecrow, Walt Disney's (1964 - 1965)

Secret Agent (1966 - 1968, two issues)

Secret Squirrel (1966, one issue)

Smokey, the Bear (continued from Dell through 1973 and adapted to "Little Golden Book" series)

Snagglepuss (1962 - 1963, four issues)

Snooper and Blabber Detectives (1962 - 1963)

Snow White (continued from Dell and adapted to "Little Golden Book" series)

Space Family Robinson (1962 - present)

Space Ghost (1967, one issue)

Spine-Tingling Tales (1975 - 1976, four issues)

Steve Zodiac (1964, one issue)

Supercar (1962 - 1963)

Super Goof, Walt Disney's (1965 - present)

Tarzan (continued from Dell through 1972 and adapted to "Little Golden Book" series (written by Gina Ingoglia Weiner); continued as a D-C title from 1972 to 1977, and continued as a Marvel title from 1977 to present (also see Section 12, United Feature's *Tip Top Comics* and *Sparkler Comics*)

Tasmanian Devil and his Tasty Friends (1962, one issue)

Three Little Pigs, Walt Disney's (continued from Dell through 1968 and adapted to "Little Golden Book" series)

Three Stooges (continued from Dell through 1972)

Tiger Girl (1968, one issue)

Time Tunnel (1967, two issues)

Tom and Jerry (continued from Dell to present)

Top Cat (continued from Dell through 1970 and adapted to "Little Golden Book" series)

Total War (1965, two issues; title changed to *M.A.R.S. Patrol* beginning at third issue)

Tweety and Sylvester (continued from Dell to present)

Twilight Zone (1962 - present)

UFO Flying Saucers (1968 - 1977)

Uncle Scrooge (continued from Dell to present)

Virginian, The (1963, one issue)

Voyage to the Bottom of the Sea (1964 - 1967)

Voyage to the Deep (1962 - 1964)

Wacky Adventures of Cracky (1972 - 1975)

Wacky Races (1969 - 1972)

Wagon Train (1964, four issues)

Wally (1962 - 1963, four issues)

Walt Disney's Comics (continued from Dell to present)

Walt Disney's Comics Digest (1968 - 1976)

Walt Disney's Showcase (1970 - present)

Wart and the Wizard, Walt Disney's (1964, one issue)

Where's Huddles? (1971, three issues)

Wild Kingdom (1965, one issue)

Wild, Wild West (1966 - 1969, seven issues)

Winnie, the Pooh (1977 - present and adapted to "Little Golden Book" series)

Wonderful Adventures of Pinocchio (continued from Dell for one issue (1963) and adapted to "Little Golden Book" series)

Woody Woodpecker (continued from Dell to present and adapted to "Little Golden Book" series)

Yogi Bear (continued from Dell through 1970 and adapted to "Little Golden Book" series; also continued by Charlton Comics, 1970 - 1976)

Yosemite Sam and Bugs Bunny (1970 - present)

Zane Grey's Stories of the West (1964, one issue)

Zorro, Walt Disney's (continued from Dell through 1968)

GILBERTON PUBLISHING COMPANY

1941 marked the peak of the superhero fantasy boom; it also saw Gilberton Company introduce the first edition of *Classic Comics*. The magazine was titled "The Three Musketeers," and according to the established trend of the times, the next issue should have been "Three Musketeers No. 2." Not so! *Classic Comics No. 2* was titled "Ivanhoe," a completely different character—or rather, a comic book adaptation of a completely different literary classic!

Gilberton had moved in a totally new direction for comic book literature. Not only did they discard the use of continuing characters in succeeding issues, but for the first time literary classics, until then the exclusive province of book publishers, were adapted into comic book format. In the months that followed, the youthful fans of comicdom made a happy discovery about Gilberton's *Classic Comics*. Not only were they entertaining to read, but they were handy references for school homework as well, especially when the homework assignment involved preparing a report on a book that just happened to have appeared in a recent issue of *Classic Comics*.

As the months rolled by, youngsters disagreed on the question of whether or not *Classic Comics* were actually comic books. Some said "yes," they were as much fun to read as the comics that featured superheroes. Others said "no," *Classic Comics* were to be used for school homework only—and school itself was the proof. The formidable institutions of secondary education absolutely forbade comic books unless, of course, they were *Classic Comics*. These were okay to read in class. In fact teachers sometimes passed them out to pupils.

Little by little, *Classic Comics* found their place in the classrooms of some 25,000 schools in the United States, Canada, and other countries as supplementary instructional material. Yet they were also sold on the newsstands along with comic books featuring Superman, Captain Marvel, Batman, and all the rest.

However, as "comics" began to become a "dirty word" in the English vocabulary, Gilberton instituted two basic changes to move their magazines away from the comic book image. In the course of reprinting the series, the first change involved dropping "comics" from the title and changing it to *Classics Illustrated*, which the series is better known as. The second change involved a new look for the cover—during the third printing of the series, the line art normally associated with comic book covers was replaced by more sophisticated illustrations. The contents, however, continued as full-length adaptations of literary classics illustrated in the standard comic book style.

As an answer to the basic question about the classification of the Gilberton titles, this section presents a review of the "uncomic" comic book, *Classics Illustrated*.

Classics Illustrated No. 77
©Gilberton Publishing Co., Inc.

Classics Illustrated No. 275
©Gilberton Publishing Co., Inc.

Homer's *Iliad*, and its companion epic, the *Odyssey*, are without a doubt among the world's greatest literary classics. Both date back to more than 3,000 years ago when people told stories and wrote poems about heroic deeds of gods and men. And Homer stood out as the greatest poet of all. The English translations of his works began in the 19th Century and were slightly modified in ensuing years. Today, there are several variations of both the *Iliad* and the *Odyssey*.

Of the 20th Century scholars who specialized in Homer, W.H.D. Rouse was probably the most highly regarded. His translations were first published in 1937, and they were generally accepted as standard works. Beginning in 1949, Rouse's version has been periodically reprinted in paperback form, and often serves as the basis for adaptations of Homeric works into other artistic forms.

Basically, the *Iliad* detailed the events of the last days of the Trojan War and the *Odyssey* recounts the adventures of Odysseus[3], one of the victorious soldiers of that war, as he travelled home to Ithaca to rejoin his wife Penelope. However, the gods would delay his return. A raging storm erupted and swept his ship to, among other places, a distant island inhabited by the one-eyed cyclops, shown on the cover here as he is about to hurl a huge boulder to sink Odysseus' ship and prevent his escape.

There are different theories about the time the story was supposed to have taken place and the exact location of the island. According to W. J. Stillman, a lifetime scholar of Homer, the *Odyssey* occurred around 1000 B. C. at the time when Greece was under the dual control of the Ionian Dorian peoples. Accordingly, the mystery island where Odysseus landed was Kaphallenia, as the Greeks had later named it after the god, Cephalus. At that time, it was located clearly in sight of Ithaca but separated by a narrow strait between two mountainous rocks jutting from the water. The area was subject to strong undercurrents and throughout the years that followed, tidal waves from those undercurrents eventually swept Kaphallenia under the sea.

Upon Odysseus' eventual return to Ithaca, the people, assuming he was killed in the Trojan War, rejoiced by retelling his experiences. The oral tradition continued from generation to generation until the stories were finally carved on the gigantic rock wall surrounding Ithaca.

2,000 years later, crumbled fragments of those walls were uncovered for archeological study. Peculiar scratchings found on the surface of the rocks seemed to contain the remains of an ancient language which, according to 19th Century experts, revealed the full account of the *Iliad* and the *Odyssey*. W. J. Stillman was a member of the archeological team who made the discovery. He prepared a treatise on the subject that was published in *Century Illustrated Magazine*, October 1884. The article also included several reproductions of line engravings made by artists Harry Fenn, A. Irwin, H. Davidson, A. J. Whitney, H. Gray, and A. Hayman who laboriously copied the ancient hieroglyphics.

The following illustration which appeared in *Century Illustrated* depicts a portion of the reconstructed wall that surrounded Ithaca.

In describing the findings, Stillman pointed out that each rock in the illustration measured about five feet in length.

In the above reproduction of another sample from the *Century Illustrated* article, artists Harry Fenn and A. Hayman combined their talents to produce an engraving based upon a vague scratching that had been partially eroded over the years.

When translated, it read: "The Voyage of King Odysseus."

When the *Odyssey* appeared in *Classics Illustrated No. 81*, this was the opening panel . . .

Ulysses, the Roman name for Odysseus, was used by *Classics Illustrated* in their comic book adaptations of the *Iliad* and the *Odyssey*.

The similarity between the comic book adaptation and Stillman's 19th century translation extends further. In the following engraving from *Century Illustrated*, artist H. Davidson reconstructed from Stillman's translation, the strait through which Odysseus' ship would have to pass to reach Ithaca. The beach in the foreground was described as the "sandy shores of Pylos," a small island visible only during low tide. Accordingly, Odysseus had to wait far out in the distance until the tide had risen high enough to cover the island before entering the strait for fear of brushing against the awesome sea gods that might have been asleep in the vicinity. However, as he waited, the clouds began to turn grey and a storm set in. Rather than wait any longer, he decided to take a chance and enter the strait . . .

©1884 by The Century Co.

Here is the corresponding scene in *Classics Illustrated* . . .

The comic book adaptation of the *Odyssey* was never accepted as a serious publication of Homer because it did not accurately follow the "recognized" 20th century translation. But the truth is, *Classics Illustrated* closely followed W. J. Stillman's version of the story.

The *Iliad* is perhaps the very foundation of almost all fantasy and adventure that is found in modern literature, and it undoubtedly inspired the creation of many superhero characters that were based on mythological concepts. Homer's work describes the tragedy of the Trojan War, but exactly when it occurred varies from translation to translation. It has been placed anywhere from 500 years before to 500 years after the *Odyssey*. However, according to Stillman, Odysseus describes being in the war against Troy and being seriously wounded by Hector on the battlefield. Stillman pinpoints the war as having taken place in the vicinity of 1000 B.C., shortly before Odysseus started his voyage towards home. The confusion about dates is most likely due to our not knowing how the war actually began, a missing link in all translations. The rock segment containing the hieroglyphics with the answer has never been found. How the war began is something that has had to be speculated upon from other available information concerning that era.

To fully grasp the complexities that lay behind the Trojan War, some insight into Greek mythology is desirable for this was a war involving the spiritual and non-spiritual gods which comprised the basic religions of the eastern Mediterranean world of that day. The spirital gods dwelled on Mt. Olympus, the tip of the world which rose far beyond the reach of mortal men. From this vantage point, the gods observed mankind. Zeus, the supreme god, would occasionally come down to Earth disguised as a man, mate with a woman, and then return to Mt. Olympus.

The result of the brief liaison was a child who in essence was part god and part mortal. Over the years, many forms of non-spiritual "demi-gods" came to inhabit Earth. Two such demi-gods, Hector and Achilles, played a dominant role in the Trojan War.

Zeus' son, Hector, was born of a Trojan woman who died in childbirth. The infant was adopted by the mother's sister Hecuba, wife of Priam, the king of Troy. She raised him with her other children, one of whom was a boy named Paris. As Hector grew to adulthood he divided his time between Troy as a warrior and hero of the Trojan people, and Mt. Olympus among the family of gods, particularly the goddess Iris, who loved him.

By contrast, Achilles' father was a mortal, Peleus, the king of Thessaly, but also a grandson of Zeus. Achilles' mother was the goddess, Thetis, a sea nymph who lived in the ocean. Thetis, fearing a prophecy that her first born son would be killed in battle, took precautions to protect his life. She led him down into the underworld of darkness ruled by the god Pluto, Zeus' brother, to Pluto's toilet of "stench" (the "magic waters of Styx" according to 20th century translations) and dipped her child into the "magic water" until it completely covered him. By this act,

the infant's flesh would become invulnerable to human weapons. However, Thetis overlooked the infant's heel which she held him by as she immersed the child in the water. And Achilles' heel would be his only weak point, although neither he nor his mother were aware of it as he grew up to be a great warrior and demi-god, dividing his time between Earth and Mt. Olympus. In essence, Hector and Achilles were half-brothers.

The Trojan War began when King Priam received a wedding invitation from King Agamemnon of Sparta. But Priam was unable to attend the wedding and he sent his son Paris in his place as the royal representative, bearing gifts and good will from Troy. Upon arriving in Sparta, Paris was greeted as a guest of honor. But when he met the bride-to-be Helena, the most beautiful woman in Greece (whose name is often shortened to "Helen"), he immediately fell in love with her. That night Paris kidnapped Helen and fled back to Troy with her. King Agamemnon promptly summoned his armies to go to Troy to rescue his intended. At the city's gates, King Agememnon told the Trojans to release Helen or else his armies would destroy the city.

However, Priam, upon confronting his son, learned that Helen loved him and had fled Sparta of her own free will. She pleaded with Priam not to surrender her to the man she loathed, whereupon Priam ordered his army to drive the Greeks away from Trojan soil. The two sides fought each other for a duration often translated as "ten years." (In that era, however, a full year was measured by altogether different standards.)

As the war went on, the gods, observing all from Mt. Olympus, could not agree on who was right, and consequently they began taking sides. Hector managed to break himself away from the charms of the goddess Iris, whose only interest was Hector and not warfare, and returned to Earth to help Troy. In one incident, Hector wounded Odysseus who was then taken out of battle and carried back to his ship.

But demi-gods, such as Ajax, aided the Greeks in their assaults upon the Trojans.

During one attack, Hector and Ajax clashed on the battlefield and fought to a draw. But since *they* were not actually at war with each other, they parted in friendship. However, in a different incident, Hector accidentally slew Patroclus, another demi-god and Achilles' best friend, who had disguised himself as a Greek soldier fighting the Trojans. The death of Patroclus created a bitter feud between Hector and Achilles who thus far had avoided taking sides upon the request of Thetis.

Unexpected events were to change Achilles' neutral position. The Greek soldiers, in order to replenish food and supplies, often took turns raiding and plundering small villages near Troy. During one raid they invaded a house and brutally raped the young maiden Briseis while she slept. And Briseis happened to be a cousin of Achilles. When Achilles found out, he angrily stormed into the Greek's encampment to confront King Agamemnon. Armed guards rushed in to the king's rescue. As Achilles was about to tear the camp apart, word came down from Mt. Olympus ordering him to lay down his sword and accept the king's apology, for his soldiers had no way of knowing they were invading a house of Achilles.

Achilles begrudgingly lowered his sword as King Agamemnon apologized to him. Achilles remained at the Greek camp to learn more about them and to decide which course of action to take. He was in the King's tent when a Trojan messenger entered under a momentary truce to offer a plan that would bring an end to further bloodshed between Greece and Troy. Under the plan, the Trojans would select one of their soldiers to fight one Greek soldier in single combat, and the victor would settle the war. If the Trojan soldier lost, Helen was to be returned, and if the Greek soldier lost, Helen would remain in Troy and the Greeks would gather their forces and leave the land.

While the plan had its merits as a solution for ending the war, King Agememnon was reluctant to accept its terms when he found out that he would have to select an opponent to face Hector—the one Trojan warrior that no Greek soldier could stand up to in single combat. At this point, Achilles announced that he would represent the Greeks, but only because of his hatred towards Hector.

The unexpected announcement surprised everyone, including the Greeks, the Trojans, and Hector himself, not to mention the gods observing from Mt. Olympus but the latter made no move to intervene.

In *Classics Illustrated's* adaptation of the *Iliad*, artist Alex Blum successfully captures that dramatic moment when the two super warriors met face to face on the battlefield . . .

When the titanic fight had ended, Hector lay dying in a pool of blood. The victorious Achilles then pierced Hector's ankles, tied his feet to the rear edge of his chariot, and then proceeded to drag him back and forth across the rugged terrain, tearing the flesh from Hector's body in the process. The Greeks cheered Achilles while the saddened Trojans mourned the loss of their hero and begged Achilles to stop. On Mt. Olympus, the gods were disgusted at Achilles' foul act and the disrespect he showed for a fallen enemy. Most enraged was the goddess Iris who had hoped to wed Hector.

Trojan soldiers atop the wall angrily hurled rocks down at the invulnerable Achilles, demanding that he surrender Hector's body to them for a proper burial. Achilles, not feeling the rocks as they bounced harmlessly off his armor, merely glanced up at the Trojans and laughed in their faces. Then he turned to continue dragging Hector's remains across the ground. Finally, Paris, the mortal half-brother of Hector and one who started the war in the first place, raised his bow, took careful aim at Achilles, and fired as soon as Achilles had turned his back.

As the poison-tipped arrow sped through the air,

ACHILLES PIERCED THE ANKLE-BONES OF THE DEAD MAN AND FASTENED THE BODY WITH THONGS OF OX-HIDE TO THE CHARIOT.

©Gilberton Publishing Co., Inc.

the goddess Iris intervened and, remaining invisible to mortal eyes, guided the arrow to Achilles' only weak spot—his heel. The fatal arrow struck its mark and sank deep. Achilles screamed in pain, a sensation he had never known before. The poison coursed through his body as he reached down and struggled to extract the arrow. Then to the amazement of all Achilles stumbled, fell off the chariot, collapsed and died.

The Greek soldiers, stunned by the death of their seemingly invincible warrior, were fearful that the gods had intervened against them, and they retreated back to their ships.

In further accounts of the Trojan War, King Agememnon had in the meantime already formulated his own plan to crush Troy. While the fighting was going on, he dismantled one of his ships whose captain and crew had been killed earlier in battle and used the wooden planks to construct a gigantic horse. The retreat of his army fit perfectly with his plan.

King Agamemnon ordered a crew of his men to haul the wooden horse to the gates of Troy under the pretext that it represented a gift, a token of everlasting peace between the two nations. Assuming that the Greeks were sincere, especially after watching them retreat at the sight of Achilles' death, the Tro-

jans opened the gates and pulled the horse into the city.

They also retrieved Hector's body and buried him with a funeral fit for a god. There was a mixture of sadness and joy as the Trojans mourned the death of their hero and simultaneously celebrated the end of hostilities by drinking large quantities of wine before falling into a stuporous sleep.

While the Trojans slept, a handful of Greek soldiers who had hidden inside the giant horse, quietly climbed out and opened the city gates for King Agamemnon and the remobilized Greek armies. Odysseus' wounds had healed, and he stood beside the king as second in command.[4] When the city gates were opened, the Greek forces stormed inside and unmercifully slaughtered the sleeping Trojans. The royal family was slain, King Agamemnon himself plunging the knife into Paris' back and seizing the startled Helen from his arms. Helen screamed at the sight of her beloved Paris lying dead beside her. She pulled the knife from his back and plunged it into her breast, preferring death to a life with King Agamemnon in Sparta. Agamemnon vengefully ordered Troy to be burned to the gound. And with the city in flames, the victorious Greeks returned to their ships with the spoils of war and departed for home.

[4] *20th century translations normally do not place Odysseus in the Trojan War. In recent books dealing with Homer, it has often been suggested that, because the* Iliad *is far more involved than the* Odyssey, *Homer wrote the* Odyssey *during his younger life and the* Iliad *during his later life—or, that he wrote one of the poems but not necessarily the other. While Stillman's 19th century translation does not either confirm nor deny Homer as the author of the hieroglyphics, further information on the subject can be found in other publications covering Homer, Helen of Troy, the* Trojan War, *and Odysseus.*

On March 9, 1950, the month is which the *Classics Illustrated* series was approaching the end of its third reprinting, Albert Cantor, president of Gilberton, announced that the series would be expanded with the introduction of new titles that would include, for the first time anywhere, illustrated adaptations of Shakespearean plays. An editorial staff of twenty literary researchers was assigned the monumental task of insuring that the comic book adaptions would adhere rigorously to the author's language and plot.

An immediate problem, of course, was finding a workable way to depict the physical characteristics, gestures and mannerisms of the characters as none of these details are described in the scripts. In the adaptation of *Hamlet,* artist Alex Blum graphically recaptured the mood of the original play. The characters and setting were drawn in such a way that the reader might sense he was viewing an artistic rendering of an actual performance of *Hamlet* on stage. The scene in which Hamlet's father is murdered is a good example of Blum's work.

Classics Illustrated No. 83
©Gilberton Publishing Co., Inc.

©Gilberton Publishing Co., Inc.

Early in Act III, Hamlet contemplated suicide and
declaimed literature's most famous soliloquy . . .

"There is no difference between TIME and any of the three dimensions of space except that our consciousness moves along with it."

- H. G. Wells, *The Time Machine* 1895

Classics Illustrated No. 133
©Gilberton Publishing Co., Inc.

In 1895, Henry Holt and Company published the first edition of *The Time Machine* in which the author H. G. Wells, while explaining within the story how the machine operated, also introduced startling new theories about time and space which until then had been totally unheard of. Wells described the molecular physics of a four-dimensional cube in which *time* was the fourth dimension, a separate plane moving about the fixed positions of the known three dimensions. It was Wells' contention that it was theoretically possible to penetrate the fixed three planes and enter the moving fourth plane and thus travel through time. The original story was concerned with scientific principles of a machine designed to accomplish this act. When the machine's operator travelled some 800,000 years into the future, he discovered that mankind had evolved into two hostile races, the backward human tribe of the Eloi and the cannibalistic half-human monsters known as the Morlocks.

But the act of getting to the future was the meat of the story and it attracted the attention of the scientific community. Wells' theories about *time* were convincing enough to be used as the basis for a revolutionary system of theoretical mathematics wherein certain equations that normally reduced to zero could acquire a new and different value when the arithmetic of the moving plane was applied to the equation. His story was also studied in depth by many who actually wanted to try to penetrate the fourth dimension. U. S. Patent Office records reveal that, during the early 1900s, a great number of patents were applied for on a variety of perpetual motion apparatuses that would operate forever provided they operated in the fourth dimension for the purpose of travelling into the future, or transport a person or persons from the three dimensional world into the fourth dimension as a means of prolonging the normal life span.

Time, as a separate and distinct dimension, was accepted as a fact until 1916 when the concept was rebutted by a noted physicist who had different ideas on the subject. Albert Einstein's *Theory of Relativity* waded through "a bit of his own arithmetic" to prove that *time* was a natural function of the three planes that moved together at the same rate in continuous motion. Wells' theories were questioned, but the validity of Einstein's theory was slow in finding acceptance. Most schools continued to adhere to the existence of a separate and distinct *fourth* dimension.

During a lecture at Princeton University in 1933,

Einstein was asked to comment on the theoretical possibility of the Wells' time machine penetrating the "other" dimension and traveling 800,000 years into the future. Einstein replied that such a machine was not even theoretically possible unless it was built for travelling through space. He added that for such a machine to travel through space *and* 800,000 years into the future, the Earth and the solar system, in the meantime, would have moved to an entirely different region of the universe, and the machine would have to race much faster than light in order to reach the same point on Earth. Einstein opined that such a machine would burn up and evaporate as its speed approached light velocity, and would therefore obviously never arrive at its intended destination.

Einstein had answered the question, and Wells' time theories were dismissed—the "Four Dimensional Cube" was replaced by Einstein's definition of the *time-space continuum*.

As a result, the world of science fiction literature was thrown into a state of confusion. Some authors would still express themselves in terms of the Wells' time theories, for although his time machine may have turned out to be an impractical physical invention, it nevertheless stood out as an ingenious *literary* device that opened the door to a miriad of fantasy concepts dealing with time travel. Other authors, however, began to express themselves in terms of Einstein's concepts on the theory that quality science fiction should not deviate from scientific fact. Yet another school of authors combined the concepts of Wells and Einstein into a *third* theory in which Einstein's time-space continuum was actually Wells' moving plane, but instead of moving in a straight line, it moved as a wave with dips and peaks—or "space warps." It was theorized that a time machine could travel in a straight line, penetrate the space warp and thus advance through time as well as space.

The story that started it all, *The Time Machine*, has been reprinted several times, but with certain later deletions. Reprint editions that came out after 1933 tactfully omitted the more detailed elements about the machine's operation as well as Wells' original time theories. The later versions concentrated upon the adventure element, upon what happened to the traveller after he arrived in the future. The actual act of getting there was no longer considered important.

The adventure element was also portrayed in the *Classics Illustrated* adaptation, although unlike the hardcover and paperback reprints of the story, the comic book remained true to Wells' time theories. Only in the comic book was the machine's construction properly disclosed. For the first time since 1895, the cover of *Classics Illustrated No. 133* reveals the time machine as an open-ended gyroscope with two outer rings spin-

ning in opposite directions. The vertical ring spins along its axis fast enough to slice through the height dimension while the horizontal ring spins along its axis fast enough to slice through the width and depth dimensions. This accomplished, the machine faded into the fourth dimension and the compound motion created by the spinning action of the gyroscope inside an escalating vacuum of ether swept the machine and its operator right through the time stream.

Day and night fused into a grey haze swirling about the operator. He experienced intervals of extreme coldness, and then periods of extreme warmth. The intervals of changing temperatures grew shorter until the environment soon reached a constant coolness. Vague shadows sprouted up like trees, rapidly growing taller and then vanishing in the twilight. He heard brief spurts of strange gibberish echoing from somewhere in the distance, gibberish that sounded almost like human voices but he couldn't be sure.

Then a spot of brightness began to penetrate the grey haze as if daylight were seeping through, and the surface beneath the machine slowly acquired a greenish hue. Something was happening. Then the gyroscope suddenly stopped spinning! The worried operator glanced down at the instrument reading and made an incredible discovery . . .

The New York Time

Copyright, 1938, by The New York Times Company.

Second-Class Matter.
New York, N. Y.

NEW YORK, MONDAY, OCTOBER 31, 1938.

PP

MEAD STANDS PAT AS A NEW DEALER IN BID FOR SENATE

Democratic Candidate Opposes Any Except Minor Changes in Labor and Security Laws

UPHOLDS THEORY OF TVA

Wants Budget Balanced, but Not if This Means 'Misery,' He Tells The Times

Text of Representative Mead's reply is printed on Page 6.

From a Staff Correspondent

BUFFALO, N. Y., Oct. 30.—Representatives James M. Mead, Democratic candidate for the short-term Senatorial seat in the election Nov. 8, today answered in a statement the six questions on campaign issues propounded by THE NEW YORK TIMES to the four New York nominees of the two major parties in an editorial Oct. 20.

Mr. Mead's answer, in the main, was a broad and little qualified defense of the New Deal legislation which he, as a member of the House of Representatives, had a part in formulating and passing.

The principles of the Social Security and National Labor Relations Acts he defended stoutly, seeing need only for revisions to extend the benefits of the former, a correction of technical defects and a tightening of administration.

Principal opposition to the Social Security Act he saw inspired by those who fear that it will "become too important a monument to the Democratic party and to men like President Roosevelt and Senator Wagner."

Opposes "Pay-as-You-Go" Policy

He unqualifiedly opposed a revision of the law to make social se-

Radio Listeners in Panic, Taking War Drama as Fact

Many Flee Homes to Escape 'Gas Raid From Mars'—Phone Calls Swamp Police at Broadcast of Wells Fantasy

A wave of mass hysteria seized thousands of radio listeners throughout the nation between 8:15 and 9:30 o'clock last night when a broadcast of a dramatization of H. G. Wells's fantasy, "The War of the Worlds," led thousands to believe that an interplanetary conflict had started with invading Martians spreading wide death and destruction in New Jersey and New York.

The broadcast, which disrupted households, interrupted religious services, created traffic jams and clogged communications systems, was made by Orson Welles, who as the radio character, "The Shadow," used to give "the creeps" to countless child listeners. This time at least a score of adults required medical treatment for shock and hysteria.

In Newark, in a single block at Heddon Terrace and Hawthorne Avenue, more than twenty families rushed out of their houses with wet handkerchiefs and towels over their faces to flee from what they believed was to be a gas raid. Some began moving household furniture.

Throughout New York families left their homes, some to flee to near-by parks. Thousands of persons called the police, newspapers and radio stations here and in other cities of the United States and Canada seeking advice on protective measures against the raids.

The program was produced by Mr. Welles and the Mercury Theatre on the Air over station WABC and the Columbia Broadcasting System's coast-to-coast network from 8 to 9 o'clock.

The radio play, as presented, was to simulate a regular radio program with a "break-in" for the material of the play. The radio listeners, apparently, missed or did not listen to the introduction, which was: "The Columbia Broadcasting System and its affiliated stations present Orson Welles and the Mercury Theatre on the Air in 'The War of the Worlds' by H. G. Wells."

They also failed to associate the program with the newspaper listing of the program, announced as "Today: 8:00-9:00—Play: H. G. Wells's 'War of the Worlds'—WABC." They ignored three additional announcements made during the broadcast emphasizing its fictional nature

Mr. Welles opened the program with a description of the series of

Continued on Page Four

OUSTED JEWS F REFUGE IN POL AFTER BORDER

Exiles Go to Relatives' or to Camps Maintain Distribution Commi

REVEAL CRUELTY O

Others Sent Back to G Pending Parleys on Is the Two Governm

Wireless to THE NEW YORK

WARSAW, Poland, Oct.
evacuation from frontier
thousands of Polish Jews
cording to official repo
12,000 according to an est
the Jewish Relief Comm
ported from Germany beg
after they had been m
frontier stations up and
border for twenty-six hou
terrible ordeal is nearing

Polish authorities have
officials of the Joint Di
Committee to send the v
relatives' homes in Pola
special camps the commit
tains. The refugees spent
less night in barracks, cro
tion buildings or empty
cars; many spent the nig
open in the no man's land
the frontiers.

The Joint Distribution C
supplied food and will also
cially reduced railway fare
interior.

It is believed that the e
will last another day or
refugees desire to remai
frontier area pending the
of the Warsaw-Berlin neg
which may result in the
the deportation order,
them to return to their
Germany.

Suffering Is Describ

Reports from various po
the frontier describe the

B. C. VLADECK DIES; CITY COUNCILMAN

American Labor Party Chief Here Was Manager of The Jewish Daily Forward

B. Charney Vladeck, American

DALADIER PREPARES TO RULE SEVERELY

Calls Cabinet Meeting to Talk Over Decrees to Promote Recovery in Industry

By P. J. PHILIP

Classics Illustrated No. 124
©Gilberton Publishing Co., Inc.

Drawn by Warwick Goble.
"THEY CUT EVERY TELEGRAPH AND WRECKED THE RAILWAYS."
"The War of The Worlds"
©1897 by John Brisben Walker

H. G. Wells also wrote *The War of the Worlds* which, when adapted to a radio script that was aired on October 30, 1938, threw the entire nation into panic. The story centered around an invasion from Mars, but the element that created the panic was not so much the plot itself but the way it was presented. The first landing of the Martian ships, and their awesome heat rays that set buildings and bridges on fire, was described through the eyes of an on-the-spot news reporter, played by Orson Welles, whose voice was choked with fear and terror. The radio audience heard a roaring explosion as a huge building blew apart, the screams and racing footsteps of people, and then abrupt silence after a swoosh of fire filled the air. The news commentor gasped, "Oh, my God! All those people! Gone in a puff of smoke! It's the end of the world!"

Many a listener who had tuned in a few minutes after the program had begun and had missed the opening disclaimer, assumed he was hearing an authentic news announcement. He, and many like him, scrambled for his life, as the following newspaper article indicates.

It wasn't until the next day that listeners found out that the Martian invasion was a fake. New York city was not levelled to the ground after all! The Federal Communication Commission initiated legal action against the Columbia Broadcasting System but later withdrew charges after W. B. Lewis, vice president of programming, explained that the network had fulfilled its obligation by amply describing the program as a radio play.

Although October 30, 1938 was the first time the general public had heard of *The War of the Worlds*, science fiction fans were quite familiar with it, for the story had been published a little more than a decade earlier as a two-part serial in *Amazing Stories*, August and September 1926. The original version, however, first appeared in *Cosmopolitan Magazine*, May 1897. It was scheduled to run as a two-part serial. Part One appeared in the May issue, but it frightened the reading public so much that managing editor John B. Walker cancelled Part Two from the June issue on the basis that the story was not appropriate for the broad family readership that *Cosmopolitan* catered to.

The part that did appear had been lavishly illustrated with realistic line drawings by Warwick Gable. His pictures may well have been the element that made the story so frightening at the time. Yet all adaptations and reprints of *The War of the Worlds* that would follow in later years utilized Gable's interpretation as the standard description.

While many educators praised Gilberton for publishing distinguished literary works in comic book form, the critics of comic books objected to the manner in which elements of violence and cruelty were portrayed in certain issues of *Classics Illustrated*. Although the violence was perfectly acceptable in text form, it was supposedly harmful to children when illustrated in a comic book. During the third printing of the series, almost all matters dealing with man's violent actions against his fellow man were changed and redrawn to dilute or eliminate the violence and brutality inherent in the original text.

For example, *Classics Illustrated No. 18*, "The Hunchback of Notre Dame," depicted the touching scene in which the hunchback Quasimodo was seized by guards, stripped to the waist, chained to the flogging wheel, and brutally lashed in front of the crowd until he passed out. Upon regaining consciousness, he pleaded for someone to give him water. The crowd sneered and spat at him—all except for the beautiful dancing girl, Esmeralda.

Here is the original version by artist Allan Simon as it appeared in the first and second printings.

The enraged critics considered it extremely poor taste to so nakedly show the disfigurement of the hunchback as he was being lashed to the flogging wheel. In later reprints, the story was redrawn and that particular scene was changed to show Quasimodo wearing a colorful wraparound and kneeling on a platform. The lashing was implied but not shown. The acceptable version in later reprints was depicted this way.

Other changes were also made. In the original
version, when Quasimodo broke free he gained his
revenge quite graphically. Here are a few scenes.

In the acceptable version, Quasimodo's acts of retribution were suggested by this single panel.

Classic Comics No. 18
©Gilberton Publishing Co., Inc.

©Gilberton Publishing Co., Inc.

©Gilberton Publishing Co., Inc.

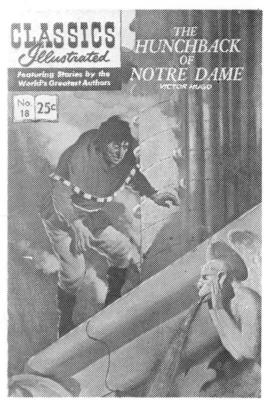

©Gilberton Publishing Co., Inc.

Yet both versions portrayed Victor Hugo's classic love story about a deformed village bell ringer and a beautiful dancing girl. One was a highly evocative version that invited the reader to identify emotionally with Quasimodo. The other was produced as a kind of illustrated textbook, satisfactory as a reference work for a student's book report.

But the critics still weren't satisfied. *The Hunchback of Notre Dame*, as originaly written, concluded with the death of both Quasimodo and Esmeralda. The critics insisted that the comic book adaptation should have a happy ending. So the fifth printing, in total contradiction to Victor Hugo's original story, ended with the agile Quasimodo accidentally falling from a tower while a caption explained, "He was never seen again." Esmeralda, meanwhile, found that her handsome admirer Phoebus was not dead after all (even though Victor Hugo very definitely killed him off early in the story) and the two joined hands and lived happily ever after.

The new comic book version of *The Hunchback of Notre Dame* appeased the critics of violence in comic books to the point that they congratulated Gilberton for publishing such excellent magazines. But the liter-

ary liberties that were taken enraged educators who severly criticized Gilberton for distorting plot and character in its later reprints, not only in *The Hunchback of Notre Dame*, but in many others as well. Many of the stories in the *Classics Illustrated* series were adapted from hardcover editions of publishers who controlled all the rights to the book. In many instances, these publishers would not authorize Gilberton to change the story in subsequent *Classics Illustrated* reprints. Gilberton had a problem.

To publish or not to publish, that was the question. Was it nobler in the mind to suffer the slings and arrows of outrageous critics or take arms against a sea of ignorance by opposing them? Caught in the middle of diametrically opposing interests, Gilberton was in a state of turmoil. With mounting pressures building up from all sides, they finally decided *not to publish*, and terminated *Classics Illustrated* during the early 1960s.

Although the series underwent several printings, there was no single printing that contained a full run of *all* the titles since several stories appeared for the first time during the third printing. In addition, many stories have two, three, and even four different versions while others have only a single version that was printed five or six times with no change except on the cover. Unravelling this maze in order to describe the differences between a "first edition" and a "revised edition" as compared to the "first edition of the original story" for every title within the series is a separate topic that can not be covered here. Most of the stories that appeared in *Classics Illustrated* have been updated and are readily available in paperback editions. However, as a general guideline for those interested in tracing the literary classics of specific authors, a complete numerical listing of *Classics Illustrated* follows with the author's name in parenthesis followed by the artist's name when known.

NUMERICAL LISTING OF CLASSICS ILLUSTRATED COMIC BOOKS

No. 1. "The Three Musketeers"
(Alexandre Dumas) Illustrated by Malcom Kildale.
No. 2. "Ivanhoe"
(Sir Walter Scott)
No. 3. "Count of Monte Cristo"
(Alexandre Dumas)
No. 4. "The Last of The Mohicans"
(James Fenimore Cooper)
No. 5. "Moby Dick"
(Herman Melville) Illustrated by Louis Zansky.
No. 6. "A Tale of Two Cities"
(Charles Dickens)
No. 7. "Robin Hood"

No. 8. "Arabian Knights"
(—) Illustrated by Lillian Chestney.
No. 9. "Les Miserables"
(Victor Hugo)
No. 10. "Robinson Crusoe"
(Daniel Defoe) Illustrated by Stanley Maxwell.
No. 11. "Don Quixote"
(Miguel de Cervantes)
No. 12. "Rip Van Winkle and The Headless Horseman"
(Washington Irving)
No. 13. "Dr. Jekyll and Mr. Hyde"
(Robert Louis Stevenson) Illustrated by Lou Cameron.
No. 14. "Westward Ho!"
(Charles Kingsley)
No. 15. "Uncle Tom's Cabin"
(Harriet Beecher Stowe)
No. 16. "Gulliver's Travels"
(Jonathan Swift) Illustrated by Lillian Chestney.
No. 17. "The Deerslayer"
(James Fenimore Cooper) Illustrated by Louis Zansky.
No. 18. "The Hunchback of Notre Dame"
(Victor Hugo) Illustrated by Allen Simon.
No. 19. "Huckleberry Finn"
(Mark Twain)

No. 20. "The Corsican Brothers"
(Alexandre Dumas)
No. 21. "Three Famous Mysteries"
(Edgar Allen Poe)
No. 22. "The Pathfinder"
(James Fenimore Cooper) Illustrated by Louis Zansky.
No. 23. "Oliver Twist"
(Charles Dickens)
No. 24. "A Connecticut Yankee in King Arthur's Court"
(Mark Twain) Illustrated by Jack Hearne.
No. 25. "Two Years Before The Mast"
(Richard Henry Dana, Jr.)
No. 26. "Frankenstein"
(Mary Wollstonecraft Shelley) Illustrated by Robert Webb.
No. 27. "Adventures of Marco Polo"
(—) Illustrated by Homer Fleming.
No. 28. "Michael Strogoff"
(Jules Verne) Illustrated by Arnold Hicks.
No. 29. "The Prince and the Pauper"
(Mark Twain) Cover illustrated by H.C. Kiefer, contents illustrated by Arnold Hicks.
No. 30. "The Moonstone"
(Wilkie Collins) Illustrated by Don Rico.
No. 31. "The Black Arrow"
(Robert Louis Stevenson) Illustrated by Arnold Hicks.
No. 32. "Lorna Doone"
(Richard D. Blackmore) Illustrated by Matt Baker.
No. 33. "Adventures of Sherlock Holmes"
(Arthur Conan Doyle)
No. 34. "The Mysterious Island"
(Jules Verne) Illustrated by Robert Hayward Webb and David Heames.
No. 35. "Last Days of Pompeii"
No. 36. "Typee"
(Herman Melville) Illustrated by Ezra Whiteman.

Classics Illustrated No. 2
©Gilberton Publishing Co., Inc.

Classics Illustrated No. 3
©Gilberton Publishing Co., Inc.

Classics Illustrated No. 5
©Gilberton Publishing Co., Inc.

Classics Illustrated No. 7
©Gilberton Publishing Co., Inc.

No. 37. "The Pioneers"
(James Fenimore Cooper) Illustrated by Rudolph Palais.

No. 38. "The Adventures of Cellini"
(—)

No. 39. "Jane Eyre"
(Charlotte Bronte) Illustrated by Harley M. Griffith.

No. 40. "Mysteries: The Pit and the Pendulum; Adventures of Hans Pfall, The Fall of the House of Usher" (Edgar Allen Poe)

No. 41. "Twenty Years After"
(Alexandre Dumas) Illustrated by H.C. Kiefer. This story is the sequel to "The Three Musketeers."

No. 42. "The Swiss Family Robinson"
(Johann Wyss)

No. 43. "Great Expectations"
(Charles Dickens)

No. 44 "The Mysteries of Paris"
(Eugene Sue) Illustrated by H.C. Kiefer.

No. 45. "Tom Brown's School Days"
(Thomas Hughes)

No. 46. "Kidnapped"
(Robert Louis Stevenson) Illustrated by Matt Baker.

No. 47. "20,000 Leagues Under the Sea"
(Jules Verne) Illustrated by H.C. Kiefer.

No. 48. "David Copperfield"
(Charles Dickens) Illustrated by H.C. Kiefer.

No. 49. "Alice's Adventures in Wonderland"
(Lewis Carroll) Illustrated by Alex Blum.

No. 50. "Tom Sawyer"
(Mark Twain)

No. 51. "The Spy"
(James Fenimore Cooper) Illustrated by Arnold Hicks.

No. 52. "The House of Seven Gables"
(Nathaniel Hawthorne)

No. 53. "A Christmas Carol"
(Charles Dickens) Illustrated by H.C. Kiefer.

No. 54. "The Man in the Iron Mask"
(Alexandre Dumas)

No. 55. "Silas Marner"
(George Eliot)

No. 56. "Toilers of the Sea"
(Victor Hugo)

No. 57. "Song of Hiawatha"
(Henry Wadsworth Longfellow)

No. 58. "The Prairie"
(James Fenimore Cooper)

No. 59. "Wuthering Heights"
(Emily Bronte)

No. 60. "Black Beauty"
(Anna Sewell)

No. 61. "The Woman in White"
(Wilkie Collins) Illustrated by Alex Blum.

No. 62. "Bret Harte's Western Stories"
(Bret Harte) Illustrated by H.C. Kiefer.

No. 63. "The Man Without a Country"
(Edward Everett Hale)

No. 64. "Treasure Island"
(Robert Louis Stevenson) Illustrated by Alex Blum.

No. 65. "Biography of Benjamin Franklin"
[This issue won the Thomas Alva Edison Award for the best comic book dealing with American history in October 1955. It was also reprinted without the *Classics Illustrated* logo as a premium giveaway.]

No. 66. "The Cloister and the Hearth"
(Charles Reade)

No. 67. "The Scottish Chiefs"
(Jane Porter) Illustrated by Alex Blum.

No. 68. Julius Caesar"
(William Shakespeare) Illustrated by H.C. Kiefer.

No. 69. "Around the World in Eighty Days"
(Jules Verne) Illustrated by H.C. Kiefer.

No. 70. "The Pilot"
(James Fenimore Cooper)

No. 71. "The Man Who Laughs"
(Victor Hugo)

No. 72. "The Oregon Trail"
(Francis Parkman)

No. 73. "The Black Whip"
(—) Illustrated by Alex Blum.

No. 74. "Mr. Midshipman Easy"
(Frederick Merryat)

No. 75. "The Lady of the Lake"
(Sir Walter Scott) Illustrated by H.C. Kiefer.

No. 76. "The Prisoner of Zenda"
(Anthony Hope) Illustrated by H.C. Kiefer.

No. 77. "Iliad"
(Homer) Illustrated by Alex Blum.

No. 78. "Joan of Arc"
(George Henry Calvert, first edition 1860)

No. 79. "Cyrano de Bergerac"
(Edmond Nostrand)

No. 80. "White Fang"
(Jack London) Illustrated by Alex Blum.

No. 81. "Odyssey"
(Homer) Illustrated by Alex Blum.

No. 82. "Master of Ballantrae"
(Robert Louis Stevenson)

No. 83. "The Jungle Book"
(Rudyard Kipling)

No. 84. "The Gold Bug"
(Edgar Allan Poe) Illustrated by Alex Blum.

No. 85. "The Sea Wolf"
(Jack London)

No. 86. "Under Two Flags"
(Ouida) Illustrated by Maurice Del Bourgo.
No. 87. "a Midsummer Night's Dream"
(William Shakespeare) Illustrated by Alex Blum.
No. 88. "Men of Iron"
(Howard Pyle)
No. 89. "Crime and Punishment"
(Feodor Dostoevski) Illustrated by Rudolph Palias.
No. 90. "Green Mansions"
(William Henry Hudson) Illustrated by Alex Blum.
No. 91. "The Call of the Wild"
(Jack London)
No. 92. "The Courtship of Miles Standish"
(Henry Wadsworth Longfellow)
No. 93. "The Tragedy of Pudd'nhead Wilson"
(Mark Twain) Illustrated by H.C. Kiefer.
No. 94. "David Balfour"
(Robert Louis Stevenson) This story is the sequel to "Kidnapped".
No. 95. "All Quiet on the Western Front"
(Erich Maria Remarque)
No. 96. "Daniel Boone"
(John Bakeless)
No. 97. "King Solomon's Mines"
(H. Rider Haggard) Illustrated by H.C. Kiefer.
No. 98. "The Red Badge of Courage"
(Stephen Crane)
No. 99. "Hamlet"
(William Shakespeare) Illustrated by Alex Blum.
No. 100. "Mutiny on the Bounty"
(Charles Nordhoff and James Hall)
No. 101. "William Tell"
(Frederick von Schiller) Illustrated by Maurice Del Bourgo.
No. 102. "The White Company"
(Arthur Conan Doyle)
No. 103. "Men Against the Sea"
No. 104. "Bring 'Em Back Alive"
(Frank Buck) Illustrated by H.C. Kiefer.
No. 105. "From the Earth to the Moon"
(Jules Verne) Illustrated by Alex Blum.
No. 106. "Buffalo Bill"
(Mrs. Ann S. Stephans[5]) Illustrated by Alex Blum.
No. 107. "King of the Kyber Rifles"
(Talbot Mundy)
No. 108. "Knights of the Round Table"
(—) Illustrated by Alex Blum.
No. 109. "Pitcairn's Island"
(Charles Nordhoff and James Hall) Illustrated by Rudolph Palais.
No. 110. "A Study In Scarlet"
(Arthur Conan Doyle) Illustrated by Seymour Moskowitz.

No. 111. "The Talisman"
(Sir Walter Scott)
No. 112. "Kit Carson"
(Mrs. Ann S. Stephans[5]) Illustrated by Rudolph Palais.
No. 113. "The Forty-five Guardsmen"
(Alexandre Dumas) Illustrated by Maurice Del Bourgo.
No. 114. "Red Rover"
(James Fenimore Cooper) Illustrated by Pete Costanza.
No. 115. "How I Found Livingstone"
(Sir Henry Morton Stanley)
No. 116. "The Bottle Imp"
(Robert Louis Stevenson)
No. 117. "Captains Courageous"
(Rudyard Kipling) Illustrated by Pete Costanza.
No. 118. "Rob Roy"
(Sir Walter Scott)
No. 119 "Soldiers of Fortune"
(Graham M. Jefferies)
No. 120. "The Hurricane"
(Charles Nordhoff and James Hall)
No. 121. "Wild Bill Hickock"
(Mrs. Ann S. Stephans[5]) Illustrated by Lorio and Trapani.
No. 122. "The Mutineers"
(Charles Boardman Hawes)
No. 123. "Fang and Claw"
(Frank Buck)
No. 124. "The War of the Worlds"
(H.G. Wells)
No. 125. "The Ox-Bow Incident"
(Walter van Tilburg Clark)
No. 126. "The Downfall"
(Emile Zola) Illustrated by Lou Cameron.
No. 127. "King of the Mountains"
(Edmund About)
No. 128. "Macbeth"
(William Shakespeare) Illustrated by Alex Blum.
No. 129. "Davy Crockett"
No. 130. "Caesar's Conquests"
(—) Illustrated by H.C. Kiefer.
No. 131. "The Covered Wagon"
(Emerson Hough)
No. 132. "The Dark Frigate"
(C. B. Hawes)
No. 133. "The Time Machine"
(H. G. Wells)
No. 134. "Romeo and Juliet"
(William Shakespeare)
No. 135. "Waterloo"
(Erckmann and Chotrion)
No. 136. "Lord Jim"
(Joseph Conrad)

No. 137. "The Little Savage"
(Frederick Merryat)
No. 138. "A Journey to the Center of the Earth"
(Jules Verne)
No. 139. "In the Reign of Terror"
(G. A. Henty)
No. 140. "On Jungle Trails"
No. 141. "Castle Dangerous"
(Sir Walter Scott) Illustrated by Stan Campbell.
No. 142. "Abraham Lincoln"
(Rufus Blanchard, first edition 1882)
No. 143. "Kim"
(Rudyard Kipling) Illustrated by Joe Orlando.
No. 144. "The First Men in the Moon"
(H. G. Wells)
No. 145. "The Buccaneer"
(—) [This was the last issue of the fourth reprint series and was renumbered as 148 during the fifth reprint series.]
No. 145. "The Crisis"
(Winston Churchill) [This was a special edition introduced during the fifth reprint series.]
No. 146. With Fire and Sword"
(Henry K. Sienkiewicz)
No. 147. "Ben Hur"
(Lew Wallace) Illustrated by Joe Orlando.
No. 148. "The Buccaneer" [See No. 145]
No. 149. "Off on a Comet"
(Jules Verne)
No. 150. "The Virginian"
(Owen Wister)
No. 151. "Won by the Sword"
(G. A. Henty) Illustrated by J. Tartaglione.
No. 152. "Wild Animals I Have Known"
(Ernest Thompson Seton)
No. 153. "The Invisible Man"
(H. G. Wells) Illustrated by N. Nodel.
No. 154. "History of the Conspiracy of Pontiac"
(Francis Parkman)
No. 155. "Lion of the North"
(G. A. Henty) Illustrated by N. Nodel.
No. 156. "The Conquest of Mexico"
(Bernal Diaz Del Castillo)
No. 157. "Lives of the Hunted"
(Ernest Thompson Seton) Illustrated by N. Nodel.
No. 158. "The Conspirators"
(Alexandre Dumas)
No. 159. "The Octopus"
(Frank Norris)

Classics Illustrated No. 161
©Gilberton Publishing Co., Inc.

No. 160. "Food of the Gods"
(H. G. Wells)
No. 161. "Cleopatra"
(H. Rider Haggard) Illustrated by N. Nodel.
No. 162. "Robur, the Conqueror"
(Jules Verne)
No. 163. "Master of the World"
(H. G. Wells)
No. 164. "The Cossack Chief"
(L. N. Tolstoy)
No. 165. "The Queen's Necklace"
(Alexandre Dumas)
No. 166. "Tigers and Traitors"
(Jules Verne)
No. 167. "Faust"
(Johann Wolfgang von Goethe) Illustrated by N. Nodel.
No. 168. "In Freedom's Cause"
No. 169. "Negro Americans, the Early Years"
(—) [The last issue.]

5. See Section 14, *The Dime Novel* (Mrs. Ann Stephans).

Classics Junior Illustrated No. 559
©Gilberton Publishing Co., Inc.

Gilberton also published other "uncomic" comic books. Their second major catagory was *Classics Illustrated Junior*—a series of seventy-six comic book adaptations of world famous fairy tales for young readers. While the series included such well known fables as *The Wizard of Oz* and others that were adapted to various artistic forms throughout the years, it also contained certain stories seen for the first time which turned out to be the lost out-of-print fairy tale classics that had not been heard of since the middle 19th century! In the latter situation, Gilberton introduced stories that were not published anywhere else.

For example, *Classics Illustrated Junior No. 559*, "The Japanese Lantern" featured the only known English pictorial translation of a highly unusual legendary fable that dates back to 12th century Japan. The story centered around a silk weaver and his two sons whom he had raised without a mother. As the boys reached adulthood, the silk weaver encouraged them to seek a bride whereupon the boys journeyed to a distant village and ultimately returned home with their new wives, Yuki and Chiyo.

The two women had added an aura of happiness to the lonely household that was lacking feminine charm and motherly love, but after a year had passed, the young wives sought permission to visit the village of their parents. The silk weaver, fearing the dreary loneliness that would again fall upon the house during Yuki's and Chiyo's absence, strongly objected to their making the trip. As a ploy to discourage the girls' interest in the trip, the silk weaver gave them an impossible challenge: he would grant them permission and his blessings only on the condition that they bring back two gifts. One gift had to be "fire carried in paper" and the other had to be "wind carried in paper." He told them he would not accept them back unless they had the gifts. Instead of being discouraged, the young women were thrilled at having permission to travel, and they promised to return with the two gifts without realizing the impossibility of obtaining them.

The weaver's plan had backfired, but he was obligated to let the girls leave. He was suddenly aware that he unintentionally turned the girls away from his house for good.

Yuki and Chiyo journeyed to the village of their parents for a brief visit. Then they set out to seek the two gifts—and they found that no one had ever heard of paper that could carry fire or the wind. Determined to find the gifts so that they would be allowed to rejoin their beloved husbands and father-in-law, the young women decided to search for the paper in every village throughout Japan and, if necessary, other lands. They hiked toward the next village, and the road led them into an enchanted forest kingdom where they found an old wise man and magician who agreed to help them.

The wise man took a sheet of paper, magically arranged twigs upon it which he tied together in an accordion fashion, and then folded the paper into the shape of a hand-fan. Upon waving it back and forth, it was found that the paper did indeed *carry the wind!* Next, he proceeded to make the second gift. The wise man caused small branches to drop from the trees and form themselves into curved loops. He tied other branches to the curved ones making a standing ribcage. Then he folded the paper around the structure until he had shaped a partially enclosed lantern. He lit a small candle, placed it inside the lantern, and affixed it firmly to the base. And as the lantern began to glow, it was found that the paper did indeed *carry the fire!*

The girls returned home and everyone lived happily ever after.

Unlike many fairy tales written solely as a bedtime story for youth entertainment, "The Japanese Lantern" presented a fanciful explanation about the origin of two popular Japanese inventions used throughout the world, the paper hand-fan and the paper lantern.

Although *Classics Illustrated Junior* seldom appeared on the newsstands with regular comic books, the series was sold extensively in stores handling all types of children's literature. And in this area, *Classics Illustrated Junior* emerged as the leader of all children's books! Unfortunately, the junior series was discontinued when Gilberton terminated the senior series.

Classics Junior Illustrated No. 510
©Gilberton Publishing Co., Inc.

Classics Junior Illustrated No. 535
©Gilberton Publishing Co., Inc.

NUMERICAL LISTING OF CLASSIC JUNIOR ILLUSTRATED COMIC BOOKS

No. 501—*Snow White and the Seven Dwarfs* (original version)
No. 502—*The Ugly Duckling*
No. 503—*Cinderella*
No. 504—*The Pied Piper*
No. 505—*The Sleeping Beauty*
No. 506—*The Three Little Pigs*
No. 507—*Jack and the Beanstalk*
No. 508—*Goldilocks and the Three Bears*
No. 509—*Beauty and the Beast*
No. 510—*Little Red Riding Hood*
No. 511—*Puss-N-Boots*
No. 512—*Rumplestilskin*
No. 513—*Pinocchio* (original version)
No. 514—*The Steadfast Tin Soldier*
No. 515—*Johnny Appleseed*
No. 516—*Aladdin and His Lamp*
No. 517—*The Emperor's New Clothes*
No. 518—*The Golden Goose*
No. 519—*Paul Bunyan*
No. 520—*Thumbelina*
No. 521—*King of the Golden River*
No. 522—*The Nightingale*
No. 523—*The Gallant Tailor*
No. 524—*The Wild Swans*
No. 525—*The Little Mermaid*
No. 526—*The Frog Prince*
No. 527—*The Golden-Haired Giant*
No. 528—*The Penny Prince*
No. 529—*The Magic Servants*
No. 530—*The Golden Bird*
No. 531—*Rapunzel*
No. 532—*The Dancing Princesses*
No. 533—*The Magic Fountain*
No. 534—*The Golden Touch*
No. 535—*The Wizard of Oz*
No. 536—*The Chimney Sweep*
No. 537—*The Three Fairies*

No. 538—*Silly Hans*
No. 539—*The Enchanted Fish*
No. 540—*The Tinder-Box*
No. 541—*Snow White & Rose Red*
No. 542—*The Donkey's Tale*
No. 543—*The House in the Woods*
No. 544—*The Golden Fleece*
No. 545—*The Glass Mountain*
No. 546—*The Elves and the Shoemaker*
No. 547—*The Wishing Table*
No. 548—*The Magic Pitcher*
No. 549—*Simple Kate*
No. 550—*The Singing Donkey*
No. 551—*The Queen Bee*
No. 552—*The 3 Little Dwarfs*
No. 553—*King Thrushbeard*
No. 554—*The Enchanted Deer*
No. 555—*The Three Golden Apples*
No. 556—*The Elf Mound*
No. 557—*Silly Willy*
No. 558—*The Magic Dish*
No. 559—*The Japanese Lantern*
No. 560—*The Doll Princess*
No. 561—*Hans Hundrum*
No. 562—*The Enchanted Pony*
No. 563—*The Wishing Well*
No. 564—*The Salt Mountain*
No. 565—*The Silly Princess*
No. 566—*Clumsy Hans*
No. 567—*The Bearskin Soldier*
No. 568—*The Happy Hedgehog*
No. 569—*The Three Giants*
No. 570—*The Pearl Princess*
No. 571—*How Fire Came to the Indians*
No. 572—*The Drummer Boy*
No. 573—*The Crystal Ball*
No. 574—*Bright Boots*
No. 575—*The Fearless Prince*
No. 576—*The Princess Who Saw Everything*

8

LEV GLEASON PUBLICATIONS

Lev Gleason was the publisher of *Crime Does Not Pay*, a comic book that would precipitate an avalanche of controversial crime titles ten years after the first issue appeared in June 1942. *Crime Does Not Pay* introduced a highly unusual innovation in which the illustrated narrative, based on police files and court records, "told it like it was" from the criminal's viewpoint. The editorial objective of the magazine was to document actual case histories of convicted or deceased criminals in an attempt to explain what motivated criminal behavior, and to impress upon its juvenile readership that the bad guys who followed an easy path of crime to achieve momentary gains of material luxuries *always* ended up on the losing end—either dead or in jail.

Crime Does Not Pay maintained this stance throughout the war years when the great majority of other comic books acquired a patriotic tone. While it stuck out as an "oddball" title it nevertheless commanded continuing attention at the newsstands. The magazine also differed from the others in that it pulled no punches in depicting the violence that often attended the real crimes that made newspaper headlines. The theme might well have been inspired by the success of the first classic crime movie *Little Caesar*, which was produced by Warner Brothers in 1931 and starred Edward G. Robinson. It was this movie that brought the wrath of the critics down on Hollywood for glamorizing the life of a gangster—Edward G. Robinson, it seemed, had played the role too well.

Similarly, *Crime Does Not Pay* was convincingly real. Yet it remained the only comic book of its type, until after the war years when other publishers frantically searched for a new theme to substitute for the costumed superheroes who were beginning to lose their

©1931 Warner Bros.

appeal. It was suddenly discovered that *Crime Does Not Pay* was not the blacksheep of the family after all, but in fact the answer to their prayers.

In 1949 a number of comic books similar to *Crime Does Not Pay* appeared with a multitude of features that were thinly disguised variations of stories that had previously appeared in Gleason's magazine. And the new crime titles seemed to be aiming toward one objective: to "out-crime" and "out-violence" *Crime Does Not Pay!*

Crime Does Not Pay No. 63 (May 1948)
©1948 Lev Gleason Publications, Inc.

Crime Does Not Pay No. 59 (Nov. 1948)
©1948 Lev Gleason Publications, Inc.

Of course the flood of titles of the "new" genre that utilized the villain's viewpoint were labelled "crime comics" for lack of a better term, and promptly caused a storm of criticism from many sectors. Policemen's Benevolent Associations charged that crime comics glorified criminal activities and emphasized disrespect for the law. The clergy charged that the comics were immoral, and schools charged that they hindered learning, were aesthetically unattractive, and on the whole a complete waste of time. Child psychiatrist Dr. Frederic Wertham charged that crime comics were the principle cause of juvenile delinquency. In lecture after lecture to various P.T.A. groups and women's clubs, Dr. Wertham solemnly pronounced that comic books, not parents, were entirely responsible for their children's misbehavior.

However, there were differences of opinion on the social effects of crime comics. Dr. Paul W. Tappan, Professor of Sociology at New York State University, held the view that the real roots of a youngster's maladjustments began long before his exposure to comic books, and were dependent solely upon the child's relationship with his family, his community, and his church. And Dr. Paul Witty, head of the psychological educational clinic of Northwestern University, claimed that comic books had little, if any, effect on the behavior of young people.

The controversy raged, fueled by heated arguments from both sides of the issue. Then on August 19, 1948, the lid blew off when newspapers published a front-page story that described how three boys in New Albany, Indiana, tortured a playmate with fire and knives as a reenactment of a story they had read in a crime comic book. The episode became the critics' chief weapon in their fight against comic book publishers, and Gleason was their main target.

On January 14, 1949, New York State Senator Benjamin F. Feinburg introduced a bill proposing that the distribution and sale of comic books be regulated by the State Department of Education, and that publishers be required to file for a special permit of approval for each book before it was published. Gleason was the only publisher to fight the Feinburg Bill, and through a series of newspaper editorials that pointed out its clear-cut violation of the constitutional right of freedom of the press, he helped block the bill's passage.

But the issue didn't stop there. Soon afterward Gleason locked horns with Dr. Wertham in a series of vigorous debates over the positive and negative effects of *Crime Does Not Pay*. But by then, Dr. Wertham had rallied support in his crusade against Gleason's comic book and its imitators, and public outcry ultimately brought the roof down on Gleason by mid-1955.

Unfortunately the powerful impact of *Crime Does Not Pay* overshadowed the other remarkable innovations Gleason brought to the comic book field, and these will be reviewed in this section.

Silver Streak Comics No. 6 (Sept. 1940)
©1940 Comic House, Inc.

Daredevil (battles Hitler) No. 1 (July 1941)
©1941 Comic House, Inc.

Lev Gleason entered the comic book arena in mid-1941 when he acquired the ownership of the failing Rhoda Publications which had introduced its first comic book, *Silver Streak Comics*, in December 1939. While this issue marked the debut of a variety of heroic characters, it also introduced the Claw, a villainous supermonster of the Orient who declared war on western civilization in his quest to dominate the world. In early stories, the Claw's schemes were always foiled by the sheer luck and good fortune of American scientist Carl Tarrant.

The third issue (February 1940) marked the debut of the Silver Streak, created by Ralph Jones, a superhero of lightning speed who appeared only a few weeks after the debut of D-C's Flash, also a superhero of lightning speed. Both characters were identical in theme, but in view of the fierce competition, both could not achieve equal popularity as "the fastest man alive." One would have to go. D-C was established whereas Rhoda was just starting. Consequently, it smothered any chances for Rhoda's fleet-footed hero to survive as the star of *Silver Streak Comics*.

However, the sixth issue introduced Jack Binder's Daredevil, a novel action character because he possessed no superpowers. Of course he was a skilled acrobat, and having no alter-identity he remained a man of mystery behind the mask and costume that covered him from head to toe. (Daredevil's origin,

however, did reveal that he was Bart Hill prior to donning his famous red-and-blue costume.) Daredevil had no partners, no romantic interests, nothing to interfere with his full-time fight against crime.

Daredevil's trademark was his uncanny skill with the boomerang, which he carried tucked in his belt. In his hands, the boomerang was a versatile instrument. Faster than a blink of an eye, Daredevil could sling his boomerang fifty paces and smash it against a gunman's Adam's apple before the latter could raise his weapon and pull the trigger. He could sail it across the room, around the corner and down the hallway to jam a vital door lock before the fleeing hoodlums could escape. He flung it at getaway cars, and villains' airplanes, jamming the propellor blades. At close range, Daredevil used it to klunk the bad guys on the back of their heads, or whack them across the bridges of their noses.

Silver Streak Comics then featured the fantastic battles between Daredevil and the Claw who was ten times the size of any human. The Claw was large and powerful enough to crush Daredevil like an insect, but Daredevil used his boomerang with noteworthy effectiveness. He hurled it to strike the Claw in one eye. And when Daredevil caught the boomerang on the rebound while the Claw was screaming in agony, he deftly returned it to strike the Claw's other eye!

Daredevil versus the Claw warranted a separate magazine of its own. The battles between the two continued in *Daredevil Comics* which began in July 1941. In the first issue, titled *Daredevil Battles Hitler*, the Claw teamed up with Adolph Hitler—and Daredevil countered by teaming up with the Silver Streak to stop them! The action-packed episode ended when Daredevil managed to trick the Claw into turning against Hitler. However, the final showdown between the two arch-enemies occured in *Daredevil Comics No. 31* when the awesome giant was finally killed.

From this point on, "Daredevil," under the ingenious guidance of Gleason's partner, writer Charles Biro, underwent a gradual change in editorial philosophy. It soon became a feature that combined a bold and dynamic human interest theme with a realistic, true-to-life approach that had never before been depicted in comics. First, Daredevil did the utterly unbelievable—he publicly unmasked himself, revealed his secret identity as Bart Hill, and announced his retirement from crimefighting!

Of course Bart Hill suddenly found himself the target of assassination attempts by underworld hood-lums. While standing in a crowded subway station, he was suddenly shoved off the platform and into the path of a speeding train. As far as the world knew, the train had crushed Bart Hill and dragged the remains of his body for miles because just the torn shreds of his jacket were found strewn along the tracks. But in reality, Bart Hill had escaped injury; the moment he was shoved off the subway platform, he landed agilely on his hands and flipped to the other side of the tracks a split second before the train whizzed past. He hurriedly took off his jacket and threw it under the wheels, and then disappeard from sight.

In *Daredevil Comics No. 45*, Bart Hill appeared in a new disguise, wearing a mustache and eyeglasses, and paid a visit to his four young orphan friends, Jock, Pee Wee, Curly, and Scarecrow. The quartet, better known as the Wise Guys, had made their first appearance in the thirteenth issue of *Daredevil Comics* and appeared from time to time afterwards, usually in stories that saw Daredevil helping them out of various jams of their own making. He now confided in them that he was adopting a new identity and needed a new name. He asked for their suggestions . . .

©1947 Lev Gleason Publications, Inc.

Jock came up with the acceptable name of Bill Hart. And so, Bart Hill , alias Daredevil, became the distinguished Professor Bill Hart and left to apply for a teaching position at a nearby university. Meanwhile, the Wise Guys signed up for some flying lessons, and unwittingly became involved in a fraudulent insurance scheme and wound up lost at sea in a downed aircraft.

When Professor Hart learned of their plight, he donned his famous red-and-blue costume, brushed the cobwebs from his boomerang, and returned to action as Daredevil. He rescued the Wise Guys and quickly smashed the insurance scheme. The story concluded this way:

On another level, this story, which was actually an adventure about the Wise Guys with Daredevil appearing as a "big brother" only at the end, was a harbinger of things to come.

The same issue included a second Daredevil adventure—the first story to take a step in Charles Biro's new direction. It began with Scarecrow's first date. She was a girl named Millie Withers who led a string of lovesick admirers around by their noses. Scarecrow soon lost interest in Millie after a picnic she had invited him to developed into a reunion of Millie's other admirers who also showed up.

After the picnic, Millie returned to the small apartment she shared with her mother. Her mother was planning to marry a handsome Casanova named Charlie, but Charlie also had eyes for Millie who encouraged his advances when her mother was out of the house. But one day, mother unexpectedly came home early . . .

236

Charlie, of course, was discovered, and the romantic triangle reached its climax in a dramatic confrontation between mother and daughter . . .

Thrown out of the only home she knew, Millie drifted downhill, going from bad to worse. She became involved with a hoodlum, and the liaison led to her arrest as an accomplice to robbery and murder. The poor girl needed help! While in jail awaiting trail, she called on her past boyfriends for assistance, but they all turned their backs on her—except for Scarecrow. In turn, Scarecrow and the Wise Guys called upon Daredevil, who entered the picture again at the end of the story to intervene on Millie's behalf.

During the trial, Daredevil convinced the judge to give Millie a light sentence in a girl's reformatory where she would be eligible for parole within a few months, and the judge went along with the plea.

The story was typical of Daredevil's adventures in the issues that followed. Each one reflected a shocking true-to-life situation, and one of the most shocking occurred in *Daredevil Comics No. 47.*

Here, the story centered around two lovely young sisters, Amy and Anita Locke, whom the Wise Guys had met during football practice for a school game. On the big day, Jock and Curly called on the two girls to take them to the game—but the girls' father wouldn't hear of it. He rudely slammed the door in Jock's face and harshly reprimanded Amy for dating "fresh young punks." Then he questioned Amy's new dress . . .

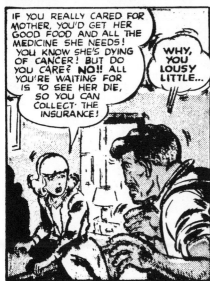

The invalid Mrs. Locke, bedridden and dying of cancer, tried to reason with her husband, but . . .

Amy and Anita decided to run away from home, but first they sneaked off to the football game to watch the Wise Guys win. After the game, Jock learned of the girls' problem and persuaded them to return home and try to patch things up with their father.

In the meantime, the girls' father had invited neighbors over for a few drinks and a friendly game of poker. But the game was not exactly friendly after the stakes were raised and Mr. Locke started losing . . .

When Jock and Curly brought the girls home, this is what they found when Amy opened the door . . .

The strain of Mrs. Locke getting out of bed was too much for her; she slumped into a chair and passed away shortly after the police arrested Howard Locke and took him off to jail. The girls were grief stricken, and they had no one to turn to except the Wise Guys. Jock called in Daredevil who once again appeared on the scene at the end of the story to tie up the loose ends. He made arrangements to have Mrs. Locke's insurance policy pay for the funeral expenses and send the girls to the exclusive Broadmoor Preparatory School.

However, the classic "Daredevil" episode that appeared in *Daredevil Comics No. 49* (July 1948) was somewhat different. It began when the Wise Guys visited a funeral home to pay their last respects to Mattie Proctor, a former schoolmate who had died of mysterious wounds. While at the funeral home they ran into Daredevil who had been investigating the case. Daredevil informed the Wise Guys that he suspected Mattie's death was linked to a vicious secret organization that had apparently been responsible for a recent outbreak of burglaries. The Wise Guys agreed to find out as much as they could on their own and keep Daredevil informed. They split up in different directions, visiting soda bars, pool parlors, and various corner hangouts, mixing in with young toughs in the hopes of somehow infiltrating the secret organization.*

*While the above sequence shows Curly with a cigarette in his mouth, it must be pointed out that the Wise Guys neither smoked nor drank. Curly lit a cigarette only as a ploy to gain Vinny's confidence and lead him to think that he was through associating with the Wise Guys.

242

Curly put on the best show. When he was taken to the organization's headquarters in an abondoned mine, he observed the inhuman torture inflicted upon one member who was accused of careless talk about gang activities to outsiders—the victim's hands were thoroughly useless afterwards. Then it came time for Curly's initiation as a new applicant for membership. Someone objected to his qualifications . . .

Fortunately, the cowardly blow from behind was not critical. Curly regained consciousness and, with his shoulder bleeding badly, struggled to his feet, realizing he would never be allowed to leave alive if he backed out. Besides, everything depended on infiltrating the Greys as a full-fledged member. He took their oath.

After the meeting adjourned and everyone had left, Curly, still weak from his shoulder wound, explored the mine to search for the arsenal of weapons. When he found it, he accidentally released a booby trap and a ton of heavy bricks fell on him . . .

Somehow he found the strength to crawl out of
the mine before he collapsed.

But Scarecrow said something that rang a bell. The secret
organization was a gang of their own age. And they had killed
Mattie Proctor. Although Curly had gone through a rugged
initiation to gain membership in the organization, he seemed to
be all right. Did his bruises mean that they had to call for help?
The question presented a formidable challenge. Jock, the spokes-
man of the Wise Guys, thought about it and decided that they
should handle the situation on their own. For the first time, the
Wise Guys *did not* call upon Daredevil! Jock's decision to assume
leadership was the turning point in the series . . .

After organizing a group of young Square Shooters to join his cause, Jock made preparations to raid the Greys' headquarters and confiscate the weapons from the arsenal. Curly, having received treatment for his wounds, led the way and pointed out the booby traps. Pee Wee remained outside as a lookout . . .

The next day, the Greys discovered that their weapons were missing and called an emergency meeting of all members. Realizing his absence would create suspicion, Curly pulled on his hood and attended the meeting. In another part of town, Jock called together the Square Shooters to organize another raid on the mine as soon as they received Curly's signal.

At the Grey's meeting, the leader pointed out that the club records with each member's name and address and evidence linking them to Mattie Proctor's murder had been stolen along with the weapons. The leader explained that a traitor was in their midst—

Meanwhile, outside the mine entrance, the Wise Guys and the Square Shooters waited for Curly to come out . . .

Curly was trapped! But with his back against the wall and nowhere to turn, he showed the mob what it was like to be a Wise Guy. He suddenly reached in his shirt, pulled out a stick of dynamite, and issued the ultimate challenge . . .

Of course the Greys immediately set out after Curly and tried to head him off. They were right on his heels when he reached the tunnel entrance, and when they charged out into the open the battle royal began! The Square Shooters, fighting side by side with the Wise Guys, tore into the startled Greys . . .

When the melee was over and the "tough" Greys were thoroughly beaten by boys their own age, Jock lined them up in front of the mine entrance to apply the *coup de grace*.

Just then, the police arrived on the scene to take charge. The Greys made a hasty dash to the safety of the patrol wagon, thus bringing to an end the first story of its kind that dealt exclusively with a boys-against-boys conflict.

It was this episode that catapulted the Wise Guys into the top slot as the leading teenage stars of comicdom. They had neither scientific gadgets nor super powers, indeed they were just average boys on the block who came to grips with "average" problems! And they became embroiled in the kind of realistic adventures that juvenile readership could readily identify with. It was an accomplishment that seriously threatened the popularity of superhero fantasy.

As the Wise Guys began handling situations on their own, Daredevil's appearances became more infrequent. In some stories, he didn't appear at all, and by 1950 he was phased out of the series altogether. The Wise Guys were the stars—and Pee Wee emerged as the star of the Wise Guys, even though the magazine still retained the title of *Daredevil Comics*.

Daredevil Comics No. 53 (March 1949)
©1949 Lev Gleason Publications, Inc.

Daredevil Comics No. 45 (Nov. 1948)
©1948 Lev Gleason Publications, Inc.

Daredevil Comics No. 47 (Mar. 1949)
©1948 Lev Gleason Publications, Inc.

Although the changeover from Daredevil to the Wise Guys was a gradual one, Gleason had experimented with the approach that emphasized youth's participation in the heroic role in other features that had originated in Rhoda's *Silver Streak Comics*. For example, *Silver Streak Comics* had featured a superhero named Captain Battle. While these stories were full of action, the actual character concept had little to offer in the way of originality, theme, or motif. Gleason phased out Captain Battle and introduced his son, Captain Battle Jr!

Captain Battle Jr., a young patriotic adventurer who served the country on special undercover assignments in the European theater of military operations, was put into his own magazine that ran for three issues and was published at irregular intervals between 1942 and 1944. His father, Captain Battle, also headlined his own magazine, *Captain Battle Comics*, which survived for just two issues. The third issue was retitled *Boys Comics No. 3* and included a new roster of juvenile stars. It was in this magazine that the junior hero concept was ultimately perfected with the introduction of young Chuck Chandler, as shown on the following pages.

Captain Battle Junior No. 2 (Winter 1944)
©1944 Comic House, Inc.

250

253

255

The story was merely a preview of what was to come in the rough-and-tumble grudge battles between Chuck Chandler, better known as Crimebuster, and Iron Jaw on the thrilling pages of *Boy Comics*. Crimebuster wore no mask and he had no scientific gadgets. He had no weapon, no car, no super power, no partners, and no girl friends—just an adopted pet monkey named Squeeks. Crimebuster operated alone, relying strictly on his rigid cadet training in military sciences and physical fitness. And he had but one objective in mind—to bring about the utter destruction of his most hated enemy, Iron Jaw.

In *Boy Comics No. 15.* Crimebuster finally accomplished his objective in a gruesome episode that ended with Iron Jaw's death. After that, Crimebuster's adventures were slanted toward true-to-life situations that were quite similar to those encountered by the Wise Guys.

Gleason did not publish many titles, but they were all blockbusters.

Boy Comics No. 41 (Aug. 1948)
©1948 Lev Gleason Publications, Inc.

Boy Comics No. 44 (Feb. 1949)
©1949 Lev Gleason Publications, Inc.

ALPHABETICAL LISTING OF LEV GLEASON COMIC BOOKS

Black Diamond Western (1949 - 1955, succeeded *Desparado*
Comics after the eighth issue.)
Boy Comics (1942 - 1956, succeeded *Captain Battle Comics*
after the second issue.)
Boy Meets Girl Comics (1950 - 1956)
Captain Battle Comics (1941, Rhoda Publications.)
Captain Battle Jr. Comics (1942 - 1944)
Crime and Punishment (1948 - 1955)
Crime Does Not Pay (1942 - 1955, succeeded *Silver Streak*
Comics after Issue 21.)
Daredevil Comics (1941 - 1956)
Desparado Comics (1949, became *Black Diamond Western*
after the eighth issue.)
Silver Streak Comics (1939 - 1942, Rhode Publications.)
Uncle Charlie's Fables (1951 - 1952)

9

E-C PUBLICATIONS

As noted before, the quest for world peace at the end of World War II had a dramatic impact on the comic book industry. Patriotic heroes and war themes were phased out by publishers who quickly discovered that adventure themes about would-be world dictators and enemy agents were losing their public appeal. Most of the comic book characters turned to fighting crime or switched to episodes of light humor.

For the most part, the comic book industry as a form of escape entertainment reached a low ebb by 1948. New fuel was needed to perk up the industry. Nothing new could be attempted in the area of super-hero fantasy simply because everything that could be done had already been tried. Nevertheless, some publishers did attempt to revive Wild West fiction, while others struggled with animal fantasy, already a closed territory that belonged exclusively to Dell Publishing Company.

In looking at other literary areas, publishers found that Hollywood was entering a science fiction period, that soap opera romance had become a popular subject in radio drama, and that the new detective magazines which emphasized sex and violence were gradually replacing pulp fiction. Many of the comic book publishers entered these three categories with an emphasis given to crime and girlie themes because the subject matter required little creative effort to produce.

The new wave of crime and girlie titles imitated each other page for page and word for word, often repeating an identical story that had appeared in a competitive comic book the month before. Sensational cover appeal was stressed. This was the modern "realism" for the upcoming generation of the 1950's— and the only topic many of the publishers could come up with as a last attempt to stay in business. With the industry in rather poor shape, publisher William M. Gaines entered the arena, inheriting a small group of educational comic books from his late father Max Gaines, one of the original founders of the industry during the early 1930s. William Gaines replaced the educational titles with a line of romance titles. After two years of imitating his run-of-the-mill competitors, Gaines terminated his first group of romance comics and introduced the "New Trend Entertainment Comics" series, a dynamic innovation that was destined to turn the entire industry around.

Weird Science was among the first of the "New Trend Entertainment Comics" series and made its debut in May, 1950. It marked the beginning of comic book adaptations of classic science fiction stories from the early pulps which had by then almost dwindled away. The striking cover of the first issue (illustrated by Al Feldstein) depicted the leadoff story that had been adapted from Henry Hasse's novellette "He Who Shrank," which first appeared in *Amazing Stories*, August 1936.

Amazing Stories (Aug. 1936)
©1936 Teck Publications, Inc.

The story concerned a man with terminal cancer who volunteered to take a new medical serum that was intended to shrink the disease out of his system. But unforeseen complications set in after the injection—the patient himself started to shrink! He dwindled down to the size of an insect on the table, then down into the surface scratches of the table which suddenly sprang up like huge canyons around him. Specks of dust emerged into monstrous germs that threatened to devour him. Soon he became small enough to vanish from their grasp.

It grew darker as he drifted aimlessly into a sea of ether, a black empty void that was sprinkled with specks of light. He brushed the specks aside but as he continued to shrink they grew into tiny pebbles of fire that scorched his flesh. The one-time specks eventually expanded into massive flaming spheres growing farther apart from each other. To escape their heat, the story's hero floated behind a huge boulder that was suspended nearby.

As he lay against the surface, he gradually became aware of sharp stings from tiny needles pricking his flesh. He brushed them away while his size allowed him to, but as he continued to grow smaller he discovered the needles were actually air missiles that were being fired at him by some microsocopic life forms that his weight was apparently crushing. Before he became small enough for the missiles to render serious harm, he pushed himself away and drifted through the ether toward another boulder farther out in the distance.

An immeasurable span of time elapsed before he finally reached it. When he did, the boulder had grown into a massive planetary body. Trapped by its gravitational pull, he plunged through the atmosphere until he fell to the surface like a falling meteor. Although he had shrunk considerably he was still large enough to withstand the fall and land safely. The planet was inhabited by intelligent beings who had been observing him since he first emerged as a dark shadow blotting out their distant stars. They offered to help him. Unfortunately, they could do no more than reduce his shrinkage rate. Before a permanent cure could be found, he had vanished down into another sea of atoms . . . down into another submicroscopic universe . . . down into worlds within worlds, shrinking infinitely while experiencing fantastic adventures at each level.

He eventually shrank to a world inhabited by beings almost identical to him. Although they lacked his ability to communicate telepathically (a gift he had acquired during his journey), they were nevertheless advanced enough to receive and understand his thought messages.

The story concluded with the shrinking traveller narrating his autobiography to one of those beings—a human on planet Earth! But he soon lost telepathic contact as he shrank down into the office chair he was sitting upon and vanished again.

When the original story was first published in 1936 it startled the scientific community. Hasse's theory that the world and the stars in the sky were all part of a universe existing among other similar universes within a single atom of a much larger dimension prompted brand new theories about time and space. Although the fictional plot was soon forgotten, numerous scientific articles began to appear which stated that the composition of atomic molecules was held together by a force similar to that which held the planets and stars together.

When the story reappeared almost twenty years later in the first issue of *Weird Science*, the concept of someone shrinking down into a sub-microscopic universe was adopted as standard plot material for later comic book literature.

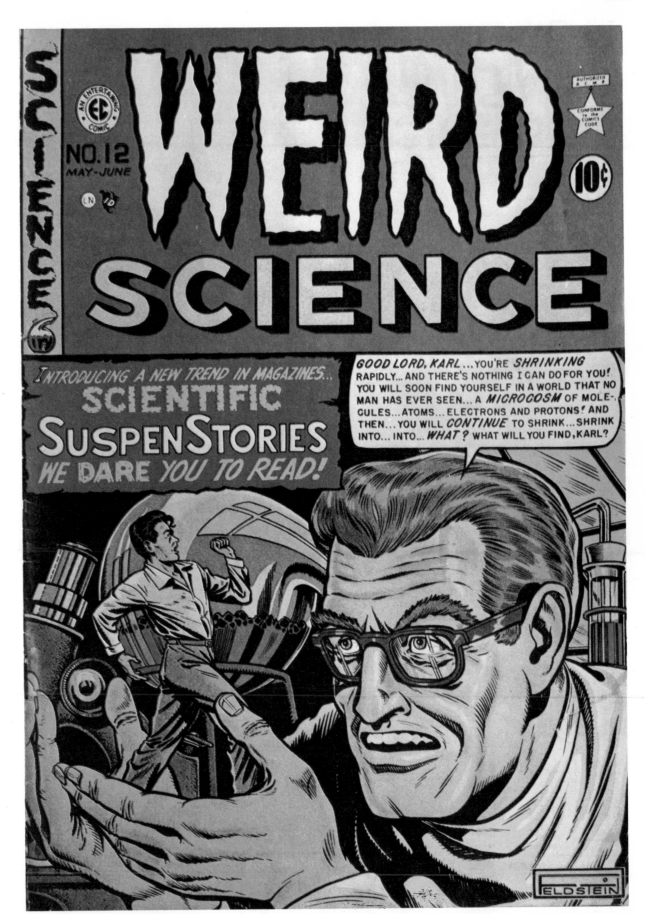

Weird Science Comics No. 12 (May-June 1950)
©1978 by William M. Gaines

266

Weird Science No. 13 (July-Aug. 1950)
©1978 by William M. Gaines

Weird Science No. 15 (Nov.-Dec. 1950)
©1978 by William M. Gaines

Weird Science No. 8 (July-Aug. 1951)
©1978 by William M. Gaines

Weird Science No. 9 (Sept. Oct. 1951)
©1978 by William M. Gaines

Weird Science No. 16 (Nov. Dec. 1952)
©1978 by William M. Gaines

The stories that appeared in the earlier issues of *Weird Science* were illustrated by Al Feldstein (who also produced the cover art), Harvey Kurtzman, Jack Kamen, Bill Elder, and Joe Orlando. After the first two years, Feldstein, Kurtzman, and Elder switched to other E-C magazines, leaving Kamen and Orlando as the regular staff for *Weird Science*. The two were later joined by artists Wally Wood and Al Williamson, both of whom had perfected a dynamic style of realistic illustration that helped turn *Weird Science* into a comic book of classic art in addition to its classic science fiction story content.

Early pulp science fiction was known for its unexpected twist endings that often threw the reader for a loop. However, when these stories were adapted into a comic book format, they usually had to be reconstructed to capture the correct mood and feeling for the surprise conclusion. Al Williamson did just that in depicting "Spaceborn," his first illustrated story for *Weird Science* which appeared in Issue 16.

Set in another century of tomorrow where space flight was commonplace, "Spaceborn" centered around an experience of two newlyweds, Lon and Enid, who decided to spend their honeymoon on one of the distant planets that were charted as uninhabited but suitable for human life. As their two-passenger deluxe space cruiser penetrated the atmosphere and landed, Enid suddenly took ill.

Realizing that Enid could not survive another takeoff, Lon decided to settle down permanently on the planet where they would spend the rest of their lives. However, Enid was in need of medical supplies and Lon realized he would have to return alone to Earth to get them. He left Enid behind with the intention of getting back to her within a few weeks, but his ship's overdrive system failed and it took him six years to reach Earth. After loading a new cargo ship with the necessary supplies, Lon rushed back to the lonely planet where his wife awaited him.

As he landed and stepped out of the cruiser, a grotesque monstrosity slithered toward him . . .

268

Weird Science No. 17 (Jan. Feb. 1953)
©1978 by William M. Gaines

Weird Science No. 18 (Mar. April 1953)
©1978 by William M. Gaines

Weird Science No. 19 (May June 1953)
©1978 by William M. Gaines

Weird Science No. 20 (July-Aug. 1953)
©1978 by William M. Gaines

Weird Science No. 17 marked the first of a special series of comic book adaptations of Ray Bradbury's classics which had been previously published in the pulp magazines, principally *Amazing Stories*.

Weird Science No. 18 featured Bradbury's

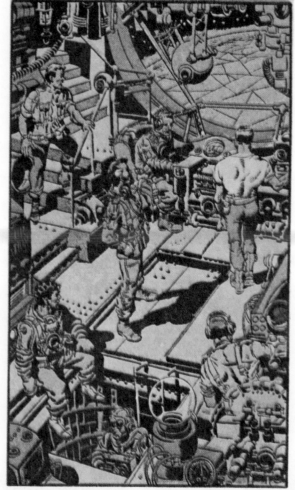

THE SHIP CAME DOWN FROM SPACE, IT CAME DOWN FROM THE STARS AND THE SILENT GULFS OF SPACE. IT WAS A NEW SHIP, THE ONLY ONE OF ITS KIND, IT HAD FIRE IN ITS BELLY AND MEN IN ITS BODY, AND IT MOVED WITH CLEAN SILENCE, FIERY AND HOT. A CROWD HAD GATHERED AT ITS NEW YORK LAUNCHING SITE AND SHOUTED AND WAVED THEIR HANDS UP INTO THE SUNLIGHT...AND THE ROCKET HAD JERKED UP, BLOOMED OUT GREAT FLOWERS OF HEAT AND COLOR, AND RUN AWAY INTO SPACE ON THE *FIRST VOYAGE TO MARS!* AND NOW, IT WAS DECELERATING WITH METAL EFFICIENCY IN THE UPPER ZONES OF MARS'S ATMOSPHERE...

The original version, first published in Fiction House's *Planet Stories* in 1948, was reprinted several times afterwards in full-length paperback editions, serialized in *Playboy Magazine,* and adapted into a popular movie under the title *The Angry Red Planet.* The story has been widely acclaimed by critics as a classic masterpiece of modern literature.

In this issue of *Weird Science,* artist Wally Wood vividly illustrated the classic in comic book format for the first and only time.

The story centered around the first space expedition to Mars where the astronaut team, commanded by Captain Black, made a startling discovery. Upon reaching the red planet they landed in the middle of a small community identical to a quaint village that could have been found anywhere on Earth at the turn of the century. Totally dumbfounded at their findings, the captain and crew set out to explore the village in search of an explanation. They approached the first house . . .

HOLLOW ECHOES SOUNDED FROM THE BOARDS AS THEY WALKED ACROSS THE PORCH AND STOOD BEFORE THE SCREEN DOOR. INSIDE THEY COULD SEE A CRYSTAL CHANDELIER AND A COMFORTABLE MORRIS CHAIR. CAPTAIN JOHN BLACK RANG THE BELL...

IF YOU'RE *SELLING* SOMETHING, I'M MUCH TOO *BUSY* AND I HAVEN'T *TIME*...

I...I BEG YOUR PARDON, BUT WE'RE *STRANGERS* HERE, MA'AM! WE'RE FROM *EARTH*, AND WE WANT TO KNOW HOW THIS TOWN *GOT* HERE AND HOW *YOU* GOT HERE!

They met other inhabitants who came to greet them and discovered they were all relatives and loved ones who had long since died on Earth but were now, amazingly, living on Mars!

272

CAPTAIN BLACK LAY PEACEFULLY, LETTING HIS THOUGHTS FLOAT...

SO THIS...IS...MARS! WHO LIVED HERE A THOUSAND YEARS AGO ON MARS? MARTIANS? OR HAS THIS ALWAYS BEEN LIKE THIS? MARTIANS? MARTIANS...

HE LAUGHED OUT LOUD, ALMOST. HE HAD THE MOST RIDICULOUS THEORY ALL OF A SUDDEN. IT GAVE HIM A KIND OF CHILLED FEELING. JUST SUPPOSE...

...SUPPOSE THERE WERE MARTIANS LIVING ON MARS AND THEY SAW OUR SHIP COMING AND SAW US INSIDE OUR SHIP AND HATED US! AND SUPPOSE THEY WANTED TO DESTROY US, AS INVADERS, AND THEY WANTED TO DO IT CLEVERLY, SO THAT WE'D BE TAKEN OFF GUARD...

WHAT A CLEVER WEAPON TO USE AGAINST EARTHMEN WITH ATOMIC WEAPONS! WHAT MORE NATURAL? WHAT MORE SIMPLE? A MAN DOESN'T ASK QUESTIONS WHEN HIS MOTHER IS SUDDENLY BROUGHT BACK TO LIFE; HE'S MUCH TOO HAPPY!

AND THE BRASS BAND PLAYED AND EVERYBODY WAS TAKEN TO PRIVATE HOMES, AND NOW WE ARE ALL IN VARIOUS BEDS, WITH NO WEAPONS TO PROTECT US, AND THE ROCKET LIES IN THE MOONLIGHT, EMPTY...

AND IT WOULD BE SO SIMPLE FOR MY BROTHER, HERE IN BED BESIDE ME, TO TURN OVER AND PUT A KNIFE INTO MY HEART WHILE CHANGING FORM, MELTING, SHIFTING...BECOMING A ONE-EYED, GREEN, AND YELLOW-TOOTHED MARTIAN...

AND IN ALL THE HOUSES DOWN THE STREET A DOZEN BROTHERS OR FATHERS SUDDENLY MELTING AWAY AND TAKING OUT KNIVES AND DOING THINGS TO THE UNSUSPECTING SLEEPING EARTHMEN!

JOHN! WHERE ARE YOU GOING?

I... I... FOR A DRINK OF WATER...

BUT YOU'RE NOT THIRSTY!

CAPTAIN JOHN BLACK BROKE AND RAN ACROSS THE ROOM! HE SCREAMED TWICE...

HE NEVER REACHED THE DOOR...

Weird Science began as *Saddle Romances*, a confession comic book which started in 1949 and ran bimonthly up to Issue 11, March-April 1950. Beginning with Issue 12, the title was changed to *Weird Science*, the romance format was dropped and the science fiction theme introduced. Although *Weird Science* was an entirely new magazine, it continued the numbering sequence of *Saddle Romances*.

The carry-over of the numbering sequence from a terminated title to a new title was then common practice in order to simplify the magazine's contract commitments with its advertisers who may have signed for page space for twelve, or twenty-four or thirty-six issues in advance. While the title, format, and story contents may have changed between two magazines, the ads remained the same.

The early issues of *Weird Science* contained three to four science fiction stories illustrated by such major artists as Al Feldstein, Harvey Kurtzman, Jack Kamen, and Wally Wood, with covers by Feldstein.

WEIRD SCIENCE

Weird Science No. 12 (May-June 1950):

The first issue, in which the contents included the comic book adaptation of "He Who Shrank." Other features were "Dream of Doom" and "Experiment in Death." In addition to comics, *Weird Science* introduced original science fiction short stories in text. This issue contained two: "Murder In The 21st Century!" and "By The Dark Side of The Moon."

Weird Science No. 13 (July-August 1950):

The contents for this issue included a story entitled "Flying Saucer Invasion" illustrated by Al Feldstein. Although the subject of flying saucers had been written about many times during the 1950s, this particular story was an adaptation of the original science fiction classic on the theme that first appeared in *Planet Stories* in 1942. The plot was concerned with the military investigation of rumors about unidentified flying objects shaped like discs that flew much faster than conventional aircraft. The military, however, failed to find concrete evidence of their existence and dismissed the entire matter as a fraud—just as an invading fleet of thousands of flying saucers from a distant world sped toward Earth.

Other contents included "The Man Who Raced Time" illustrated by Harvey Kurtsman, and a short story in text, "Sands of Time."

Weird Science No. 14 (September-October 1950):

The contents included "Destruction of The Earth," a story about the end of the world illustrated by Al Feldstein, "Sounds From Another World" illustrated by Harvey Kurtsman, "Eternal Man" by Wally Wood, and "Machine From Nowhere" by Jack Kamen.

Weird Science No. 15 (November-December 1950):

The contents included "Panic!", a clever spin-off of the radio dramatization of H. G. Wells' classic *War of the Worlds*.

The story, illustrated by Al Feldstein, concerned a television remake of the famous radio broadcast that once panicked the nation in 1939. To avoid causing a similar panic, the television studio sent out publicity releases to all newspapers to promote the show and to inform the public that everything they would be watching was pure fantasy. So when the program depicting an alien invasion was televised, the public laughed it off as a big joke.

The twist was that the program had coincided with an actual alien invasion and the unsuspecting public who thought they were watching science fiction when the news commentator began to insist it was a true report, were totally unaware, until too late.

Other contents included "Radioactive Child" illustrated by Harvey Kurtzman. This story was unique offbeat sci-fi centering around a young boy with super intelligence who designed the hydrogen bomb—then lost his extraordinary mental ability when it was needed most to thwart an enemy army.

Weird Science No. 5 (January-February 1951):

The new numbering sequence began with this issue and continued to Issue 22 when the magazine was merged with *Weird Fantasy*. The contents of *Weird Science No. 5* included "Made Of The Future" illustrated by Al Feldstein, "Return", illustrated by Wally Wood, "Killed In Time" illustrated by Jack Kamen, and "The Last War On Earth" illustrated by Harvey Kurtzman. This issue also included a short story in text entitled "Progress," one of the best in the series.

Weird Science No. 6 (March-April 1951):

The contents included "Man and Superman," a semi-humorous tale illustrated by Harvey Kurtzman which centered around two brothers: one was a frail but brilliant young atomic physicist and the other was a muscular body builder with the mind of a ten-year-old. They communicated on two entirely different levels, neither one understanding the other. While the body builder talked about the Mr. America contest he was going to win, the scientist explained his experimental work on increasing the mass of an atom without changing its structure. The most bizarre events occurred when the two mixed their work together.

©1978 by William M. Gaines

Other stories in this issue included "Spawn of Venus," a tale about an alien amoeba that devoured living matter on Earth and was illustrated by Al Feldstein, and "Sinking of The Titanic," a time-twister illustrated by Wally Wood.

Weird Science No. 7 (May-June 1951)

The contents included "Monster From The Fourth Dimension" illustrated by Al Feldstein, "Something Missing" illustrated by Jack Kamen, "The Aliens" illustrated by Wally Wood, and "Gregory Had a Model-T" the last story to be illustrated by Harvey Kurtzman for *Weird Science*. Kurtzman was by this time producing stories and cover art for the other E-C titles that his bold and zany style was more ideally suited for.

Weird Science No. 8 (July-August 1951):

This issue included "Seeds of Jupiter," a tale about an alien seed that fell to Earth and changed into an indestructible life form that threatened to devour humanity—and it was also the last story that Al Feldstein illustrated for *Weird Science* prior to his taking over as the editor of E-C's *Mad Magazine*. Other contents included "Beyond Repair" illustrated by Jack Kamen. This was an unusual romance story of the future where a handsome playboy, upon returning home from a lengthy space journey, met and wooed his best friend's girl, and then ran off with her as she joked that her former boy friend was building another robot sweetheart.

©1978 by William M. Gaines

Weird Science No. 9 (September-October 1951):

This issue contained the first cover art by Wally Wood who continued doing covers through Issue 22 (with an occasional Feldstein cover art in between). The contents included two action space adventures that were also illustrated by Wood, one of which was "Grey Cloud of Death" as depicted in the following scene.

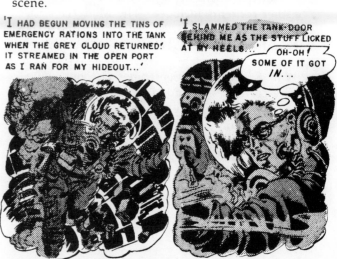

©1978 by William M. Gaines

Weird Science No. 10 (November-December 1951):

This issue contained two unusual tales illustrated by Wally Wood. The first, "The Maidens Cried", concerned a trip to a distant planet inhabited by beautiful women—who were actually insects that experienced a physical transformation during various life cycles similar to the manner in which a caterpillar changed to a moth. The second, "Transformation Completed," concerned a scientist experimenting with changing sex hormones in rabbits—he imprudently carried the experiment an extra step further in an attempt to prevent his daughter from marrying.

Weird Science No. 11 (January-February 1952):

The contents included an autobiography of artist Jack Kamen, and a story entitled "Why Papa Left Home" that was illustrated by Joe Orlando. This was a unique time-twister in which a young scientist, resentful because of his father's desertion many years before, built and tested a new time machine, went twenty-five years into the past, became stranded, met a woman, fell in love and married her. They had a son, and then when he was suddenly catapulted back to his own time, he made an incredible discovery when he went home to his mother. . .

©1978 by William M. Gaines

Issue 11 also included "Only Human" illustrated by Kamen, an adaptation of one of the first science fiction stories with a computer theme. A female programmer, feeding information into the newly-built machine's memory bank, unknowingly projected her own inner feelings of loneliness and desire to love and be loved into the input data. As a result, the computer failed to function properly because of internal emotional stress in its circuit panels—it had fallen in love with its programmer!

Weird Science No. 13 (May-June 1952):

The contents included "Weighty Decision" illustrated by Wally Wood. This was a unique classic on the journey-to-the-moon theme where an astronaut crew, enroute to their lunar destination, discovered that the commander's girl friend had secretly stowed away inside the food compartment. She wanted to be near the man she loved but her extra weight, which was not accounted for during blast-off, had placed the entire mission in jeopardy—too much fuel was being consumed. Midway between Earth and the moon the commander had a decision to make about the excess weight problem. Something or someone had to be ejected into space, and it was either part of the vital scientific instruments, a member of his highly trained crew—or his girl friend. He reluctantly made his choice.

©1978 by William M. Gaines

Issue 13 also contained another story illustrated by Wood, "He Walked Among Us." The story told of an astronaut's trip to a distant world where primitive beings accepted him as a god. His experiences on the planet paralleled the life of Christ, except that instead of being crucified the astronaut was tortured and put to death on the rack.

"Say Your Prayers," illustrated by Joe Orlando, was another entry in Issue 13. This was a highly unusual tale about space travel from an alien's viewpoint. In this story a crew of intelligent insects that looked something like the praying mantis journeyed across the stars to colonize Earth. After barely escaping being trampled to death by gigantic monsters (humans), the insects hastily boarded ship and blasted away.

However, two members of the crew, Bfan and Glun, were accidently left behind and had to begin a new life on the strange world. When translated into the language of the humans, Bfan and Glun meant Adam and Eve.

Weird Science No. 14 (July-August 1952)

The contents for this issue included "There'll Be Some Changes Made" illustrated by Wally Wood. This was a thought-provoking exploration of the sex theme and concerned an astronaut who journeyed to a distant planet where he met and fell in love with an exotic alien beauty. Luwana was the most beautiful woman he had ever seen and he married her—only to discover later that she was in fact a hermaphrodite!

©1978 by William M. Gaines

Weird Science No. 16 (November-December 1952):

Al Williamson's art began with this issue and continued through Issue 22, with occasional combinations of Frank Frazetta pencil layouts and Williamson inkings and vice versa. The major stories in this issue included Williamson's "SpaceBorn," and Wally Wood's "Down To Earth," an action adventure on the alien invasion theme in which the aliens win.

©1978 by William M. Gaines

Weird Science No. 17 (January-February 1953):

This issue introduced "Long Years," the first of the Ray Bradbury classics. It also included "Island Monster" illustrated by Al Williamson. This story, in the tradition of *King Kong*, concerned a colossal beast that was tracked down on a remote island, captured and brought back to civilization for exhibition. It escaped, went on a destructive rampage, and was eventually killed. However, a scientific expedition that later explored the island discovered the wreckage of a spaceship and other evidence that indicated the monster was actually a peaceful ambassador from another world who was bringing a message of friendship to Earth.

"Plucked," illustrated by Wally Wood, was the third story in Issue 17. This was a tale about alien invaders who periodically came to Earth under a hypnotic screen and kidnapped groups of healthy humans for their dinner table, much in the same way humans gathered unsuspecting turkeys for their holiday feasts.

Weird Science No. 18 (March-April 1953):
The Ray Bradbury "Mars Is Heaven" issue.

Weird Science No. 19 (May-June 1953):

The contents included an autobiography of Ray Bradbury and his classic "The One Who Waits" illustrated by Al Williamson. This story was in the first-expedition-to-Mars tradition where an astronaut crew was accidentally devoured by a vaporish form of life that was lonely and only trying to seek companionship.

Also in this issue was "The Precious Years" illustrated by Wally Wood. This was an unusual futuristic tale about a man and woman, bored with eternal youth, who sought to escape the ennui of their lives by volunteering for death. Except in this particular age, death had an entirely different meaning which the couple did not discover until it was too late.

©1978 by William M. Gaines

Weird Science No. 20 featured Bradbury's "Changeling" that was first published in 1949 in *Planet Stories*. Here artist Jack Kamen reconstructed the story as a unique one-act play with two characters, a couple named Martha and Leonard, and displayed a rare skill in dramatically capturing the changing emotions of a frustrated and jealous woman deeply in love.

The opening scene began in Martha's apartment as she impatiently waited for her boyfriend Leonard to make his nightly visit. She believed he was dating other women and intended to confront him with her suspicions. When Leonard finally did come and held her in his arms, she acted coldly.

She accused him of dating her best friend, Alice Summers. He denied it. Then Martha presented proof—a newspaper picture showing Leonard and Alice holding hands. He still denied it. They argued. One word led to another until she couldn't take it any longer. She pulled out a gun.

The phone call confirmed all the proof she needed. In a rage she slammed the phone down with one hand and pulled the trigger with the other hand.

Unable to move with life ebbing away, Leonard confessed the truth—that he had actually left her long ago.

Leonard keeled over and collapsed on the floor. Suddenly Martha came to her senses. She realized what she had done, and she wanted him back. But it was too late. The damage was done.

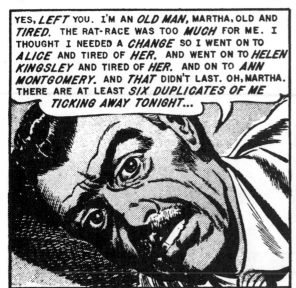

278

I'VE GOT TO *TELL* YOU, MARTHA. YOU *CUT* SEVERAL *VITAL ELEMENTS* WITH YOUR *BULLETS*. I CAN'T GET *UP*. THE *DOCTORS*, IF THEY *CAME*, WOULD *FIND ME OUT ANYWAY*, I'M NOT *THAT* PERFECT!

OH, MARTHA, I DIDN'T WANT TO *HURT* YOU. *BELIEVE* ME. I WANTED ONLY YOUR *HAPPINESS*. I SPENT *FIFTEEN THOUSAND DOLLARS* FOR THIS REPLICA, *PERFECT IN EVERY DETAIL*.

THERE *ARE VARIABLES*. THE *SALIVA* FOR ONE. A *REGRETTABLE* ERROR. IT SET YOU *OFF*. BUT YOU *MUST* KNOW THAT I *LOVED* YOU...

SHE WOULD FALL AT ANY MOMENT, WRITHING INTO INSANITY, SHE THOUGHT. HE *HAD* TO BE STOPPED FROM *TALKING*...

AND WHEN I SAW HOW THE *OTHERS* LOVED ME, I HAD TO PROVIDE REPLICAS FOR *THEM*, POOR DEARS. THEY *LOVE* ME *SO!* YOU WON'T *TELL* THEM, *WILL* YOU, MARTHA? *PROMISE?* I'M A VERY TIRED OLD MAN, AND I WANT MY PEACE, A BOOK, SOME MILK AND A LOT OF *SLEEP*...

ALL THIS YEAR, THIS *WHOLE YEAR*, I'VE BEEN *ALONE*... ALONE *EVERY NIGHT!* TALKING TO A *MECHANICAL HORROR!* IN *LOVE* WITH *NOTHINGNESS. ALONE ALL THE TIME* WHEN I COULD HAVE BEEN OUT WITH SOMEONE *REAL*...

I CAN *STILL* LOVE YOU, MARTHA.

OH, GOD...

SHE SEIZED UP THE HAMMER...

SHE SMASHED AT HIS HEAD AND BEAT AT HIS CHEST AND HIS THRASHING ARMS AND WILD LEGS. SHE BEAT AT THE SOFT HEAD UNTIL STEEL SHONE THROUGH, AND SUDDEN EXPLOSIONS OF WIRE AND BRASS COGGERY SHOWERED ABOUT THE ROOM WITH METAL TINKLES. THE MOUTH SAID...

I... LOVE YOU...

SHE STRUCK THE MOUTH WITH THE HAMMER AND THE TONGUE FELL OUT. THE GLASS EYES ROLLED ON THE CARPET. SHE POUNDED AT THE THING UNTIL IT WAS STREWN LIKE THE REMAINS OF A CHILD'S ELECTRIC TRAIN ON THE FLOOR...

The same issue also included Wood's illustrated dramatization of

THE LOATHSOME!

The title of this extraordinary classic pertained to a little girl who was disfigured at birth by a rare hereditary disease, the result of her father's overexposure to radiation from a hydrogen bomb explosion. Life was cruel to her from the moment of her birth when the attending physician explained the sad news to the father.

One glance at the child and the father immediately accepted the doctor's advice. The hospital placed her in a special orphanage managed by the ambitious Miss Ferby whose only interest was receiving government payments for caring for the child.

As the girl grew into early childhood she experienced constant ridicule and physical abuse. Because of her misshapen appearance, the matrons detested her and sought any trivial excuse for punishing the child. When she accidently broke a mirror . . .

IT WAS THE TEN YEAR OLD MUTANT CHILD. SHE DRAGGED HERSELF ACROSS THE GRASS-CARPET, STOPPING EVERY SO OFTEN TO LOOK AROUND, SEARCHING INTO THE SHADOWS FOR PRYING EYES. SHE HELD A NOTE IN HER HAND, COLD WHITE IN THE MOON'S LIGHT...

Isolated in her room during the day, the girl was only allowed to use the playground at night after the other children were tucked into bed. With no playmates or toys, the girl amused herself by scribbling notes and hiding them. When the watchful matrons failed to find any of her notes they accused the child of secretly scheming conspiracy against the orphanage and set a trap to catch her in the act of writing one of her secret messages. They watched her closely the next night . . .

THE MUTANT-CHILD MOVED TOWARD THE GROVE OF TREES AT THE FAR END OF THE ORPHANAGE GARDEN. SHE LOOKED AT THE NOTE, LOOKED AROUND HESITANTLY, THEN PUSHED IT INTO A HOLLOW IN ONE OF THE OLD TREES...

THE THREE ADULTS, EXPLODING FROM THE ORPHANAGE BUILDING, MADE HER SPIN AROUND, WIDE-EYED AND FRIGHTENED...

THE MONSTER REACHED INTO THE HOLLOW TREE, PULLING OUT THE NOTE. THEY WERE ALMOST UPON HER NOW...

THE MUTANT *WAS* RUNNING...WILDLY TRYING TO ESCAPE. SHE SCRAMBLED UP A TREE GROWING NEAR THE SPIKED ORPHANAGE WALL...

SUDDENLY, THE NIGHT WAS RENT BY A BLOOD-CURDLING SCREAM. THE MUTANT-GIRL TUMBLED FROM THE LIMB THAT OVERHUNG THE WALL...

A SCALLOPED CURTAIN OF RED DESCENDED FROM THE IMPALED CREATURE'S BODY...RINGING DOWN OVER THE CONCRETE THAT HAD ENCLOSED HER FOR TEN YEARS...

MONA AND DOCTOR SIMMS AND MISS FERBY STARED UPWARD IN HORROR. THE COLD WHITE SHEET OF PAPER SLIPPED FROM HER HAND AS THE LAST SPARK OF LIFE SLIPPED FROM HER BODY. IT FLUTTERED QUIETLY, LIKE A DEAD LEAF ON A GREY FALL DAY, TO THEIR FEET. THE DOCTOR WHISPERED...

MISS FERBY KNELT AND PICKED UP THE FALLEN LEAF WITH TREMBLING HAND. SHE HELD IT UP SO THE MOONLIGHT ILLUMINATED THE HEAVY SCRAWL. THE WORDS WRITTEN THERE CHOKED IN HER THROAT...

Weird Science No. 21 (September-October 1953):

This issue contained Ray Bradbury's classic "Punishment Without Crime," a thought-provoking tale whose ending was, and still is, open for legal debate. The story centered around the perplexing court trial of a man who killed an illegally manufactured marionette that was a duplicate of his girlfriend, in fact the marionette was in many respects more human than the real person. The fact that the victim was not a human being was unimportant; the crucial point hinged on the accused man's frame of mind when he committed the act. And based on that point, he was found guilty of murder in the first degree and convicted!

This issue also featured "Two's Company" illustrated by the team of Al Williamson and Frank Frazetta. This was a superbly drawn story about a man marooned on an isolated planetoid who fell in love with an attractive female inhabitant without realizing she was just a figment of his imagination.

Weird Science No. 22 (November-December 1953):

The last issue! Early in 1954 this title was merged with *Weird Fantasy* and the two became *Weird Science-Fantasy* and published as issue No. 23 (March 1954). The new title ran for six issues and then was terminated at No. 29 (June 1955). It was later revived as *Incredible Science Fiction* which ran for four issues, and was then terminated altogether in January 1956. In addition to other Ray Bradbury stories, the new magazine included comic book adaptations of Otto Binder's "Adam Link" series which had originally appeared in *Amazing Stories* during the early 1940s. (Adam Link was the famous robot who earned the right to be acknowledged as a human being.)

Weird Fantasy No. 13 (May-June 1950)
©1978 by William M. Gaines

Amazing Stories (Aug. 1926)
©1926 Experimeter Publishing Co.

Weird Fantasy, the sister comic book of *Weird Science* made its debut in May 1950. The first issue featured "Am I Man or Machine?", a story illustrated by Al Feldstein and adapted from the once famous science fiction novelette "The Talking Brain" by M. H. Hasta, and first published in *Amazing Stories* in August 1926. At the time the story appeared, man's knowlege of medical science was limited, and "The Talking Brain" was considered important enough to take cover precedence over two other classics by G. G. Wells and Jules Verne that were included in the same issue. In addition, this story was introduced by a brief article by Dr. Flexner, a surgeon and university medical instructor, who explained that under certain conditions it was theoretically possible to maintain life in organic tissue that was separated from its body.

The story concerned the crushed victim of a car accident. Although nothing could be done to save the victim's body, his head was carefully removed and his brain miraculously kept alive by a team of scientists. Al Feldstein's cover for *Weird Fantasy No. 13* effectively depicted this unusual tale, the first of its kind to provide comprehensive medical directions for reconstructing a man with a completely artificial body. The tragic story concluded when the mechanically remade victim returned to his sweetheart "Butterfly"—only to leave her with the impression he was a stranger after realizing he, as a living machine, could never give her his love.

Weird Fantasy No. 20 (July-Aug. 1953)
©1978 by William M. Gaines

Weird Fantasy also featured adaptations of other Ray Bradbury's stories. "There Will Come Soft Rains," illustrated by Wally Wood, appeared in Issue 17 (January-February 1953). The next two issues carried adaptations of Bradbury's "Zero Hour" and "King of The Grey Spaces." Then came *Weird Fantasy No. 20* with the cover scene depicting the deteriorated rocket ship that was featured in Bradbury's rarest classic "I, Rocket."

At the time *Weird Fantasy No. 20* was published it was virtually unknown that "I, Rocket" happened to have been Bradbury's very first story of science fiction. When "I, Rocket" was first published in *Amazing Stories,* May 1944, it was hailed as a literary innovation because the story was narrated by the sensory perceptions of an electronic instrument system in an inanimate rocket ship.

However, the pulp literature of 1944 was overshadowed by the hard news of national and international events and *Amazing Stories* as well as all other magazines suffered limited readership during this period. "I, Rocket" was forgotten a few months after it appeared, never to be reprinted again until its appearance in *Weird Fantasy No. 20* almost ten years later. This literary classic was turned into a classic work of art by Al Williamson.

"I, Rocket," Bradbury's first, as illustrated by Williamson at his best, is reprinted here in part, with the permission of E. C. Publications.

I, ROCKET

AT THE RATE THINGS ARE COMING AND GOING, IT'LL TAKE A FEW HUNDRED YEARS TO BREAK ME DOWN INTO RUST AND CORROSION... MAYBE LONGER. IN THE MEANTIME, I'LL HAVE MANY DAYS AND NIGHTS TO THINK IT OVER. YOU CAN'T STOP ATOMS FROM REVOLVING AND HUMMING THEIR LIFE-ORBITS INSIDE METAL. THAT'S HOW METAL LIVES ITS OWN SPECIAL LIFE. THAT'S HOW METAL THINKS. WHERE I LIE IS A BARREN, PEBBLED PLATEAU, WITH PALE, WEEDY GROWTHS AND A FEW HUNCHED TREES COMING UP OUT OF PLANETOID ROCK. THERE'S A WIND COMES OVER THE PLATEAU EVERY MORNING. THERE'S RAIN COMES IN THE TWILIGHT, AND A SILENCE COMES DOWN EVEN CLOSER IN THE NIGHT. THAT'S MY WHOLE LIFE, NOW... LYING HERE WITH MY JETS TWISTED AND MY FORE-PLATES BASHED...

AL WILLIAMSON

BUT WHILE I'M RUSTING AND WONDERING, I CAN THINK IT ALL OVER... HOW I CAME TO BE HERE, HOW I CAME TO BE BUILT...

ADAPTED FROM A TALE BY
RAY BRADBURY

I WAS A WAR ROCKET. MY BIRTH-PERIOD, AND THE BASE WHERE I WAS INTEGRATED... SKELETON, SKIN, AND INNARDS... WENT THROUGH THE USUAL BIRTH-PAINS. IT IS A DIM PORTION IN MY MEMORY, BUT WHEN THE FINAL HULL WAS MELTED TO ME, THE AWARENESS WAS THERE, A *METAL* AWARENESS. I COULD THINK, BUT TELL NOBODY THAT I THOUGHT...

FORE AND AFT THEY PLACED THEIR SPACE-ARTILLERY NOZZLES, AND WEIGHTED ME WITH SCARLET AMMUNITION. I BEGAN TO FEEL MY PURPOSE, EXPECTANTLY, PERHAPS A BIT IMPATIENTLY. MEN HUSTLED IN AND OUT OF ME WITH SMALL RUBBER-TIRED TRUCKS BEARING EXPLOSIVES. THE MUNITIONS-LIEUTENANT PRODDED THEM...

HURRY IT UP! HURRY IT UP! SKIP! WE'VE GOT A *WAR* TO MEET.

COPYRIGHT, 1944, BY RAY BRADBURY

THEN THERE WAS SOME FANCY BUSINESS ABOUT A CHRISTENING. SOME OFFICIAL'S DAUGHTER CRASHED A BOTTLE OF FOAMING LIQUOR ON MY PROW. A FEW REPORTERS FLICKED THEIR CAMERAS. AND A SMALL CROWD PUT UP THEIR HANDS, WAVED THEM, AND PUT THEM DOWN, AS IF THEY REALIZED HOW STUPID IT REALLY WAS WASTING THAT FINE CHAMPAGNE...

AND THEN I SAW THE CAPTAIN, METAL BLESS HIM, FOR THE FIRST TIME. HE CAME RUNNING ACROSS THE FIELD, THE MASTER OF MY FATE... THE CAPTAIN OF MY SOUL. I LIKED HIM RIGHT OFF. HE STOMPED ABOARD AND CRACKED OUT ORDERS...

SNAP IT! GET RID OF THAT DAME, AND THOSE REPORTERS OUT THERE. CLEAR THE APRON! SEAL THE LOCKS! CLAMP PORTS! WE'RE PUSHING THE BLAZES OUT OF HERE!

THEY RAPPED ME TIGHT. THEY EXPELLED THE CROWD. SIRENS SHOUTED ACROSS THE BASE APRON. THE CREW DID THINGS TO MY ALIMENTARY CANAL. THE CAPTAIN SHOUTED. THAT WAS THE SLAP ON MY BACK THAT BROUGHT ME MY FIRST BREATH, MY FIRST SOUND, MY FIRST MOVEMENT. MY CAPTAIN POUNDED ME INTO LIVING...

I THREW OUT WINGS OF FIRE AND SMOKE. SUDDENLY I WASN'T METAL LYING IN THE SUN ANY MORE. I WAS THE BIGGEST DARN BIRD THAT EVER SANG INTO THE SKY. MAYBE MY VOICE WASN'T ANYTHING BUT THUNDER, BUT IT WAS STILL SINGING TO ME. I SANG LOUD AND I SANG LONG...

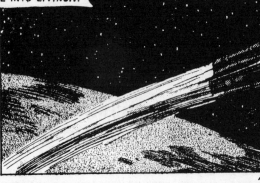

IT WAS THE FIRST TIME I'D SEEN THE WORLD. I WAS SURPRISED TO FIND THAT IT WAS ROUND...

YES, I LIKED MY CAPTAIN. HIS NAME WAS LAMB...IRONIC FOR A MAN LACKING LAMB-LIKE QUALITIES. CAPTAIN LAMB SAT IN MY CONTROL ROOM, CRACKING HIS KNUCKLES...

YES. SHE'S A GOOD SHIP! A FINE SHIP! WE'LL POUND THE HOLY MARROW OUT OF THOSE MARTIANS.

THE YOUNG MAN NAMED CONRAD SAT BESIDE THE CAPTAIN AT THE DUO-CONTROLS...

WE'D BETTER. THERE'S A GIRL WAITING IN YORK PORT FOR US TO COME BACK.

US! BOTH OF YOU? YOU AND HILLARY?

THE TWO OF US. BOTH ON THE SAME WAR-ROCKET. AT LEAST I CAN KEEP MY EYE ON HIM. I'LL KNOW HE'S NOT DOWN THERE SCUDDING ALONG ON MY ACCELERATION...

SPACE IS A FUNNY PLACE TO TALK ABOUT LOVE. IT'S LIKE LAUGHING OUT LOUD IN A BIG CATHEDRAL...TRYING TO MAKE A WALTZ OUT OF A HYMN.

2

THEY WERE *PART* OF ME... *LAMB* AND *CONRAD* AND THE *CREW*. LIKE *BLOOD CORPUSCLES* PULSING IN THE ARTERIES OF A *WARM BODY*. AND LIKE *ANY* BODY, THERE WERE *MICROBES* TOO. *DESTROYING* ELEMENTS. THEIR NAMES WERE *LARION* AND *BELLOC*...

NOW AS FAR AS *KILLING* LAMB GOES... THAT'S *OUT!* WE'RE ONLY *TWO* AGAINST THE *REST*. I WANT TO COLLECT THAT *MONEY* WE'RE GUARANTEED...

SO DO I! THEN WE HIT THE *ENGINES*, EH, LARION?

A *WELL-PLACED TIME BOMB* SHOULD WORK *MIRACLES* WITH THE *MAIN JET-ENGINE*. AND WHEN IT *HAPPENS*, WE CAN BE *OUT* AND *AWAY IN SPACE* IN *PLENTY* OF TIME.

SEEMS A *SHAME*. NICE NEW ROCKET, NEVER *TESTED* BEFORE. AND IT ALL GOES *BOOM* BEFORE IT HAS *PROVEN* ITSELF...

DON'T GET *SENTIMENTAL*, BELLOC. YOU'RE GETTING *PAID* FOR IT. NOW HERE'S THE PLAN. THERE'S A CERTAIN AMOUNT OF *CONFUSION* DURING THE SH?FT CHANGE-OVER. *HALF* THE CREW'S *GROGGY*. THE *OTHER* HALF'S TOO *TIRED* TO *WORRY*. NOW, DURING THE *NEXT* CHANGE-OVER, WE'LL...

SELF-PRESERVATION IS AN ALL-ENCOMPASSING THING. YOU FIND IT IN METAL AS YOU FIND IT IN MEN. MY BODY WAS TO BE ATTACKED. FROM OUTSIDE I FEARED NOTHING. FROM INSIDE, I WAS UNCERTAIN. I DIDN'T APPROVE OF THE IDEA...

LARION. BELLOC. GOING BELOW? I'LL BE DOWN IN THIRTY MINUTES. WE'LL CHECK THE AUXILIARIES TOGETHER.

RIGHT, SIR.

C'MON, BELLOC.

LARION AND BELLOC WENT BELOW TO THEIR STATIONS. THE CHANGE-OVER PROCEEDED. THE POISON WAS IN MY HEART... WAITING...

DID YOU CHECK THE *LIFE-BOATS*, BELLOC?

NUMBER *THREE* BOAT'S READY TO *GO*. LET'S GET THIS *OVER* WITH...

MARS CAME UP AHEAD LIKE A RUDDY DROP OF DRIED BLOOD. THE WAR I'D NEVER SEEN BUT ALWAYS HEARD ABOUT WAS OUT THERE. I WANTED TO BE PART OF IT. I WANTED TO GET THERE WITH LAMB AND HILLARY AND CONRAD AND THE OTHERS. LARION CLIMBING RUNGS, ON HIS WAY TO GET THE TIME-BOMB, BELLOC, WAITING BELOW. TIME GETTING SHORTER... SHORTER...

I THOUGHT ABOUT CAPTAIN LAMB AND THE WAY HE BARKED ORDERS, ABOUT HILLARY AND CONRAD THINK-ING ABOUT A WOMAN'S LIPS, ABOUT BELLOC, WAITING. AND SUDDENLY... THERE WAS A *HISS*, AN *EXPLOSION*...

WHAT IN...!

GOOD LORD!

WHAT WAS THAT?

SOMEBODY SCREAMED. I KNEW *WHO* IT WAS AND *WHERE* IT WAS AND *WHAT* IT WAS...

3

286

WARNING BELLS CLAMORED THROUGH ME. CONRAD SCUTTLED DOWN THE RUNGS, YELLING. HE VANISHED TOWARD THE ENGINE ROOM...

IT'S DOWN THERE...

HILLARY GRABBED THE SHIP'S CONTROLS AND FROZE THEM, LISTENING AND WAITING. HE SAID ONE WORD...

ALICE...

THE CAPTAIN GOT THERE FIRST. HE TOOK ONE LOOK AND SCREAMED...

CUT THE FEED VALVE... FOR GOD'S SAKE!

CONRAD GRASPED A VALVE-WHEEL GLINTING ON THE WALL, TWISTING IT, GRUNTING. THE LOUD GUSHING NOISE STOPPED. STEAM-CLOUDS BILLOWED IN MY HEART, WRAPPING CAPTAIN LAMP AND THE OTHERS TIGHT... MAKING THEM COUGH...

CHOKE... *WHAT HAPPENED...* *IT'S BELLOC...*

MY VACUUM VENTILATORS BEGAN HUMMING, CLEARING THE STEAM. THEY SAW BELLOC, LYING THERE. HE SAID NOT A WORD TO ANYBODY. HE JUST BLED WHERE THE EXPLODED OIL-PIPE HAD CAUGHT HIM ON THE NOSE AND CHEEK AND PLUNGED ON BACK INTO HIS BRAIN...

HE'S... DEAD.

I... I CAN'T UNDERSTAND IT. I CHECKED THOSE OIL-LINES THIS MORNING. THEY WERE OKAY! I DON'T SEE...

FOOTSTEPS ON THE RUNGS. LARION CAME DOWN. HE LOOKED AS IF SOMEBODY'D KICKED HIM IN THE STOMACH WHEN HE SAW BELLOC LYING THERE. HIS FACE SUCKED BONE-WHITE, STARING, HIS JAW DROPPED...

YOU.. YOU KILLED HIM! YOU FOUND OUT... FOUND OUT WHAT WE WERE GOING TO DO AND YOU KILLED HIM. WELL, I'LL SHOW YOU... *WHAT?*

LARION BEGAN TO LAUGH. HE DARTED ABOUT SUDDENLY AND LEAPED UP THE LADDER RUNGS...

I'LL SHOW YOU... *STOP HIM...*

CONRAD RUSHED UP THE LADDER AT LARION'S HEELS. CAPTAIN LAMB WATCHED THEM GO, LISTENING TO THE FADING FEET ON THE RUNGS, GOING UP AND UP...

WATCH IT...

A FEW MINUTES LATER, CONRAD CAME BACK DOWN THE LADDER. HE HELD UP THE TIME-BOMB...

IT'S A GOOD THING THAT OIL-PIPE *BURST*, CAP. LARION TRIED TO *HIDE* THIS IN SUPPLY. IT'S A *BOMB*. HE AND *BELLOC*...

WHAT *ABOUT* LARION?

HE TRIED TO ESCAPE THROUGH AN EMERGENCY LIFE-BOAT AIR-LOCK. THE FOOL WAS IN TOO MUCH OF A HURRY. HE OPENED THE OUTER DOOR TOO SOON AND WAS SUCKED OUT INTO SPACE. HE'S GONE FOR GOOD...

THE CAPTAIN LOOKED PUZZLED...

THAT'S FUNNY. HE *KNEW* HOW THOSE AIR LOCKS WORK. HE *WOULDN'T* HAVE MADE SUCH A *STUPID* MISTAKE. IT...IT MUST HAVE BEEN AN *ACCIDENT*...OR... OR...*SOMETHING ELSE!*

MY BODY WAS CLEANSED. THE ORGANIC POISON WAS ELIMINATED. MARS WAS VERY CLOSE NOW. RED. *BRIGHT* RED. IN ANOTHER SIX HOURS WE WOULD BE ENGAGED IN COMBAT...

I HAD MY TASTE OF WAR. WE DROVE DOWN, CAPTAIN LAMB AND THE MEN INSIDE ME, AND I PUT OUT MY ARMS FOR THE FIRST TIME, AND I CLOSED MY FINGERS OF POWER AROUND MARTIAN SHIPS...FIFTEEN OF THEM...

I SCREAMED. I TALKED TO THE STARS. I DISSECTED MARTIAN ROCKETS WITH QUICK CALM STROKES OF MY RAY-ARMS. AND SPUNKY LITTLE CAP LAMB GUIDED MY VITALS, SWEARING AT THE TOP OF HIS LUNGS...

LET'S GO, YOU DIRTY ◎#⨯?!!S! LET'S KNOCK 'EM OUT OF THE UNIVERSE!

5.

ONE DAY CONRAD COLLAPSED UPON THE CONTROL DECK WITH A SHARD OF SHRAPNEL WEBBED IN HIS LUNGS...

AND IT WAS HILLARY WHO TOOK THE NEWS BACK TO YORK PORT, TO THE GIRL THEY BOTH LOVED...

AND OTHERS OF THE CREW DIED WITHIN ME, THEIR BLOOD SPILLING OUT UPON MY DECK PLATES, WARM AND THICK. SLOP, THE COOK, AYRES, THE NAVIGATOR...

WE KNOCKED HOLES IN THE VACUUM. WE GOT WHAT WE WANTED OUT OF WAR, AND THEN... QUITE SUDDENLY ONE DAY... SPACE WAS SILENT. CAPTAIN LAMB SHRUGGED HIS SHOULDERS...

WELL, MEN. IT'S ALL OVER. THE WAR'S OVER... THIS SHIP IS BEING CONVERTED INTO A CARGO-FREIGHTER...

THE CREW MUTTERED, SHIFTING THEIR FEET...

IT'S BEEN GOOD, I WON'T DENY IT. I HAD A FINE CREW AND A SWEET SHIP. WE WORKED HARD. WE DID WHAT WE HAD TO DO. AND NOW IT'S ALL OVER. WE HAVE PEACE.

PEACE. IT MEANS GETTING DRUNK AGAIN... LIVING ON EARTH AGAIN. IT MEANS FORGETTING HOW FREE-FALL FEELS ON YOUR GUTS. IT MEANS LOSING FRIENDS. AND IT MEANS LEAVING THIS ROCKET...

WE LANDED IN YORK PORT WITHOUT FANFARE. THE CREW PACKED THEIR DUFFLE BAGS AND LEFT. CAPTAIN LAMB LINGERED AWHILE, WALKING THROUGH ME, SWEARING UNDER HIS BREATH...

...AND AFTER A WHILE, HE LEFT TOO...

I WASN'T A WAR-ROCKET ANYMORE. THEY CRAMMED ME WITH CARGO AND SHIPPED ME BACK AND FORTH TO VENUS FOR THE NEXT FIVE YEARS. I HAD A NEW CAPTAIN AND A STRANGE CREW AND A STRANGE PEACEFUL ROUTINE COMING AND GOING ACROSS THE STARS...

6

After many cargo flights, the rocket, whose mechanical sensors still continued to think, had finally seen its day and was abandoned on an isolated planetoid. She began to rust and her seams showed signs of cracking. As the internal mechanisms gradually began to crumble under the silent winds and rains, her ability to think started to falter in a manner very similar to a human whose mind grows senile after living for more than a century. It could only lay there like a helpless metal child, recalling the good old days when she served as a mighty war-rocket for Captain Lamb and his crew. But with each passing night, those memories also grew weaker.

The rocket knew she was dying!

Then one day, she saw a silver speck fleeting across the sky; a spaceship was approaching and eventually landed nearby. The pilot climbed out and walked over to the airlock; the rocket could sense the pilot stepping inside of her—and she experienced a strange sensation when she heard the voice of Captain Lamb calling out to himself how happy he was to have finally located his favorite ship. Captain Lamb swore to get a repair crew there as soon as possible, to put the rocket back in shape again. A complete overhaul was necessary—*there was another war to be won!*

Here is the opening scene of "I, Rocket" as it appeared in *Amazing Stories* . . .

I, ROCKET

A thing of steel and alloy—a rocket ship. Yet it claimed respect and gave a great enduring loyalty

Illustrated by Brady

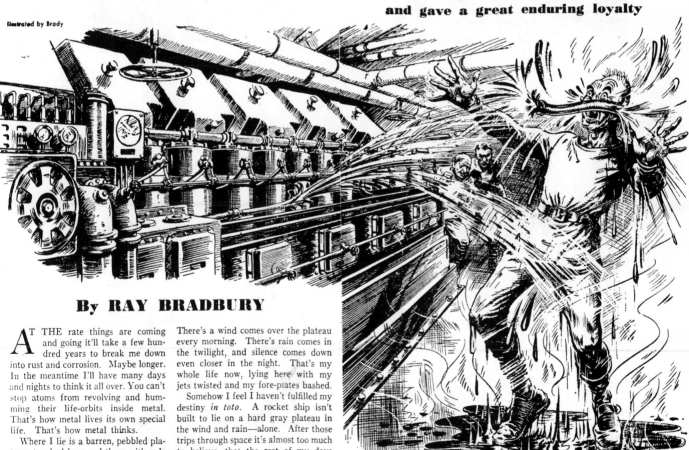

Gushing oil followed the flying length of pipe as Belloc reeled back

By RAY BRADBURY

AT THE rate things are coming and going it'll take a few hundred years to break me down into rust and corrosion. Maybe longer. In the meantime I'll have many days and nights to think it all over. You can't stop atoms from revolving and humming their life-orbits inside metal. That's how metal lives its own special life. That's how metal thinks.

Where I lie is a barren, pebbled plateau, touched here and there with pale weedy growths, a few hunched trees coming up out of planetoid rock.

There's a wind comes over the plateau every morning. There's rain comes in the twilight, and silence comes down even closer in the night. That's my whole life now, lying here with my jets twisted and my fore-plates bashed.

Somehow I feel I haven't fulfilled my destiny *in toto*. A rocket ship isn't built to lie on a hard gray plateau in the wind and rain—alone. After those trips through space it's almost too much to believe, that the rest of my days will be wasted here——

But while I'm rusting and wonder-

290

Weird Fantasy No. 8 (July-Aug. 1951)
©1978 by William M. Gaines

Weird Fantasy No. 10 (Nov.-Dec. 1951)
©1978 by William M. Gaines

Weird Fantasy No. 16 (Nov.-Dec. 1952)
©1978 by William M. Gaines

Weird Fantasy No. 21 (Sept.-Oct. 1953)
©1978 by William M. Gaines
(cover art by Frank Frazetta)

WEIRD FANTASY

The first bimonthly issue of *Weird Fantasy* began as No. 13 (May-June 1950) and continued the numbering sequence from *"A Moon, a Girl, Romance Comics."* The magazine included material similar to that of *Weird Science* and was illustrated by the same artists. After the first four issues, a new numbering sequence was introduced with the fifth issue as *Weird Fantasy No. 5* (January-February 1951).

Weird Fantasy No. 6 (March-April 1951):
The contents included "Space-Warp" illustrated by Al Feldstein, "The Dimension Translator" by Harvey Kurtzman, "Rescued" by Wally Wood, and "And Then There Were Two" by Jack Kamen.

Weird Fantasy No. 7 (May-June 1951):
The contents included "7-Year-Old Genius" by Al Feldstein, "Come Into My Parlor" by Jack Kamen, "Across the Sun" by George Roussos, and "Breakdown" by Wally Wood.

Weird Fantasy No. 8 (July-August 1951):
The contents included "Origins of the Species," the last story illustrated by Al Feldstein for this magazine, and centered upon a speculative concept on the evolution of mankind. Other stories were "It Didn't Matter" by Jack Kamen, "The Slave Ship" by George Roussos, and "Enemies of the Colony" by Wally Wood.

Wood's story concerned an Earth colony which had settled on a distant planet and were eventually devoured by tiny creatures that at first appeared to be as friendly and as harmless as rabbits.

Weird Fantasy No. 9 (September-October 1951):
This issue contained Wally Wood's adaptation of the classic "Spawn of Mars." The story concerned the first Mars expedition which included a lady astronaut, Jean Belmont, who fell in love with the team's navigator Dr. Fairbanks. While on Mars, the crew ran afoul of a monstrous life form that Fairbanks supposedly killed, but in reality it was the other way around. The monster killed Fairbanks and took his place by the use of hypnotic illusion. When the crew returned to Earth, Jean and the monster she assumed to be Dr. Fairbanks were married. The truth emerged the following year when the two were involved in a car accident. Jean's husband was killed and the hypnotic screen faded away, revealing the body of the loathsome, disgusting Martian creature. Jean became hysterical and was taken to the hospital for treatment—where she learned that she was pregnant!

Weird Fantasy No. 10 (November-December 1951):
The major contents included "Secret of Saturn's Ring," an action space adventure, and "The Mutants," both illustrated by Wally Wood. "Mutants" followed the same theme as "The Loathsome." Other entries in this issue were "Timely Shock!" by Jack Kamen and "Not On The Menu" by Joe Orlando.

Weird Fantasy No. 11 (January-February 1952):
This issue contained an autobiography of Al Feldstein, and an interesting tale entitled "Two-Century Journey" illustrated by Wally Wood. This story centered around mankind's problem of overpopulation. The solution to the problem was a mass exodus to a distant star in search of another planet. After landing on what seemed to be the ideal world, the Earth travellers met the friendly inhabitants only to learn that they too had an overpopulation problem and that a great number of them had already made a mass exodus to Earth.

Wood's second entry here was "The 10th at Noon," a credible story about a team of meteorologists who were unconcerned about the threat of atomic war as they perfected a camera system for photographing weather conditions as they existed in the future. The team used this technique for making accurate weather forecasts—until they developed a picture showing New York destroyed by the mushroom cloud of a hydrogen bomb explosion on the tenth at noon.

Other stories included "Shrinking From Abuse" by Jack Kamen and "The Thing in the Jar" by Joe Orlando.

©1978 by William M. Gaines

Weird Fantasy No. 14 (July-August 1952):

The contents included "The Exile," the last story that Wally Wood illustrated for *Weird Fantasy*, and "Mad Journey," the first story that Al Williamson illustrated for this magazine. Another entry was Jack Kamen's adaptation of "Close Call," a last-woman-on-Earth theme in which a lonely miss, the only living person in the world to have survived an atomic holocaust, heard her telephone ring—only to have the caller hang up when she picked up the receiver.

Weird Fantasy No. 15 (September-October 1952):

This issue contained three stories illustrated by Al Williamson, two of which introduced an experimental story-telling technique that had been used occasionally in earlier science fiction pulps—a single plot with alternate endings. The story of the first version, "Quick Trip," concerned a journey to a nearby star where the travellers got fouled up in the time plane and reached their destination fifty-five years after the star had exploded and destroyed its solar system. "Quick Trip" was followed by a second version of the same journey entitled "Long Trip." Here the travellers reached their destination safe and sound in accordance with their thirty-year flight schedule. After landing on the planet Pollux they were greeted by Earthmen who told them the world had been colonized seventeen years earlier; the invention of a space overdrive system reduced star travel to a mere two days.

Weird Fantasy No. 16 (November-December 1952):

This issue featured Al Williamson's "Skeleton Key," a unique story about an archeological team who uncovered the fossil remains of a prehistoric mammal with a human skull inside its ribs. Stunned at the finding that suggested the mammal, which existed millions of years before man, could have devoured a human during a period when man did not exist, the archeologists made a careful survey of the grounds they were digging. They ran into another group of scientists who by coincidence were testing a newly built time machine in the same isolated area. The time travellers told the archeologists how they had journeyed into the past back to the beginning of Earth but had unfortunately lost one of their members who was eaten alive by a ferocious beast. After a gruesome battle with the beast which they eventually killed with grenades, the time travellers returned to the present.

Upon a close examination of the skull, the archeologists realized it was the lost time traveller from the 20th century.

Other contents included "What He Saw!" by Jack Kamen, and two short stories by Joe Orlando.

Weird Fantasy No. 17 (January-February 1953):

The adaptation of the Ray Bradbury classics began in this issue, starting with "There Will Come Soft Rains" illustrated by Wally Wood. Set in the early 21st century after mankind was destroyed by atomic fallout, the story concerned an empty city whose automatic machines continued their normal programmed functions as dictated by the recorded tape of a "voice-clock" which called out the hourly assignments. A look into one typical home revealed that its machines were following the daily schedule of preparing the dehydrated meals for their human masters, setting the table, clearing the table the following hour, washing the dishes, changing the bed linen, cleaning the house, watering the lawn, and a host of similar household tasks. At the story's climax the automatic fire alarm went off and the sprinkler robots of each building joined together to battle the raging flames that threatened to destroy the city. But the fire was too large and the city was reduced to ruins. Only the voice-clock in the remains of one house remained intact; it continued calling out the hourly routines even though there were no more machines to heed its commands and, of course, no more people who required the machines. Finally the recording apparatus inside the voice-clock became damaged; it kept repeating, "Today is August 5, 2026 . . . Today is August 5, 2026 . . ."

©1978 by William M. Gaines

Other contents included "The Aliens" illustrated by Al Williamson, "Ahead of The Game!" by Bill Elder, and "In The Beginning," an interesting concept on the evolution of the species illustrated by Joe Orlando.

Weird Fantasy No. 18 (March-April 1953):

The contents included Bradbury's classic "Zero Hour" illustrated by Jack Kamen. Here the children of the world played a new and unusual game and innocently paved the way for a Martian invasion of Earth.

"Homesick" was an artistic masterpiece by Al Williamson who vividly captured a moment of passion between two people desparately in love.

©1978 by William M. Gaines

However, the adaptation of "Judgment Day," illustrated by Joe Orlando, was the milestone epic appearing in this issue. The story concerned astronaut Tarlton who visited Cybrinia, a distant world colonized entirely by robots which humans of previous generations had built to develop and manufacture themselves as an independent government. Tarlton was there to inspect the progress of the robot society and determine if it was advanced enough to be admitted to the Galactic Republic as an extension of Earth.

©1978 by William M. Gaines

As Tarlton toured the cities, he discovered that the mechanical society was manufacturing itself into a caste system: there were the orange robots which had all the superior advantages of an elite class of citizens, and blue robots that were restricted to menial labor assignments and totally lacking the technologies and luxuries of the elite orange citizens.

Black astronaut Tarlton, the official star representative of Earth decided that Cybrinia was still in a primitive stage and not yet ready to become part of the Galactic Republic. He climbed in his spacecraft and returned home.

©1978 by William M. Gaines

Weird Fantasy No. 19 (May-June 1953):

This issue contained an autobiography of artist Al Williamson, Ray Bradbury's "King of Grey Spaces," a story which concerned cadet training at the Space Academy, "Brain-Child" illustrated by Williamson, a story along the theme of "I, Rocket," and "Time For A Change," a unique time-twister illustrated by Joe Orlando who also produced the cover art.

Weird Fantasy No. 20 (July-August 1953):
The famous Ray Bradbury "I, Rocket" issue.

Weird Fantasy No. 21 (September-October 1953):
The contents included Ray Bradbury's "Million Year Picnic" illustrated by Severin and Elder. The story was a brief excerpt from Bradbury's "Martian Chronicles" in which the children of the first space colony settlers explored the surface of the planet in search of Martians and finally realized that, upon glancing down at their own reflections in the water, *they* were the new Martians.

Weird Fantasy No. 22 (November-December 1953):
The last issue! *Weird Fantasy* merged with *Weird Science.*

And then there was *Mad!*—the forerunner of the currently popular magazine that began as a comic book of satire about other comics. The first bimonthly issue (October-November 1953) featured the stylized humor of artist Harvey Kurtzman whose work pre-viously appeared in the early issues of *Weird Science* and *Weird Fantasy.* Kurtzman's *Mad* art was entirely different. Beginning with the first issue, he introduced a mysterious and zany character called "Melvin," but tactfully avoided showing him completely.

Mad Comics No. 1 (Oct.-Nov. 1952)
©1952 by E.C. Publications, Inc.

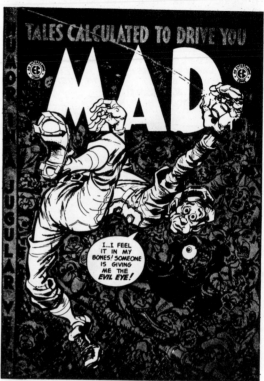

Mad Comics No. 2 (Dec.-Jan. 1953)
©1952 by E.C. Publications, Inc.

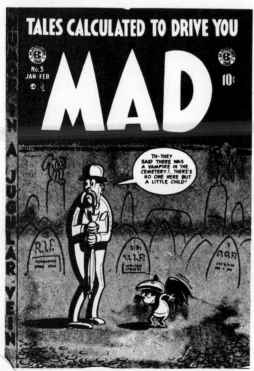

Mad Comics No. 3 (Feb.-Mar. 1953)
©1953 by E.C. Publications, Inc.

Mad Comics No. 4 (April-May 1953)
©1953 by E.C. Publications, Inc.

Melvin's true identity was not revealed until *Mad No. 5* where, in a rare editorial, he was finally exposed as the "mad" *Mad* publisher William M. Gaines! Yet Melvin had another identity which would come to light in a later issue.

Kurtsman's second *Mad* creation was the one and only Shadowskeedee Boom-Boom, a character spoof on the Shadow, the popular crimefighter of early pulp fiction, radio drama, and Street and Smith comic books. Shadowskeedee is the little guy on the cover of *Mad No. 4* and is shown here as he challenges his arch rival "Manduck" to a duel of hypnotic power.

One thing that gets us about the cartoon world is . . . you have these strong guys! . . No matter what happens . . . no matter how bad things are . . . no matter what . . . who . . . how . . . who . . . who . . . how . . . ha . . . who . . . ha . . . who . . . who-ha. . . . These guys wind up being the strongest! . . . Like forinstance . . take this guy . .

POOPEYE!

We've decided that the trouble with The Comics today is that they just ain't got no literary value! Things might have been a lot different if they'd started off right in the first place. We're convinced that comics would be considered high-class reading matter if only they'd hired some famous authors, poets and playwrights to handle the actual writing. So, if you have a strong stomach, keep reading and see what would've happened

IF FAMOUS AUTHORS WROTE THE COMICS

PICTURES BY WALLACE WOOD   **TEXT BY FRANK JACOBS**

©1959 by E.C. Publications, Inc.

If Tennessee Williams Wrote: LITTLE ORPHAN ANNIE

If Mickey Spillane Wrote: NANCY

If Paddy Chayefsky Wrote: DONALD DUCK

Mad No. 5 was one of the most controversial comic books of 1953.

During the early 1950s critics of comic books began attacking the sex, violence and sensationalism that were often essential ingredients of many of the comic books that flooded the market. Parents, educators, clergymen, and even policemen embarked on wide-ranging campaigns to get rid of what they considered "comic book trash." Newsstands and bookstores displaying comic books that were deemed unfit for children were often subject to police raids—and some comics were even confiscated and burned.

Ironically, the theme of *Mad No. 5* happened to be a satire on the sex and violence themes that the critics objected to. The theme was cleverly reflected in an unusual cover by Bill Elder that simultaneously depicted two different features that were contained in that issue: a satire on *Inner Sanctum Mysteries*, a popular radio program, and on *Martin Kane, Private Eye*, then a new television program.

But the cover also depicted a corpse with an ax and an arrow embedded in its skull plus four knives and a dart protuding from its chest. Something in a perambulator was drinking blood from a plasma bottle, and a man in the background was hanging a small girl by the neck.

Mad Comics No. 5 (June-July 1953)
©1954 by E.C. Publications, Inc.

The critics screamed in outrage—not only at the cover but at certain contents inside the book. They saw no humor in a scene like this from the satire on *Inner Sanctum Mysteries* . . .

Nor were they amused by these scenes from the takeoff on *Martin Kane, Private Eye* . . .

Mad Comics No. 20 (Feb. 1955)
©1954 by E.C. Publications, Inc.

Mad was probably the most ingenious comic book ever published, but its sense of the original occasionally backfired as in the case of *Mad No. 20*, February 1955. Here, the cover was designed to look like a student composition notebook so that, presumably, students could sneak the book into their schoolrooms to read during class. Unfortunately when it was released for newsstand circulation it was often mistaken for an actual composition book, and as a result it was not displayed on the racks with other comic books. Stores and dealers everywhere who handled hundreds of monthly magazines of all sorts plus other assorted merchandise unknowingly buried their copies of *Mad No. 20* in the warehouse with the school supplies! When the error was discovered during annual inventory checks it was too late to sell an eight-month-old comic book as a new issue. For the most part, all the *Mad* "notebooks" were discarded and destroyed.

The contents of this issue with its deceptive cover featured takeoffs on "The Katzenjammer Kids" and "Paul Revere." It also included Wally Wood's unique feature on "Sound Effects" and Jack Davis' classic satire of the "Cowboy," part of which is shown here.

COMPARISON DEPT.: DID' YOU EVER READ ANY AUTHENTIC STUFF ON THE OLD WILD WEST?... I MEAN REAL AUTHENTIC!... NEXT, DID YOU EVER COMPARE IT WITH THE MOVIE AND TELEVISION VERSION OF THE OLD WILD WEST? AIN'T IT A HOWL?... FOR INSTANCE, TO BE SPECIFIC, TAKE THE...

COWBOY!

FIRST OF ALL, IN MOVIES AND TELEVISION, THE COWBOY IS USUALLY NAMED SOMETHING LIKE... *LANCE STERLING!*... NOT THAT YOU'D MEET ONE GUY IN A HUNDRED WITH SUCH A NAME!...MAINLY PEOPLE HAVE NAMES LIKE... GEORGE FREEBLE... IGGY SIEDENHAM ... MELVIN POZNOWSKI...! COULD YOU EVER PICTURE A COWBOY HERO CALLED MELVIN POZNOWSKI?... SO HIS NAME IS LANCE STERLING!... AND HIS CLOTHES... OH BROTHER!... HAND TAILORED!... WITH GLOVES!... IN THE HOT SUN ALL DAY LONG, WITH GLOVES!... ANYBODY HERE EVER WEAR GLOVES IN THE HOT SUN ALL DAY LONG?... YOU BETCHA YOU DIDN'T! YOU'D GET A RASH AND YOUR HANDS WOULD ROT OFF!

NOW IN REAL LIFE... THE 100% GENUINE COWBOY HAD AN ORDINARY OLD NAME LIKE MAYBE... *JOHN SMURD!*...THEY'D HANG ANYBODY WITH A NAME LIKE LANCE STERLING! AND IF THEY COULD GROW THEM, MOST GENUINE COWBOYS HAD BIG WALRUS MUSTACHES WHICH WERE THE CUSTOM OF THE TIMES! CAN YOU IMAGINE ANYTHING MORE NAUSEATING THAN THE HOLLYWOOD COWBOY WITH SUCH A NAUSEATING MUSTACHE, GOING INTO A CLINCH WITH THE LEADING LADY?... NAUSEATING MAINLY SINCE THESE MUSTACHES OFTEN HAD TOBACCO JUICE SOAKED IN!... AS FOR CLOTHES... LET'S FACE IT! WHAT DO YOU HAVE TO WEAR TO TEND COWS BESIDE A GOOD PAIR OF BOOTS?

IN MOVIES... LANCE STERLING NEVER WORKS!
...HE RUNS FROM POSSES!...HE HAS FIST FIGHTS!
...HE SHOOTS IT OUT WITH THE BAD GUYS!...BUT
HE NEVER WORKS! NOW TELL ME HOW CAN A
GUY SUPPORT HIMSELF IF HE NEVER WORKS?

OLD JOHN SMURD WORKED LIKE A HORSE!
HIS HORSE WORKED LIKE OLD JOHN SMURD!
THERE WASN'T NO COWBOY UNION THEN!
WHO HAD TIME FOR RUNNING FROM POSSES?
WHO HAD TIME FOR SHOOTING IT OUT WITH BAD GUYS?

LANCE STERLING ALWAYS HAS PLENTY TIME
FOR TROUBLE...AND IS USUALLY SOME NO-GOOD-
NICK HANGING AROUND WITH A THIN BLACK
MUSTACHE AND A BLACK HAT! EVERY TIME... A
THIN BLACK MUSTACHE AND A BLACK HAT...

AS FOR VILLIANS IN JOHN SMURD'S TIME...
ONLY A GIGOLO FURRINER'D WEAR A THIN
BLACK MUSTACHE! VILLIAN'S MUSTACHE IN JOHN
SMURD'S TIME (EXCEPT MAYBE FOR SMELL)
WAS JUST LIKE JOHN SMURD'S MUSTACHE!

NOW IN THE MOVIES
WHEN THE HERO PULLS
HIS GUN, HERE'S WHERE
THE REAL PHONEY
BALONEY BEGINS!

OLD LANCE STERLING,
SIMPLE COWPOKE,
WHIPS OUT HIS GUN
LIKE THE CIRCUS
TRICK SHOOTER!

JOHN SMURD DIDN'T
HAVE MUCH EQUIPMENT
AND HAD TO DRAG HIS
SHOOTING IRON OUT OF
HIS SHIRT OR PANTS POCKET!

...MAIN THING WAS TO
HAVE RIGID ARM...STEADY
EYE...OR IN OTHER WORDS,
MAIN THING WAS NOT
TO BE SCAIRT.

THE WAY LANCE FANS OFF SIX SHOTS IN ¼ OF A SECOND... HE'D HAVE TO PRACTICE FIVE HOURS A DAY!

NOW I DON'T CARE IF YOU'RE ANNIE OAKLEY! YOU *GOT* TO MISS YOUR TARGET *SOME-TIMES!*...NOT OLD LANCE!

NOW GET THIS!... HERE'S THIS VILLIAN WHO'S JUST TRIED TO MURDER LANCE... JUST TRIED TO *MURDER* HIM... I ASK YOU... WHAT DOES LANCE DO?... OLD LANCE *THROWS HIS GUN AWAY AND GOES TO FIGHT THE VILLIAN FAIR FIST-FIGHT STYLE!*

JOHN SMURD... HIS VILLIAN, MIGHT'VE BEEN NERVOUS AND MISSED HIM WITH ALL SIX SHOTS! OLD JOHN MIGHT'VE THROWN HIS GUN AWAY TOO... ONLY THE REASON HE'D THROWN IT WAS BECAUSE HE WAS TRYING TO BUST THE VILLIAN'S HEAD OPEN!

NOW COMES THE FIST-FIGHT! HERE THIS GUY HAS JUST TRIED TO MURDER HIM... LANCE STERLING COMES OUT FIGHTING WITH ONLY FISTS ALLOWED! NATURALLY, VILLIAN BUSTS HIM ON THE HEAD WITH A NEARBY ARMCHAIR!

NOW IF JOHN SMURD GOT HIT WITH AN ARMCHAIR ...YOU THINK THAT CHAIR WOULD FLY TO FLINDERS LIKE THEM HOLLYWOOD BALSA-WOOD CHAIRS? THAT CHAIR WOULDN'T FLY TO FLINDERS! MORE THAN LIKELY, JOHN SMURD'D FLY TO FLINDERS!

CRUNK!

When complaints poured in to the E-C office from irate fans claiming they could not find *Mad No. 20* anywhere on the newsstands, the next few issues carried this advertisement for subscription orders.

IF YOU HAVEN'T BEEN ABLE TO FIND 'MAD' ON YOUR LOCAL NEWSSTAND...

Ⓐ Look harder! It may be at the bottom of the pile...

or...Ⓑ Ask your dealer to send threatening letters to his wholesaler, demanding *MAD*...

or...Ⓒ Send the attached subscription coupon which gets you 60¢ worth of comic books for 75¢...

or...Ⓓ Give up the whole business and spend your dime on something worth while!

MAIL THIS COUPON TO:
ENTERTAINING COMICS GROUP
225 LAFAYETTE STREET, ROOM 706
NEW YORK 12, NEW YORK

Please send me the next six issues of *MAD* (mailed in strong manila envelopes) for which I enclose 75¢.

NAME

ADDRESS

CITY   ZONE   STATE

Mad No. 23 (May 1955) was the last issue—as a comic book!

In July 1955, Issue 24 marked the beginning of the new *Mad Magazine* with Harvey Kurtzman as its art director. The satirical content was expanded in all directions, from sports and politics to business and science, and while it still contained illustrated features, the contents was basically straight text material.

And the following picture of the new Melvin appeared for the first time!

©1955 by E.C. Publications, Inc.

Mad Magazine No. 24 (July 1955)
©1955 by E.C. Publications, Inc.

Melvin also appeared as one of the panel experts in a feature article on space travel.

DR. X. FLINE SAUCER   CAPT. BUCK ROGER   MELVIN COZNOWSKI   COMMDR. ZORK ARGH

SCIENTISTS ANSWER IN LIGHT OF POSITIVE PROOF OF MAN'S CONQUEST OF FLIGHT AND EVIDENCE OF MAN'S ABILITY TO EXPLORE OUTER SPACE: IN OTHER WORDS . . . NO!

©1955 by E.C. Publications, Inc.

Although later issues always carried Melvin's picture, they never referred to his name, only his famous motto: "What? Me worry?" Melvin began appearing on the cover and was eventually adopted as the identifying character-logo for *Mad Magazine*. During the 1960s, he became Alfred E. Neuman!

Mad Magazine also underwent changes on its staff. Harvey Kurtzman, who had been instrumental in shaping the new format, left E-C Publications in 1958 to begin his own magazine called *Frenzy*, the first true competitor to *Mad*.

Exit Harvey Kurtzman, enter Don Martin . . .

DON MARTIN DEPT. PART II

Being both a member of the literati and the illiterati, Don Martin is familiar with the soul-searching torment

ON CHOOSING A BOOK

The basic ingredients of the supernatural . . .

©1978 by William M. Gaines

. . . highlighted a story category that dealt with such matters as pacts with the devil, reincarnation, voodooism and witchcraft, communicating with spirits of the dead, journeys into hell, vampire legends, possessed souls, plus numerous theories about afterlife, as well as confrontations between God and the Devil.

Inasmuch as the supernatural themes often ran contrary to many religious beliefs, they were never exploited in non-pulp mediums like the wild west or detective themes were. Hollywood played it safe, carefully limiting such films on the subject to Dracula-type fantasy. Early radio drama also tred lightly on the supernatural theme in such programs as *Inner Sanctum Mysteries, Lights Out,* and *The Whistler,* where evil was always punished or destroyed at the end. But even then critics voiced strong opposition to the "fright" programs, claiming they were psychologically harmful to children. *Inner Sanctum Mysteries,* popularized by its famous squeaking door, underwent heavy screening before the program was allowed on the air.

By contrast, early pulp literature explored the supernatural without limit. In such pulp magazines as *Weird Tales* and *Ghost Stories,* evil was treated as an awesome powerful force and not necessarily destroyed or punished in the end. For example, in a story in which the Devil possessed a man's soul and would not release him until he slew his loved one, the story, which focused upon the man's emotional torment, might have abruptly ended when he seized a butcher knife and plunged it into his wife's heart while she slept, and then sighed in relief that the Devil was gone. This particular theme had numerous variations. In other stories the wife was possessed, or the love of the husband and wife was strong enough to overcome the Devil's influence.

However, the few pulps specializing in this subject had faded away by the mid-1940s and the basic story themes lay dormant as a forbidden literary genre no one would touch.

In 1950, William Gaines dared to reopen the door to the supernatural realm and bring out a series of "fright comics" as part of the E-C New Trend series—not comics about monster fantasy, but illustrated story adaptions of previously published hard-core supernatural pulp fiction. *Haunt of Fear No. 15,* the first issue, represented one of three fright titles which began in May 1950 and ran bimonthly to December 1954. The other two were *Crypt of Terror* (later changed to *Tales From The Crypt* due to complaints by critics who objected to the word "terror" in a comic book title) and *Vault of Horror* (later changed to *Crime SuspenStories* due to complaints by the same critics who also objected to the word "horror." The three titles shocked the nation and made other comics exploiting sex and violence look like books of fairy tales!

Illustrated stories of the supernatural was something brand new. The stories that were presented often reflected themes from well-respected literary classics, but in a comic book format they were received and read quite differently! A twelve-year-old child, the typical comic book fan, looked upon fright comics as a fun thrill in much the same manner as riding a roller coaster. The adult critics, however, viewed the subject in a much different light.

While critics fumed at the 419 different crime comic books and the three E-C fright titles already in the market place, *Shock Suspenstories No. 1* made its debut in January 1952 as the fourth and most shocking fright title of them all. The critics promptly went to Congress about it, protesting, among other things, that comic books were entirely responsible for juvenile delinquency.

Senator Estes Kefauver, Democrat of Tennessee, promised he would take time out from his schedule to read some of the comic books in question.

In June 1953, a Senate subcommittee was formed under the chairmanship of Robert C. Hendrickson, then Republican of New Jersey, to investigate the critics' complaints. Supposedly, the subcommittee sat down every month to read comic books.

On April 21, 1954 after *Shock Suspenstories No. 14* had been released, William Gaines was called in to a Senate hearing.

Holding up a copy of the latest issue of *Shock Suspenstories*, Senator Kefauver asked Gaines if he considered the cover depicting an ax-wielding man holding aloft the severed head of a blond woman to be in good taste.

Gaines replied: "Yes, I do—for the cover of a horror comic. I think it would be in bad taste if he were holding the head a little higher so the neck would show with blood dripping from it."

Senator Kefauver pointed to the woman's face on the cover and commented, "You've shown blood dripping from the mouth."

The closed hearing continued for two days while several of the fright comics were reviewed. Thomas C. Hennings, a Missouri Democrat, pulled out a back issue of *Tales from The Crypt* to elaborate on one of the stories in which a possessed ten-year-old girl shot and killed her alcoholic father, then framed her stepmother and stepmother's boy friend who were ultimately tried, convicted, and executed for the murder. Gaines pointed out that the child had lived a miserable life throughout the story and triumphed in the end and that in fact the story was based on a *Weird Tales* classic written by the famous author O. Henry!

Then a rare file copy of *Mad No. 5* was brought out for discussion of its cover. Both sides expressed their views both pro and con. There were heated differences of opinion.

Subcommittee Director Richard Lendenen reported that various research studies had generally agreed that such comic books would not cause well-adjusted children to commit crimes. But, he added, they *might* have a harmful effect on disturbed children who appeared to be the most avid consumers.

Dr. Harris Peck, then Director of Mental Health Services for the Domestic Relations Court in Washington, testified that most of the 2,000 juvenile delinquents that came into the court's clinics each year did read such comic books and were most likely influenced by them.

Attorney Henry E. Shultz, legal counsel for the Association of Comics Magazine Publishers, insisted that to blame comic books for turning children into "little monsters" was a lot of rubbish.

Dr. Frederick Wertham, the most outspoken critic of comic books and author of *Seduction of the Innocent*, said that his studies of several thousand children had shown that any normal child was harmed by the crime and fright comics.

Gaines immediately blasted back, asserting that it would be just as difficult to explain the harmless thrill of a horror story to a Dr. Wertham as it would be to explain the sublimity of love to a frigid old maid! "The truth is," Gaines concluded, "that delinquency is a product of the real environment in which a child lives—and not the fiction he reads!"

When asked for an opinion, Walt Kelly, creator of the famous "Pogo" comic strip and also president of the National Cartoonists Society, conceded that the comic books in question could pose a danger, but added that he objected to any form of new censorship legislation that would restrict creativity.

After evaluating testimony from all sides, the Senate Subcommittee, overlooking Gaines' summation of the matter, concluded that some regulation was needed to control the content in comic books published for children. This decision led to the formation of the Comics Code Authority with censorship powers over comic book publishers.

The E-C line of titles was among the group of publications that the Code Authority flatly refused to give their Seal of Approval to. As a result, Gaines was forced to suspend his comic book line in mid-1955, and this marked the end of another milestone in the era of the Golden Age of Comics.

Haunt of Fear Comics No. 8 (July-Aug. 1951)
©1978 by William M. Gaines

Two Fisted Tales No. 18 (Nov.-Dec. 1950)
(First Issue) ©1978 by William M. Gaines

Haunt of Fear Comics No. 15 (May-June 1950)
(First Issue) ©1978 by William M. Gaines

ALPHABETICAL LISTING OF E-C COMIC BOOKS

Aces High (1955, five issues)
Animal Fables (1946-1947)
Animated Comics (1948, one issue)
Blackstone, the Magician (1947, one issue)
Crime Patrol (1948-1950)
Dandy (1947-1948)
Extra! (1955, five issues)
Fat and Slat (1947-1948)
Frontline Combat (1951-1954)
Gunfighter (1948-1950)
Happy Houlihans (1947, two issues)
Haunt of Fear (1950-1954)
Impact (1955, five issues)
Incredible Science Fiction (1955-1956)
International Crime Patrol (1948, six issues)
Land of the Lost (1946-1948)
Mad (Comics) (1952-1954)
Mad (Magazine) (1954-present)
Mad Follies (1963-1969)
Mad Special (1970-present)
MD (1955-1956)
Modern Love (1949-1950)
Moon Girl (1947-1949)
A Moon, a Girl—Romance (1949-1950)

More Trash from Mad (1958-1969)
Picture Stories from the Bible-2nd Series (1946, two issues)
    (The First Series was a D-C title)
Picture Stories from World History (1947, two issues)
Piracy (1954-1955)
Psychoanalysis (1955, four issues)
Saddle Justice (1948-1949)
Saddle Romances (1949-1950)
Shock Illustrated (1955-1956, magazine format)
Shock Suspenstories (1952-1954)
Tales from the Crypt (1950-1955)
Tales of Terror Annual (1951-1953, three issues which
    included reprints from assorted fright titles.)
Terror Illustrated (1955-1956, magazine format)
Tiny Tot Comics (1946-1947)
Valor (1955, five issues)
Vault of Horror (1950-1955)
War Against Crime! (1948-1950)
Weird Fantasy (1950-1953)
Weird Science (1950-1953)
Weird Science-Fantasy (1954-1955)
Weird Science-Fantasy Annual (1952-1953, two issues
    which included reprints from *Weird Science* and
    Weird Fantasy.

10

FOX FEATURES SYNDICATE

During the late 1940s and early 1950s as the trend shifted away from superhero fantasy and war themes, Fox Features emerged as the leading publisher of romance comic books, an innovation that brought a brand new readership of teenage girls to the comic book market. With such titles as *All Great Confessions, Book of Love, Intimate Confessions, My Desire,* and *Romantic Thrills,* Fox introduced some of the most fashionable and gorgeous lovelies that ever strutted across the pages of a comic book. When the unexpected success of the romance theme sparked competition from other publishers (who quickly exhausted the eleven basic story plots of girl-meets-boy with every conceivable variation possible for a happy ending), Fox shifted from the "fairy tale" type of romance story to more compelling true-to-life material that delved into such controversial subjects as common-law marriage, teenage pregnancy, rape, and prostitution.

In addition, Fox Features interjected the romance theme into a series of short-lived crime comic books that featured stories about gangsters' girl friends who acted as accomplices in crime. Although Fox's approach to comic book literature during this period did not generate any significantly new literary concepts, it did nevertheless stir up outrage and criticism from parents, educators, clergymen, and other sectors of the adult population who considered such magazines damaging to children—a crusade that led to the inevitable termination of the full line of Fox titles by 1955.

However, there was another phase to Fox Features that is not generally known. As one of the very early magazine publishers that switched from detective pulps to comic books during the 1939 boom, Fox had originated several remarkable concepts in quality fantasy. Had these features continued throughout the years, there is no doubt that some would have achieved superstar status along with the greatest. This section is a review of the *original* Fox Features during that period.

Wonderworld Comics No. 9 (Jan. 1940),© 1939 Fox Publications, Inc.

Flame Comics No. 2 (Fall 1940)
©1940 Fox Publications, Inc.

Fox's first comic book title *Wonder* began in May, 1939—and it ran head-on into a legal clash with Hugo Gernsbach, noted founder of the science fiction pulp magazine *Amazing Stories*, and publisher of a second science fiction pulp that also happened to be called *Wonder*. Fox promptly changed their title to *Wonderworld Comics* which went into effect with the third issue. *Wonderworld Comics No. 3* also marked the debut of an exotic superhero, the Flame, created by Basil Berold and illustrated (mostly) by Lou Fine.

In the unusual origin (undisclosed until the eighth issue), it was revealed that the Flame, during infancy, was the son of an American missionary in China. When a sudden deluge threatened to destroy the city, the desperate parents, as a last hope to save their child's life when all else appeared lost, placed the infant inside a basket which the raging flood swept across the Chinese countryside and into Tibet.

The basket was retrieved by a fishing crew of Buddhist priests who adopted the child and trained him in the art of self defense and the sacred secrets of the Grand High Lamas, which included the mystical power over fire. Upon reaching adulthood, the orphan pledged to use his skills against evil and departed for America to begin his war against crime.

As a character whose power was derived from fire, the Flame's specific abilities were somewhat vague during the first few issues and had to be refined as the feature progressed from month to month. Of course

he was immune to gunfire. Whenever armed thugs shot at him, the hail of bullets simply melted away upon striking his body. But the Flame was vulnerable to other dangers. He tactfully avoided being struck by wooden clubs or stabbed with a knife. Worst of all was getting drenched by a rainfall or waterhose—this seemed to drain his strength and almost literally put the Flame "out."

One of his unique traits was a special "flame-pistol" that he used as a weapon for setting the bad guys on fire, or for blowing up their getaway car. He also used it as a torch for burning through locked doors and brick walls. In addition, the weapon provided him with a clever method of flight. By spraying a cone of fire at his feet, the Flame could stand on top of the blaze and rise into the air with the fire, then race through the sky by running along the fiery path wherever he aimed it. He could also skim across water and scale tall buildings in a similar manner.

Artist Lou Fine was largely responsible for perfecting the Flame's unique traits as shown in the following story that appeared in *Wonderworld Comics No. 9*. This was the story that followed the original episode in the eighth issue and generally set the pattern for the remainder of the series, both in *Wonderworld Comics* and the full length *Flame* comic book which began in 1940 and ran quarterly for eight issues until its termination in Winter 1941 (January 1942).

THE FLAME

By Basil Berold

OVER A SUBMARINE INFESTED SEA, THE FLAME BATTLES THE UNDERWATER RAIDERS OF THE DEEP..........

THROUGH THE CHOPPY WATERS OF THE ATLANTIC, AN AMERICAN FREIGHTER PATIENTLY PLODS TOWARDS WAR-TORN EUROPE...

WITHOUT WARNING A LONG GRAY TORPEDO STRIKES THE BOAT AMIDSHIP.

AMID CRIES OF AGONY AND PANIC, THE LUMBERING SHIP SINKS BELOW THE SURFACE

THOSE SWINE WILL PAY FOR THIS!

RETIRING TO HIS MAGNIFICENT LABORATORY, THE FLAME BEGINS HIS PLAN FOR WREAKING VENGEANCE ON THE HEARTLESS KILLERS.

FIRST, I SHALL NEED AN EXPLOSIVE MORE POWERFUL THAN ANY KNOWN

FOR HOURS, HE WORKS TIRELESSLY. FINALLY.

THERE! THIS CAPSULE CONTAINS ENOUGH POWER TO DESTROY THE LARGEST SHIP AFLOAT!

MEANWHILE, ON AN ISLAND DEEP IN THE SOUTH ATLANTIC............

GEN. DOYOFF IS VISITED BY A HIGH OFFICIAL OF A GREAT FOREIGN POWER.........

YOU HAVE DONE WELL, DOYOFF. HERE IS YOUR FEE..

IT IS NOT ENOUGH..IF WE ARE TO COMPLETE YOUR PLAN, WE WANT TWICE THE AMOUNT!

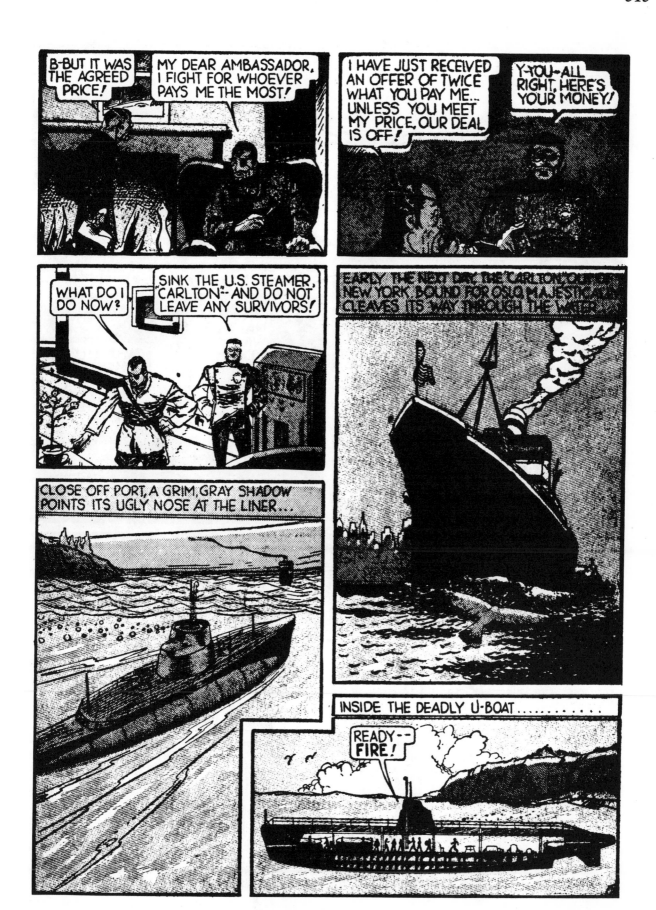

EXCELLENT! A DIRECT HIT!! NOW TO LIQUIDATE THE CREW---

QUICKLY, THE SUBMARINE COMES TO THE SURFACE AND OPENS FIRE ON THEM...

HA! THAT WILL GET THEM!

CAPTAIN! LOOK! COMING OUT OF THE FIRE!

AS THE HUNGRY FLAMES EAT AT THE SHIPS VITALS...

A TALL FIGURE BEGINS TO APPEAR

...AND SUDDENLY, THE FLAME STANDS IN THE ROARING INFERNO...

317

318

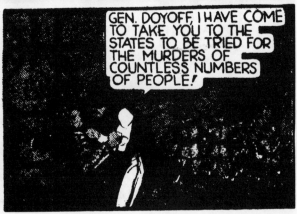

SUDDENLY, DOYOFF'S MEN, WITH CLUBS AND BLUDGEONS, FALL UPON THE FLAME..

THE TREMENDOUS ODDS PROVE TO BE TOO MUCH FOR THE MIGHTY FLAME.........

HURRY, PUT HIM IN THAT GLASS TUBE, WHILE I TURN ON THE WATER!

OH! MY HEAD! WHAT'S THIS? WATER!

DRAWING HIS GUN, THE FLAME AIMS IT AT THE SURGING WATER........

THE WATER BEGINS TO BOIL VIOLENTLY, AS THE HUGE TONGUE OF FLAME STRIKES IT...

(COUGH) UGH, THIS STEAM IS STIFLING ME! MY PLAN HAS TO WORK SOON, OR.....

AS THE WATER BOILS FASTER AND FASTER, THE GLASS EXPANDS, AND WITH A SHARP SNAP, SHATTERS TO BITS..........

THERE! FREE! FIRST, I'LL DESTROY THIS PLACE, AND THEN I'LL GET THOSE CULPRITS!

LEAPING FROM THE WINDOW, THE FLAME TURNS, AND HURLS ONE OF HIS LETHAL CAPSULES...

BOOM!

NOW FOR THAT KILLER, DOYOFF!

MEANWHILE, ABOARD A U.S. DESTROYER...

HMM..SOUNDED LIKE AN EXPLOSION COMING FROM THAT ISLAND!

LOOK, SIR, THERE'S THE KILLER SUBMARINE

AFTER THEM, FULL SPEED AHEAD!

CONFOUND IT! A DESTROYER! I'LL ESCAPE IN MY PLANE, WHILE THE OTHERS GO BY SUBMARINE..

321

JUMPING INTO HIS PLANE, THE COWARDLY LEADER TAKES OFF AS THE FLAME RUNS ACROSS THE FIELD

CATCHING ONTO THE TAIL, THE FLAME EDGES UP BEHIND GENERAL DOYOFF.

SLUGGING HIM INTO UNCONSCIOUSNESS, THE FLAME TAKES OVER THE CONTROLS.

DIVING LOW, HE DROPS THREE OF HIS TINY PELLETS ON THE SUBMERGING U-BOAT.

DOWN, DOWN THEY SPIN, HITTING THE SHIP FORE AND AFT, BLOWING IT TO BITS.

LANDING QUICKLY, THE FLAME TURNS DOYOFF OVER TO THE DESTROYER'S CAPTAIN

GOOD WORK, MAN, B-BUT WHO ARE YOU?

I AM KNOWN AS THE FLAME, AND YOU WILL KNOW ME BY THAT NAME UNTIL I'VE WON MY FIGHT AGAINST CRIME, AND UNTIL IT DISAPPEARS FROM THE EARTH!

DON'T DARE TO MISS THE NEXT THRILLING ADVENTURE OF THE FLAME

Fox's second title, *Mystery Men Comics*, began in August 1939 and introduced Charles Nicholas' Blue Beetle, one of the most exciting characters in the early years of comics. The Blue Beetle, illustrated by several different artists, was unique in many respects. His costume, for example, which looked like a routine comic book disguise, was actually made of a special lightweight cellulose material that shielded him from gunfire. Although the protective qualities of the costume were important in the beginning, the costume became such a minor element as the series developed that it seldom came into play in later episodes.

Blue Beetle's exceptional abilities were enhanced by periodic dosages of vitamin 2-X, a secret pharmaceutical compound invented by Dr. Franz, a proprietor of a drugstore and the only person who knew that Blue Beetle's true identity was police officer Dan Garrett.

Mystery Men Comics No. 13 (Aug. 1940)
©1940 Fox Publications, Inc.

Here is a brief scene from the origin of Blue Beetle . . .

©1940 Fox Publications, Inc.

In terms of superhero fantasy, almost all costumed crimefighters had their "nonhero" alter-identities. And although the nonhero-identity was an essential part of the overall character concept, it seldom served any meaningful purpose in the series. For the most part, he was just a faceless character in a crowd. Not so with Blue Beetle!

His alter-identity, Officer Dan Garrett, served a very definite purpose in glorifying the uniform of the policeman at a time when the policeman's role in society was often looked upon with distrust. As a rank-and-file cop on the beat, Dan Garrett patrolled the crime-infested streets, and was right in the thick of the gang slayings, muggings, and robberies that so often prevailed. And he was there to enforce the law with no nonsense!

Officer Dan Garrett on the job . . .

Of course there were trying times when even a policeman faced overwhelming odds. But instead of calling headquarters for help, Dan Garrett would casually stroll to the drugstore and step into the back room where Dr. Franz would give him a dose of vitamin 2-X. . .

©1940 Fox Publications, Inc.

He would then slip out of his police uniform, don the other blue suit hanging in the secret closet, and charge out the back door as the awesome, brutalizing, bulldozer known to the underworld as the Blue Beetle! He took on all odds like a one-man death squad. . .

©1940 Fox Publications, Inc.

Blue Beetle encountered many obstacles in his gruesome fights with the underworld. The battle zone was a violent one and the opposing sides played for keeps. In one thrilling episode, while pursuing a ruthless gang of kidnappers in a rip-roaring 100-mile-an-hour car chase through the city streets, Blue Beetle was led to the waterfront section where the thugs made an unexpected turnoff into a concealed alleyway. Unable to stop his car in time, Blue Beetle crashed through the guard wall. . .

Was this the end of the Blue Beetle?

As to the helpless girl whom the dastardly villains had kidnapped...

Just when all appeared lost...

Needless to say, the enraged Blue Beetle slaughtered the villains in his usual unmerciful style and saved the girl, concluding a gripping adventure that skyrocketed his popularity up to the number one position. Letters from everywhere poured in to Fox Features requesting back issues of *Mystery Men Comics*.

Blue Beetle's dramatic victory in that adventure was used in an advertisement that appeared in all Fox Features' titles during 1939 and 1940.

The Blue Beetle comic book, Fox's leading title, debuted in late 1939 and ran for eleven issues up to the end of 1941. It was one of the top sellers on the newsstands during this period, and was loaded with violent excitement from first page to last page as Officer Dan Garret and his alter-identity Blue Beetle smashed down one hoodlum empire after the other.

Ironically, Blue Beetle had a very perplexing problem living as two separate identities. As Officer Dan Garrett, he followed the law strictly according to the book. Wherever possible, the apprehended suspects were treated fair and square, and permitted their day in court. But as Blue Beetle, he threw the book away and administered justice on the spot as sole judge and executioner. For instance, during the outbreak of a gang war, Blue Beetle stepped in and wiped out both sides to prevent innocent people from getting hurt. As a result, he was wanted by the authorities for taking the law in his own hands.

The assignment was given to the toughest cop on the force, Dan Garrett. His job: *Bring in the Blue Beetle!*

Blue Beetle Comics No. 3 (Summer 1940)
©1940 Fox Publications, Inc.

Among the many other superhero features appearing in *Mystery Men Comics*, the interplanetary adventures of Rex Dexter of Mars (created by artist Dick Briefer) was perhaps the next most important character. Although Briefer's style reflected a crude simplicity that was typical in many comic books of that era, he did nevertheless introduce some unique literary concepts.

For example, in one story where Rex Dexter and his girl friend Cynde were enroute to Mars (Rex's birthplace), they picked up a radio distress signal from the distant world of Tarsis calling for experienced space pilots to assist in a massive evacuation. The couple swerved off their course and sped to Tarsis to offer their services. Upon landing, they were escorted to the Elder Leader who explained the crucial situation: Tarsis' scientists discovered that the core of their planet was overheating and that it would explode within a few days. It was essential for the people to leave immediately for another star system. As the Elder Leader continued, Rex and Cynde watched the visascreen and saw the spaceport where the panic-stricken population was crowding into massive vessels. Although there were enough spaceships to hold everyone, there was a disastrous shortage of navigators. The two new arrivals were anxious to help out.

The Elder Leader realized that Cynde's claim made good sense and the matter was promptly settled. Cynde was shown to her new ship . . .

The above scene which appeared in *Mystery Men Comics No. 16* (July 1940) had unknowingly established a revolutionary milestone in the early days of science fiction stories dealing with space travel. Here, the fate of a world population rested on the delicate shoulders of Rex Dexter's lovely girl friend, one Captain Cynde of Earth, and comicdom's first Lady Astronaut Commander.

In this particular episode, however, mutiny and foul play entered the scene as Cynde's ship departed from the doomed planet . . .

©1940 Fox Publications, Inc.

The bad guys take over . . .

But Rex, piloting a sister ship, was alert and raced to the rescue . . .

©1940 Fox Publications, Inc.

©1940 Fox Publications, Inc.

Rex and his men donned spacesuits, left their own craft and boarded Cynde's ship to thwart the evil-doers in a savage battle. Afterwards, when Cynde was able to resume full command once again and Rex and his men returned to the sister ship, both vessels rejoined fleet formation. The exodus finally reached their new home, the planet Mercid . . . .

Although the story concluded here, it actually served as the beginning of new adventures on Mercid in which Rex Dexter, Cynde, and the settlers clashed with hordes of flesh-eating monsters that inhabited the world. From this point, the series expanded further into the full-length magazine, *Rex Dexter Comics*, which unfortunately survived for only two issues.

©1940 Fox Publications, Inc.

Samson, a direct descendent of the strongest man in the world, was the super fist of the Fox Features family of comic book heroes. Although this particular character was not entirely Fox's creation, Samson's leadoff in the first issue of *Fantastic Comics* in December 1939 did mark the beginning of a new direction in superhero fantasy that linked character origins with mythological concepts as opposed to laboratory sciences.

Fantastic Comics' Samson, even though he paraded about in a simple loin cloth and strapped sandals, was in essence a modern crimefighter who used his enormous strength to crush those who would destroy the peaceful progress of civilization. Actually, Samson had a tendency to be a bit rough on the bad guys. He often broke their necks and backs, and sometimes flung their lifeless bodies off mountainsides or slammed them into brick walls as though they were plastic dolls. When Samson went into action he split open skulls with his bare hands. He would strike fiercely and suddenly as shown in this typical scene where the villain lured him into a dungeon, locked the massive steel door to prevent his escape, and then opened the water valves to drown him like a trapped rat...

Fantastic Comics No. 2 (Jan. 1940)
©1939 Fox Publications, Inc.

©1940 Fox Publications, Inc.

In addition to starring as the main attraction in *Fantastic Comics*, Samson was placed in his own full-length magazine as another leading title from Fox Features. *Samson Comics* ran quarterly for six issues between 1940 and 1941.

Although Samson didn't soar through the air, he was nevertheless quite capable of leaping tremendous distances—he could even jump out of a plane 5,000 feet in the air and land on the ground unharmed.

Samson was a totally invulnerable being, except for one weakness—*his hair!* If it was clipped he would lose his strength. And there were indeed situations when the bad guys threw hair-nibbling lice at him, or sprayed him with a deadly acid that had no effect on flesh, but could destroy hair.

Later on in his adventures, Samson adopted a not-so-super junior sidekick by the name of Little David.

Fantastic Comics had more than just the mighty Samson to offer. Another feature was the superbly constructed adventures of Sub Saunders who originally had been a naval officer of the United States submarine fleet in the year 10,000. Assigned to an expedition that was exploring the ocean depths for new minerals, Saunders' vessel was wrecked by a mysterious ray near the bottom of the Atlantic Ocean. He found that he was trapped in the midst of an incredible undersea war between the Atlanteans and the Octo-people who worshipped a gigantic octopus god. It was the Atlanteans who retrieved the submarine and saved the lives of Saunders and his crew by treating them with a special light that allowed them to live underwater.

The American crew allied themselves with the Atlanteans, and Saunders fell in love with Queen Lantida, heir to the throne of Atlantis. He became a member of the war council, offering his expertise in naval military strategy. In one dramatic episode, warriors of the Octo-people slaughtered the Atlantean guards on duty at the city's entrance, penetrated the city's fortified defenses, seized the queen, and escaped to their stronghold with their prisoner where they laid plans to sacrifice her to the octopus god. Alarmed at the queen's sudden disappearance, Saunders left the city and set out to search for her. However, he also was captured by the Octo-people and was slated to be fed to their god. But unknown to the Octo-people, Saunders, through his wrist-radio, managed to send out a coded distress signal to his crew members who in turn notified the Atlantean war council of the impending danger.

Weird Comics, another Fox title that ran for twenty issues from 1940 to 1942, headlined Dr. Mortal, quite an unusual character for the main attraction of a comic book during the days when superheroes ruled the newsstands. Created by Godfrey Clarke, Dr. Mortal was an evil scientist who engaged in all sorts of diabolical experiments in his mad quest to dominate the world. His work ranged from shrinking people to doll size, to transferring human brains into ape skulls, raising the dead and creating various living monstrosities that were part animal, part human, and part machine.

The "Sorceress of Zoom", another *Weird Comics'* feature, introduced a highly original concept for a fantasy series, but it did not continue long enough to achieve any major recognition. "Zoom" referred to a mystical city inside another dimension between Earth and Hades, and it was ruled by an evil queen who had acquired magical powers from the Devil. She commanded a brigade of "undead" creatures, who in essence were lost souls the Devil had sent up from hell, to aid the sorceress in her quest to conquer mankind.

Opposing her at every move was Rani-Bey, an aged Hindu magician dedicated to saving mankind from evil domination.

The series was created by Sandra Swift, one of the first women to enter the comic book field as both writer and artist. When "The Sorceress of Zoom" was terminated, she continued as a crackerjack story writer for other features in the Fox Features line, including some of the Blue Beetle adventures. Later, Sandra Swift became senior editor and writer for many of the romance comics that Fox Features became famous for.

Weird Comics also carried "Thor," another feature that starred a superhero with a mythological theme. Here Dr. Grant, a young scientist engaged in an experiment with a new electrical conductor, was almost electrocuted when a bolt of lightning suddenly struck him—and discovered he was the surviving heir to the supernatural powers of the ancient god of thunder. Whenever Grant's life was endangered, a bolt of lightning struck him and the spirit of Thor would take over his body. Grant then automatically acquired superpower.

"Thor" was discontinued in 1942 when Fox Features terminated *Weird Comics*. However, some twenty-five years later, the character concept of Thor was revived by Marvel Comics Group.

Although *Weird Comics* never became a major title, the fifth issue, August 1940, was perhaps an exception. It featured the classic origin of the Dart (created by Jerry Abus) and the story began in ancient Rome where the gods had entrusted a young, courageous

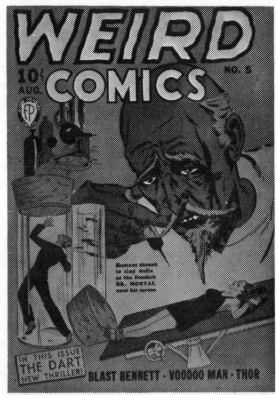

Weird Comics No. 5 (Aug. 1940)
©1940 Fox Publications, Inc.

gladiator, Caius Martius, with the power of flight so that he might oppose the tyranny that was spreading through Rome. When an invading army had conquered an isolated village and sent its people fleeing into the hills, Caius arrived on the scene. He gathered the villagers together and formulated a plan to take back the city. But first he would have to cripple the enemy defenses long enough for his own men to launch a surprise attack.

The small group of villagers armed themselves and remained well hidden in the hillsides to wait for Caius' signal. As dusk approached, the lone gladiator darted silently through the sky, over the city walls and into the heart of the enemy camp to battle the entire regiment. The diversion was sufficent for the villagers to ease up to the city unnoticed. But when they stormed through the gates to aid Caius they found he had already succumbed to overwhelming odds. He had been taken prisoner, and a sorceror had unleashed a deadly curse upon him that dissolved his body into a rock!

The curse finally wore off in the 20th century, and Caius came to life inside a museum. He awoke to a strange new world where crime and tyranny still existed. Armed with his sword, the power of light, plus gladiatorial combat experience, Caius assumed a new role to fight against crime—as the Dart!

From the sixth issue on, the Dart became *Weird Comics'* main attraction.

THE BLUE BEETLE - SAMSON - THE FLAME

Big-3 Comics No. 2 (Winter 1940)
©1940 Fox Publications, Inc.

The Blue Beetle, Samson, and the Flame were Fox's leading characters, and they were featured together in the famous *Big 3* comic book. Ironically, this comic book was the most sensational and eye-catching title of *any* magazine published in 1941, and it was also the most confusing. Everybody knew the "Big 3"; President Franklin Roosevelt, Prime Minister Winston Churchill, and Premier Joseph Stalin dominated newspaper headlines almost every day.

When Fox's *Big 3* comic book appeared on the newsstands, adults, misled by the prominent title, scooped up the book in great numbers, assuming they were buying a news magazine reporting on the world tensions that were leading up to a probable world war (which had started in Europe but had not yet involved America). But when they opened the cover and flipped through the pages, all they found were stories about the Blue Beetle, Samson, and the Flame!

Among comic fans, it became the hilarious pun of the year for Fox's "Big 3" did have their political counterparts: Blue Beetle represented Roosevelt, the Flame was Churchill, and Samson portrayed Stalin. And newspaper editorial cartoons often carried the joke one step further by depicting Blue Beetle, Samson, and the Flame with briefcases in hand, rushing to the White House to attend a "Big 3" conference, or Blue Beetle making a presidential speech with Roosevelt's famous leadoff, "My fellow countrymen. . .", or the Flame seated at a desk and sporting Churchill's derby while making a transatlantic telephone call from London to Washington ("Hello, Franklin? This is Winston."), or Stalin, wearing a loin cloth and cap, pressing 2,000-pound dumbbells.

However, certain members of congress did not consider the joke particularly funny. In fact, they felt the *Big 3* comic book was making political ridicule of the President of the United States and the other two world leaders, and they clamped down on Fox Features. As a maneuver around the constitutional guarantee of freedom of the press, someone in the Senate sent word to Fox Features (via a personal visit from the FBI) that the comic book had to be suspended. The buck was then passed to the newly formed War Production Control Board which had been authorized by presidential order to stop the manufacture of non-essential products and goods that utilized materials needed for military use. Normally, this was supposed to apply to products made of steel, but restrictions were also extended to certain industries that used paper. Supposedly, the Board just happened to pick out a few titles of Fox Features as a handful of magazines to be sacrificed in the interest of national defense as part of the paper conservation drive.

The *Big 3* comic book was terminated at the seventh issue in December 1941, at the outbreak of World War II. The clampdown also forced Fox Features to discontinue its other comic book titles featuring the *Big Three*, thus bringing an end to *Wonderworld Comics*, *Mystery Men Comics*, and *Fantastic Comics*, as well as the full-length magazines of the Flame, Blue Beetle, and Samson.

But no other comic book publishers had been affected!

Fox's few remaining titles to which Congress found no objection were not strong enough to carry the ball. At this point, Fox Features began concentrating on publishing other periodicals, mostly photo illustrated magazines. *Green Mask Comics, Rocket Kelly Comics,* and a few other Fox comic book titles were continued, but on an irregular basis. Fox also introduced *All Great Comics* which came out about once a year as a 100-page magazine that mostly contained reprints of newspaper comic strips from the 1930s.

Meanwhile, rights to the "Blue Beetle" feature were acquired on a temporary basis by Holyoke Publishing Company who ran the second series, apparently without conflict with the U. S. Government, during the war years up until 1945. After the war ended and the War Production Control Board was dissolved, Fox Features returned to comic books in full gear and resumed Blue Beetle for the third series. By this time, however, Fox had drifted away from superhero fantasy and they dropped their leading star after a few issues to concentrate on the new field of romance comics.

The other two stars of *Big-3 Comics*, Samson and the Flame, were later revived for a brief spell during the 1950s by Ajax Publications who also published a few crime comics. The second series of Samson and the Flame ran until 1955 when the Comics Code Authority stepped into the picture and closed the door on Ajax—not because of Samson and the Flame, but because of its crime titles.

Years after Fox Features discontinued comic books, Blue Beetle—or rather, the *son* of Blue Beetle—would be revived as the fourth series by the upcoming Charlton Comics Group. Charlton published *Blue Beetle Comics* at irregular intervals between 1955 and 1968.

ALPHABETICAL LISTING OF FOX FEATURES' COMICS BOOKS

All Famous Crime Stories (1949, one issue)
All Great (1944 - 1946, three issues)
All-Great Confessions (1949, one issue)
All-Great Crime Stories (1949, one issue)
All Great Jungle Stories (1949, one issue)
All Top Comics (1945 - 1949)
All Your Comics (1944, one issue)
Almanac of Crime (1948, one issue)
Big-3 (1940 - 1942)
Blue Beetle (1939 - 1941)
Book of Love (1950, one issue)
Bouncer (1944 - 1945, three issues)
Captain Kidd (1949, two issues)
Captain Rocket (1950, one issue)
Colossal Features Magazine (1950, three issues)
Cosmo Cat (1946 - 1949)
Crime Incorporated (1950, three issues)
Crimes By Women (1948 - 1949)
Dagar, Desert Hawk (1948-1949)
Dorothy Lamour, Jungle Princess (1950, three issues)

Eagle (1941 - 1942)
Everybody's Comics (1944 - 1947)
Famous Crimes (1948 - 1953)
Fantastic Comics (1939 - 1941)
Feature Presentations Magazine (1950, two issues)
Feature Stories Magazine (1950, two issues)
Flame (1940 - 1942)
Frank Buck (1950, three issues)
Full Color Comics (1946, one issue)
Green Mask (1940 - 1946)
Hoot Gibson Western (1950 - 1951)
Inside Crime (1950, two issues)
Jo-Jo Comics (1945 - 1949)
Journal of Crime (1949, one issue)
Jungle Lil (1950, six issues)
Jungle Thrills (1950 - 1952)
Junior Comics (1947 - 1948)
Little Pan (1947, eight issues)
Love Stories (1950 - 1954)
March of Crime (1950, three issues)

Martin Kane, Private Eye (1950, one issue)
Murder, Inc. (1948 - 1952)
My Confessions (1949 - 1950)
My Experience (1949 - 1950)
My Great Love (1949 - 1950)
My Intimate Affair (1950, two issues)
My Life (1948 - 1950)
My Love Affair (1949 - 1950)
My Love Life (1949 - 1950)
My Love Memoirs (1949 - 1950)
My Love Secret (1949 - 1950)
My Love Story (1949 - 1950)
My Past Confessions (1949 - 1950)
My Private Life (1950, one issue)
My Secret Life (1949 - 1950)
My Secret Story (1949 - 1950)
My True Love (1949 - 1950)
Nutty Life (1946, two issues)
Pedro (1950, two issues)
Phantom Lady (1947 - 1949)
Range Busters (1950 - 1951)
Revealing Love Stories (1950, one issue)
Rex Dexter of Mars (1940, two issues)
Ribtickler (1945 - 1947)
Rocket Kelly (1944 - 1947)
Rocket Ship X (1951, one issue)
Romantic Thrills (1950, one issue)
Romeo Tubbs (1950, one issue)

Rulah, Jungle Goddess (1948 - 1949)
Sabu, Elephant Boy (1950, two issues)
Samson (1940 - 1941)
Science Comics (1940, eight issues)
Science Comics, 2nd Series (1946, five issues)
Snarky Parker (1950, one issue)
Spectacular Stories (1950, one issue)
Star Presentation (1950, one issue)
Sunny, America's Sweetheart (1947 - 1948)
Tegra, Jungle Princess (1948, one issue)
They Ring The Bell (1946, one issue)
Truth About Crime (1949, one issue)
U. S. Jones (1941 - 1942)
Variety Comics (1946; 1950, two issues)
V-Comics (1942, two issues)
Weird Comics (1940 - 1942)
Western Killers (1948 - 1949)
Western Outlaws (1948 - 1949)
Western Thrillers (1948 - 1949)
Will Rogers Western (1950 - 1951)
Women Outlaws (1948 - 1949)
Wonder Comics (1939, two issues)
Wonderworld Comics (1939 - 1942)
Wotalife Comics (1946 - 1947)
Zago, Jungle Prince (1948 - 1949)
Zegra (1948 - 1949)
Zoot (1946 - 1948)

©1940 Fox Publications, Inc.

11

TIMELY/MARVEL COMICS

The Marvel Comics Group is the publisher of the famous Spider-Man series and the full galaxy of Marvel superheroes that range from the incredible intergalactic epics of Fantastic Four, to the savage sword-and-sorcery tales of Conan the Barbarian, to the zany miscapades of Howard the Duck who, in January 1976, hatched into a world he never made. Under the creative ingenuity of editor Stan Lee, the Marvel Comics Group has molded its own universe of heroes and villains who live and breathe and fight on and on—but never die. In this universe, everyone crosses over into each other's adventures. Super villains like Dr. Doom have clashed with almost every superhero within the Marvel roster. And minor characters that appear in the supporting cast in a particular adventure often end up headlining their own magazine when that adventure is continued. In addition, one adventure will often overlap with an entirely different adventure in another comic book with different characters involved in different situations. Yet the overlap of the two adventures become a third adventure that might be a continuation of a story in a magazine that was terminated a few months previously!

Superhero fantasy, as a form of escape literature, had practically evaporated by the late 1950s when the Marvel Comics Group, then producing a line of romance titles, made a bold and daring move. In November, 1961 it introduced a new superhero feature, "Fantastic Four," and from that point, the Marvel universe of fantasy began to evolve into a never-ending cycle that has forged the present-day comic book into one of the nation's leading forms of escape entertainment.

Actually, the Marvel Comics Group was an outgrowth of Timely Publications which entered the comic book field in October 1939 with the first edition of *Marvel Mystery Comics* (titled *Marvel Comics No. 1*). This issue marked the debut and origin of the famous Human Torch who soon afterwards branched out in his own magazine, and then appeared as a leading feature within a score of other Timely titles. Although the character was eventually phased out in 1949, its basic concept of the superhero of fire was later revived in the person of Johnny Storm, one of the Fantastic Four.

Marvel Comics No. 1 also introduced that famous superhero of the water, Sub-Mariner, who was also phased out in the early 1950s and then revived fifteen years later.

As early as 1936 Columbia Pictures, one of the three Hollywood leaders that specialized in movie serials, made plans to produce its full-length technicolor extravaganza film *The Lost Atlantis* after its major competitor, Republic Pictures, had released a twelve-chapter smash hit thriller *Undersea Kingdom*. *Lost Atlantis* was planned to be much bigger! The story was to have centered around the legendary undersea kingdom inhabited by an advanced culture of semi-human amphibians that were divided into two warring factions that fought for control of Atlantis. The violent explosions emitting from the underwater battles caused powerful whirlpools on the surface that capsized a fishing vessel. An Atlantean scouting party, hunting for its enemy, discovered the sinking ship and managed to rescue a survivor who had not yet drowned. Equipping him with an air-breathing helmet, they took him down to the city under the sea where he met the queen of Atlantis.

During the midst of the warfare, a strong love developed between the surface stranger and the queen. In the end, she gave up her throne and helped her loved one escape to the surface where she expected to join him for a life of everlasting happiness. However, the queen discovered that she could not breathe on the surface and the two sadly bid farewell to each other as she returned to the sea.

The sequel *Prince of Atlantis* was expected to center upon a son who was born of the love affair.

The well-publicized picture meant a tremendous undertaking that involved entirely new photographic effects to achieve screen realism in the underwater scenes, such as Atlanteans fighting giant squids with ray guns, tractor tanks crawling the ocean floor and firing bombs at the city walls of Atlantis, and Atlanteans engaged in hand-to-hand combat with swords, hacking away at each other while swimming between the rocky walls of steep mountains on the ocean floor. Various filming techniques were experimented with but none proved successful.

At this same time, Edward Nassour had invented a method of producing animated films which employed the use of movable puppets for stop-motion photography in place of drawings. The Walter Lantz Animation Studio, famous for its *Woody Woodpecker* cartoons, acquired the rights to Nassour's invention and joined with Columbia Pictures to produce *Lost Atlantis* using the new process. However, it was soon discovered that successful employment of puppet animation required that the puppets be draped with a flexible material that would allow free movements of the limbs for life-like action. Unfortunately, the ideal material, latex rubber, had not yet been devised, and Lantz's test efforts using other materials, such as paper and cloth, failed to achieve the desired realism. (The process, now perfected, can be seen in a number of current television commercials.)

Inasmuch as Columbia Pictures could not solve the production problem even with Walter Lantz's dedicated efforts, it cancelled its plans for the film even though it had been promoting it for more than three years. As part of the promotion, Columbia Pictures had engaged First Funnies, Inc., an art studio headed by Bill Everett, to produce a black-and-white comic book premium to be given away free to young patrons who attended the movie. The inside front and back covers were intended to carry advertisements of the movie and its sequel *Prince of Atlantis*.

A handful of advance copies of the comic book was circulated to a few of the theaters that showed Columbia's movie serials. But when Columbia announced cancellation of the film, it also meant cancellation of the comic book premium, now bearing the title *Motion Picture Funnies Weekly*, which included Bill Everett's creation of the origin of Prince Namor, the Sub-Mariner which was generally based on the film that never saw completion.

Meanwhile, Timely Publications, searching for dynamic publishing ideas, acquired the rights to Everett's material in *Motion Picture Funnies Weekly* and used Sub-Mariner as a main attraction in *Marvel Comics*. However, in 1939 the comic book field was growing more competitive than its sister pulp field, and Timely Publications, having experienced failure with *Marvel Science Stories,* could not afford to rely on just one main feature to get a new comic book entry off the ground—not when it had to fit between *Action Comics* and *Detective Comics* on the newsstands. An additional attraction was needed, something equally fantastic and bizarre like Carl Burgos' Human Torch!

Torch's origin was unique. It began when Professor Norton demonstrated his newly created android which was mounted inside an airtight cylinder. As Horton opened the oxygen valve to let air flow into the vacuum chamber, the android moved, then suddenly burst into flames and began radiating fire. Horton quickly closed the valve, the flames were snuffed out and the undamaged android became still again. But frightened newsmen who had observed the spectacle insisted that the android was a monster and should be destroyed before it caused harm. Although Horton objected to complete destruction, he did agree to entomb the entire apparatus within a block of cement.

Supposedly, the matter of the flaming android was brought to an end. But air seeped in through a tiny crack in the concrete, penetrated the cylinder, and ignited the android again. Once on fire, the android came to life and melted his way free. During his struggle to adjust to life as a synthetic human, he learned how to control the flames, and how to sail through the air on a burst of fire. His first human contact was a gangster who attempted to exploit him for evil purposes. But the android was not an obedient servant—he destroyed the gangster and the mob by burning them to a crisp. His second human contact was his creator Professor Horton, who also attempted to exploit him. Of course the android objected, and after learning how he had come into being, he leaped toward the ceiling, burned a hole through it, and sailed away.

The Human Torch was regarded as a menace to society and to avoid attracting attention to himself, he adopted the alter-identity of Mr. James Hammond. He began to use his flaming powers constructively to benefit society and soon emerged as a hero. As Jim Hammond, he acted so much like a human that he often forgot he was an android—and so did the readers! However, the dual role proved to be a bit awkward. Every time the well-dressed Jim Hammond ignited himself to spring into action as the Human Torch his clothes went up in flames. The dual role was eventually discarded, and Jim simply remained the Human Torch.

When Torch was elevated to his own full-length magazine, which began as a quarterly publication in December 1940, he adopted a junior sidekick, Toro, a circus fire-eater who was somehow immune to flames. Torch taught Toro to ignite himself and sail through the sky. Although the character concept of Toro lacked the same creative insight that had been applied to the feature's central figure, he nevertheless was as convincing as the average superhero character of the 1941 era who had little if any explanation at all for his amazing powers. The important element about Toro was that he was the junior sidekick of the Human Torch and that was all that really mattered. They shared many action-packed adventures in which they used their flaming ability as an effective weapon to thwart the forces of evil. The story of Toro's origin, which first appeared in *Human Torch Comics No. 1*, was also reprinted a few months later in *Marvel Mystery Comics No. 18*.

Marvel Mystery's other star, Sub-Mariner, was the super amphibian being whose mother, Princess Fen of Atlantis, was betrayed by her love for a surface human, Naval Commander McKensie, who accidentally caused the near annihilation of the Atlantean people. Guided by his mother, Sub-Mariner sought vengeance against the human race and declared all-out war on the upper world. The awesome wrath of Sub-Mariner's vengeance reached its peak in *Marvel Mystery Comics No. 8* when the Human Torch, defender of the human race, set out to stop Sub-Mariner in what might be termed as comicdom's most spectacular battle.

Even though they fought each other like wild animals, it was more than just a battle between the two—it was a battle of the elements, water versus fire, Atlantis against the surface world! Earth was threatened with destruction when Sub-Mariner led his powerful amphibian forces against the combined armies of the United States and Europe, led by the Human Torch. The battle continued in *Marvel Mystery Comics No. 9* and then in *Marvel Mystery Comics No. 10*. And it had to be reprinted in its entirety in *Human Torch Comics No. 5*. It was mid-1941 when in a stalemate: Sub-Mariner discovered that only part of the surface world was his enemy—the part comprised of Nazi Germany and the Axis powers! Sub-Mariner made friends with the Human Torch, and *Marvel Mystery Comics No. 17* (March 1941) presented Part One of an unbelievable twist: "The Human Torch and Sub-Mariner Fighting Side By Side!"

Of course the battle between Human Torch and Sub-Mariner and then their team-up had more or less overshadowed the other fascinating features appearing in *Marvel Mystery Comics*. The first issue also introduced Paul Gustavson's "Angel," a well-illustrated series about a costumed crimefighter which ran as a regular feature for almost seven years. In addition, stories of the Angel appeared in *Sub-Mariner Comics*. *Marvel Comics No. 1* marked the debut of Ka-Zar, a superhero of the jungle whose adventures ran for two years. Ka-Zar was terminated in January, 1942, and then revived during the 1970s.

Marvel Mystery Comics No. 4 introduced Electro, the wonder robot invented by Professor Zog. While the first few episodes saw Electro crushing routine criminal activities, the series, as created by Steve Dahlman, soon acquired a high level of ingenuity. For example, in *Marvel Mystery Comics No. 14*, Professor Zog sent Electro down to the center of the Earth to battle the awesome subterranean "Onees" who had devised the means for magnetically extracting iron from metal alloys and concentrating its stockpile so that Earth's gravitational stability would be thrown out of balance, thus causing the world to drift out of orbit and speed away from the sun. It was the Onees' plan for destroying all life on the surface so that they could rule the world. In a titanic struggle against overwhelming forces, Electro managed to crush the scheme and wipe out the Onees. Then in the next issue, he clashed with the Green Terror that threatened mankind. In Issue 19, Electro appeared for the last time in an action-packed adventure that pitted him against the Anton Invaders of Korpu.

Issue 13 introduced the "Vision" series, created by Joe Simon and Jack Kirby. The Vision was a supernatural being from another dimension who visited Earth to battle the eerie forces of evil which he was quite familiar with. Ordinary smoke provided the dimensional doorway for the Vision to cross between the two worlds.

And besides comics, the center-page spread of *Marvel Mystery* often featured short action stories by Mickey Spillane.

Motion Picture Funnies Weekly No. 1 (1939)
©1939 Funnies, Inc.

Marvel Comics No. 1 (Nov. 1939)
©1941 Marvel Comics Group
All Rights Reserved

Human Torch Comics No. 5 (Fall 1941)
©1941 Marvel Comics Group
All Rights Reserved

Marvel Mystery Comics No. 17 (March 1941)
©1941 Marvel Comics Group
All Rights Reserved

September 1, 1939: Nazi Germany invaded Poland and set international events in motion that led to the outbreak of World War II. The United States did not become officially involved until after the bombing of Pearl Harbor, even though arms and material had been shipped overseas to allied nations. To inspire the spirit of national patriotism, Congress urged various publishing media to encourage those literary themes that were consistent with the government's position on the war.

In response to the request, Timely Publications, in March 1941, introduced the first edition of the Joe Simon-Jack Kirby classic Captain America, an all-new character who blasted Nazi aggression with a double-barreled dose of American patriotism—first, as a superhero garbed in a colorful red-white-and-blue costume of stars and stripes, and second, in his alter-identity as Pvt. Steve Rogers, U. S. Army. The cover of *Captain America Comics No. 1* was, at the time, a sensational newsstand shocker—it was the first of its kind to depict a fictional character of American origin striking Adolph Hitler months before America declared war on Germany!

In the first story, the origin of Captain America was revealed. Nazi agents had infiltrated the military services and various governmental positions to embark on a campaign of sabotage to paralyze critical defense industries. At a special White House conference, the President (who bore an uncanny resemblance to President Roosevelt) held a meeting with FBI Director J. Arthur Grover and senior military officers of the Joint Chiefs of Staff to reveal a top-secret plan for combating the impending crisis. The group was taken to the research laboratory near the Pentagon to witness a revolutionary medical experiment for creating a tactical fighting force made up of super-soldiers. A doctor explained how a wonder serum had been designed to advance body chemistry to near superhuman capacity. A slight young man in poor physical condition had been selected from a group of enlistees for military service to test the effectiveness of the serum.

As the serum was injected into the patient's veins, his frail body amazingly changed into a dynamic, muscular physique. His code name: Captain America, the first of the new tactical force.

However, a Nazi spy was among the government officials observing the test. Without warning, he pulled his revolver and opened fire, killing the doctor and the other officials. (The story implied that everyone in the audience was killed.) The transformed patient immediately leaped into action and tackled the killer. But during the battle, the vial of the wondrous serum was destroyed!

To maintain secrecy about what had happened, the new superhero donned mask and costume and set out to crush the remaining members of the spy ring.

Captain America Comics No. 1 (March 1941)

No one realized that Captain America was, in reality, Pvt. Steve Rogers. However, his secret was accidentally discovered by the regimental mascot, Bucky Barnes, who then became a junior sidekick to Captain America.

In the same issue, Captain America battled the notorious Red Skull. And though the Red Skull was supposedly killed at the end, he bounced back two issues later to become Captain America's number one arch enemy. The powerful impact of the series was not fully realized until 1942, *after* the country was at war, when Captain America became an outstanding character in comic book literature—and the headliner of Timely's leading titles.

In 1944, Republic Pictures introduced the action-packed movie serial adaptation of Captain America. However, the screen version was somewhat different from the character in the comic book version. In the movie serial, Captain America's alter-identity was District Attorney Grant Gardner, whose lovely secretary served as his assistant both in and out of costume. The Captain America of the screen also holstered a gun. And the story line, although exciting as a movie serial, was not based on the patriotic theme that made the comic book character so outstanding. In the movie version, Captain America crushed the diabolical scheme of a power-mad museum curator who assumed the masked role of the Scarab.

©1944 Republic Pictures

A REPUBLIC SERIAL in 15 Chapters

RETURN of CAPTAIN AMERICA

THE NUMBER ONE CHOICE OF YOUNG AND OLD — CAPTAIN AMERICA!

RETURN of CAPTAIN AMERICA

FORMERLY ENTITLED "CAPTAIN AMERICA"
Based on the Character appearing in CAPTAIN AMERICA Comics

DICK PURCELL
LIONEL ATWILL
LORNA GRAY

A REPUBLIC SERIAL IN 15 CHAPTERS

©1944 Marvel Comics Group and Republic Pictures
All Rights Reserved by Marvel Comics Group

Captain America Comics No. 59 (Nov. 1946)
©1946 Marvel Comics Group

Captain America Comics No. 66 (April 1948)
©1948 Marvel Comics Group

Captain America, with his code name, his red-white-and-blue costume of stars and stripes, his alter-identity of a serviceman, and his stories based on the war theme, set a standard that was followed by most of the patriotic superheroes that emerged on the comic book scene from 1942 to 1944. The strip's creator, Jack Kirby, well-known to comic fans for his seemingly endless flow of superhero characters of past and present, left the "Captain America" series in the early 1940s and it was continued by other artists. Kirby, meanwhile, joined the D-C staff to begin another patriotic feature, "Boy Commandos" (which began in *Detective Comics No. 64* as the backup feature to "Batman"), but he would return to Marvel years later to begin "Fantastic Four."

When World War II ended in 1945, the parade of patriotic superheroes also came to an end. For the most part, they were phased out within a few months following the end of the war. Captain America, the leader of the crowd, was one of the very few to make a successful transition to civilian life. (Curiously enough, the other exception was Kirby's "Boy Commandos.")

Captain America's changeover occurred in *Captain America Comics No. 59* (November 1946) in the opening story that began with Pvts. Steve Rogers and Bucky Barnes receiving their honorable discharges from the army. Steve Rogers, a school teacher in civilian life, returned to his former occupation and accepted a position at Lee High School. But between classroom hours, he fought crime as Captain America!

Steve Rogers' new role, created by Stan Lee, continued to play a significant part in the feature's story lines. The social image reflected by an intelligent and understanding school teacher was of a higher standard than the image reflected by a comparative personality such as millionaire playboy Bruce Wayne. The new adventures of Captain America often depicted Steve Rogers in the classroom giving lectures in mathematics, history, science, and other subjects, or counselling students about their personal problems. As an example of how the classroom element served to give background to a story, Captain America, in one adventure, had to smash a racket in which hoodlums used school kids to start fires in order to draw attention away from places they intended to rob. Needless to say, Steve Rogers, as counselling teacher, discovered the plot!

Captain America Comics No. 66 marked the last appearance of Bucky Barnes as a junior sidekick, and the first appearance of Golden Girl, Captain America's new female partner. The series was discontinued in 1950 as superhero fantasy gave way to Marvel's new trend of love and romance titles. But April 1968 marked the dramatic comeback of Captain America by Stan Lee and Jack Kirby!

And crashing through the defensive line of super-heroes was the one and only . . .

Mighty Mouse Comics No. 1 (Fall, 1946)
©1946 Terry Toons, Inc.

Created by the Paul Terry Animation Studios in 1943 for animated film shorts, Mighty Mouse, in 1946, was adapted to comic book format for four semi-annual issues by Timely Publications. Mighty Mouse was the perfect blend of superhero and animal fantasy, a dynamic fusion of Superman and Mickey Mouse, and perhaps one of the most ingenious creations of all. Mighty Mouse, champion of oppressed mice, took on everyone from cats and dogs to humans and robots. When the feature was adapted for television, the critics who searched for sex and violence could find none, they declared: "Great entertainment—recommended for mice only."

After the fourth issue, the "Mighty Mouse" comic book series went from Timely Publications to St. John Publishing Co. who introduced the character in the first 3-D comic book, an innovation that would become a popular fad during the 1950s. When the fad wore off, Dell Publishing Company picked up the "Mighty Mouse" series and kept it going until their comic book line was phased out. But Mighty Mouse was continued as a Gold Key title which ran up through 1968. The series is currently being readied for another revival.

©1946 Terry Toons, Inc.

Today, however, Spider-Man is Marvel's top banana. In May, 1970, Spider-Man did the unbelievable—he challenged the Comics Code Authority!

The story that appeared in *The Amazing Spiderman Comics No. 96* (May 1970) was the first of its kind to deal with the drug issue, then a taboo subject. Spider-Man tackled the touchy subject anyway. When the Comics Code Authority confronted Marvel Comics on the matter, it was revealed that the drug story had been published at the request of the National Institute of Mental Health, a branch of the Department of Health, Education, and Welfare and an organization that carried more weight than the Comics Code Authority. As a result, the Comics Code Authority was forced to relax its rigid standards for the first time since its inception in October, 1954. And everyone cheered Spidey.

Since then, the Marvel Comics Group has emerged a giant, bumping heads with the other giant of the industry, D-C Comics, for the number one position. The two have often blasted and attacked each other on their editorial pages. Finally, when they were at a state of war, the two publishers agreed to settle their feud by selecting a superhero from each line to slug it out on the comic pages.

D-C called upon Superman, and Marvel called upon Spider-Man. And the two met on the battlefield of the following issue . . .

ALPHABETICAL LISTING OF MARVEL/TIMELY TITLES

Adventures Into Weird Worlds (1975 - 1976)

All-Select Comics (1943 - 1946 (Timely)

All Surprize Comics (1943 - 1946 (Timely))

All Teen Comics (1947, one issue (Timely))

All Winners (1941 - 1947 (Timely), and continued under western format as *All Western Winners* through 1948)

Amazing Adventures (1970 - 1976)

Amazing Fantasy (1961 - 1962)

Amazing Fantasy No. 15 (The origin and first appearance of Spider-Man)

Amazing Adventures (1970 - 1976)

Amazing Comics (1944, one issue (Timely))

Amazing Spider-Man (1963 - present)

Annie Oakley (1948 - 1956)

Apache Kid (1950 - 1956)

Arrgh! (1974 - 1975)

Astonishing Tales (1963 - present)

Avengers (1963 - present)

Best Love Comics (1949 - 1950)

Beware! (1973 - 1974)

Black Goliath (1976 - present)

Black Panther (1973 - present)

Black Rider (1950 - 1955)

Blackstone, the Magician (1948, four issues)

Blaze Carson (1948 - 1949)

Blaze, the Wonder Collie (1949 - 1950)

Blonde Phantom (1947 - 1949)

Captain America (1941 - 1950 (Timely, first series), and resumed in 1968 through the present (Marvel, second series))

Captain Britain (1976 - present)

Captain Marvel (1968 - present (Note: not the same as *Captain Marvel* by Fawcett Publications))

Captain Savage (1968 - 1970)

Casey, Crime Photographer (1949 - 1950)

Cat Comics (1972 - 1973)

Chamber of Chills (1972 - 1976)

Chamber of Darkness (1969 - 1970)

Champions (1975 - present)

Chili (1969 - 1973

Cindy (1947 - 1950 (Timely))

Combat Kelly (1972 - 1973)

Comedy Comics (1942 - 1946 (Timely), and continued in 1948 to 1949)

Complete Comics (1944 - 1945 (Timely))

Complete Mystery Comics (1948 - 1949)

Conan, the Barbarian (1970 - present)

Cowgirl Romances (1950, one issue)

Crazy Magazine (1973 - present, black-and-white magazine format)

Crazy Comics (1973, three issues)

Creatures On The Loose (1971 - 1975)

Crime Can't Win (1950 - 1953)

Crime Cases (1950 - 1952)

Crime Exposed (1948 - 1950)

Crimefighters (1948 - 1949)

Crypt of Shadows (1973 - 1975)

Cupid (1950, two issues)

Daredevil (1964 - present (Note: not the same as *Daredevil* by Gleason Publications))

Daring Comics (1944 - 1945 (Timely))

Daring Mystery Comics (1940 - 1942 (Timely))

Deadly Hands of Kung Fu (1974 - present, black-and-white magazine format)

Dead of Night (1973 - 1975)

Defenders (1972 - present)

Doc Savage Comics (1972 - 1974)

Doc Savage Magazine (1975 - present, black-and-white magazine format)

Doctor Strange (1968 - 1969, and continued in 1972 to present)

Dolly Dill (1945, one issue (Timely))

Dracula Lives! (1973 - 1975, black-and-white magazine format)

Eternals (1976 - present)

Evil Knievel Comics (1974, one issue published as an advertising premium)

Fantastic Four (1961 - present)

Fantasy Masterpeices (1966 - 1967)

Fear (1970 - 1975)

Film Funnies (1949 - 1950)

Frankenstein (1973 - 1975)

Frankie Fuddle (1947 - 1949)

Funny Frolics (1945 - 1946)

Gay Comics (1944 - 1949)

Ghost Rider (1973 - present)

Giant-Size Chillers (1974 - 1975)

Giant-Size Creatures (1974, one issue)

Giant-Size Dracula (1974 - 1975)

Giant-Size Superheroes (1974, one issue about Spider-Man)

Giant-Size Superstars (1974, one issue)

Girl Comics (1949 - 1952)

Groovy Comics 1968, three issues)

Gunhawk (1950 - 1951)

Gunslinger (1973, two issues)

Haunt of Horror (1974 - 1975, black-and-white magazine format)

Howard, the Duck (1976 - present)

Human Torch (1940 - 1949 (Timely, first series), and resumed in 1974 to 1975 (Marvel, second series))

Ideal, A Classical Comic (1948 - 1949 (Timely))

Ideal Comics (1944 - 1946 (Timely))

Inhumans (1975 - present)

Iron Fist (1975 - present)

Iron Man (1968 - present)

Iron Man and Sub-Mariner (1968, one issue)

It's a Duck's Life (1950 - 1952)
Jeanie Comics (1947 - 1949)
Joker Comics (1942 - 1950 (Timely))
Journey Into Mystery (1972 - 1975)
Jungle Action (1972 - 1976)
Ka-Zar (1970 - 1971, and resumed in 1974 to present)
Kellys, The (1950, two issues)
Kent Blake of the Secret Service (1951 - 1953)
Kid Colt, Outlaw (1948 - 1976)
Kid Comics (1943 - 1946 (Timely))
Kid Movie Comics (1946, one issue (Timely))
Komic Kartoons (1945, two issues (Timely))
Krazy Comics (1942 - 1946 (Timely), and resumed in 1948 to 1950)
Krazy Krow (1945 - 1946 (Timely))
Kull and the Barbarians (1975, three issues in black-and-white magazine format)
Kull, the Conqueror (1971 - present)
Lana (1948 - 1949)
Lawbreakers Always Lose (1948 - 1949)
Life with Millie (1958 - 1962)
Little Aspirin (1949, three issues)
Li'l Kids (1970 - 1973)
Little Lana (1949 - 1950)
Little Lenny (1949, three issues)
Little Lizzie (1949 - 1959)
Li'l Pals (1972 - 1973)
Li'l Willie (1949, two issues)
Logan's Run (1977 - present)
Love Adventures (1949 - 1952)
Love Dramas (1949 - 1950)
Love Romances (1949 - 1963)
Lovers (1949 - 1957)
Love Tales (1949 - 1957)
Luke Cage (1972 - present)
Mad about Millie (1969 - 1970)
Man-Thing (1974 - 1975)
Margie Comics (1947 - 1949 (Timely))
Marvel Chillers (1975 - 1976)
Marvel Classics Comics (1976 - present)
Marvel Collectors Item Classics (1965 - 1969)
Marvel Comics (1939, one issue and then becomes Marvel Mystery Comics beginning with the second issue (Timely))
Marvel Double Feature (1973 - 1977)
Marvel Feature Comics (1971 - 1973, and resumed in 1975 to 1976)
Marvel Mini-Books (1966, six issues)
Marvel Movie Premiere (1975, one issue ("The Land That Time Forgot") published in black-and-white magazine format)
Marvel Mystery Comics (1939 - 1949 (Timely))
Marvel Premiere (1972 - present)
Marvel Presents (1975 - present)

Marvel Preview (1975 - present, black-and-white magazine format)
Marvel's Greatest Comics (1969 - present)
Marvel Special Edition (1975, one issue about Spiderman)
Marvel Spectacular (1973 - 1975)
Marvel Spotlight (1971 - present)
Marvel Superheroes (1972 - present)
Marvel Superheroes Special (1966, one issue)
Marvel Tales (1949 - 1957, and resumed in 1964 to present)
Marvel Team-Up (1972 - present)
Marvel Treasury Edition (1974 - present)
Marvel Treasury Special (1974 and 1976, two issues)
Marvel Triple Action (1972 - present)
Marvel Two-In-One (1974 - present)
Master of Kung Fu (1974 - present)
Masters of Terror (1975, two issues published in black-and-white magazine format)
Men's Adventures (1950 - 1954)
MGM's Marvelous Wizard of Oz (1975, one oversize issue published in collaboration with D-C Comics)
Mighty Marvel Western Comics (1968 - 1976)
Mighty Mouse (1946 - 1947, four issues and continued by St. John Publishing Company)
Millie, the Model (1945 - 1961, and continued for thirteen annual issues through 1974)
Miss America Comics (1944, one issue (Timely))
Miss America Magazine (1944 - 1957, magazine format)
Miss Fury (1943 - 1946, eight issues (Timely))
Mitzi's Boy Friend (1948 - 1949)
Mitzi's Romances (1949, two issues)
Molly Manton's Romances (1949, two issues)
Monsters On the Prowl (1971 - 1974)
Monsters Unleashed (1973 - 1974, black-and-white magazine format)
Motion Picture Funnies Weekly (1939, one premium issue published by Funnies, Inc. with part of contents later adapted to Marvel Comics No. 1)
Movie Tunes (1946, three issues)
Ms. Marvel (1977 - present)
My Love (1949 - 1950, and resumed in 1969 to 1975)
My Own Romance (1949 - 1951)
My Romance (1948, two issues)
Mystic Comics (1940 - 1945 (Timely), and resumed in 1951 to 1957)
Namora (1948, three issues)
Nick Fury, Agent of S.H.I.E.L.D. (1968 - 1971, and continued as S.H.I.E.L.D. through 1973)
Night Nurse (1972 - 1973)
Night Rider (1974 - 1975)
Not Brand Echh (1967 - 1969)
Nova (1976 - present)
Official True Crime Cases (1947 - 1948)
Omega, the Unknown (1976 - present)

Oscar (1947, one issue)

Our Love Story (1969 - 1975)

Outlaw Kid (1970 - 1975)

Peter, the Little Pest (1969 - 1970)

Planet of the Apes (1974 - present, black-and-white magazine format)

Powerhouse Pepper (1943 - 1948, five issues (Timely))

Pussycat (1953, three issues published in black-and-white magazine format)

Red Raven (1940, one issue (Timely))

Red Sonja (1977 - present)

Red Warrior (1951, six issues)

Red Wolf (1972 - 1973)

Ringo Kid (1970 - 1976)

Romance Diary (1949, one issue)

Romances of the West (1949 - 1950)

Romance Tales (1950, nine issues)

Savage Sword of Conan (1974 - present, black-and-white magazine format)

Savage Tales (1971 - 1975, ten issues published in black-and-white magazine format)

Sgt. Fury (1963 - present)

Shanna, the She-Devil (1972 - 1973, five issues)

S.H.I.E.L.D. (1973, five issues)

Silly Tunes (1945 - 1947, seven issues (Timely))

Silver Surfer (1968 - 1970)

Skull, the Slayer (1975 - 1976)

Son of Satan (1975 - 1977)

Spectacular Spider-Man (1968, two issues published in black-and-white magazine format)

Spectacular Spider-Man Comics (1976 - present)

Spidey Super Stories (1974 - present)

Spoof! (1970 - 1973, five issues)

Sport Stars (1949, one issue)

Spy Fighters (1951 - 1953

Star Wars (1977 - present)

Strange Tales (1953 - 1976)

Strange Worlds (1958 - 1959)

Sub-Mariner (1942 - 1949 (Timely), and resumed in 1968 to present)

Sun Girl (1948, three issues (Timely))

Superman Vs. Spider-Man (1976, one issue published in collaboration with D-C Comics)

Supernatural Thrillers (1972 - 1973)

Super Rabbit (1943 - 1949 (Timely))

Super Villain Team-Up (1975 - present)

Tales of Asgard (1968, one issue)

Tales of the Zombie (1973 - 1975, black-and-white magazine format)

Tarzan (1977 - present)

Terry-Toons Comics (1942 - 1947 (Timely), and continued by St. John Publishing Co.)

Texas Kid (1951 - 1952)

Tex Dawson, Gunslinger (1973, one issue)

Tex Morgan (1948 - 1950)

Tex Taylor (1948 - 1950)

Thor (1966 - present)

Tiny Tessie (1949, one issue (Timely))

Tomb of Darkness (1974 - 1976)

Tomb of Dracula (1972 - present)

Tough Kid Squad Comics (1942, one issue (Timely))

Tower of Shadows (1969 - 1971)

True Adventures (1950, three issues)

True Complete Mystery (1949, one issue)

True Life Tales (1949 - 1950)

True Mysteries (1949, one issue)

True Secrets (1951 - 1954)

True Western (1949 - 1950, two issues)

Two-Gun Kid (1948 - present, published at irregular intervals)

Two-Gun Western (1950 - 1952)

2001: A Space Odyssey (1976 - present)

Uncanny Tales (1973 - 1975)

Unknown Worlds of Science Fiction (1974 - 1975, published in black-and-white magazine format)

USA Comics (1941 - 1945 (Timely))

Vampire Tales (1973 - 1975, black-and-white magazine format)

Vault of Evil (1973 - 1975)

Venus (1948 - 1952)

Wacky Duck (1946 - 1948)

Warlock (1972 - 1976)

War is Hell (1973 - 1975)

Weird Wonder Tales (1973 - present)

Werewolf By Night (1972 - present)

Western Gunfighters (1956 - 1957, and resumed in 1970 to 1975)

Western Kid (1971 - 1972)

Western Life Romances (1949 - 1950)

Western Outlaws and Sheriffs (1949 - 1952)

Western Team-Up (1973, one issue)

Western Winners (1949, three issues)

What If ? (1977 - present)

Whip Wilson (1950, three issues)

Wild West (1948, two issues, and continued as *Wild Western Comics* through 1957)

Willie Comics (1946 - 1950)

Witness (1948, one issue)

Wonder Duck (1949 - 1950, three issues)

Worlds Unknown (1973 - 1974)

X-Men (1963 - present)

Young Allies (1941 - 1946 (Timely))

Young Hearts (1949 - 1950)

Young Men (1950 - 1954)

Ziggy Pig and Silly Seal (1944 - 1946 (Timely))

Further information on who's who in the current Marvel lineup of characters appears in the two softcover book publications *Bring On The Bad Guys* by Stan Lee, and *Origins of Marvel Superheroes*, also by Stan Lee both of which were published in 1976 (Simon & Shuster).

12

UNITED FEATURE SYNDICATE

United Feature Syndicate is the marketing institution behind Charles Schulz's famous comic strip "Peanuts," which for the past twenty years has appeared in newspapers throughout the world, and in a host of paperback and hardcover books. Charlie Brown and his friends have also appeared in over a half-dozen animated television specials and several full-length feature films.

United Feature's other well-known humor strip, "Nancy," centers around an adorable little girl who has been with us somewhat longer than Charlie Brown. "Nancy," created by Ernie Bushmiller, dates back to the 1930s, a time when United Feature reprinted its famous newspaper comic strips in comic books, most notably *Tip Top Comics*. Although the contents of *Tip Top Comics* was basically humorous, it did carry a few adventure strips, the most popular of which were reprints of the original comic strip adaptation of Edgar Rice Burrough's "Tarzan of the Apes."

Tarzan, who was introduced in *All Story Magazine* October 1912, was one of the few classic heroes of literary fiction to achieve equal fame and popularity in other media—the pulps, movies, hardcover books, and comics. However, when adapted to the comic strip under the able hands of artist Hal Foster, "Tarzan" became an outstanding art classic as well. The origin of Tarzan was introduced on the newspaper comic pages on January 27, 1929.

The strip, based on the epic "Tarzan of the Apes" as it appeared in *All Story Magazine*, ran for ten weeks as a daily feature and was reprinted in its entirety in 1939 in United Feature's black-and-white *Single Series Comics No. 5*. Foster's rendition in color for Sunday pages, which came later, was reprinted as a continuation series that began in the first issue of *Tip Top Comics*, United Feature's first comic book title which started in April 1936. *Tip Top Comics* was one of the earliest titles to feature heroic adventures in its contents. In 1940, reprints of the Foster-illustrated "Tarzan" from *Tip Top* were published in United Feature's *Single Series Comics No. 20*, the first full-length comic book of "Tarzan" in color.

Tarzan Comics, Single Series No. 20 (1940)
©1933 By Edgar Rice Burroughs, Inc.

Tip Top Comics No. 52 (August 1940)
©1940 United Feature Syndicate
("Tarzan" © by Edgar Rice Burroughs, Inc.)

In developing the strip, Foster introduced a novel technique in story illustration by placing all the dialogue in captions rather than the more conventional speech balloons. The practice was especially helpful for the feature because speech represented a peculiar problem—Tarzan, according to Burroughs' original concept, did not speak any specific language, yet he could understand all men and all animals. Although Tarzan lacked a formal education, he was extremely intelligent—he could analyze men at a glance, and he easily knew friend from foe. And he kept a keen jungle-sense of justice, which was roughly parallel to a civilized approach to questions of right and wrong.

When Tarzan's dialogue was put into captions, the strip gave the illusion that an unseen narrator was translating whatever Tarzan said. In the original Tarzan adventures in text form, the narrative described the dialogue in such a manner that it was understood the characters were speaking different languages. In the silent screen adaptations of "Tarzan," the speech peculiarity did not present a problem—important conversations were just flashed across the screen to be read.

However, in later sound film adaptations, the character concept was changed by every actor who starred in the role. Tarzan spoke fluent English with either an American or British accent, or spoke broken English, or he spoke like an intellectual philosopher.

Occasionally he grunted. None of these were true to the authentic Tarzan.

The film adaptations[1] and Foster's comic strip defined Burrough's character in two different ways, and from the point of view of dialogue the comic strip undoubtedly remained closer to Burrough's original creation than the movie versions did. However, when Foster left the series to begin "Prince Valiant," "Tarzan" was taken over by different artists, and only two followed Foster's technique of placing the dialogue in captions. The others used speech balloons which gave the impression that everyone in the story, including foreigners, natives, Tarzan, and even the animals, were speaking fluent English.

After Foster left, Rex Maxon took over the daily feature and, for a short while, the Sunday feature (which was reprinted in United Features' other comic book titles, *Comics On Parade*). Although Maxon's style was not as polished as Foster's, he nevertheless maintained the true feeling of the character by placing the dialogue in captions as translated by the "off-stage" narrator.

---

1. Further information on film versions appears in *Tarzan of the Movies* (Citadel Press, New York, 1973). This book covers the complete history of the Tarzan films.

Burne Hogarth was the next artist. When he took over the Sunday feature, he initially followed the exact tone and style which Foster had established for depicting "The Bull Ape," but later he began to introduce an electrifying realism that gave the illusion that everything in the story was in motion. Under Hogarth, Tarzan ascended from "The Bull Ape" to "The Ape Man." And there was a difference!

"The Bull Ape" seemed almost human—he could smile, feel sympathy, and even fall in love. He was also occasionally slow and awkward when taken out of his familiar jungle environment.

By contrast, "The Ape Man" became a savage superhero . . .

"The Ape Man" never smiled. He was deadly serious at all times. And love was entirely out of the question. Hogarth's characters reflected only perfect people—the men were tall and muscular and the women were shapely and beautiful.

A typical Hogarth-illustrated adventure took Tarzan into the Earth's core where he fell prisoner to Prince Jagurt of the Sea City. Prince Jagart wanted to kill Tarzan for saving Princess Leecia, but the princess, who owed her life to the Ape-Man, sacrificed herself by leaping into a pool of demon-fish as a means of diverting attention. Tarzan could have escaped, but he was not concerned about his own freedom, just the fate of the helpless princess . .

Onlookers formed a human chain, lowered themselves down the wall, and pulled the princess to safety. But before they could rescue Tarzan, one of Jagurt's men reached through a secret trap door beneath the pool, seized Tarzan's foot and dragged him under before he could catch his breath. Tarzan's limp body was carried down an underground water tunnel which emptied into a small pool inside the prince's private chambers. Various ways of doing away with Tarzan were discussed as he lay unconscious on the floor.

Meanwhile, the city was beginning to tremble from earthquakes. The wall enclosure that protected the city from the ocean started to crack and water began seeping through the ceiling. The panic-stricken people sought to flee to the surface by the only route available—a hidden water filled tunnel that barred all except experienced swimmers. Upon the next tremor, the wall burst open and water poured through with the force of a tidal wave. The swimmers were trapped in the tunnel as the raging undercurrent slammed their bodies into the rocks. Meanwhile, Tarzan had regained consciousness.

Here, Burne Hogarth, the Michaelangelo of comic strip illustration, depicts the desparate plight of Tarzan as he struggles to outswim the awesome tidal wave that has destroyed the city and its people . . .

The Hogarth-illustrated "Tarzan" series was reprinted in United Feature's *Sparkler Comics* beginning in July 1940, and in a few full-length editions of *Tarzan Adventures,* an international comic book published in Great Britain by Westworld Publications in association with United Feature. After the reprint series was discontinued in *Sparkler Comics,* Dell introduced the next version utilizing original story material in the full-length *Tarzan Comics* in the "Dell 4-Color Comics" series, which later continued as a Gold Key comic book and then was adapted to a series of hardcover children's books. "Tarzan" was finally dropped from newspaper syndication on February 28, 1967 when United Feature began stressing their humorous strips.

Sparkler Comics No. 42 (March 1945)
©United Feature Syndicate
("Tarzan" © by Edgar Rice Burroughs, Inc.)

Edgar Rice Burroughs' classic creation of the "Jungle Lord" made a comeback for a short-lived television series, then faded away again. He made another comeback in the literary sphere when Ballantine Books introduced a new and updated version of the Tarzan novels in paperback, many of which had been reprinted previously by other publishers throughout the years following their first appearance in *Argosy-All Story Magazine* and *Blue Book Magazine* during the 1920s. (The adventure, "The Triumph of Tarzan," which appeared only in *Blue Book* and was never reprinted anywhere else, was adapted to comic strip in the Hogarth-illustrated series.) In addition,

Ballantine also published a two-volume biography *Edgar Rice Burroughs, the Man Who Created Tarzan.* Compiled and written by Irwin Porges, these volumes provide invaluable information about Burroughs and development of the many characters he created, from Tarzan to John Carter of Mars.

In 1972, D-C revived "Tarzan" for another comic book series which ran for five years up through early 1977 and included adaptations of the same Tarzan novels which Ballantine was producing in paperback. Then in June 1977, the Marvel Comics Group picked up the series and introduced the first issue of the new *Tarzan Comics.*

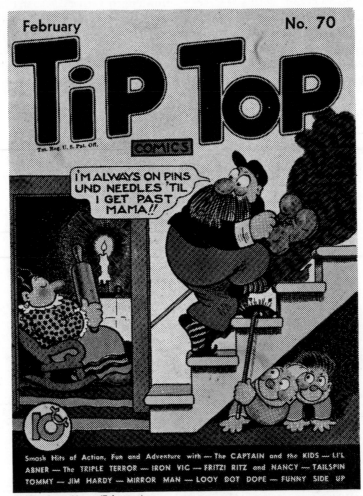

Tip Top Comics No. 70 (Feb. 1942)
©1942 United Feature Syndicate

Other stars of *Tip Top Comics* were those two mischievous rascals, Hans and Fritz, otherwise known as the Katzenjammer Kids. It was September 1897 when Rudolph Dirks originally created the feature as "Katzenjammer Kids" for the Hearst newspaper syndicate. However, in 1912, Dirks left Hearst and moved to the Pulitzer offices. He took his comic strip with him and offered it to his new employer—or at least tried to. A legal battle promptly followed between the two newspapers concerning ownership of the feature. The courts finally ruled that Hearst owned the title "Katzenjammer Kids" and that Dirks, if he wanted to continue the strip for Pulitzer, would have to change the name. For several years following, Dirks continued the feature as "Hans and Fritz" but due to anti-German sentiment during World War I, he changed the name to "The Captain and the Kids."

In the meantime, Hearst had hired another artist to keep the feature going as "The Katzenjammer Kids," following Dirks' style and signing the strip as "R. Dirks." King Features Syndicate ultimately acquired the rights to the Hearst strip and later acquired the rights to the Pulitzer strip which, in the meantime, had been distributed by United Feature Syndicate.

Tip Top Comics also included reprints of "Nancy" which was then titled after her aunt "Fritzie Ritz", Al Capps's "Li'l Abner," and a few other features that were popular during the 1930s but were eventually phased out during the 1940s. The ill-fated ones included "Broncho Bill," one of the early Wild West comic strips created by Harry O'Neill, and "Tailspin Tommy," one of the first flying aces created by Hal Forrest. In addition, *Tip Top Comics* introduced a few original features that never appeared in the newspapers. The original contents included two adventure series created by Fred Methot and Reg Greenwood: "The Mirror Man," a costumed crimefighter, and "The Triple Terror," three adventuresome brothers, each of whom possessed a different skill.

THE KING WAVES A NEW COMMAND AND THE MAN-OFINS FORM A RING AROUND THE CAB.

THE MANOFINS LOCK TOGETHER TO CRUSH THE CAB.

AT THAT MOMENT A GIANT CREATURE FROM THE OCEAN'S DEPTHS RAIDS THE MANOFIN'S LAIR!

THE CAB ARISES FROM THE WATERY DEPTHS!

Sparkler Comics No. 7 (Feb. 1942)
©United Feature Syndicate

Sparkman Comics No. 1 (1941)
©1941 Francis M. McQueeny

The Sparkman, created by Fred Methot and Reg Greenwood, became an original United Feature superhero who appeared for one issue in his own magazine and then became a major attraction in *Sparkler Comics* which was carrying "Tarzan" and other reprint features. The Sparkman had discovered the secret of harnessing static electricity within his body and discharging it as an active current through two artificial fingertips that extended from his insulated gloves. After the first twelve episodes, however, the Sparkman donned a new costume and discarded his special gloves which had proved awkward and cumbersome during slugfests with villains. From then on, he became a straight costumed crimefighter. The feature was discontinued during the early 1940s.

Sparkler Comics, which was generally named after the Sparkman, continued as a monthly magazine until it was terminated in January 1955.

During the 1940s, many of the characters in *Tip Top Comics* were also put in their own full-length magazines, or were transferred into *Sparkler Comics*. In 1959, *Tip Top Comics No. 176* introduced reprints of "Peanuts" which ran as the leading feature for the next thirty-six issues until the magazine was discontinued in 1961.

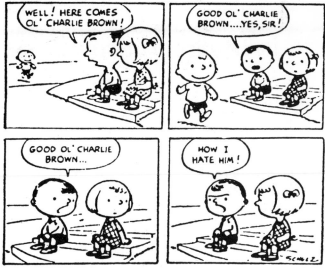

The First "Peanuts" cartoon (Oct. 2, 1950)
©1950 United Feature Syndicate

"Fritzi Ritz" (1926, later retitled "Nancy")
©United Feature Syndicate

ALPHABETICAL LISTING OF UNITED FEATURE COMIC BOOKS

Abbie and Slats (1947-1948, with earlier issues published in the "Single-Series" editions)

Broncho Bill (1939-1940, two issues in the "Single-Series" editions and resumed as a monthly title by Better Standard Publications from 1949 to 1950)

Comics on Parade (1938-1955)

Curly Kayoe (1946-1948)

Ella Cinders (1938-1940, two issues in the "Single-Series" editions and resumed as a monthly title for five issues from 1948 to 1949)

Fight for Love (1952, one issue about "Abbie and Slats")

Fritzi Ritz (1948-1958)

Giant Comics Edition (1941-1943, two issues)

Jim Hardy (1939-1940, two issues in the "Single-Series" and resumed in 1947 for two issues)

Lil 'Abner (1939-1940, two issues in the "Single-Series" editions and resumed in 1947 by Toby Press then continued through 1955 by Harvey Publications)

Nancy and Sluggo (1949-1954, and resumed in 1955 by St. John Publishing Company, then continued as a Gold Key title through 1963)

Okay Comics (1940, two issues)

Single-Series Editions (1938-40)

Sparkler Comics (1940-1955)

Strange As It Seems (1939, three issues in the "Single-Series editions (also see Section 13, *Famous Funnies*))

Tarzan (1939, one black-and-white issue of daily strip reprints by Foster; 1940, one color issue of Sunday strip reprints by Foster (also see Section 6, Dell Publications))

Tip Top Comics (1936-1961)

Tip Topper (1949-1954)

EASTERN COLOR
PRINTING COMPANY

Toward the end of the nineteenth century, two revolutionary inventions paved the way for the mechanization of the printing industry—the rotary printing press and the Mergenthaler Linotype machine. Both were a tremendous boon to book and newspaper publishing. The Linotype machine sped up the hitherto cumbersome typesetting process, while the new printing presses sped up paper feed-through and produced printed copies of books and magazines a hundred times faster than the hand-operated presses of the past. The rotary printing press offered another new feature: through the use of special engraving plates, multi-color printing based on overlaps of the four basic colors was possible.

However, since both machines were hand manufactured, and only approximately six could be produced each year, the changeover to the new equipment was a gradual one. And the intricate engraving techniques called for in color reproduction were, therefore, confined to only a handful of pioneering institutions. The first color press was sold to the newly formed U. S. Bureau of Engraving for printing dollar bills; another was sold to the *New York World* which experimented with printing Richard Outcault's "Yellow Kid" series in color during 1896. However, at that time the color printing process proved to be too costly for widespread use in comics and its application in *this* area was uneconomical until almost three decades later.

Eastern Color Printing Company was another pioneer. Previously one of the few firms that specialized in printing color covers for the pulp maga-

zines, Eastern became the first major institution to perfect an engraving process that would allow for the addition of color to black-and-white comics, and it proved a godsend for the newspaper syndicates who were just beginning to introduce full-page Sunday funnies. For a brief period between 1929 and 1932, the Sunday comic pages combined strips that were printed both in black-and-white and in color. By 1933, color for the Sunday comics and black-and-white for the daily strips had become the universal standard. As newspaper comics became a popular entertainment form, a few publishing firms began reprinting collections of black-and-white comic strips bound in book format with cardboard covers, all of which varied in size and number of pages. Some were almost as large as the newspaper itself while others were long and narrow, proportional to the trim size of the comic strip panel.

In 1933, Eastern printed a soft cover magazine called *Funnies on Parade* which carried reprints of some of the first color comics for the Sunday newspapers, including the popular "Mutt and Jeff." Here the comic strip was reduced to about half the size of the newspaper version and was spread across two facing pages so that the magazine, when opened, had to be turned sideways to read the panels. This was originally published as an advertising premium for Proctor and Gamble and was offered free with the purchase of a new breakfast cereal that was being introduced at the time. A few months later Eastern followed up with a second magazine premium called *Century of Comics*, a whopping 100-pager with a different format. This time the comic strips were reduced to almost one-fourth the size of the newspaper version and easily fit a single 8½" × 11" page. A third 32-pager, *Famous Funnies, Carnival of Comics,* followed on the heels of the second. The trim size measured 8" × 10".

Early in 1934, Eastern published a fourth magazine entitled *Famous Funnies* as a special edition for Dell Publishing Company. The new magazine sold for ten cents in candy stores, stationery stores, and newsstands along with Dell's dime western and detective novels. It contained, in addition to reprints of color comic pages, advertisements for Dell's line of pulps for that year.

A few months later, in May 1934, Eastern published its own edition of *Famous Funnies, the Nation's Comic Monthly,* and Issue No. 1 became the first such monthly publication of its kind! Its 64-page format and ten-cent pricetag set the standards for what was soon to become the comic book magazine industry, and was universally adopted as the "standard form" by all other publishers from that time on.

Comics blossomed into a full-grown entertainment media, and Eastern's role in the industry grew with it. First, it serviced the newspaper syndicates by printing the Sunday comics in color. Second, it was the leader in producing comic book premiums for national advertisers. Third, it printed comic books for the new, smaller publishers, who did not have their own printing facilities.

When the major pulp publishers entered the comic book field as a sideline to keep their presses running, they did not have the engraving facilities for making their own color plates. Eastern filled the gap. It supplied color plates to Fawcett, Dell, D-C, Timely, Gleason, Gilberton, Fox Features, Fiction House, and most of the others until the early 1940s when the color reproduction process was simplified by new photolithographic methods.

While performing these functions, Eastern also continued to publish its own classic title, *Famous Funnies, The Nation's Comic Monthly.* Although the early issues contained reprints from the Sunday comics which were then mostly humor features complete within a single page, Eastern made a happy discovery when it started reprinting the continuous adventure strips. In the original newspaper versions that were continued on a weekly basis, it was necessary to remind the reader what had gone on before, and the plots often included large amounts of repetitive material when the story ran for a period of several months. However, when the same feature was adapted to a comic book format, it was no longer necessary to remind the reader on page 4 about what had occurred on page 1.

In addition, the adventure comic strip, in telling a long story, often contained more wordage in the balloon conversations and the panel captions than humor strips, and the size of the lettering was often much smaller. When the newspaper page was reduced to fit a 7" × 9" printing plate for a comic book page, the word portions of the adventure strip often shrank to a nearly unintelligible state.

Eastern, therefore, adopted the policy of reworking its adventure strip reprints. Larger lettering was incorporated in the dialogue balloons and captions, and this meant reconstructing the story with less dialogue and descriptive material, and eliminating the repetitive passages. Thus the "reprint" adaptions in *Famous Funnies* read slightly differently from the newspaper version, and often presented a concise, and more smoothly flowing version of the story. (Of course the original artists handled the reworking of the strip.)

Eastern perfected the comic book in more ways than one. During the twenty-year history of *Famous Funnies,* more than 100 different features on a wide variety of subjects appeared between its covers. While some ran for only twelve issues or less, others ran for a decade or more to become some of comicdom's best classics. A few of these features, representing a sampling of the broad spectrum of material that appeared in *Famous Funnies,* are reviewed in this section.

Famous Funnies, A Carnival of Comics (1933)
©1933 Famous Funnies, Inc.
(First Comic Book Magazine, value: $12,5000)

Famous Funnies No. 85 (Aug. 1941)
©1941 Famous Funnies, Inc.

"Roy Powers" was a remarkable comic strip that was linked to the Boy Scouts of America, the national youth organization founded in 1910 by Chicago newspaper publisher William D. Boyce who was inspired by a boys' training program developed in England in 1907 by Lord Baden-Powell, author of *Scouting For Boys*. After Congress had granted the Boy Scouts of America a federal charter on June 15, 1916, the organization underwent several changes, and the comic strip played an important role in them. On February 9, 1927, Boyce established the Eagle rank as the scout's highest grade, and it was earned by only those few young individuals who performed lifesaving feats at great personal risk, or engaged in outdoor camping and pathfinding in thick forest areas which had not yet been explored.

It was important to the growing organization to find some means of promoting the Eagle rank as a coveted goal for scout members to achieve. The answer came a few years later when artist Paul Powell, himself a former Boy Scout, created the fictional comic strip character Roy Powers, the Eagle Scout who braved the elements, fighting his way through forest fires, hurricanes, flash floods, and blizzards to get to the side of someone needing assistance. Roy Powers was portrayed as a 17-year-old who patrolled the shorelines with the U.S. Coast Guard, flew on rescue missions with the U.S. Air Corps and, on one occasion, courageously aided the police in bringing notorious gangs of Barbary Coast hoodlums to justice.

The character was immediately adopted as the official symbol of the Boy Scouts of America and developed as a continuing adventure strip for newspaper syndication in 1935. In 1937, Eastern reprinted the strip in *Famous Funnies,* starting with Issue 39, where it ran as a regular feature for a decade.

The first adventure began with Roy Powers and a few of his friends of the Beaver Patrol setting out on an overnight hike in a deep forest. The group was accompanied by a biology professor who nearly lost his life in a fall while climbing a mountain. Of course the scouts rushed to his aid, and this introductory episode portrayed the ability and ingenuity of Boy Scouts. The young men treated the professor's broken leg, made a stretcher from tree branches, and carried him across rugged terrain, mountain streams, and through thick foliage (all during the darkness of night), following trails they had marked earlier in the day. They managed to successfully transport their patient to the nearest medical facility where he received prompt professional attention.

While the story may not have been overly imaginative, it did present a dramatic true-life situation that empasized what an Eagle Scout was all about!

After the professor's injuries healed, he invited Roy and the Beaver Patrol to accompany him on an archeological expedition to the Arizona plains to search for historical evidence of an ancient Indian people that were believed to have occupied the area several centuries earlier. But the government had officially declared the territory off limits, and turned the land over to the last of the Apache tribes—anyone who ventured into the area was doing so at his own personal risk. Despite the potential danger, Roy Powers and the Beaver Patrol departed on their dramatic adventure—the first of many that would follow. Of course they clashed with the Apaches, but they ended up on peaceful terms with them.

Upon their successful return, the Beaver Patrol was granted a small island on which to set up a permanent Boy Scout campsite. But there was a price to be paid! They had to first solve the "Big Bird Mystery" that haunted the island. The beginning of this episode, shown on the following pages, was typical of the "Roy Powers" feature.

As it turned out, Roy eventually discovered that the "Big Bird" was actually a radio-controlled aircraft in disguise that was the creation of a deranged scientist who was using the island to secretly develop weapons of war for a foreign power. The Boy Scouts had accidentally uncovered the plot and notified the government authorities who in turn set out to arrest the scientist and his accomplice.

During the 1930s, "Roy Powers" became a very popular comic strip and it encouraged many readers to join the Boy Scouts so that they could do the same things Roy Powers did. Additionally, "Roy Powers" served as the lead-off feature in *Famous Funnies* for several months until Issue No. 81.

In 1939, Universal Pictures produced a controversial movie serial entitled *Scouts to the Rescue*, a direct adaptation of the comic strip with one change—Roy Powers' name was changed to "Bruce Scott." Inasmuch as the Boy Scouts of America was chartered as a nonprofit organization, legal complications prevented theatrical use of Roy Powers for commercial exploitation. Yet it was quite obvious that the star of the serial, regardless of what he was called on the screen, was Roy Powers. Moreover, movie star Jackie Cooper, who played the main role of Eagle Scout Bruce Scott, looked almost exactly like Roy Powers! And that was enough proof to convince eager young movie fans that they were watching their favorite Boy Scout hero in action for the first time on the screen.

The movie serial plot centered around the scouts' accidental discovery of a buried cache of counterfeit money, and this eventually led to a clash with a gang of counterfeiters whose secret headquarters was a supposedly abandoned ghost town in the mountains. To add more excitement, the story also involved a marauding band of Apache Indians who used the mountains for their hunting grounds and who opposed the presence of whites anywhere on their land.

Between counterfeiters, Indians, grizzly bears, mountain cats, wolf packs, snakes, bear traps, rainstorms, landslides, brush fires, whizzing arrows and speeding bullets, the scouts found many problems to overcome in their courageous struggle to survive. In the end, however, they finally brought the counterfeiters to justice and made peace with the Indians.

Although the names of the characters had been purposely changed to avoid legal conflict, Universal Pictures still encountered problems with distributing the serial because some critics labeled it as commercial exploitation of a nonprofit organization. As a result, the serial was generally restricted to free showings in schools.

The movie serial also raised a question about "Roy Powers" as a newspaper comic strip, and to avoid similar legal complications "Roy Powers" was soon dropped from newspaper syndication and had to be separated from the Boy Scouts as its official symbol in order to continue running in *Famous Funnies*.

Artist Paul Powell kept the feature going as his own strip until he retired in 1944. Afterwards, "Roy Powers" was taken over by another artist who continued the feature until it was dropped from *Famous Funnies* because of a page cutback that was effected at that time.

In the meantime, the Boy Scouts of America continued to grow. By 1960, its national membership had swelled to two million and that figure did not include its junior counterpart, the Cub Scouts of America, nor its sister counterpart, the Girl Scouts of America. By 1976, total combined scout membership exceeded five million!

Although "Roy Powers" lies buried in the literary graveyard of yesterday's long forgotten comic book features, his spirit still lives on today in each member of the Boy Scouts who dreams of becoming an Eagle Scout.

©1939 Universal Pictures and Boy Scouts of America

Famous Funnies No. 76 (Nov. 1940)
©1940 Famous Funniues, Inc.

Napoleon and Uncle Elby Comics No. 1 (1942)
©1933 Arthur J. Lafave Syndicate and
©1942 Eastern Color Printing Co.

The canine star of the early 1930 Sunday comics was Napoleon, an overgrown, lovable animal whose hilarious antics were reprinted in the first issue of *Famous Funnies* and continued as a regular feature for over a decade. Created by artist Clifford McBride for the Arthur J. Lafave Syndicate, "Napoleon" made its first appearance as a black-and-white daily strip in May 1929 (then titled "uncle Elby") and gradually evolved into the classic of pantomine humor, undoubtedly the most difficult art expression to keep alive and interesting for an extended period of time.

Napoleon never uttered a word of dialogue in conversation or thought balloons. He expressed his feelings and moods entirely through physical action typical of a domesticated pet. Although the strip occasionally included dialogue, human characters did the talking, and this usually amounted to a few words issued by Napoleon's master, Uncle Elby.

Like most humor strips, the entire act was complete within a single page. As such, "Napoleon" occupied a special position in *Famous Funnies*—the feature was often placed between each adventure strip. And Napoleon was often featured on the cover! McBride had the uncanny skill of depicting a complete sequence of action within a single illustration with such clarity and simplicity that the idea was obvious at a glance. In the midst of the many superhero titles displayed on the newsstand, the Napoleon covers made *Famous Funnies* stand out like a shining star.

In 1942, Eastern published a full-length comic book edition of "Napoleon," reprinting sixty-four pages of his hilarious adventures and misadventures that had previously appeared in *Famous Funnies*. Although McBride retired a few years later, the newspapers reran his popular "Napoleon" repeatedly until its eventual termination in the early 1950s.

In 1954, Dell Publishing Company acquired rights to "Napoleon," hired another artist to illustrate it, and published a new edition of the feature. However, it just didn't work. "Napoleon" was a product of Clifford McBride's own special style and embodied a personal touch that could never be duplicated. Napoleon, when drawn by someone else, just didn't look or act like Napoleon!

©1935 Arthur J. Lafave Syndicate

NAPOLEON
By Clifford Mc Bride

Prior to 1940, the term comics was generally applied to the newspaper comic strips that were created primarily for adult readership. During 1940, however, comic books had become a separate branch of the genre as more and more magazines were created for juvenile readership. Very few features had equal appeal both on comic pages and in comic books. Often a feature that was highly successful as a newspaper comic strip became a total flop when it was put into a comic book. Similarly, a feature that lacked appeal as a newspaper strip often became extremely popular when it appeared in a comic book.

Such was the case in 1939 when artist Russell Stamm developed "Invisible Scarlet O'Neil" as a newspaper strip for the Chicago Times Syndicate. Scarlet, considered too absurd and radical in its portrayal of the weaker sex, never captured the adult audience. Relatively few newspapers carried the strip, and it was soon phased out of syndication.

Eastern, however, reprinted the strip as the lead-off feature in *Famous Funnies No. 81* (April 1941). The kind of fantasy employed in "Invisible Scarlet O'Neil" fascinated juvenile readership, and Scarlet became one of the first superheroines of comicdom. It is worthwhile noting that Scarlet was also the first character[1] to employ invisibility as a superpower, a gift that would be adopted by other characters later on.

Scarlet also introduced the world's fastest technique for changing identity—she disappeared and reappeared simply by pressing a sensitive nerve on her left wrist, as shown here in the origin of Invisible Scarlet O'Neil.

Famous Funnies No. 81 (April 1941)
©1941 Famous Funnies, Inc.

Famous Funnies No. 81 through *No. 88* reprinted the original newspaper series, a human-interest story in which Scarlet protected a young blind youth from his wicked uncle who sought control of the youngster's trust fund. The plot, hardly of interest to a juvenile reader during the period of superhero fantasy, concluded in Issue 89, but then was carried over into the next issue when Scarlet, by employing her power of invisibility, forced the uncle to sign the boy's release papers as well as any claim to the youth's trust fund. From this point on, Russell Stamm created separate story material specifically for *Famous Funnies*.

Having aided the blind youth in enrolling in a special clinic for an eye operation that would eventually restore his sight, Scarlet departed from the human-interest story and embarked on a new kind of adventure. In her first escapade she boldly confronted a ruthless gang of Nazi agents engaged in stealing America's top secret war plans. Scarlet was hurled out of airplanes, run over by speeding cars, and shot at with machine guns. Yet she always escaped and finally managed to foil the enemy plot by using her power of invisibility.

Scarlet's adventures explored the invisibility concept as it had never been explored before, and resulted in the discovery of several brand new story themes. In one situation, she fell victim to amnesia while invisible, and a most bizarre chain of events occurred when she thought she didn't exist. Perhaps the strangest episode—and one that rates as a Golden Age classic in creative fantasy—occurred when Scarlet discovered that her invisible power was contagious. It began with a casual stroll down the street during an invisible state when a youth, coming in the opposite direction, bumped into her and knocked himself silly. Thrown to the ground, the dumbfounded lad scratched his head and tried to figure out what had happened. As a gesture of apology, Scarlet kissed the boy on the cheek. Result: the boy became invisible!

The boy's name was Hobble-De-Hoy, and he discovered that invisibility had its problems.

Unable to adjust to his new life, Hobble-De-Hoy ran away from home. His parents notified the police who began an intensive search for the missing (in more ways than one) youth. The search was futile for all involved, but Scarlet, as mystified as everyone else, was determined to find him. Fortunately, she was successful when the two, neither seeing the other, accidently bumped into each other in the park. . .

©1945 Famous Funnies, Inc.

Scarlet tried to correct the situation and make Hobble-De-Hoy visible again. She pressed his pulse and kissed him on the cheek—but nothing happened. While Scarlet pondered the problem, the youth slipped out of her grasp and darted away. Scarlet called out for him but he didn't answer. As he dashed into the street he crossed the path of a speeding truck and was struck down!

No one was aware of the misfortune until Scarlet, now visible, accidently stumbled and tripped over the unconscious body lying in the street. She carried him to a doctor whose administration of various injections finally dissolved the boy's invisibility. After his injuries had been treated and Scarlet had escorted him home, she moved on to another adventure that pitted her against a gang of racketeers.

©1945 Famous Funnies, Inc.

"Invisible Scarlet O'Neil" remained a regular feature in *Famous Funnies* for almost ten years and often made the cover spotlight. When Scarlet was terminated in 1950, readers demanded she be brought back. In response, Eastern published three full-length editions of *Invisible Scarlet O'Neil Comics,* which included reprints of some of her most exciting adventures from her earlier years in *Famous Funnies.* After the third issue, Scarlet dropped out of sight again.

However, her experiences had no doubt made a strong impression on comicdom; many other characters would soon adopt the use of invisibility in one form or another. In addition, Scarlet's seemingly trivial gesture of pressing her wrist was borrowed by other characters. *Quality Comics'* Captain Triumph, for example, discovered that by pressing the birthmark on his left wrist, he could instantly change from "average" to "super."

During 1952, the enterprising Harvey Publications acquired full rights to Scarlet for their "Comics Hits Revival" series, which was devoted solely to bringing back the cream of the crop: Flash Gordon, Mandrake, Phantom, Dick Tracy, and many others. *Comics Hits No. 50* introduced the all-new "Tales of Invisible Scarlet O'Neil." Ironically, this issue marked the end of the revival series.

By strange coincidence, Harvey's next book happened to introduce Casper, the Friendly Ghost, a character of their own creation who was also blessed with the gift of invisibility. Casper, though, became invisible at will, quite like Sue Richards of Fantastic Four.

In the beginning, when the contents of *Famous Funnies* consisted of reprints of Sunday features, the pages were photographically reduced to fit the standard page size of the comic book. However, with the outbreak of World War II in 1941, wood pulp became an essential material to the war effort, and the publishing industry participated in national drives to conserve the use of paper. As a conservation measure, newspaper editors requested that the syndicates reduce the size of the full-page Sunday comic strip to either three-fourths or one-half the size of the newspaper page. But inasmuch as the comic strips were prepared several months in advance, the change to the smaller size was a gradual one, and it did not become fully effective until January 1943. The modified proportion of the new comic strip size also meant that Eastern could no longer use the newspaper feature to fit the page size of *Famous Funnies.*

At the same time comic book publishers, as a means of conserving paper, made plans to cut back on the number of pages of new editions. During 1942, the standard 64-page format had dropped to a 52-page format and, in some cases, a 48-page format. Eastern made plans to comply with both changes.

Famous Funnies No. 88 (November 1941) carried the last sets of reprint material from the full-size newspaper page. Beginning with the next issue, the magazine converted to a new format. Many of the features were terminated and the features that were retained were developed with story material made just for the comic book. (In this case, the artists had to turn their strips into dual features—one for newspaper syndication to fit the new size requirement with emphasis on

Famous Funnies No. 89 (Dec. 1941)
©1941 Famous Funnies, Inc.

adult appeal, and the other to fit the page size of *Famous Funnies* with emphasis on juvenile appeal.)

The new format of *Famous Funnies No. 89* was set off by the dramatic introduction of Fearless Flint, the first superhero feature created specifically for the magazine by Stephan Douglass and H. G. Peters.

Flint's origin began when construction worker Jack Bradley was drilling a tunnel through a mountain. A sudden explosion caused a landslide and the dust that almost buried Bradley had a strange effect on his flesh. At first the dust seemed harmless, but Bradley soon discovered that whenever he brushed against metal his skin would change into an extremely hard, flint-like substance. Although the effect was only temporary, the condition returned whenever he became good and angry. He also discovered that when his skin had hardened to flint he was invulnerable to pain or physical injury. In fact, as a man of flint, Jack Bradley was a super being!

With the construction site destroyed, Bradley set out to track down the party responsible for dynamiting the mountain. His search led to a group of Pacific Islands inhabited by a tribe of natives who were under the hypnotic influence of a strange and sinister being known as the Lava Man, a sworn enemy of the human race. Fearless Flint immediately pitted his newly acquired power against the Lava Man in a dynamic action-packed adventure that continued over the next four issues.

After finally destroying the Lava Man, Fearless Flint slammed his way through a new adventure, battling the awesome Gargoyle Monsters who posed a serious threat to humanity.

In creating Fearless Flint, H. G. Peters introduced a highly distinctive style of illustration, purposely distorting human anatomy and perspective in order to convey the feeling of bold dramatic action, as shown here in the following scenes from the Gargoyle adventure . . .

Unfortunately, Fearless Flint fizzled out after eight episodes and was terminated when *Famous Funnies* instituted its page cutback. Stephan Douglass, one half of the creative team remained on Eastern's staff to become a regular cover artist for *Famous Funnies* and other titles of Eastern. H.G. Peters, the other half of the team, left Eastern and moved to D-C Publications to join "Charles Moulton" (alias Dr. William Moulton Marston) to develop the new "Wonder Woman" for the first issue of *Sensation Comics*. It was Peters who designed Wonder Woman's costume and endowed her with an "invisible" airplane.

As we have seen, Eastern's introduction of a practical way to print comics in color marked a new era for the industry, and the field began to grow as many features of all types were introduced for newspaper syndication. However, it was rare for a new comic strip to be perfectly formed in terms of its story, theme, and character development—or even its art style. More often than not, these elements were somewhat crude in the beginning and were only perfected by many months—and even years—of trial and error. Unfortunately, many features did not last long enough for their creators to develop them fully. Those that did manage to survive beyond the crucial first year of publication usually underwent varying degrees of change.

An example of one successful feature that underwent a complete overhaul, changing from humor to science fiction adventure, was Frank Godwin's "Connie." "Connie" started in the newspapers in 1927 as a feature of the Ledger Syndicate and was reprinted in the first issue of *Famous Funnies* where it continued as a regular series until the page cutback in the 1940s. In the beginning, artist Frank Godwin created "Connie" as a satirical comedy about a happy-go-lucky socialite who was much involved in the comings and goings of people connected with the motion picture industry. Inasmuch as Hollywood's talking films were beginning to fascinate the public, Connie's jibes at the medium was very much in vogue at the time. In fact newspapers carried several comic strip features that followed a similar theme, but "Connie" remained the most famous of them all.

"Connie" ©1936 Ledger Syndicate

Godwin had Connie continually changing wardrobes to reflect the latest clothing styles worn by the movie stars in their films. Every week Connie would wear a different dress, or a different hat, or a different evening gown, or pair of shoes, or fur coat, or bathing suit, and sometimes a different hair sytle. Normally, if an artist kept changing his character's appearance, the character would lose his or her identification. But Connie's constant change of wardrobe was an integral part of her character, and it strongly appealed to young female readership. No one outdressed Connie, and Connie always dressed for the occasion. She dressed formally when attending a social party given by Hollywood's hierarchy, and casually when stopping by the local movie house. Connie loved the movies, and she often had hilarious dreams about the pictures she had seen whether they were western films, gangster films, musical comedies, or of the horror variety. Because the motion picture industry covered a broad spectrum, Godwin was always able to inject new ideas within the theme of the strip.

But changes were on the horizon. At one point, Connie came across two tickets which she assumed were for a theatrical performance. Close inspection, however, revealed that she had in her possession two tickets to a demonstration of a time machine which she and her friend Jack attended. The sequence abruptly ended when the demonstrator, Dr. Chrono, faded from view. What was going on? This seemingly pointless idea lacked the usual "Connie" humor and besides, she was still wearing the same riding pants she had on the week before! Apparently, artist Frank Godwin had missed the boat this time. . . *or had he?*

In *Famous Funnies No. 84*, the "pointless" idea was expanded into the first adventure of the *new* Connie. Dr. Chrono, reappeared, still sitting in the chair of his time machine. He explained to the audience that he had just returned from another time. He asked Connie if she would like to take a short trip into the future. Of course she was excited and thrilled and quickly hopped into the chair. But she was also a bit cautious—she would only go one year into the future.

However, as Dr. Chrono was about to turn on the power, his pet cat became ensnarled in the motor compartment and its tail accidentally brushed against the timing lever, shoving it ahead ten centuries. Connie materialized in the Year 2941 when the world government of the new society was under control of women! But the world government was also on the brink of collapse. The sinister forces of the Yellow Combine were planning to take over, and Connie was seized as one of their spies. Fortunately, the women scientists probed Connie's mind with thought translators and verified that she had come from the past, an innocent spectator to an impending war. Connie was invited to serve the lovely brunette who was the President of the world!

Meanwhile, back in the 20th Century, Jack and Dr. Chrono became worried when Connie failed to return. Dr. Chrono then sent Jack ahead in time to the same year to find Connie. But when Jack arrived, the war had already broken out and the space fleets of both sides were engaged in heavy battle.

Here are comparative samples of the early Connie and the later Connie . . .

374

The feature that underwent the most spectacular change of all was "Big Chief Wahoo," a humorous newspaper strip of Publishers Newspaper Syndicate that was picked up by *Famous Funnies* in 1937. The team of Allen Saunders and Elmer Woggon originally created Wahoo as a tough little Indian chief who bumbled his way through the big city trying to comprehend the confusing ways of the paleface environment.

Wahoo was usually accompanied by his charming niece Minnie Ha-Cha who tried to educate him about the new life. But the chief was a stubborn student—he preferred to abide by old tribal customs. And in the event of a conflict between the new ways and the old, he would settle the disagreement with a good old fashioned slugging match. While the series was usually set in the big city, the scene occasionally shifted to the reservation as it did in *Famous Funnies No. 88* when a young white youth who was visiting Wahoo's tribe, ran away because he couldn't comprehend the confusing ways of the red man's environment.

Beginning with *Famous Funnies No. 89* as part of the magazine's new format, the series acquired a more serious tone and became an altogether different feature. It began on the same reservation during the course of a sacred ceremonial dance. A photographer was caught taking pictures of the affair and a fight broke out as the Indians attacked him. But Wahoo, who was nearby at the time, intervened and stopped the altercation. The photographer, who introduced himself as Steve Roper, was anxious to repay Wahoo for saving his life. Wahoo had gained a new ally who would help in the search for the white youth who had run away from the reservation and was presumably lost in the mountains.

The search turned into an exciting adventure that spanned several issues before the youth was finally found safe and sound. Based on the belief that the experiences of a young white boy on an Indian reservation would make a sensational news story, Roper sent photographs of the event to the magazine editor who had originally assigned him to cover Indian tribal customs. But when Roper inquired about the boy's background, Minnie Ha-Cha revealed a startling secret.

In reality, the youth was a prince and legal heir to a foreign throne in Europe, but rival uncles were warring over control of the throne after the king and queen, the boy's parents, were mysteriously poisoned. Loyal servants of the queen had smuggled the young prince out of the country and brought him to America to safeguard his life. To avoid international complications with a friendly government and yet provide political asylum for the prince, United States authorities had secretly placed him in protective custody on the Indian reservation—an "independent" government that was not tied to Washington's diplomatic obligation to return the prince to his country.

Upon realizing that the published story would expose the prince's whereabouts and create all types of problems, Chief Wahoo and Steve Roper flew to the city to stop the editor from using the pictures. He considered them and the story the news sensation of the year. Wahoo interceded and quite forcibly persuaded the editor to surrender the photos. As a result, Roper was promptly fired from the magazine.

Wahoo planned to return to the reservation as soon as he was assured that Roper had found new employment. Roper's next job, however, involved a hazardous photo assignment in the kingdom of Kashbar, a small country that was pocketed between friendly and enemy nations. Inasmuch as the assignment was far too dangerous for one person, Wahoo agreed to accompany Roper. The daring two then took off for a Nazi-occupied sector of the Orient and became involved in an exciting adventure of foreign intrigue.

Naturally, Wahoo and Steve Roper survived their ordeal in the Orient and returned to the United States with the photographs. But upon their return, Roper was notified that his father was in serious trouble. Roper, with Wahoo accompanying him, immediately left for home. Unknown to the two, Minnie had secretly stowed away inside Steve's plane.

In *Famous Funnies No. 124*, the three were united en route to Steve's home. A budding romance was developing between Steve and Minnie, but the romantic element brought unexpected complications to the feature. Roper told his mother that he did not love Minnie, although he reassured Minnie that the reverse was true.

In the newspaper version the romance continued, exploring the sensitivities of the mixed relationship. But in the comic book the romance ended abruptly when Minnie left for a new career in Hollywood. With romance out of the way, Wahoo and Roper returned to business.

As it turned out, Roper's father was a scientist whose research laboratory had been developing the formula for the atomic bomb which was urgently needed by the government. Because enemy agents had made previous attempts to steal the formula, Dr. Roper was anxious to deliver it safely to the War Department in Washington. Achieving a successful delivery, however, would pose a major problem. The mails could not be trusted, nor could any of Dr. Roper's assistants. Secrecy was essential and that eliminated the possibility of using a military or police escort.

Dr. Roper would not entrust anyone with the formula—except his son, Steve. Inasmuch as someone had already made an attempt on Steve's life, it became obvious that enemy agents were determined to prevent the formula's delivery. A daring plan was devised: surely the spy ring would overlook an inconspicuous Indian as the all-important courier of the formula for the atomic bomb . . .

However, Soko, Dr. Roper's "devoted Philipino butler who could hardly speak English," overheard the plan. In reality, Soko was the chief officer of the Japanese spy organization responsible for securing the formula. He radioed his men in Washington to intercept the Indian at all costs.

While Wahoo, Steve, and Dr. Roper continued to discuss the ideal routes to take, Wahoo's keen ears detected that someone was eavesdropping through the wall of the adjoining room. He motioned to Steve and his father to continue talking while he tiptoed out of the room to catch the eavesdropper—who turned out to be Soko. Soko sought to escape, but found that his Japanese judo chops could not break Wahoo's deadly hammer lock! Soko was exposed as a Japanese spy and placed under arrest. But when Soko's radio

transmitter was discovered, Dr. Roper realized that the spy ring was now aware of Wahoo's role, and that a change of plan was necessary. A new figure had to be brought into the picture, someone as equally trustworthy as Wahoo.

Steve wired Minnie Ha-Cha in Hollywood. Minnie, absent from the strip for several months, returned as an altogether different character—she was now the super shrewd secret agent who would mastermind the plan to move the formula safely through the spy network and into the hands of the War Department. Minnie's first step was to translate the complex formula into tribal language then weave it into a decorative pattern on an otherwise ordinary shawl . . .

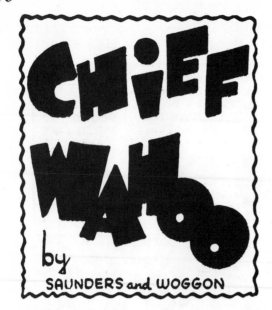

by
SAUNDERS and WOGGON

car and had surmised that Minnie's shawl somehow contained the secret formula. Watsiki tried to wreck the bus, but only succeeded in knocking the driver unconscious. Its brakes burned out, the bus sped out of control toward a steep ravine, and Wahoo, who had never driven before, leaped to grab the wheel . . .

©1945 Famous Funnies, Inc.

Next, the shawl was cut into two parts. Steve would take one half, wear it as a scarf, and fly to Washington by private plane. Minnie would wear the other half in accordance with the tribal customs of a newlywed. She and Wahoo would travel to Washington on commercial airliner, posing as an Indian couple on their honeymoon trip to the "Land of the Great White Father." If all went well, the three would meet at the Washington National Monument and then deliver the two halves to the War Department. But should the enemy capture either of them, the formula would still remain safe, for its translation was virtually impossible to decipher unless both halves of the shawl were fitted together. Even then, no one but an Indian maiden could read it—no one but Minnie Ha-Cha!

Dr. Roper approved Minnie's strategy, and the threesome parted. Wahoo and Minnie left for the airport, while Steve boarded his private plane.

Unknown to Steve, however, Soko had cleverly punctured the fuel lines of his plane prior to his capture, and at an altitude of 20,000 feet the plane suddenly ran out of gas! It plunged into a nose dive and crashed in the Ozark mountains.

Meanwhile, Wahoo and Minnie had also experienced complications. Enemy agents were waiting to intercept them while they changed planes. Wahoo managed to overcome their adversaries, and he and Minnie decided to continue the journey by train. This time they were intercepted by a different team of spies who attacked them with knives. Again Wahoo went on the warpath, whipping out his tomahawk and fighting his way to freedom. But he and Minnie had missed their train. The only alternative was to take a bus.

Enter Mr. Watsiki, new chief of the Kymarian Spy Operation. Mr. Watsiki had been trailing the bus by

With only seconds to spare, Wahoo turned the vehicle away from the edge of the cliff and onto a freshly-paved highway. The bus gradually coasted to a stop as the wheels became clogged in the wet cement. Wahoo and the busload of passengers sat back to wait for the next bus to pick them up while Minnie tended the driver's head wound. Wahoo and Minnie eventually reached Washington but didn't realize that Watsiki, upon finding that the bus did not crash into the ravine, had picked up their trail again.

Wahoo and Minnie waited for Roper at the designated meeting place. But when Roper didn't show up, Minnie decided that they should report directly to the Office of War Intelligence. They confided the secret of the shawl to a man who greeted them and identified himself as an officer of the War Department, but who, in actuality, was a double agent working for Watsiki. Wahoo and Minnie were cleverly led into a trap under the pretext that the officer was taking them to a secret houseboat headquarters where other government officials along with Steve Roper were impatiently waiting for them. But once Wahoo and Minnie arrived at the houseboat, they were promptly imprisoned—and Watsiki seized Minnie's half of the shawl!

Meanwhile, in the Ozark Mountains, a wilderness family discovered the plane wreckage and Roper's unconscious body. As they nursed him back to health,

Roper discovered he was being forced into marrying the daughter in the family. Roper managed to escape and reach Washington—and walk into the waiting arms of Watsiki's men.

Inasmuch as Watsiki now possessed both halves of the shawl, he tortured the prisoners until Minnie had no choice but to translate the formula. Having completed his objective, Watsiki prepared to dynamite the houseboat and blow up his prisoners. But while Wat-

siki was lighting the fuse, Roper had picked up a small piece of broken glass and was busily cutting the ropes that bound him. The fuse started burning as Watsiki and his men prepared to leave in the waiting motorboat. Roper severed his ropes and hastily cut Wahoo and Minnie free. In the ensuing battle royal that saw both sides scramble desparately for their lives, the heroic trio managed to leap into the motorboat and speed away a split second before the explosion . . .

©1945 Famous Funnies, Inc.

With the spy ring destroyed and the formula safe, Wahoo, Steve, and Minnie finally delivered the shawl to the proper authorities, thus marking the conclusion of a patriotic classic that ran as a continuous adventure in *Famous Funnies* during the war years, ending finally in June 1946.

Following this episode, the feature underwent

other changes; first, its title became "Chief Wahoo and Steve Roper." Then the series introduced the solo adventures of Minnie Ha-Cha during which time she emerged as the most beautiful woman in comicdom. Minnie, however, was soon afterwards phased out of the series which was followed by Wahoo's eventual departure and the new strip became "Steve Roper."

While the first and second editions of *Famous Funnies* carried all humor features, the third issue introduced the first reprint of "Buck Rogers"—and a new definition for the "funny book magazine" was born.

The monumental impact of this comic strip is best appreciated by reviewing that state-of-technology as it existed when the Buck Rogers idea was devised by the team of writer-inventor Phil Nowlan and artist-aeronautical engineer Lt. Dick Calkins of the U. S. Air Corps.

The era was the 1920s. The turn of the century had seen the birth of inventions that would gradually shape the future of America. Hand labor was replaced by steam-powered mechanization, and steam power paved the way for mass production of the new horseless buggies. A contraption called the telephone was being introduced for home use in 1920. Hollywood produced its first talking movie in 1927. Everyone raved about Charles Lindbergh's historic flight from New York to Paris on May 20, 1927. And the perfection of the vacuum tube in 1923 paved the way for establishing the nation's first radio broadcasting network. Transmitting stations were slowly being constructed as more and more crystal receiving sets were placed on the market as luxury items for the wealthy.

The turn of the century had also marked the beginning of scientific publications that explained, among other things, how to build a homemade crystal receiving set. This small group of technical journals, founded by Hugo Gernsbach, led to the first magazine of science fiction, **Amazing Stories,** *which was introduced in April 1926. Two years later, the August 1928 issue featured Phil Nowlan's classic novelette "Armageddon-2419." This was the story of a pilot who survived an airplane crash and sought temporary shelter inside an abandoned coal mine which, moments later, collapsed on him. The pilot was asphyxiated by a peculiar carbon vapor that preserved his body in a state of suspended animation. The shaft was opened some 500 years later and upon exposure to fresh air the pilot, Anthony Rogers, miraculously revived. He awoke to a strange new world of scientific marvel—and a world at war!*

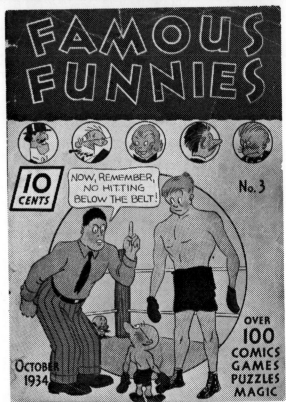

Famous Funnies No. 3 (Oct. 1934)

In view of the infant state of electronic technology during the 1920s when Nowland wrote this story as the origin of Buck Rogers, his exacting description of the world of the future, which introduced unheard of concepts relating to atomic warfare, surface-to-air missiles, television communication systems, laser beams, and anti-gravity propulsion, was extraordinary. Or was it fantasy?

In the following illustration which accompanied that story, artist Frank R. Paul depicted Buck Rogers for the first time. We see Buck inside an airship propelled by liquid helium, observing a battle scene on a closed-circuit television monitoring screen, and talking into a microphone. Buck is revealing the enemy's position to a ground soldier who is aiming a bazooka loaded with an atomic firing shell . . .

Seen upon the ultroscope viewplate, the battle looked as though it were being fought in daylight, perhaps on a cloudy day, while the explosions of the rockets appeared as flashes of extra brilliance.

Scene from "Armageddon-2419" (Origin of "Buck Rogers")
as published in *Amazing Stories,* August 1928

Considering that closed-circuit television did not become a reality until the 1960s, and that the bazooka was not devised for the U.S. Army until 1943, Paul's illustration depicting what would quickly become known as "Buck Rogers stuff" was an unusual work of art to appear in a pulp magazine in 1928. It was this illustration that suggested the potential of a comic strip on the subject.

Within a few months following the publication of "Armageddon-2419," Nowlan teamed up with Dick Calkins to develop the "pilot-in-the-25th-Century" idea into a comic strip for the John F. Dille Newspaper Syndicate. On January 7, 1929, the daily newspapers introduced the scientific adventures of Buck Rogers. The March 1929 issue of *Amazing Stories* featured Nowlan's sequel, "Airlords of Han," that set forth the technological concepts of interstellar space travel that would later be used in the comic strip. The following year, on March 23, 1930, "Buck Rogers" began in the Sunday comics section—which, of course, was being printed in color by Eastern.

While the newspaper was the nation's most effective mass communication medium, radio was slowly emerging as an important alternative. And with it came a new art form—radio drama. The first dramas were Wild West programs and detective programs, and then, in 1932, came the Nowlan-Calkins "Buck Rogers" series that captivated the nation. Special sound effects were created for rocket ships soaring through outer space, metal robots clanking across the countryside, people equipped with jet-belts sailing through the atmosphere, and nuclear-powered submarines bubbling to the ocean's surface.

When a twelve-year-old tuned in to "Buck Rogers" on the radio, he was not just listening to a story—he was also listening to the incredible sounds of life and technology 500 years in the future! The "Buck Rogers" radio program came to an end in 1934, just a few months before Eastern began publishing the nation's first monthly color comic book for the juvenile audience. And *Famous Funnies No. 3* started the Buck Rogers fever all over again!

Buck's role in the state of interstellar affairs soon rose to that of a special agent for Space Patrol Headquarters, and his assignments took him throughout the universe. His regular teammates included female companion Wilma Deering (who had originally discovered his body in the coal mine), her teenage brother Buddy Deering, and Alura from the Mars colony. The other principle character was Dr. Huer, Chief Scientist of Earth, whose research projects for the Space Patrol generally kept him confined to his laboratory. The 1935 adventure that brought Buck and Dr. Huer together scored new heights in the annals of science fiction. It seemed that the fixed state of equilibrium between the planetary bodies was being se-

Famous Funnies No. 82 (May 1941)
©1941 Famous Funnies, Inc.

riously threatened by Mars' tendency to shift out of its normal orbital path around the sun and soar away from the solar system. Buck's job: to find the cause and put a stop to it. The cause: super intelligent alien beings from another galaxy who were determined to steal a planet!

In 1939, Universal Pictures introduced the movie serial adaptation of Buck Rogers. Generally following the framework of the comic strip, the movie serial centered around an underground revolutionary struggle that was resisting the dictatorial regime of President Kane who was planning conquest of various space colonies within the United Solar Federation. In the midst of the action as always, Buck came to the aid of the revolutionist cause that was led by Dr. Huer. He successfully penetrated Kane's air defenses and sought help from the Saturn space colony which was unaware of Kane's activities.

Meanwhile, Kane's army was attacking the arctic region in an attempt to wipe out the revolutionaries' stronghold in a hidden city beneath the polar cap. Dr. Huer's men, observing the surface through their visascreens, waited for the enemy patrols to reach the proper position. Then, sections of ice glaciers slid open. Hidden space artillery guns telescoped out and pointed down at the troops who were storming across the snow toward the tunnel entrance. Devastating

You followed Buck Rogers' adventures in the newspapers! You heard him on the radio! Now *SEE him for the first time* in the most fantastic adventures ever filmed!

12 AMAZING THRILL-THRONGED CHAPTERS

BUCK ROGERS

WITH LARRY CRABBE

Constance MOORE · Jackie MORAN
Henry BRANDON · Wheeler OAKMAN
Philson AHN · Jack MULHALL

Screen play by Norman HALL and Ray TRAMPE · Original cartoon strip by Dick Calkins and Phil Nolan
Based on the Buck Rogers newspaper feature owned and copyrighted by John F. Dille Co.
Directed by FORD BEEBE and SAUL GOODKIND · Associate Producer: BARNEY SARECKY

©1939 Universal Pictures

rocket bombs were fired. The few who survived the merciless cross fire were buried by huge avalanches created by the shattering explosions of shell fire.

Kane's own space squadron headed toward the arctic region to support whatever was left of his ground forces. Dr. Huer's men observed the approaching ships and waited until they were within firing range. With a few adjustments of the remote control dials, the guns swung upward and pointed toward the sky. Rocket bombs were fired, ripping the ships apart. But the ships released their own fire. Glaciers of ice were levelled. Artillery guns exploded.

Dr. Huer's visascreens began blinking out as the observation cameras on the surface were destroyed. However, Dr. Huer was still able to observe President Kane in his "Palacedrome." They watched him issue an emergency security alert! All military personnel were to report to their artillery stations and all patrol squadrons were to form a defensive blockade—an invading battle fleet had been sighted approaching Earth!

It could only mean one thing: Buck Rogers had gotten through to the Saturn Space Colony!

The first defending squadron flanked outward in straight-line formation. They streaked up through the atmosphere to meet the Saturn warships, and precipitated the most spectacular space battle ever produced in motion pictures. Thunderous explosions ripped through the air as rocket bombs whizzed in all directions. Sizzling heat rays sprayed across the skies. Flaming fragments of exploding vessels rained down from the heavens. Cities caught fire and complete buildings evaporated in sweltering billows of smoke. It was the ultimate war—"Armageddon-2419!"

When the United States entered the war in December 1941, the *Buck Rogers* movie serial was quickly cancelled; Oriental actors had starred as the people of the Saturn space colony, and when they attacked Earth, it was the yellow good guys from Saturn fighting white Earthmen who were the bad guys. By 1942 the movie serial was forgotten. By then the famous comic strip was portraying similar interplanetary warfare, but white Earthmen were the good guys fighting the yellow bad guys from Mars. As such, the *Buck Rogers* movie serial, produced in 1939 and cancelled in 1941, remains virtually unknown as one of Hollywood's first science fiction film classics.

After Phil Nowlan's death in 1940, Dick Calkins took over the comic strip as both writer and artist. At the time, Calkins had a different strip, "Skyroads," which he turned over to artist Russell Keaton so that he could devote his full time to "Buck Rogers." When *Famous Funnies* converted from reprints to original stories, Calkins acquired a new partner, artist Rick Yaeger, and together they developed "Buck Rogers" into a dual feature that presented separate and unrelated stories—one for newspaper syndication and the other for *Famous Funnies.*

At the same time, Eastern, in tribute to the late Phil Nowlan, introduced a set of six full-length comic book editions of "Buck Rogers" with the original adventures that Nowlan and Calkins had created in the 1930s.

In the new newspaper feature, Dr. Huer and Buddy Deering faded out of the picture as Buck and Wilma Deering returned to Earth in the midst of an interplanetary war against Mars. Having saved each other from innumerable hazards, Buck and Wilma emerged as the romantic couple of the 25th century. Their story situations often led toward marriage, but something unexpected always happened to prevent it.

Then Buck mysteriously disappeared, leaving a heartbroken Wilma to carry on as the main star. Her relentless search for Buck took her everywhere on Earth as well as back and forth to Mars and Venus where she met many other suitors. And the ultimate question was posed: if she failed to find Buck, could Wilma find happiness with another man?

In *Famous Funnies*, however, it was Buck and Wilma who were phased out, while Dr. Huer and his band journeyed into distant galaxies. In one episode, they found themselves stranded on a remote world with barbaric creatures in close pursuit. The chase led through the depths of the planet, where they discovered the ancient ruins of a spaceship from Twentieth-century Earth which had crashed there during the dawn of space travel. Fortunately, Dr. Huer was able to repair the ship just as the monsters came charging over the mountainside. The ship blasted off! But while the group had escaped, their antiquated vessel couldn't travel very far and they were forced to land on a nearby planet. There they were overwhelmed by a society of "metal monkeys." One, who spoke the Earth language, led them away, and the conversation went like this . . .

©1944 Famous Funnies, Inc.

Buck Rogers Comics No. 2 (1940)
©1932 John F. Dille Syndicate;

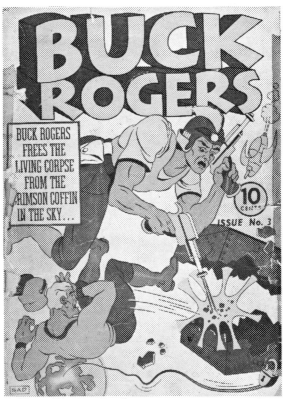

Buck Rogers Comics No. 3 (1941)
©1933 John F. Dille Syndicate

Dr. Huer had his hands full trying to outsmart his adversary, who had devised the means for transplanting the human mind into a battery-operated mechanical body. Buck had unknowingly fallen victim to the scientist, and Dr. Huer was scheduled to be next.

From the 1940s to the mid-1950s, the dual features of "Buck Rogers" continued in the newspapers and in the comic book. During these years, the famous "Buck Rogers" trademarks—robots, ray guns, antigravity jet-belts, spaceships, and interplanetary warfare—became commonplace in pulp science fiction as well as in comic book literature. In September 1946, Buck Rogers made a comeback on radio just when the medium was beginning to experience its first threat from television that was then evolving out of its experimental stage. (Shortly afterwards, the appeal of the continuous adventure comic strip in the newspaper would be affected by the coming of television.) The *Buck Rogers* radio program was soon cancelled along with other once-popular radio shows. In 1952, the "Buck Rogers" comic strip was dropped from newspaper syndication when Calkins retired. Eastern recruited topnotch artist Frank Frazetta to keep the feature going in *Famous Funnies,* where it appeared until June 1955 when the magazine, after leading the parade for twenty years as "The Nation's Comic Monthly," finally ceased publication.

Afterwards, other comic book publishers made a few attempts to revive Buck Rogers, the last such edition appearing in 1964.

In 1969, Chelsea House, publishers of hardcover books, introduced a 370-page hardcover volume en-

titled *The Collected Works of Buck Rogers* which featured a selection of newspaper reprints from the 1940s through the 1950s, and a few from the 1930s. Additional information on Buck Rogers appears in the first issue of *All Rare Magazine* which contains the original classic "Armageddon-2419" exactly as it was published in the August 1928 issue of *Amazing Stories.* In addition, *All Rare Magazine* includes a detailed description of the *Buck Rogers* movie serial, the 1932 radio program, and a reprint of a comic strip adventure from the 1930s.

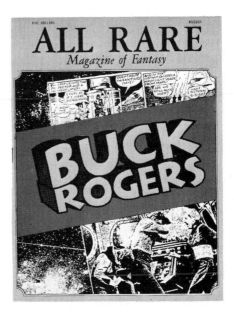

Here are a few examples that show how the "Buck Rogers" stories often included accurate technological forecasts of Space Age inventions of today . . .

YESTERDAY'S COMIC BOOK FANTASY	TODAY'S REALITY

BUCK ROGERS, 1931

Decelerating principle for re-entering atmosphere.

©1931 John F. Dille Syndicate

NASA, 1977

Decelerating principle for re-entering atmosphere.

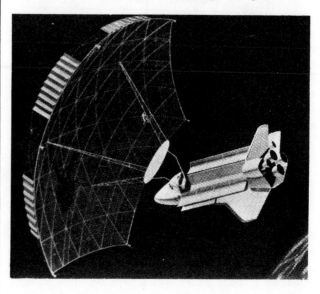

BUCK ROGERS, 1944 *(Famous Funnies)*

Piggyback principle for launching a spacecraft from a spacecraft.

©1944 Famous Funnies, Inc.

NASA, 1977

Piggyback principle for launching a satellite from the space shuttle.

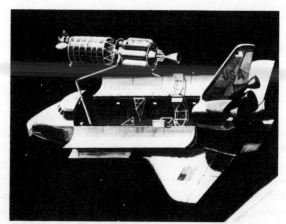

Shuttle operational modes under continuing study include **(A)** tug in relation to orbiter, **(B)** manned space station, **(C)** tug service craft, shown here repairing a multipurpose satellite, and **(D)** construction of large structures, here a radio-telescope.

In addition to reprinting such famous strips as "Buck Rogers," *Famous Funnies* also introduced other historic milestones in comic book literature which are described within the following summaries of the lesser-known features of this title:

Adventures of Patsy (Mel Graff)

"Patsy," which first appeared in the newspapers in 1934, was initially a comic strip about a young girl who wandered through fairy tale kingdoms inhabited by witches, giants, and even mechanical men. During the second year, however, Patsy woke up from her dream world and moved into more adventurous situations. She went to Hollywood to become a child actress and the unknowing assistant to a villainous stage magician who placed her under a hypnotic spell and made her part of a diabolical scheme to steal important plans for a powerful war machine. Of course, her uncle Phil Cardigan, who assumed the role of a private detective, came to the rescue and thwarted the plot. The series was reprinted in *Famous Funnies* from 1937 to 1939 as one of the first adventure strips with a child in the heroic role.

Babe Bunting (Fanny Young)

"Babe Bunting," the classic soap opera comic strip that centered around the heart-warming experiences of a young orphan girl who became embroiled in one dramatic true-to-life family situation after the other, was one of several brainstorm ideas of artist Fanny Young who is better known for her creation of the world-famous *Mother Goose* fairy tale and the "Little Miss Muffet" comic strip which appeared after "Babe Bunting" and emerged as the more popular of the two in the newspapers, running until the mid-1950s. Fanny Young resigned from "Babe Bunting" after the first few episodes and this strip was taken over by artist Roy L. Williams who continued the feature until its termination in the early 1940s. "Babe Bunting," as illustrated by Roy L. Williams, was reprinted in *Famous Funnies* from 1936 to 1939 as the first soap opera feature in comic book literature.

Dan Dunn (Norman Marsh)

"Dan Dunn, Secret Operative 48," which debuted in the newspapers in October 1933, was reprinted in the first issue of *Famous Funnies* and became the comic book's first adventure feature dealing with good-versus-evil. In this case, the threatening evil element was Wu-Fang, the infamous villain of the Orient who devised one diabolical scheme after the other in his insane quest to rule the world but was thwarted each time by our daring hero of the Secret Service. Although the feature was not especially successful as a comic strip and was phased out of newspaper syndication during 1940, its action packed theme about "the secret agent versus the master criminal from the Orient" was nevertheless adapted to early pulp fiction where it became a classic. Indeed, Wu-Fang, along with Dr. Fu-Manchu, emerged as pulp literature's most infamous characters whose names still invoke a few chills today while the heroes who fought them have long since faded away into limbo.

Daredevils of Destiny (Frank Rentfrow and Don Dickson)

This was a feature based largely on true-life events about military heroes of World War I and made its debut as a comic strip in the Sunday newspapers in August 1937. It began with an illustrated narrative about Lieutenant Christian Schilt, the first marine to be awarded the Congressional Medal of Honor!

The second episode told the tragic story of General Greely—a Civil War hero who was wounded in action on three separate occasions. The episode, however, is post-Civil War. In 1881, General Greely was assigned to command the first naval expedition to explore the Arctic Circle and collect scientific data for use in map charting. The party of twenty-four made several important discoveries during their journey. All this was marred, however, by an iceberg which smashed their ship and marooned the crew at the top of the world for more than a year. Facing death by starvation and freezing, Greely led his crew on an endless hike across the snow-covered regions to another part of the arctic where he sent distress signals to a foreign vessel that eventually rescued them. Only seven survived.

The full story of General Greely's courage, as told by one of the survivors, did not come out until 1937, long after Greely had retired from service and was in ill-health. It was at this time—a few months before his death and fifty-five years after the journey—that General Greely was awarded the Congressional Medal of Honor.

"Daredevils of Destiny" appeared in just a handful of newspapers during 1937 and was reprinted in *Famous Funnies* the following year.

Dickey Dare (Coulton Waugh)

The first version of this strip, which was for the most part a fairy tale fantasy centering around the daydreams of a young boy, began in the newspapers in July 1933 and was initially created by Milton Caniff for the Associated Press Syndicate. The strip was in trouble within a year.

To save it, Milton Caniff introduced several revisions and converted the story theme into a serious adventure with the introduction of soldier-of-fortune Dan Flynn who served as Dickey's guardian. However, Caniff abruptly left the feature but used the revised theme to create a new comic strip called "Terry and the Pirates" which began in October 1934 and was distributed by the Tribune-News Syndicate.

Meanwhile, "Dickey Dare" was resumed by artist Coulton Waugh who continued the feature over the next ten years and expanded Caniff's theme into a classic adventure strip with a young boy in the heroic role. "Dickey Dare," as illustrated by Coulton Waugh and then by his wife and former assistant Mabel Odin Burvik, who occasionally signed the strip as "Odin," was reprinted in *Famous Funnies* beginning in 1937 and continued to run as one of the magazine's major attractions through the 1950s.

During the mid-1950s when the critics began attacking objectionable elements in comics, they raised a furor over twelve-year-old Dickey Dare not attending school! Apparently, young Dickey was spending too much time as a prisoner of pirates in the South Sea islands, running from head-hunters in Africa, or trapped as a child-slave in the Orient . . . and not enough time in school. The comic strip was supposedly responsible for influencing juvenile truancy and subsequently was dropped from newspaper syndication in 1954.

Dixie Dugan (J.P. McEvoy and J.H. Strebi)

The "Dixie Dugan" series, originally titled "Show Girl," was created as a comic strip spin off of McEvoy's hit novel "Show Girl" which was first published as a serial in *Liberty Magazine* during 1928 and soon afterwards adapted for live stage performance (which was also a Broadway success), and then made into a feature-length movie for another hit. The romantic epic made its debut as a comic strip in 1929 and centered around the disappointing love affairs of a young attractive starlet named Dixie Dugan. But in 1930, the title of the comic strip was changed to "Dixie Dugan," and the heroine herself underwent a slight modification in character concept as she became more involved in serious adventure. "Dixie Dugan" was also among the original family of features that appeared in the first issue of *Famous Funnies*.

After a two-year run in the nation's first monthly color comic book, "Dixie Dugan" appeared again in *Feature Funnies* along with "Joe Palooka" and other comic strips of the McNaught Syndicate, all of which were later transferred to Columbia Features' *Big Shot Comics*. During the 1940s, Columbia introduced several full-length editions of *Dixie Dugan Comics* which became one of Columbia's leading titles.

Hairbreadth Harry (C.W. Kahles)

"Hairbreadth Harry," created in 1906 by C.W. Kahles, was the original melodrama which centered around the humorous escapades of hero Harry Hollingsworth and his never-ending efforts to save his lovely and innocent sweetheart Belinda Blinks from the dastardly clutches of arch-rival Rudolph Rassendale, the character who sported the black mustache and wore the black hat and was obviously the villain. In fact, Rassendale introduced the villain image that was later popularized by Hollywood in the silent melodramatic films and then in the sound western films where the bad guy was always recognized by his black mustache and black hat.

After Kahle's death in 1931, F. O. Alexander continued the strip for eight years and expanded it as well into a full-color Sunday feature which the Ledger Syndicate distributed in newspapers across the country. Alexander also increased the tempo of suspense by having the Sunday feature end each week with Belinda facing a terrible fate. The most famous "Hairbreadth Harry" sequence (which has been adapted numerous times with many variations in other features) was the one where Rassendale seized Belinda and threatened to do away with her if she didn't consent to marry him. When she refused, Rassendale promptly tied her to the railroad tracks as the speeding train approached . . .*could Harry save her in time?*

Of course in the next episode, our hero Hairbreadth Harry who had been observing all from the top of a steep cliff, frantically races down the hillside to engage the track control switch in time to guide the train onto the next track and away from Belinda. Then he unties her as Rassendale slips away grumbling "Curses! Foiled again!"

No doubt, Alexander's technique for portraying cliff-hanging suspense was quite influential in the making of many movie serials. "Hairbreadth Harry," as illustrated by Alexander, was reprinted in the first issue of *Famous Funnies* and ran as a regular series until 1939 when it was terminated in the newspapers.

Joe Palooka (Ham Fisher)

The "Joe Palooka" series, which is described in further detail in Section 14 as a major attraction in Columbia's *Big Shot Comics*, was another comic strip that appeared in the first issue of *Famous Funnies* and depicted Joe Palooka as he first started out—a good natured and sometimes mischievous 15-year-old youth who was constantly getting into fist fights with the neighborhood bullies. Young Joe gradually began to age as the series progressed. And the other comic books which featured "Joe Palooka," depicted the character in his adult life as the famous Heavyweight Boxing Champion of comicdom.

Lightning and The Lone Rider (Jack Kirby)

When rancher Jim Larrimore donned a black hood to disguise his face, he became the other masked rider of the plains who led the fight for law and order in the early days of the Wild West. And his white horse "Lightning" was acclaimed as the fastest stallion between Texas and the Wyoming territory. Although the Lone Rider had no faithful Indian companion at his side, he was nevertheless an exciting character whose thrill-packed adventures pitted him against the likes of Dr. Chuda . . . an immortal telepath who had been around for some 50,000 years and sought to uncover certain Aztec treasures that contained secrets of his ancient race. Dr. Chuda had enlisted the aid of a ruthless gang of outlaws to go after the treasure. Of course the Lone Rider was determined to stop them; he had traced the gang's hideout and pulverized the guards in a knock-down-drag-out battle. Then he met Dr. Chuda for the first time and this is what happened . . .

©1940 Famous Funnies, Inc.

"Lightning and The Lone Rider" was Jack Kirby's first feature, an ill-fated newspaper comic strip created during 1938 a few months after "The Lone Ranger" debuted in the newspapers. But Kirby's hero of the Wild West was reprinted in *Famous Funnies* beginning at Issue 62 (September 1939) and ran for a year until its termination at Issue 80 in March 1941 . . . the same month when Kirby introduced Captain America to the nation!

Mutt & Jeff (Bud Fisher)

Bud Fisher's famous comedy team made their debut in the newspapers in November 1907. It started out as a cartoon panel about sports with our hero Augustus Mutt in the role of an eccentric gambler at the horse races. However, the feature evolved into one of the best straight-humor comic strips of the day and was soon shifted from the sports page to the regular funny pages. "Mutt & Jeff" was also reprinted in a variety of odd-size hardcover books published by the Ball Company during 1910 and then by the Cupples and Leon Company during the 1920s. In 1930, the Walter Lantz Studios adapted the zany twosome to screen life for a series of animated cartoon shorts which were as classic and equivalent to the famous "Laurel and Hardy" films. Then a few years later "Mutt & Jeff" became the leading feature in Eastern's initial color comic book premiums as well as the cover attraction for the first few issues of *Famous Funnies*.

After a brief run in *Famous Funnies*, "Mutt & Jeff" was reprinted again in D-C's *All American Comics* and then branched out into a series of full-length comic book editions as a leading D-C title during the 1940s. Comicdom's favorite comedy team also appeared in Dell's line of comic books as well as in the group of Harvey Publications. In addition, "Mutt & Jeff," currently drawn by cartoonist Al Smith, still continues to run in many newspapers today and ranks as the oldest American comic strip feature (second only to the "Katzenjammer Kids").

Ned Brant (Bob Zupke)

Created by professional football coach and artist Bob Zupke for the McNaught Syndicate, Ned Brant of Carter University was the all-American star athlete and one of the earliest comic strip characters to deal exclusively with the sports theme. The feature was the first of its kind to illustrate the game excitement and thrill of football and other college sports as well as to describe the players' experiences of tension and anxiety that took place behind the scenes in the locker room and on the training field the day before the big game event.

McNaught Syndicate launched the "Ned Brant" series in the Sunday newspapers during the fall of 1933, coinciding with the peak of the football season, and it was reprinted in *Famous Funnies* during 1935 to mark the beginning of the sports theme in comic book literature.

Oaky Doaks (R.B. Fuller)

"Oaky Doaks," which the Associated Press Syndicate introduced in the newspapers in 1935, was perhaps one of the most offbeat humor classics in the history of comics. Its unique theme centered on Oaky Doaks as a good-natured, muscle-headed stumblebum of a wandering knight in rusty grey armor whose zany miscapades took place during the Middle Ages and often employed light-hearted elements of sword-and-sorcery fantasy. He fought dragons and

wild animals of all sorts and usually defeated them with a powerful wallop right between the eyes . . . or by pulling their tails until they yelped in pain and ran away. Here is a typical sequence in which Oaky, his chubby buddy King Cedric, and his ever-faithful stallion Nellie have escaped the clutches of a lunatic sorceror by stealing his magic carpet to flee to the skies. Then they unwittingly pick up an unwanted hitchhiker—a vicious-looking vulture who gleefully considers them for its meal . . .

©1937 Associated Press Syndicate; ©1940 Famous Funnies, Inc.

"Oaky Doaks" was reprinted in *Famous Funnies* in 1937 and continued as a regular feature until the magazine ceased publication in 1955. During these years Oaky Doaks often made the *Famous Funnies* cover attraction, and in addition he headlined one issue of his own full-length comic book which Eastern published in 1942. On the other side of the fence, the feature ran in the newspapers until 1961 and was dropped only because Associated Press Syndicate discontinued business and folded.

Scorchy Smith (Noel Sickles)

Scorchy Smith was among the first of comicdom's soldiers-of-fortune whose high-flying adventures debuted in the daily newspapers during March 1930. The feature was originally created by John Terry whose sudden illness forced him to retire within a few months. And "Scorchy Smith" was then taken over by Noel Sickles who developed the comic strip into an adventure classic comparable to Milton Caniff's "Terry and the Pirates."

Curiously enough, Sickles and Caniff often worked together as a team combining their talents to produce both "Scorchy Smith" and "Terry and the Pirates" during the mid-1930s. However, Noel Sickles left the "Scorchy Smith" series in 1936 and the feature was then taken over by artist Bert Christman until 1938. Following Christman, the feature changed hands again and was continued by many other artists who kept it going until its eventual demise in 1961. But it was Noel Sickles who had perfected the dynamic art style and tone of story plot excitement which his successors had closely followed to keep "Scorchy Smith" a leading adventure comic strip in the newspapers for thirty years. It was reprinted in *Famous Funnies* between 1937 and 1947.

Sergeant Stony Craig (Frank Rentfrow and Don Dickson)

"Sergeant Stony Craig of the U. S. Marines," which debuted in the newspapers in August 1937, was the first adventure comic strip about the armed services and was reprinted in *Famous Funnies No. 65* to run concurrently with the non-fiction "Daredevils of Destiny," also created by the Rentfrow-Dickson team. When both features first appeared in *Famous Funnies,* it marked the beginning of the military theme in comic book literature which would later become a dominant trend during the 1940s. Although "Sergeant Stony Craig" was a fictional character, his action-packed off-base assignments reflected an uncanny level of authenticity about the Marine Corps Division of Naval Intelligence . . . the story plots were based on the true experiences of the strip's creators, Sergeant Frank F. Rentfrow and Lieutenant Donald L. Dickson, both formerly of the U.S. Marine Corps!

Skyroads (Dick Calkins)

The 1927 newspaper serialization of the true-story account of Charles Lindbergh's historic airplane flight across the Atlantic had immediately triggered the explosion of aviation fiction as a new literary genre in pulp fiction which started in Fiction House's *Wings Magazine* and then filtered through into the comic strip media with the introduction of "Skyroads," created by Air Corps Lieutenant Lester J. Maitland in 1929 for the John F. Dille Syndicate. When the feature was expanded into a full-color comic strip for the Sunday newspapers in 1932, it was taken over by Air Corps Lieutenant Dick Calkins who, along with two talented assistants, perfected the strip's technical accuracy for depicting aircraft detail.

Curiously enough, one of Calkins assistants was Zack Mosely who left the feature within a year to create "Smilin' Jack," another comic strip on the aviation theme which the News-Tribune Syndicate launched in the newspapers in October 1933 . . . *for a forty year run!* "Smilin' Jack" was reprinted within Dell's line of comic books and in 1943, Universal Pictures brought Mosely's popular character to screen life in an exciting movie serial adaptation. Basically, "Smilin' Jack" Martin was a commercial pilot who operated a private airplane to deliver special cargo shipments as well as passengers to all points around the globe. Of course this activity brought him in contact with a cluster of fascinating and well-remembered characters as well as a series of romantic entanglements, the most famous of which was his love affair with Joy whom he eventually married. But Joy mysteriously vanished from his life after giving birth to their son "Jungle Jolly" who became the focal point of the feature for many years.

Calkins' other assistant was professional flying instructor and artist Russell Keaton who aided on the "Buck Rogers" series as well as "Skyroads." When Calkins decided to devote full time to "Buck Rogers," he turned "Skyroads" over to Keaton to manage completely. But within a few years, Keaton had resigned from "Skyroads" to create the "Flying Jennie" series, an altogether different comic strip on the aviation theme which centered around the high flying adventures of Jennifer Dare, comicdom's first lady flying ace. "Flying Jennie" was reprinted in Eastern's second monthly title, *Heroic Comics.*

"Skyroads" was a technical comic strip about aviation and was not developed around a central hero. Each artist who managed the series was an expert in the aviation field and had created story situations around a different group of characters which included at various intervals such aviators as Ace Ames, then Hurricane Hawk, and then Speed McCloud. Artist Leon Gordon succeeded Keaton on "Skyroads" and effectively maintained the aviation theme by introducing Clipper Williams and the Junior Flying Legion. Of the many characters that appeared in the series, the junior heroes of the Flying Legion were the most popular and indeed they emerged as the main stars of "Skyroads" when the comic strip was ultimately dropped from newspaper syndication in the mid-1940s. During its prime years of popularity, "Skyroads" was reprinted for a five year run in *Famous Funnies* from 1936 to 1941 and also appeared in a host of other publications including the fifth and sixth issues of *Buck Rogers Comics* and several editions of Whitman's Big Little Books.

"S'Matter, Pop?" (Charles M. Payne)

"S'Matter, Pop?" debuted in the *New York World* in 1910 as one of the first family-humor comic strips and appeared in the newspapers for thirty years. It was also among the original family of comic strips reprinted in the first issue of *Famous Funnies* and remained as a regular feature for two years. "S'Matter, Pop?" was also published in the third issue of *Comic Monthly* which began in 1921 as the black-and-white predecessor to *Famous Funnies* and is described in further detail in Section 14.

"Strange At It Seems" (Elsie Hicks)

"Strange As It Seems," which debuted in the newspapers at the turn of the century during the early 1900s, introduced a unique trend in the non-fiction comic strip category and was created by lady artist Elsie Hicks who used the pen-name of "John Hix." She developed the feature around subject matter consisting of incredible oddities in history and in nature which, as strange as it may seem, was a generic idea that inspired Robert Ripley's "Believe It Or Not" series which began later in 1918 and a host of other similar features of the 1930s as Stookie Allen's "Above The Crowd" and Roscoe Fawcett's "Screen Oddities." "Strange As It Seems" was also among the original family of comic strips reprinted in the first issue of *Famous Funnies* and continued to run until 1936, often appearing in the select position of the inside front cover of the comic book. In addition, Elsie Hicks' feature was reprinted for a second go-around in *Feature Funnies* during 1938 and again for three full-length issues in United Feature's "Single Series" comic book editions during 1939 and 1940.

Famous Funnies No. 86 (Sept. 1941)
©1941 Famous Funnies, Inc.
(cover art by Bill Everett)

Famous Funnies No. 139 (Feb. 1946)
©1946 Famous Funnies, Inc.

Famous Funnies No. 141 (April 1946)
©1946 Famous Funnies, Inc.

Heroic Comics No. 1 (Aug. 1940)
©1940 Eastern Color Printing Co.

In the midst of the 1940 explosion of superhero fantasy, Eastern introduced its second monthly title *Heroic Comics* as the official publication of "Reg'lar Fellers of America," a junior athletic organization founded by Clair F. Bee, then Director of Health Education at Long Island University. "Reg'lar Fellers of America" was dedicated to developing wholesome summer recreation for 12 to 15-year-olds through competitive sports, and Eastern's second publication was to serve as the vehicle for promoting the organization to the nation's youth.

While *Heroic Comics* would in time undergo a major change, it started out as a magazine of superheroes featuring some of the most imaginative characters ever created. Its star attraction was Hydroman, created by artist Bill Everett a few months after he had created the classic Sub-Mariner for Timely Publications' popular *Marvel Mystery Comics*. The two characters were quite similar. In addition to their striking physical resemblance, Hydroman and Sub-Mariner were both unique heroes "of the water" but for quite different reasons: whereas water to Sub-Mariner was his natural environment and source of strength, water was Hydroman's physical composition!

Between the two characters, Everett had perfected a fascinating pen-and-ink technique that right-fully earned him the title of "King of the Water Artists." The technique is exemplified best by Everett's portrayal of Hydroman—a liquid being of dripping wetness who could flow through the air with the smooth fluidic rhythm of a waterspout. Yet Hydroman was flexible—he could become a pool of water as easily as he could become human.

Here is the origin of Hydroman . . .

HYDROMAN

By Bill Everett

THIS IS THE STORY OF HARRY THURSTON'S GREAT DISCOVERY-"HYDRO-MAN"~HARRY IS A YOUNG CHEMIST WHO DEVOTES ALL HIS SPARE TIME TO CONSTRUCTIVE INVENTION-CONFINING HIMSELF DAY AND NIGHT TO HIS LABORATORY ~ HIS TWO DEAREST FRIENDS ARE BOB BLAKE AND JOYCE CHURCH ~ BOTH OF WHOM ARE GREATLY CONCERNED WITH OUR STORY. BOB, YOU SEE, IS ~ WELL, SUPPOSE YOU READ IT FOR YOURSELF!

OUR STORY OPENS IN HARRY'S LABORATORY IN NEW YORK CITY ONE DAY IN EARLY SUMMER—

HARRY AND HIS PARTNER, TOM KINSMAN, ARE TESTING SOME NEW REVOLUTIONARY CHEMICAL, WHEN—

BOB BLAKE

HARRY THURSTON   JOYCE CHURCH

HARRY, BE CAREFUL—THAT STUFF'S DANGEROUS!

DON'T WORRY-IT'S ONLY ALCOHOL AND WATER-WITH A LITTLE SULPHURIC ACID-LET'S SEE WHAT HAPPENS!

YEOW!

CRACK!

CONTINUED NEXT PAGE

HOLY SMOKE, HARRY! WHAT'S HAPPENED TO YOUR HAND?

I DON'T KNOW, TOM ~ GET BOB BLAKE ON THE PHONE ~

HELLO ~ MR. BLAKE? OH, MISS CHURCH ~ THIS IS KINSMAN, HARRY THURSTON'S PARTNER ~ SOMETHING'S HAPPENED TO HARRY, AND HE WANTS BOB TO COME OVER RIGHT AWAY ~ YES ~ HE LOST HIS LEFT HAND IN A FREAK ACCIDENT!

GOOD GRIEF, BOB! HARRY JUST BLEW OFF HIS HAND IN AN EXPLOSION OR SOMETHING!

HUH?

SAY, JOYCE, THAT'S BAD! COME ON, LET'S GET OVER THERE!

NOW HOW THE DEUCE COULD HE DO A THING LIKE THAT? HARRY'S GENERALLY PRETTY CAREFUL ~ THIS WOULD HAVE TO HAPPEN JUST WHEN I WAS GETTING HIM INTERESTED IN THIS CASE OF THE ORIENTAL INVADERS!

A FEW MINUTES LATER, AT HARRY'S LABORATORY ~

HARRY! WHAT HAPPENED?

GLAD YOU CAME, BOB ~ I THINK I'VE MADE AN IMPORTANT DISCOVERY! I JUST MIXED A CHEMICAL THAT TRANSFORMED MY HAND INTO A WATER-SPOUT ~ YET THERE'S NO PAIN ~ I'LL HAVE TO CHECK ON WHAT CHEMICAL WAS IN THE TUBE BEFORE

CONTINUED NEXT PAGE

I CAN'T UNDERSTAND IT MYSELF ~ HEY TOM, BRING IN THE REST OF THAT MIXTURE, WILL YOU?

HOLY MACKEREL!

YEAH - SU —! OUCH !!!!

HEY!

LOOK OUT, STUPID!

TOM TRIPS AS HE HURRIES INTO THE ROOM~

AND THE WIERD CHEMICAL SPLASHES ON BOB'S SHOULDER~

INSTANTLY BOB GOES UP IN A GEYSER OF WATER!

QUICK, TOM! GET THE ANTIDOTE!

HOLY THUNDER, HARRY! WHAT HAVE YOU DONE TO ME?

TOM THROWS A GALLON OF COUNTERACTIVE CHEMICAL ON THE POOL

AND BOB RISES, LIKE A SPECTRE, FROM THE MAGIC LIQUID!

CONTINUED NEXT PAGE

CONTINUED NEXT PAGE

398

CONTINUED NEXT PAGE

SUDDENLY *HYDROMAN* LEAPS, HIS GEYSER POUNDING OVER THE FAT GUNMAN ~

~THEN TIGHTENING AROUND HIS HEAD, DRENCHING HIM ~

HE SINKS INTO A COMA, SLOWLY DROWNING!

LET'S GET OUT OF HERE! THAT THING AIN'T HUMAN!

HYDROMAN, LEAVING THE FAT ONE, SWEEPS AROUND IN FRONT OF THE OTHERS, CUTTING OFF THEIR ESCAPE ~

HOLD IT! I'LL LET YOU GO ALL RIGHT, FOR I WANT YOU TO TAKE A WARNING TO YOUR LEADER -- TELL HIM THAT *HYDROMAN* IS ON HIS TRAIL !!!

HE RE-APPEARS FROM THE SWIRLING TORRENT

BAH! THE GREAT ONE IS FAR TOO POWERFUL FOR YOU OR ANY OF YOUR MISERABLE COUNTRYMEN! *OUT OF MY WAY!!!*

NOT SO FAST, CHUM! I'M AN AMERICAN, AND SO ARE MY PEOPLE AND AMERICANS JUST WON'T BE WHIPPED!

TELL *THAT* TO YOUR BOSS, IMBECILE! I'M LEAVING YOU NOW, BUT REMEMBER THAT *HYDROMAN* NEVER LEAVES ANYTHING UN- FINISHED!

WATCH NEXT ISSUE, FELLERS, FOR AN EXCITING ADVENTURE WITH *HYDROMAN* THE WATER WONDER!

Heroic Comics No. 6 (May 1941)
©1941 Eastern Color Printing Co.
(cover art by Bill Everett)

The first issue of *Heroic Comics* also featured Flash Gordon's closest rival, Don Dixon, a science fiction hero created by Bob Moore and Carl Pfeufer which had debuted six years previously as a newspaper comic strip. The original series was reprinted in Dell's first comic book *The Funnies* (which was printed in color by Eastern for Dell). After Dell had terminated the "Don Dixon" reprint series, Eastern picked it up and used it in *Heroic Comics*, beginning with a series of new adventures that continued over twelve issues. The Don Dixon episodes took place in the "Hidden Empire of Lumaria," a city somewhere near the center of the Earth that was populated by robots preparing to invade the surface.

Another *Heroic* character was the Purple Zombie, created by Tarpe Milles. Originally, the Purple Zombie was a cadaver dug up from the grave and used in a laboratory experiment concerned with reviving the dead. When the Purple Zombie was brought to life as the first of an army of the "undead" who would conquer the world, he turned the tables on his evil creator and set out to rid the world of crime.

Tarpe Milles also created a second feature for *Heroic Comics*, "Mann of India." Mann was an American Soldier of fortune whose adventures took him to India to fight a bandit regime working with Nazi Germany.

"Daredevils of Destiny" and "Sgt. Stony Craig" were two military adventure features created by Frank Rentfrow and Donald Dickson which ran in the newspapers for a few months during the late 1930s and appeared for a short run in the early issues of *Famous Funnies* and were later brought back in *Heroic Comics*.

Artist Russell Keaton who had formerly assisted Dick Calkins of "Buck Rogers," and the once popular aviation feature "Skyroads," had taken over "Skyroads" which appeared in *Famous Funnies*. "Skyroads," however, was terminated after Keaton created "Flying Jenny" for *Heroic Comics*. Lovely Jennifer Dare was comicdom's first woman flying ace whose adventures paralleled those of Captain Midnight. The rest of *Heroic Comics* was devoted to news about the "Fellers."

New features were constantly introduced to replace old ones. H. G. Peters who had created Fearless Flint as the first superhero for *Famous Funnies* also created another superhero, Man O'Metal, for *Heroic Comics*. Man O'Metal made his appearance in the seventh issue when he, as steel worker Pat Dempsey, was buried in white hot molten steel when a vat accidentally overturned above him . . .

HERE SOMETHING *AMAZING* HAPPENS. A HUMAN BEING, THROUGH AN IN-EXPLAINABLE CHEM-ICAL REACTION OF THE SKIN-TEXTURE, IS BEING TRANS-FORMED INTO A *MAN OF METAL.* THIS STRANGE PHENOMENON THAT SHOULD HAVE BEEN BURN-ED TO DEATH WHEN THE MOLTEN WHITE-HOT METAL SPILLED ON HIM, IS NOW TRANS-FORMED, CAPABLE OF BURNING HIS WAY THROUGH THE THICKEST BARRIERS.

Origin of "Man O'Metal"
©1941 Eastern Color Printing Co.

Heroic Comics No. 14 offered something quite unique: the introduction of Rainbow Boy as junior sidekick to Hydroman. In the following issue, Rainbow Boy, created by artist Ben Thompson as assistant to Bill Everett, became a separate feature in *Heroic Comics*. Everett and Thompson developed both series jointly and had Hydroman and Rainbow Boy make guest appearances in each other's adventures. Hydroman and Rainbow Boy made a perfect superhero team, yet they often worked independently of each other. When Everett first brought the two characters together, he started a vogue of teaming superheroes that had not been attempted before.

Everett would later crisscross characters again, but in a different magazine where it became more famous—it was in *Marvel Mystery Comics* where Everett would have Sub-Mariner battle Carl Burgos' superhero of fire, the Human Torch.

Heroic Comics No. 12 introduced Ben Thompson's "Music Master" series about violinist John Wallace who came into possession of the "musical pipes of death" and learned the ancient secrets that revealed the power of flying through the air on musical tones. The Music Master pitted his skill against the evil genius of the Mad Fiddler. Three issues later, Music Master acquired a junior sidekick, "Downbeat."

With *Heroic Comics No. 32*, the magazine underwent a drastic overhaul. The superhero features were terminated and replaced by stories based on true-life heroic acts of teenagers. Whereas *Famous Funnies* carried Roy Powers as a fictional adventure series about the Boy Scouts, *Heroic Comics* now featured true episodes of heroic deeds Boy Scouts had actually performed. *Heroic Comics* also featured true stories of courageous acts by youngsters who were not associated with the scouts. One story told of the bravery of a young baby sitter who, when a sudden fire broke out, risked her life to save two infants from the upstairs bedroom and got them safely out of the house before it burned to the ground.

Then, in January 1943, Eastern introduced a second edition of *Heroic Comics*, which featured true stories of America's servicemen on the battlefront. Throughout 1943, Eastern published the two different editions of *Heroic Comics* on alternate months. Then the "Reg'lar Fellers" *Heroic Comics* was terminated at Issue 40 and the military edition was published on a monthly basis as an adult-oriented magazine.

Heroic Comics was practically the only title to continue to use a war theme after the end of World War II. While other publishers quickly dropped war theme features and patriotic superheroes, Eastern continued to run *Heroic Comics* every month for another decade. Although the magazine never attracted juvenile readership, it appealed strongly to veterans and servicemen on active duty. Newsstand sales were negligible, but one yardstick for measuring a comic book's popularity, the military mail-order subscription figures, showed that *Heroic Comics* sold over 250,000 copies per month in that area alone!

During the 1950s when the opponents of the medium suggested that violence in comic books caused juvenile delinquency, they attacked every comic book in which a character used (or threatened to use) a gun. And they were outraged at the weapons and savage violence of war pictured on every page of a *Heroic Comics* issue. They charged that *Heroic Comics* was one of the primary magazines responsible for inciting violent crimes among the young!

Eastern's clash with the Comics Code Authority over the right to publish *Heroic Comics* as an illustrated magazine of military history led to Eastern's decision to suspend publication of all of its comic books in June 1955. That year marked the end of *Heroic Comics*, the end of *Famous Funnies*, and the end of an era—the Golden Age of Comics.

ALPHABETICAL LISTING OF TITLES BY EASTERN COLOR PRINTING

Amazing Willie Mays (1954, one issue)
Big Chief Wahoo (1942 - 1944)*
Buck Rogers (1940 - 1942)*
Buster Crabbe (1952 - 1953)
Conquest (1953, one issue)
Dickey Dare (1941, four issues)*
Dover, the Bird(1955, one issue)
Famous Funnies (1934 - 1955)
Heroic Comics (1940 - 1955)
Invisible Scarlet O'Neil (1950 - 1951)*
Jingle Jangle (1942 - 1949)
Movie Love (1950 - 1953)
Napoleon (1942, one issue)*
Oaky Doaks (1942, one issue)*
Steve Roper (1948, five issues)*
Strictly Private (1942, two issues)
Sugar Bowl (1948 - 1949)
Tales From The Great Book (1955 - 1956)

*Reprints from *Famous Funnies*

OTHER PUBLISHERS

During the period from 1938 to 1942, the comic book industry included many publishers who did not introduce any significant trends or new character innovations, but merely added to the industry's growth with titles that borrowed from existing concepts. Others like Street & Smith, the giant publisher of pulp fiction whose famous titles included *Astounding Stories, Doc Savage,* and *The Shadow,* entered the comic book field during 1940 but only as a sideline to expand the readership of their topflight pulp crime busters Doc Savage and the Shadow. Street & Smith adapted both characters to comic books and added a few other titles such as *Supersnipe Comics* and *Super-Magician Comics.*

Street & Smith was founded in 1855, and under the direction of Francis Smith, a co-founder, the company introduced as its first publication *The New York Weekly,* a small tabloid that contained historical and humorous articles and short stories of romantic fiction. During the next year, Street & Smith introduced *Tip Top Weekly,* a new version of the original dime novel which featured the first short story fiction with a continuing hero, namely the "Frank Merriwell" series created by Burt L. Standish.

Frank Merriwell was an all-American star athlete and honor student of Yale University whose adventures generally centered around sports, but he also journeyed out West and fought outlaws and Indians, and he often travelled around the world to exotic locales searching for hidden treasures. Frank Merriwell also worked as a special undercover agent to aid police in tracking down gangsters, and he occasionally travelled to England to assist Scotland Yard in breaking up international smuggling rackets. Between April 1896 and March 1915, *Tip Top Weekly* featured more than 500 thrilling adventures of Frank Merriwell. In 1936, the character was adapted to the screen for Universal's *Frank Merriwell* movie serial.

Although Frank Merriwell never appeared in the later Street & Smith comic books, the character concept was highly influential in comics, and indeed was the forerunner of all other athletic adventure heroes, such as "Yale graduate and world renowned polo player" Flash Gordon.

Tip Top Weekly No. 253 (Feb. 1901)
©1901 Street & Smith

The Shadow Magazine (July 1941)
©1941 Street & Smith

In April 1949, Street & Smith discontinued both its pulp and comic book lines to devote full attention to family oriented "slick" magazines such as *Mademoiselle*, and *Living and Charm*. While its science fiction pulp, *Astounding Stories* was immediately taken over by Conde Nast Publications and changed to *Analog Science Fiction/Science Fact*, Doc Savage, created by Lester Dent, was later revived during the 1960s in a paperback series published by Bantam Books, and revived again in 1972 as a leading comic book feature of Marvel Comics. Similarly, the Shadow, created by Walter B. Gibson under the pen name Maxwell Grant, became famous in radio drama as well as on the movie screen during the 1940s and was later revived as a comic book feature. In 1964, Archie Publications introduced the next series of *Shadow Comics* which ran for eight issues through 1965. Then in 1972, National Periodical revived the Shadow for another series as a D-C title.

On the other hand, Whitman Publishing Company, who was not a pulp publisher and who did not produce comic books, did introduce a highly innovative publication known as the *Big Little Book* which, except for its oddball size of 3¼" × 4½" with approximately 430 pages, was in essence very much a comic book. Whitman's *Big Little Book* series, which began in 1933, was published as a succession of illustrated books with text on the left-hand page and a picture on the opposite page. For the most part, the volumes were special adaptations of newspaper comic strip features such as "Buck Rogers," "Flash Gordon," "Tarzan," "Dick Tracy," "Phantom," "Mandrake," "Lone Ranger," and many others, but the balloon dialogue and captions were blanked out and replaced with text description. Here, the story of a complete adventure was often expanded into greater detail than was afforded by the space limitations of the comic strip panel. Whereas the Sunday page adventure in color was reprinted in the comic book, the black-and-white daily adventures were adapted to the *Big Little Book*.

However, the *Big Little Book* series also contained the only published version of certain movies, most notably the "Tarzan" films and the "Gene Autry" western films, and these issues utilized stills from the film in place of hand-drawn artwork for the picture on the right-hand page. The text pages described the movie in narrative form.

In addition, Whitman also introduced coloring books based on characters in the comics. Quite often, the picture pages of the coloring book included brief descriptive captions that formed a mini-story about the character. No doubt, Whitman's publications also added to the growth of the industry.

By 1943, the major publishers of comic books, and those indirectly linked to the industry, were firmly established. The next splash of comic book publishers occurred during the post-war period, 1946 to 1949, and with few exceptions they brought forth a barrage of single-issue titles whose contents fell into the crime or romance category. Then between 1953 and 1955 the industry underwent a general upheaval. The one-time giants left the business, and the smaller publishers became the giants. During the 1960s as the industry moved uphill again, new publishers, such as Charlton Comics, entered the field with a fresh approach. Charlton, for instance, introduced such series as *Six Million Dollar Man Comics* and *The Flintstones Comics* which were based on the popular television programs, and included adaptations of each story produced for the program. The 1960s also brought forth the offsprings of the comic book, most notably the black-and-white magazines produced by Warren Publishing Company which included comics with text and subject matter closely related to comics. Then in 1975, Seaboard Periodicals entered the field and introduced the "Atlas Comics" series that featured such superhero titles as *The Scorpion*, *The Destructor*, and a few others that attempted to recapture the mood of the Golden Age of Comics as it had been in the 1940s. But the short-lived series was terminated after a few months.

This section is a brief summary of the highlights of the rest of the industry outside of the major publishers of comic books.

Embee Distributing Company

Comic Monthly No. 8 (Aug. 1922)
©1922 International Feature Service, Inc.

One of the forerunners of the regular color comic book was the black-and-white *Comic Monthly*, first published by Embee Distributing Company in January 1922. This was a twenty-four page booklet that featured reprints of some of the then current daily newspaper strips. However, *Comic Monthly* was discontinued in September 1922 when Embee suddenly went bankrupt with the eighth issue barely off the press.

Comic Monthly No. 8 was not distributed because Embee was besieged with lawsuits arising from complaints from thousands of people who claimed they had paid for a two-year subscription to the magazine but had never received a single copy. It was apparent that someone had passed himself off as an Embee sales representative and had collected subscription payments from the unsuspecting public who were also promised a variety of free gifts with the first six issues. Of course nothing was ever delivered. Embee, who claimed they were unaware of the unauthorized solicitations, either acknowledged the subscriptions or returned payment to the customers.

During its brief duration, *Comic Monthly* included the following:

No. 1 - "Polly and Her Pals" (January 1922)
No. 2 - "Mike & Ike" (February 1922)
No. 3 - "Barney Google" (March 1922)
No. 4 - "Tillie, the Toiler" (April 1922)
No. 5 - "Indoor Sports" (May 1922)
No. 6 - "Little Jimmy" (June 1922)
No. 7 - "S'Matter Pop?" (July 1922)
No. 8 - "Toots and Caspar" (August 1922)

Although *Comic Monthly* was discontinued in 1922, a few of its features which continued to run in the newspapers also appeared several years later in other comic books. "S'Matter Pop?", created in 1919 by C.M. Payne for the Bell Syndicate, also ran as a regular reprint series in *Famous Funnies* during 1934 and 1935. "Tillie, the Toiler," created in 1922 by Russ Westover for King Features Syndicate, headlined eight full-length irregular size black-and-white magazine publications by Cupples and Leon Company between 1926 and 1933. It then appeared in more than twelve issues in Dell's "4-Color" series between 1941 and 1949 while the newspaper strip continued to run until 1959. Similarly, "Barney Google," created in 1919 by Billy DeBeck for King Features Syndicate, appeared in two issues of Cupples and Leons' irregular size black-and-white publications between 1923 and 1928, and again in Dell's "4-Color" series for six issues between 1942 and 1950. "Barney Google" was also revived for the comic book for three issues in 1951 as a Toby Press title, and again for one issue as a Gold Key title in 1964, and then was taken over by the Charlton Comics Group for six issues between 1970 and 1971. Curiously enough, "Barney Google," which debuted as a newspaper comic strip in June 1919, remained popular enough through the years to be adapted for television animation in 1962.

And on the other hand, "Polly and Her Pals," created in December 1912 by Cliff Sterrett for the National News Company, was later adapted to the *Big Little Book*.

Hillman Periodicals

Hillman Periodicals, formerly a publisher of photo-illustrated magazines about movies and Hollywood stars, entered the comic book field in November 1941 with *Air Fighters Comics*, a title that stressed aviation fiction with a patriotic slant. The first issue introduced several straight adventure flying aces with the "Black Commander" serving as main attraction.

The "Black Commander" adventure told about American pilot Barry Haynes, who was arrested on charges of collaborating with an enemy spy—his girl friend. Haynes was court-martialed, convicted, and sentenced to be shot as a traitor. While awaiting execution, he receives a mysterious visitor, the Chief of British Military Intelligence, who arranges his escape from prison and enlists him as a secret agent for the Allied Forces. On his first air assignment, Haynes is shot down by the Nazis and taken prisoner. Seriously wounded, the Germans piece him together again, but the plastic surgery alters his appearance.

The Germans had learned of Haynes' court-martial that arose from his romance with one of their spies, and his subsequent miraculous escape from prison. They enlist him to serve as a Nazi spy and send him on a mission to England to clear the way for a raid on a strategic airfield. Upon returning to England, Haynes discovers that the only man who can identify him as a British agent has been captured by the Nazis. Realizing that no one will believe his story, Haynes goes into action on his own to stop the air raid. He steals Britain's highly innovative experimental aircraft called the "Black Commander" and successfully fights off the enemy planes approaching the airfield. Of course Haynes is wanted by the Germans for double-crossing them. He is also wanted by the Americans as a convicted traitor, and he is wanted by Scotland Yard for the theft of the new aircraft which, during wartime, was a crime that also carried the death penalty.

Unfortunately, the theme of the "Black Commander," a man without a country, was regarded as a bit too complex for the leading patriotic feature of a comic book—it appeared in only the first issue. While the pilot heroes of the other *Air Fighters* features did not contain the plot complexities that the "Black Commander" had, they lacked the dynamic innovation required to make the magazine appealing. *Air Fighters Comics* was temporarily discontinued.

The second issue, which came out almost a year later, introduced a roster of all new characters which included Airboy, Skywolf, Black Angel, the Flying Dutchman, and Iron Ace. Of the lot, Airboy (created by Charles Biro who soon after left Hillman Periodicals to become a partner with Lev Gleason Publications) was the most popular. Airboy had several novel elements that captivated the juvenile audience, the most notable of which was his remarkable airplane. It was named "Birdie" because of the manner in which its mechanical wings flapped as it soared through the skies. Moreover, the affection that Airboy showed towards Birdie was comparable to the affection that the average youth might show toward a pet animal. To Airboy, Birdie was not just a machine but rather, a loyal friend and companion that could outfly and outmaneuver the fastest of enemy planes, glide silently like a bird in the night, hover in midair, land on rooftops, float on water, and instantly transform into a nearly indestructible battleship.

Another captivating element was the youthfulness of Airboy. He was depicted as a 14-year-old, a mere kid fighting a man's war, and undoubtedly comicdom's youngest flying ace. In his early years Airboy was young orphan Davy Nelson and was raised in a monastery under the personal guidance of Father Martier, the monk who originally designed Birdie and was subsequently killed during its first test flight when the plane crashed. On the day of the test flight Father Martier had told Davy that if unforeseen complications set in, the plane, its plans and materials would become Davy's to carry on with. After the crash and Father Martier's death, Davy recovered the wreckage and managed to repair the plane. In the meantime, other monks had converted the monastery into a gambling casino, an act that was totally contradictory to Father Martier's teachings.

Out of vengeance for the disrespect shown to his deceased teacher, young Davy Nelson took Birdie into the air and proceeded to bomb the monastery, levelling it to the ground. As Airboy, his next adventure would pit him against Japan's top flying ace who had set out to find and capture the mystery plane that flew like a bird so that it could be used for building a fleet of superior Japanese aircraft. High above the clouds, Airboy met and clashed with his adversary in a dramatic sky duel—the first of many that would prove to all that Airboy was a highly skilled fighter pilot.

In the issues that followed, Airboy slowly began to age and by the end of 1945 when the title of *Air Fighters Comics* was changed to *Airboy Comics*, Davy Nelson had matured into a young man of nineteen. During his action packed career, he fought many opponents. One of his most interesting opponents was an exotic lady pilot named Valkyrie, the leader of Hitler's special squadron of female pilots who were known as the Airmaidens. The confrontations between Airboy and Valkyrie soon led to a warm friendship between the two. Neither one wanted to hurt the other. And on occasion, they fought together as a team against the kind of enemy that was neither American nor German. Valkyrie herself often switched roles; she was a deadly villain in one story and then a courageous heroine in the next.

Skywolf, another *Air Fighters* star who debuted in the second issue, was a self-appointed defender of democracy whose international team of freedom fighters safeguarded the skies of foreign lands against Nazi bombing attacks. In Skywolf's first adventure, created by Mort Leav, Skywolf came to grips with Colonel von Tundra, one of Hitler's right-hand officers whose mangled body was held together with mechanical limbs, rivets and bolts, the result of a previous air battle with Skywolf. Von Tundra sought revenge against the man responsible for his physical disfigurement.

In *Air Fighters Comics No. 3*, the grudge battle between Skywolf and Colonel von Tundra was interrupted by a brief flashback to an incident in World War I that concerned neither. The episode centered around Baron Emmelman, a top German flying ace who engages in a bitter air duel with an allied pilot and is ultimately shot down. The baron's plane burst into flames and crashed in the dense swamps of Poland. Somehow, the half-conscious Baron Emmelman dragged himself out of the flaming wreckage and, badly burned and screaming in agony, he finally collapsed. He lay there, motionless but not quite dead. Days . . . weeks . . . months . . . years passed and the slimy marshes began to grow over around and within the remains of Baron Emmelmann. A strange transformation in nature was taking place. Something was growing out of that undefinable mass of human decay and swamp vegetation covered with entangling vines, weeds, and leaves.

One day it moved!

That indomitable form that had once been human slowly raised itself upright, then pulled through the slushy, sucking mud and slithered forward, balancing first on one vertical growth extension that vaguely resembled a leg and then on the other—*and the Heap walked the Earth!*

After the flashback explained the origin of the Heap, the story returned to the present era where Colonel von Tundra plans a bombing raid to wipe out an isolated village in Poland. But the German planes run into the Skywolf squadron. The entire sky becomes a vast battle arena as the two opposing sides desperately try to blast each other's ships. During the aerial warfare, von Tundra zeroes in on Skywolf's plane and rakes it with machine gun fire. Skywolf's plane plunges toward the ground and crashes into a swamp—the same swamp that the Heap roams! In order to verify the death of his most hated enemy, von Tundra lands his plane near the crash.

Von Tundra searches the marshes for the wreckage—and is seized by the Heap! However, his terrified cries in German seem to ring a familar chord within the creature. Instead of killing his helpless victim, the Heap carries him to a nearby village which the Germans have gained control of and where they are preparing a mass execution of its citizenry. Skywolf and his men are among the prisoners.

The sight of the Heap carrying von Tundra throws the firing squad into a panic. During the ensuing confusion Skywolf escapes, frees his men, and they reorganize for the final battle against the German soldiers who are busily trying to capture the Heap and free von Tundra. The Heap allows himself to be taken prisoner and chained—for a brief two seconds! Then pandemonium breaks loose as the Heap suddenly goes on a hungry rampage!

Meanwhile, Skywolf and his men reach their planes, take to the skies and circle around to attack the Germans on the ground who are now scrambling for their lives. The Heap stops in his tracks—the planes, the shell fire, the explosions, the German shouts, all seem to bring back a distant and familiar memory. For a brief moment, a small fraction of his human characteristics seem to dominate the creature for in the midst of the blazing crossfire between Skywolf and the Germans the Heap senses the helplessness of one of the women prisoners who had faced the firing squad and was searching frantically for someplace safe to hide. As the Heap slithers toward the girl through a hail of gunfire that has no effect on him, Skywolf, misinterpreting the monster's motives, drops a bomb on the Heap in an attempt to save her. There was a terrific explosion. After defeating the Nazis and the incredible swamp creature, Skywolf and his men streak towards the clouds—but was the Heap destroyed?

Hardly. The Heap was invulnerable. And he returned in a later story which also concluded with his apparent destruction. But the Heap could not and would not die. He returned again and again and was eventually placed in his own feature where he, as part monster, part human, part swamp vegetation, part immovable mountain that was unable to speak or communicate, slithered from one compelling adventure to another in an unyielding, almost childlike quest to survive in a world that was cruel to him. Owing to the small amount of human characteristics that still functioned within his being he sought something which he did not understand—something called love! As Baron von Emmelman, he did at one time know and understand love. He had had a wife and child whom he cherished. The Heap was thrust into situations in which he battled various forms of evil, many of which were supernatural, whether he wanted to or not. But it was this vague and distant memory of his family that gave him the fantastic will to live.

In spite of Skywolf, Airboy, and Airboy's unique airplane, it was *The Heap* that emerged as the classic creation of Hillman Periodicals.

Harvey Publications

Sad Sack Comics No. 5 (May 1950)
©1950 Harvey Features Syndicate, Inc.

Astro Comics No. 1 (1973)
©1973 Harvey Famous Cartoons
All Rights Reserved

In 1940, Harvey Publications introduced the comic book adaptation of "The Green Hornet," then a popular radio program created by Fran Striker, the author of the "Lone Ranger" series (see Section 6, page 00). Originally, the Green Hornet, alias newspaper editor Britt Reid, was the great-grandson of the Lone Ranger, who adopted the role of the masked crusader to carry on the family's tradition of fighting crime. The Green Hornet was also featured in two different movie serials during the 1940s and had made a successful comeback as a television series in 1967. In this series movie star and international martial arts champion Bruce Lee's performance of Kato, Britt Reid's mild mannered oriental butler and the Green Hornet's judo chopping masked sidekick, made the program a world-wide smash hit. Harvey also introduced All New Comics which featured a host of superheroes such as Shock Gibson, Scarlet Phantom, the Stuntman, and several others, but most of them were based on existing concepts.

One exception was "The Black Cat" series which featured actress Linda Turner in the role of the first female costumed crimefighter to use judo as a lethal weapon. The thinly clad and glamorous Black Cat debuted in her own bimonthly comic book which began in June 1946 and ran through 1951, and she made occasional guest appearances in All New Comics. The popular series, created by Al Gabriele, was another one to be sharply criticized in Dr. Wertham's book Seduction of the Innocent.

During the late 1940s, Harvey phased out most of its superhero titles and introduced its "Comics Hits Revival" series which was an attempt to bring back the adventure classics from earlier newspaper strips. The series included reprints of "Flash Gordon," "Dick Tracy," and a few others. During the same period, Harvey also introduced the first comic book series of George Baker's "Sad Sack" which became a leading title. George Baker created "Sad Sack" while in the military service during the 1940s, and the feature first appeared in the June 1942 issue of Yank Magazine, then one of the leading publications for military servicemen. "Sad Sack," featuring the humorous "miscapades" of Pvt. Sack, U. S. Army, became a sensation and was soon afterwards syndicated in newspapers across the country through Bell Syndicate. Although its newspaper syndication was discontinued in 1950, "Sad Sack" appeared in more than 650 full-length comic book issues between 1949 through the present.

Harvey's major feature, however, is "Casper, the Friendly Ghost." When Casper was introduced in 1953, Harvey terminated its "Comics Hit Revival" series and built a brand new line of characters around Casper which was soon adapted to a popular animated television series. Casper and his friends Wendy, the Witch, Spooky, and Nightmare were clever character concepts in the animal fantasy category with wide appeal to the very young audience. Casper is also merchandised in a variety of toys and appears in many coloring books (published by Whitman).

Columbia Comics Group

The Columbia comic book titles ran during the 1940s and included reprints of popular newspaper comic strips of McNaught Syndicate as well as original superhero characters. Both categories appeared in *Big Shot Comics*, Columbia's first title that began in May 1940 and ran for seven years. On the reprint side, *Big Shot Comics* featured "Joe Palooka," comicdom's original heavyweight boxing champion created by Ham Fisher in 1928. The "Joe Palooka" feature, which was generally developed around boxing and other sports, had previously appeared as a reprint series in *Famous Funnies* during 1934 and 1935 and then again in the early issues of Quality's *Feature Funnies* before it became *Feature Comics*. Joe Palooka became one of the outstanding patriotic figures on the comic pages during 1942 when he stepped down from the ring as heavyweight champ to enlist in the military service as Pvt. Joe Palooka, U. S. Army. For a while, his adventures took place overseas. After the war was over, Joe returned to civilian life and resumed his boxing career—where he met Humphrey! Humphrey, who tipped the scales at 400 pounds, was the only opponent Joe could not knock down. The two met in the ring to battle for the championship title in one of the most fascinating fights ever depicted in the comics. Humphrey could take everything that Joe dished out, but he lost the match because he became entangled in the ring ropes and couldn't get free in time to return to his neutral corner when the bell ended the round. The two became friends, and Humphrey emerged as a popular co-star of the feature and was soon elevated to his own strip.

Joe Palooka's eventual retirement from the ring opened the doorway to new adventures for him. In one episode he met Little Max, a lovable mischievous youth whose popularity grew among young readers and eventually earned him his own feature.

In the meantime, *Big Shot Comics* was introducing original story material about the adventures of Joe Palooka and this warranted a separate full-length *Joe Palooka Comics,* another Columbia title that ran between 1942 and 1944. (The feature was later taken over by Harvey Publications which introduced the second series of *Joe Palooka Comics* and an all new series of *Humphrey Comics* and *Little Max Comics.*)

The *Big Shot* superhero was Skyman who, in reality was Allen Turner whose parents were killed in an airplane crash when he was a child. He was raised by his uncle Dr. Peter Turner, a scientist and inventor. Upon graduating from college, Allen returned to assist his uncle in the laboratory and adopted a costumed identity to fight crime. Created by Gardner Fox and illustrated by Paul Reinman, Skyman was equipped with an array of sophisticated scientific devices. One of his unique instruments was the "Stasimatic Gun," a hand weapon that unleashed a ray which was capable of halting the flow of blood thus creating instant paralysis. Another was the Wing, Skyman's custom-made airplane that resembled a huge boomerang and was able to hover in midair while he swung down from it on his skyhook. Skyman also headlined his own magazine that ran at irregular intervals between 1941 and 1948.

Big Shot Comics also featured the Face, Sparky Watts, Captain Yank, and a magician called Marvello, all of whom embraced variations of the superhero concept. In addition, the magazine featured reprints of the "Charlie Chan" and "Vic Jordon" series which were popular newspaper strips at the time. Columbia's other titles included full-length issues of *The Face Comics* and *Sparky Watts Comics,* and *Dixie Dugan Comics,* the latter containing reprints of the once-famous newspaper strip "Dixie Dugan." By 1949, however, Columbia had discontinued its comic book line.

Dixie Dugan No. 2 (1943)
Sparky Watts No. 2 (1943)
Skyman No. 2 (1943)
©1943 Columbia Features

Novelty Press

Target Comics No. 1 (Feb. 1940)
©1940 Funnies, Inc.

Target Comics No. 7 (Aug. 1940)—498
©1940 Funnies, Inc.

Novelty was among the smaller publishers of the 1940s. They produced only three titles—*Blue Bolt Comics, Target Comics,* and *4-Most Comics* which ran between 1940 and 1949 and featured an assortment of superheroes. During the first two years the story material for the three titles was created by Funnies, Inc., the studio comprised of such artists as Bill Everett, Carl Burgos, Ben Thompson, Joe Simon and Jack Kirby who created many of the initial features for Timely's *Marvel Mystery Comics* and Eastern's *Heroic Comics.*

Novelty's first title, *Target Comics,* which began in February 1940, featured as its lead-off character Bulls-Eye Bill, a western gunslinger created by Bill Everett and later taken over by another artist when Everett, teaming up with writer Paul Quinn, created the "Chameleon" series. The Chameleon, whose adventures began in *Target Comics No. 6,* was basically a straight-action crimefighter who cleverly disguised his appearance in different ways to foil the bad guys. Quite often, he would make himself up to look like the gang's boss, a hotel bellhop, a taxi driver, a policeman, a murdered victim, or whatever role best suited the circumstances at hand. The unique element here was that the Chameleon's true identity—or what appeared to be his true identity—was always just another disguise, and no one, not even the reader, knew who he really was.

Target Comics No. 1 introduced Carl Burgos' Man-

owar who was actually a super humanoid built in an ancient era by a defeated Utopian civilization as their historical monument, and also as a warning symbol to future generations who would destroy themselves in war. The humanoid was entombed in a mountain and designed to activate itself to life to save mankind in the event of a world disaster. In the 20th century the mountain was levelled by the bombing that heralded the outbreak of the Nazi invasion—and Manowar, the White Streak, awoke! Utilizing his ability to emit lightning from his optical slits that vaguely resembled human eyes, Manowar springs into action battling against the evil warmongers who prey on defenseless nations.

Other features in the first issue included "Fantastic Feature Films," created by Tarpe Milles as a series of exciting short story adventures that had no continuing hero; "City Editor," featuring the crime-smashing episodes of reporter Joyce Bellamy; "Calling 2-R," a futuristic-type adventure series about a league of boy rangers who were equipped with advanced ray guns, planetary strato-cruisers, television, and a host of electronic gadgets; "T-Men," created by Joe Simon and Jack Kirby; and "Lucky Bird," an aviation ace created by Harry Campbell.

Then *Target Comics No. 5* introduced Basil Wolverton's "Spacehawk," a stratospheric adventurer with vast physical and mental powers whose super airship

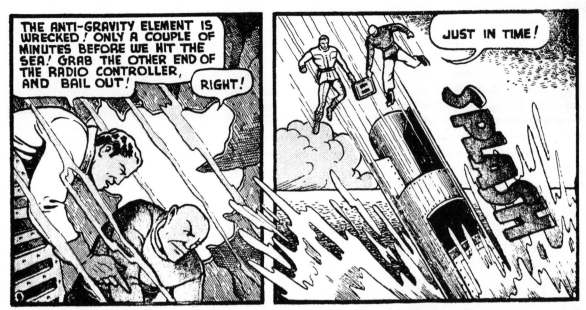

"Spacehawk" by Basil Wolverton ©1940 Funnies, Inc.

carried him beyond the atmosphere and throughout the solar system to crush evil and tyranny regardless of whatever world it was.

However, Funnies, Inc. began to fall apart when its artists joined Timely Publications and other publishers. Their original features in *Target Comics* were gradually phased out and replaced by others which Novelty Press acquired from other sources. The first new feature was "The Target," a costumed crime fighter who made his debut in Issue 10 and then, in the next issue, was joined by his two buddies who donned similar costumes and called themselves the Targeteers.

Another new feature was "The Cadet," a patriotic adventure series about cadet Kit Carter of West Point, and a semi-humorous patriotic adventure series, "Spec, Spot and Sis." "The Chameleon" was one of the few carry-overs to the new format but it was continued under a slightly different concept—the aura of mystery was removed as the Chameleon adapted the permanent true identity of Pete Stockbridge, publisher of the *Daily Star* newspaper.

Later issues of *Target Comics* featured a continuing series adapted from James Fenimore Cooper's classic "Last of the Mohicans." It was illustrated by Harold Delay, a master draftsman of the pen-and-ink technique.

Novelty's second title, *Blue Bolt Comics*, which began in June 1940, featured a costumed superhero called "Blue Bolt," created by Joe Simon and Jack Kirby, whose unique origin was revealed in the first issue. It began when three college athletes rented a small airplane to fly to a mountain resort to spend their vacation. But upon landing, a violent storm erupted

and the trio raced for shelter under the trees—only to meet with disaster when lightning struck a tall oak that toppled down and crushed them. Fred Parrish, one of the students, managed to survive and crawl free. Seeking help for his two friends, Fred struggled back to the plane and in spite of the hazardous storm, he set the controls in operation and bravely took to the skies. The storm raged on, and lightning struck again. This time it hit the plane! The flaming craft plummeted down toward the rocky mountains and crashed.

However, the scene was observed by strangely garbed, unhuman creatures who sprinted down the wall of the canyon towards the crash, dragged the unconscious pilot of the flaming wreckage, and carried him down into the depths of the Earth—down to the ultra-modern laboratory of Dr. Bertoff whose research experiments with new methods for harnessing raw electrical energy had caused the storm in the first place, and had drawn the lightning flashes to the area. Dr. Bertoff immediately went to work to save Fred's life by charging his body with electricity.

Origin of "Blue Bolt by Simon and Kirby
©1940 Funnies, Inc.

When Fred Parrish regained consciousness, he found himself endowed with the awesome power of lightning! Fred resigns himself to carrying on Dr. Bertoff's work whose principle objective is to combat the evil hordes of the Green Sorceress and thwart her ambitions to conquer mankind. But in another part of subterranean Earth, the Green Sorceress, through her power of black magic, was observing Dr. Bertoff's laboratory, and she destroyed it with terrible rays of fire. Then she sent her legion of monstrous flying creatures to feed upon the remains of Dr. Bertoff, the injured pilot, and the rest of her enemies who had served the scientist.

Of course, Fred survived the explosion—and he was ready for action when the fearful winged creatures arrived. He battled them back to the stronghold of the Green Sorceress. And a titanic tug of war ensued which extended over several fantastic adventures that took place in subterranean Earth as well as on the distant world where the Green Sorceress came from.

"The Sub-Zero Man"—one of the short-lived Golden Age classics in superhero fantasy created by an unknown artist of Funnies, Inc.—was another entry in *Blue Bolt Comics No. 1*. His origin began on the planet Venus where the scientists of that world had developed powerful atom ships for travelling through space. An expedition team had set out to journey to their nearest planetary neighbor and explore it for signs of life. While en route to Earth, an asteroid swirled into their path and the ship's crew, unable to turn the ship in time to avoid collision, crashed into the celestial body—which turned out to consist of an extremely cold vapor substance rather than solid matter. As the ship passed harmlessly through the vapor, its exterior hull suddenly acquired a thick layer of ice that had disasterous effects inside the ship. All controls and operating mechanisms froze and jammed, and the crew members were frozen and turned into ice. However, one of the Venusian astronauts who was able to move his limbs struggled to chip the ice from the steering mechanism and miraculously guided the ship to a safe landing on Earth. Although he himself was covered completely with ice, he crawled out of the ship and made his way to the nearest building to seek help for his comrades who were still frozen to their seats.

The man from Venus barged into the building—and unknowingly interrupted a crucial experiment with gamma rays. The rays penetrated his body, melted the ice, and returned him to normal. He explained his story to the interested Earth scientists. The scientists rushed to the ship but discovered that everyone aboard was beyond help.

In the meantime, the lone survivor found that as soon as he stepped out of the path of gamma rays, he turned into a being of ice and that everything he touched also froze and turned to ice. Moments later, the police arrive on the scene to investigate the spaceship. And Sub-Zero Man, upon seeing the police and assuming that they will think he murdered his companions, flees for his life, and unintentionally creates general havoc when everything he touches freezes and turns into ice. Branded as a dangerous menace to society, Sub-Zero Man is hunted by the police and is eventually captured when he dives into a lake to escape the dragnet—the water freezes and he is encased in the ice. After a welding crew cuts him free, he is carted off to jail to thaw, but he escapes during the night.

While racing across a poorly constructed dam, his weight causes the wall to crack and tons of water pour through, rushing down toward the unsuspecting town in the valley. Sub-Zero Man dashes ahead of the awesome wave and plunges into it just as the water reaches the edge of the town—and the water instantly freezes! Having saved the town from disaster, Sub-Zero Man breaks away from the frozen wave and disappears.

In further adventures, he returns to his normal self through the application of gamma ray, learns how to control his power over coldness, and uses it as an uncanny weapon to combat crime and evil.

Blue Bolt Comics No. 1. also introduced Dick Cole, an all-American college athlete and cadet, and Sgt. Spook, a policeman who was killed in the line of duty and had come back as an unseen spirit to continue his fight against crime. However, Dick Cole and Sgt. Spook were transferred to *4-Most Comics*, Novelty's third title which began in December 1941 as a quarterly magazine.

Novelty Press folded in 1949, but their features were taken over by *The Saturday Evening Post* who had decided to enter the comic book field as a sideline under the name of Star Publications. Star Publications introduced a new series of *Blue Bolt Comics* that featured reprints of "Blue Bolt," "Spacehawk," and "Sub-Zero Man," and the magazine ran for eighteen issues until its termination in 1953. In addition, Star Publications introduced a short-lived title called *Spook Comics* which included reprints of Sgt. Spook, and *Target Romance Comics* as a new format of *Target Comics*.

Between 1949 and 1954, Star Publications also introduced a variety of other titles in the animal fantasy category as *Frisky Animals* and *Mighty Bear* and in other categories that reflected the trend of the early 1950s. The horror titles included *Ghostly Weird Tales*, *Horrors of Mystery*, *Shocking Mystery*, *Startling Terror Tales*, and *Terrifying Tales*; and the crime entries included *Guns Against Gangsters* and *Thrilling Crime Cases*. *Intimate Secrets of Romance* and *Top Love Stories* were the romance titles of Star Publications.

Aragon Magazines

Aragon Magazines was one of the many new publishers which plunged into the comic book field in the early 1950s and then abruptly disappeared after producing less than a dozen issues. The difference with Aragon, however, was that they made a strong effort to produce a quality science fiction comic book in their sole title *Weird Tales of the Future*, which ran for eight issues between 1952 and 1953. Artist Basil Wolverton, whose ingeniously constructed short story narratives appeared in almost every issue, was generally responsible for the magazine maintaining its high level of artistic and literary excellence. Wolverton's classic story "Man From the Moon," which appeared in *Weird Tales of the Future No. 5* (February 1953), was typical of the magazine's contents, and the story is reproduced here.

Weird Tales of The Future No. 2 (June 1952)
©1952 S.P.M. Publications, Inc.

Weird Tales of The Future No. 3 (Sept. 1952)
©1952 Aragon Magazines, Inc.

"The Man From The Moon" ©1952 Aragon Magazines, Inc.,
and renewed ©1978 Comicade Enterprises

Weird Tales of The Future No. 5 (Jan.-Feb. 1953)
©1952 Aragon Magazines, Inc.

THE THINGS SEIZED ME AND HAULED ME INTO THE MACHINE! THERE WAS A SICKENING SENSATION OF BEING JERKED UPWARD! WHEN I CAME TO, I LOOKED OUT UPON A DISTANT EARTH!

IT CAN'T BE! IT ISN'T POSSIBLE!

I DIDN'T REALIZE UNTIL MUCH LATER THAT I'D BEEN ABDUCTED BY MEN FROM THE MOON! THEY HAD BEEN ABLE TO ENTER THE EARTH'S ATMOSPHERE FOR ONLY A BRIEF PERIOD, DURING WHICH THEY HAD CAPTURED ME AS PROOF OF THEIR LANDING! I WAS VERY ILL DURING THEIR RETURN TRIP. ABOUT ALL I REMEMBER WAS THAT THE MOON MEN KEPT CONSTANT WATCH OVER ME....

AFTER WE ARRIVED INSIDE AN AIR-FILLED CRATER, THOSE WHO HAD MANNED THE SHIP DIED FROM EFFECTS OF THE TRIP. BUT INGENIOUS LUNARITE SURGEONS SPARED ME BY CREATING IN ME AN ARTIFICIAL RESPIRATORY SYSTEM! GRADUALLY I WENT ABOUT AND LEARNED THE CUSTOMS, CONDITIONS AND LANGUAGE OF THESE PEOPLE....

PROBABLY YOU ARE RESENTFUL TOWARD US FOR TAKING YOU FROM YOUR NATIVE PLANET.

NOT ANY MORE. THIS HAS BEEN AN AMAZING EXPERIENCE! BUT I HOPE TO ONE DAY RETURN TO EARTH!

BY DEGREES MY BODY HAD TO BE ALTERED TO OVERCOME ALIEN CONDITIONS. AS THE DECADES WORE ON, LUNAR SCIENTISTS REPEATEDLY SAVED MY LIFE BY REPLACING MY BODY PARTS WITH METAL, PLASTIC AND ELECTRONIC DEVICES! EVENTUALLY ONLY MY BRAIN REMAINED INTACT. PRESERVED AND FED BY CHEMICALS, IT WAS DEFTLY TAPPED TO CONTROL THE MANY INVOLVED FUNCTIONS OF MY ROBOT BODY!

THANKS TO YOU SCIENTISTS, I'VE ALREADY OUTLIVED TWO OF YOUR GENERATIONS! CAN'T YOU DO THE SAME FOR YOUR OWN PEOPLE?

WE HOPE TO SOME DAY. OUR ORGANIC STRUCTURE IS MORE COMPLICATED THAN WAS YOURS!

I GREW VERY FOND OF THE PEACEFUL MOON PEOPLE. LONG SINCE I HAD BECOME THE MOST OUTSTANDING FIGURE ON THE PLANET. BUT I STILL LONGED TO RETURN TO EARTH AND LEARN WHAT PROGRESS HAD BEEN MADE BY MY NATION. THEN--

WE ARE AT LAST PLANNING ANOTHER SPACESHIP! YOU WILL HAVE THE OPPORTUNITY TO TRY TO REACH EARTH IN IT!

THAT'S THE BEST NEWS I'VE HEARD IN A HUNDRED YEARS!

WHEN THE MAGNETICALLY-PROPELLED SHIP WAS FINISHED, THE LARGEST MOON CROWD EVER ASSEMBLED WATCHED THE TAKE-OFF...

DO YOU THINK THE ROBOT EARTHMAN WILL RETURN WITH OUR TWO PILOTS?

I DO. WE LIKE AND RESPECT HIM, BUT ON EARTH HE'LL BE ONLY A MECHANICAL FREAK! NO ONE WILL BELIEVE HIS HISTORY!

416

SHE SUDDENLY SAT UP! I WAS SHOCKED WHEN I SAW HER FACE -- BUT I DESPERATELY WANTED TO TALK TO HER...

DON'T BE AFRAID! I AM YOUR FRIEND!

SCREAMING IN TERROR, SHE BOUNDED AWAY. I FOLLOWED -- AND FOUND MYSELF CONFRONTED BY THE UGLIEST MEN I HAD EVER SEEN! SOME FLED; OTHERS CROUCHED AND GIBBERED AND GROWLED LIKE ANIMALS!

I AM HERE AS YOUR FRIEND! LET ME TALK TO YOU! I HAVE MUCH TO ASK YOU -- AND MUCH TO EXPLAIN!

FOR ANSWER, THE MEN CAME AT ME WITH ROCKS AND CLUBS!...

SEEING THAT THEIR WEAPONS WERE HARMLESS AGAINST ME, THEY ATTACKED BODILY! BUT MY STEEL MUSCLES WERE TOO MUCH FOR THIS SAVAGE REMNANT OF HUMANITY!

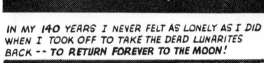

CIVILIZATION -- GONE! BUT WHAT CAUSED IT? SURELY MAN WASN'T SO STUPID AS TO HAVE DESTROYED HIMSELF!

OR WAS HE?

IN MY 140 YEARS I NEVER FELT AS LONELY AS I DID WHEN I TOOK OFF TO TAKE THE DEAD LUNARITES BACK -- TO RETURN FOREVER TO THE MOON!

THE END

During the early 1950s, the adverse publicity arising out of the controversy over the crime content in certain titles focused national attention on the industry, and comic books, for the first time, were recognized as a media of communication. While the critics took a firm stand against comic books, there were other institutions who viewed the media from an entirely new perspective. A few leading educators expressed the revolutionary idea that textbooks could be made in comic book format and used as an effective learning tool for young children. Some publishers, such as D-C Comics, went along with the idea and did produce special educational issues about their characters. But their concept was suppressed by opposing parties and the educational issues of *Superman*, for example, did not go very far.

Renville H. McMann, president of the United States Lawn Tennis Association had an altogether different idea. He felt that the comic book was an ideal tool for promoting and teaching tennis to the nation's youth, and in October 1956 his organization introduced the first issue of *Tennis Comics*, created by William H. Hutton Associates, the studio that produced the story material for many of the later issues of the *Classics Illustrated* series.

Tennis Comics No. 1 tells a story about two high school students, Steve Granger and Red Martin, who are interested in sports. They learn that tennis develops speed, stamina, strength, and skill and that it is a sport that can be enjoyed for a lifetime. The two boys meet former heavyweight boxing champion Gene Tunney, and Ralph Kiner, ex-major league baseball star, plus a few other famous sports celebrities, each of whom tells Steve and Red that playing tennis is the finest physical conditioning exercise in the world. Steve and Red naturally become interested in tennis and begin practicing for the Junior Davis Cup Championship.

Tennis Comics No. 1 (Oct. 1956)
©1956 William H. Hutton Associates, Inc.

The federal government also took a close look at the comic book as an educational device. In April 1956, the Social Security Administration introduced *Social Security Comics No. 1* featuring "John's First Job." The sixteen-page comic book told the story that lay behind a person's social security number. Here is a page from that issue . . .

Social Security Administration (April 1956)

Better Publications, Inc.

Thrilling Comics No. 3 (April 1940)
©1940 Better Publications, Inc.

Startling Comics No. 1 (June 1940)
©1940 Better Publications, Inc.

"Thrilling Magazines" was the once famous trademark of Better Publications, Inc., a major publisher of pulp fiction during the 1930s and 1940s whose titles included *Thrilling Wonder Stories, Thrilling Detective, Thrilling Sports, Thrilling Love, Thrilling Ranch Stories, Thrilling Western, Thrilling Spy Stories, Thrilling Mystery, Startling Stories, Black Book Detective, Captain Future, Everyday Astrology,* and several others.

In January 1940, Better Publications entered the comic field and placed its "trademark" on the first title *Thrilling Comics,* a magazine of superhero fantasy featuring Dr. Strange. When Dr. Hugo Strange invented "Alosin," a miraculous medical ingredient, and swallowed periodic dosages of it, he acquired incredible superhuman powers which he used to combat crime and evil around the world. *Thrilling Comics* also included the Ghost, a costumed crime fighter who, as George Chance, was raised and tutored in India where he mastered the "magic" skills of a form of yoga which he deftly applied to combat crime upon his return to America. In addition, the magazine contained several western and adventure features, one of which was "Three Comrades," created by Howard Sherman who is better known for his outstanding work on the early "Dr. Fate" stories in D-C's *More Fun Comics.*

When *Thrilling Comics* debuted on the newsstands, the titles created legal problems for Fawcett Publications. Fawcett had planned to introduce their own *Thrill Comics* a few weeks later but cancelled it after circulating a few complementary samples to the dealers. Fawcett reprinted their book as *Whiz Comics No. 2* (see Section 4, Captain Marvel).

In June 1940, Better Publications introduced *Startling Comics,* a title borrowed from their popular science fiction pulp magazine, *Startling Stories.* But the influence of the pulp did not stop at the title. *Startling Comics* introduced a superhero called "Captain Future," a name borrowed directly from Better Publications science fiction hero also called Captain Future who had headlined his own pulp magazine many years before. However, the character concept of the Captain Future in the comic book was quite different from the pulp hero. Here, research scientist Dr. Andrew Bryant, while experimenting with crossing gamma rays with infrared light waves, had one of those laboratory accidents so typical of the genre that suddenly transformed him into an invulnerable super being with flying ability. And Captain Future followed the path of other crime fighting superheroes.

Startling Comics also contained "The Mysterious Dr. X," a clever feature created by an unknown artist which ran for only a few issues. In the introductory episode, Dr. X, a master of the occult sciences, engages in an experiment to project the astral body of his niece Cynthia across space to the distant world of Inus. By hooking up a televisor screen to Cynthia's brain, Dr. X could observe her thought impressions as the astral form arrives on Inus as shown here . . .

Cynthia encounters several hostile monstrosities, but since she exists as an ethereal spirit she can not be physically harmed. But she can be frightened to the point that she might suffer a fatal heart attack, which would be disastrous to her physical being on Earth. Upon observing Cynthia's astral form fleeing to escape the hideous creatures that pursued her and then checking Cynthia's heartbeat, Dr. X summons her fiance Bob Stone and projects his astral body to Inus to rescue her. But complications arise when Bob reaches Cynthia for the two can not determine if they are alive or experiencing a dream—and then they become aware of pain as the creatures attack them. Something has gone wrong with Dr. X's projection equipment, and Bob and Cynthia are stranded on Inus!

Mystico, the Wonder Man, also made his debut in *Startling Comics No. 1.* In this feature a crazed scientist seeking to resurrect the dead as a means for building an invincible army, steals a mummy from a nearby museum to test the effectiveness of his "vita-ray" machine. The mummy slowly responds to the experiment, but as the scientist increases the machine's power it suddenly explodes and the building collapses, killing everyone inside—except the revitalized mummy. Returned to life, the mummy finds that he still possesses the same magic powers he had when he lived during an ancient era. Adopting a 20th century guise, he assumes the identity of Mystico and sets out to serve humanity and fight crime and evil.

Startling Comics No. 10 introduced the Fighting Yank, a patriotic superhero created by Richard Hughes and Jon Blummer. In reality, the Fighting Yank was mild-mannered Bruce Carter III who discovered a peculiar cloak that once belonged to one of his ancestors. Upon donning the cloak, Carter found that it gave him the power of flight and protected him from gunfire. He fashioned a skintight costume, a triangular hat reminiscent of Paul Revere, and a face mask, and leaped into action to defend America against the Axis Powers. The Fighting Yank became the star attraction of *Startling Comics* and also headlined his own quarterly magazine between 1942 and 1949.

Better Publications also introduced *Exciting Comics* which began in April 1940 and ran until 1949. The ninth issue introduced "Black Terror," created by Richard Hughes and David Gabrielsen. The Black Terror, who emerged as the most popular of the Better Publications' family of superheroes, was in reality druggist Bob Benton who accidentally discovered a revolutionary pharmaceutical compound that endowed him with superhuman strength. In addition to starring in *Exciting Comics*, the Black Terror was featured in his own full-length magazine which also ran between 1942 and 1949.

Dr. Strange, Captain Future, the Black Terror, and the Fighting Yank were featured together in *America's Best Comics*, another title which Better Publications produced during the 1940s. There were also a few non-superhero titles as *Mystery Comics, Best Comics*, and one 196-page issue of *America's Biggest Comics Book*. However, by 1950, Better Publications had discontinued its comic book line and soon after dropped its line of pulp magazines. The latter move, along with Street & Smith's departure from the pulp field, had for the most part brought an end to the era of pulp fiction.

Startling Stories, Vol. 18, No. 2 (Nov. 1948)
©1948 Better Publications, Inc.
includes: "The Visitor" by Ray Bradbury

Better Magazines of 1940
©1940 Better Publications, Inc.

Culture Publications

Spicy Adventure Stories (Dec. 1942)
(Last Issue) ©1942 Culture Publications, Inc.

Spicy Mystery (March 1941)
©1941 Culture Publications, Inc.

Culture Publications was one of the short-lived obscure publishers of pulp fiction between 1939 and 1942 whose two *Spicy* magazines never quite captured a large readership. However, the company did introduce an unusual innovation in their magazines that heralded an important phase in the history of comic books. *Spicy Adventure Stories,* which was essentially a pulp magazine with short story fiction of high adventure, sex, and violent action, also included the comic strip feature "Diana Daw," created by artist Clayton Maxwell. Although the feature was not exceptional, it did nevertheless represent the first attempt for a pulp magazine to include comics within its text contents.

The feature centered around the interplanetary adventures of female explorer Diana Daw. When Diana's spaceship ran out of fuel and drifted into the asteroid belt between Mars and Jupiter, she crash-landed on one of the tiny worlds and was captured by sinister flying harpies who placed her in a glass cage for exhibition while they debated whether to kill her and eat her or just kill her. When her boy friend Ted set out to find her, he located the planetoid where her ship had crashed. After he landed and set out on foot to trace Diana, he was seized by the Harpies and thrown into the same cage with her. The two plotted a daring escape as shown here . . .

"Diana Daw" ©1942 Culture Publications, Inc.

Culture's companion title, *Spicy Mystery*, included short stories that often fell into the science fiction category—and the comic strip "Vera Ray" that featured an adventurous heroine who found action and excitement in a hidden city near the center of the Earth.

Avon Periodicals

In July 1950 Avon Periodicals, now a major publisher of mass market paperback books, carried the idea of the "comic-pulp" one step further by including thirty-two pages of color comics in their new science fiction pulp magazine *Out of this World Adventures.* While the text section included stories by such noted science fiction authors as Ray Cummings, A. E. Van Vogt, and Lester Del Rey, the color comics section included "Lunar Station," a science fiction adventure written by John Michel and illustrated by Joe Kubert, and the classic origin of "Crom, the Barbarian," written by Gardner Fox and illustrated by John Guinta.

In the tradition of first class sword-and-sorcery fantasy, Crom lives in the ancient legendary era during the dawn of civilization when a man's sword and wits were his only defense against the greed that arose from the arts of black magic that ruled the day. One day while a caravan of the Aesir tribe was travelling through the countryside and had stopped at a small lake to water their horses, a renegade band of Cymri warriors suddenly sprang out of hiding in the hills and attacked them. The Aesir tribe was slaughtered—except for Crom and his sister, Lalla. Crom fought courageously as the Cymri seized his sister and carried her off to a waiting boat. Crom swam out to rescue her and a vicious battle followed after he climbed aboard. Although Crom slew his enemies, a mortally wounded Cymri whacked him on the head with the blunt edge of the ax before toppling over the side and into the water.

The boat drifted aimlessly for days as Lalla attempted to revive her brother. When Crom eventually awoke their boat had drifted toward an island ruled by a strange sorcerer who claimed that he had witnessed the barbarian's fight in the smoke of herb fires and had directed the wind to send their boat to him. The sorcerer revealed that he sought eternal youth and needed a vial filled with the mystical water that flowed from a special fountain in the distant city of Ophir. He commands Crom to go to the city to fill the vial and bring it back to him. The sorcerer further informs Crom that the city is filled with untold treasures in gold and jewels which are his for the taking—but that if he refuses to go or if he does not return with the vial filled with the precious water, his sister, who would be held as a hostage, will be slain.

Before Crom can draw his sword, the sorcerer's gaze places him under a hypnotic spell to carry out the order.

With Lalla a prisoner of the sorcerer, Crom takes the empty vial and sails to Ophir where he eventually finds the black tower that houses the fountain of youth. He fights his way past the guards until he comes upon the forbidden chambers whose doors

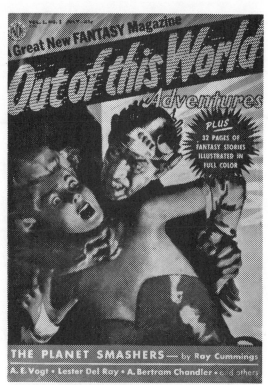

Out of This World Adventures No. 1
(July 1950) ©1950 Avon Periodicals, Inc.

open to a corridor leading to the fountain—but the corridor is blocked by a gigantic flesh-eating serpent which uncoils itself and lunges at him. After a desperate struggle, Crom drives his sword through the serpent's head and kills it. As he reaches into the fountain to fill the vial, Queen Tanit quietly enters the room and creeps up behind him with a knife poised to plunge into his back. But Crom ducks the thrust, seizes her, and takes her as a hostage to insure his safe passage through the city. He propels Queen Tanit aboard his boat to prevent her soldiers from following him. On the way back to the sorcerer's island, the queen falls in love with Crom and begs him to return to Ophir to rule beside her after he has delivered the vial and his sister is released.

Upon reaching the island, the sorcerer takes the vial, hurriedly drinks the water, and then advises Crom and the queen that they must die for they have learned his secret. The sorcerer's appearance begins to change. His aged wrinkles vanish and his white hair grows black! With each passing moment, he grows younger . . . and soon he becomes an adolescent . . . then a little boy . . . then a baby . . . and finally he disappears!

Queen Tanit explains that the sorcerer gulped the water too fast and it had a disastrous effect he hadn't counted on. Crom, his bride-to-be, and his sister depart for Ophir—but do they reach the city?

The question was to be answered in the next adventure of "Crom" which was never published. Donald A. Wollheim was the magazine's editor, and he incorporated different comic stories in the next two issues. *Out of this World Adventures* was terminated with the third issue, and Wollheim left Avon Periodicals to form his own publishing company, DAW Books which is currently a leader in paperback science fiction.

Meanwhile, Avon had entered the comic book field and introduced the popular "Avon Fantasy Classics" series. One of the best issues in the series was *An Earth Man on Venus* (1951), a novel-length science fiction adventure written by Ralph Milne Farely and illustrated by Wally Wood. The story centered around Miles Cabot, a radio specialist who, while experimenting with an invention for transmitting physical objects by radio waves, unknowingly caused a phenomenal lightning flash that catapulted him through space to Venus before he realized what had happened. Here, Miles encounters fantastic experiences with all types of intelligent insect life, some of which are friendly and others which are hostile and dangerous. He forms a close alliance with a giant ant who saves his life on many occasions, and he falls in love with a beautiful "Cupian" princess who is part human and part insect. In the midst of a civil war that erupts within the Cupian society, and the all-out world war that erupts between the Cupian species and the giant ants, Miles, together with his ant colleague and the princess, eventually overcome all obstacles and succeed in bringing peace to the strife-torn planet which becomes Miles' new home.

A few of the other Fantasy Classics' issues included *Flying Saucers* and *The Mask of Dr. Fu Manchu*. Avon, however, published only a handful of titles within the series which ran between 1950 and 1951 and soon after ceased its activities in comic books altogether (which had also included other titles in the crime and romance categories).

An Earthman on Venus No. 1 (1951)
©1951 Avon Periodicals, Inc.

©1951 Avon Periodicals, Inc.

Komos Publications

In 1940, Komos Publications burst upon the comic book field and then just as abruptly left it within the same year after producing three issues of an obscure title called *Superworld Comics*. However, the company behind *Superworld Comics* was established by Hugo Gernsbach, who is better known as the founder of *Amazing Stories,* the first magazine of science fiction, and as previously noted a magazine that contributed greatly to the growth of the comic book industry. In addition to featuring the first story of Buck Rogers in 1928, *Amazing Amazing Stories* also introduced such famous authors as Ray Bradbury whose classic stories were later adapted to comic book format in E-C's *Weird Science* and *Weird Fantasy,* and Otto Binder, who started in *Amazing Stories,* and then switched from writing science fiction to write the bulk of the story material for Fawcett's "Captain Marvel" and the "Marvel Family" during the mid-1940s and early 1950s.

Amazing Stories also introduced the famous art of Frank R. Paul who painted the dynamic cover illustrations for the early issues during the 1920s. Paul's unique style of depicting spaceships, alien life forms, robots, and complex machinery which did not exist at the time, shaped a surrealistic art form of scientific fantasy which in itself became a major influence in the graphic execution of many comic book features that would come later.

Gernsbach, however, was only associated with *Amazing Stories* as its publisher during the first three years from 1926 to 1929. Due to mounting financial problems, Gernsbach sold his original firm, Experimenter Publishing Company (which included *Amazing Stories*), to Radio-Science Publications who assumed ownership of the magazine in May 1929 and continued it, following the science fiction format that Gernsbach had originated.

Then in September 1931, Gernsbach formed a new company, Stellar Publications, to produce another science fiction pulp magazine, *Wonder Stories,* and a few science trade journals that included *Radio-Craft* and *Everyday Science and Mechanics,* with Frank R. Paul as the art director for the three publications. Nine years later, Gernsbach formed Komos Publications as a special comic book division of Stellar Publications, and the one title, *Superworld Comics,* included cover art by Frank R. Paul and two original science fiction features created by Frank R. Paul—"Marvo 1-2 Go," about a teenage space explorer of the 26th Century who was programmed with super intelligence, and "Mitey Powers," that featured an Earth ambassador to Mars who helped the Martian people overthrow a tyrannical government.

Superworld Comics No. 3 (Aug. 1940)
(Last Issue) ©1940 Hugo Gernsbach

Superworld Comics also included reprints of Winsor McKay's classic "Little Nemo" series about the fantasy dream sequences which first appeared as a newspaper comic strip in the *New York Herald* on October 15, 1905. In addition, the comic book contained several illustrated science articles.

In March 1953, Gernsbach introduced the first large-size "slick" science fiction magazine, *Science Fiction Plus,* with Frank R. Paul as its art director. The first issue included stories by John Campbell, and Otto Binder who had returned to writing science fiction in collaboration with his brother Earl under their joint pen name "Eando Binder."

Meanwhile, *Amazing Stories* had changed hands again. It is currently owned by Ultimate Publishing Company headed by Sol Cohen, who also owns *Fantastic Adventures,* a science fiction pulp which was produced during the 1940s and 1950s by Ziff-Davis Publications. In the early 1950s, Ziff-Davis introduced a line of more than two dozen comic book titles on a wide variety of topics such as *Bill Stern's Sports Book, Perfect Love, Crime Clinic, Weird Thrillers, Teenie Weenies,* and *Kid Cowboy,* to name a few. Sol Cohen, the present publisher of the first magazine of science fiction was associated with D-C Publications in 1937 as the sales manager, and was responsible for promoting "Superman" as the first national comic book of superhero fantasy.

Amazing Stories (Aug. 1927)
©1927 Experimeter Publishing Co., Inc.
includes: "War of The Worlds," Part I
(cover art by Frank R. Paul)

Amazing Stories (Sept. 1927)
©1927 Experimeter Publishing Co., Inc.
includes: "War of The Worlds," Conclusion
(Cover art by Frank R. Paul)

Amazing Stories (Aug. 1928)
©1928 Experimeter Publishing Co., Inc.
includes: "Armaggeddon-2419" (Origin of Buck Rogers) (cover art by
Frank R. Paul)

Amazing Stories (March 1929)
©1929 Experimeter Publishing Co., Inc.
includes: "Airlords of Han" (Sequel to Origin of Buck Rogers) (cover
art by F.R. Paul)

The Dime Novel

Beadle Pocket Library No. 20
©1860 Eratus F. Beadle

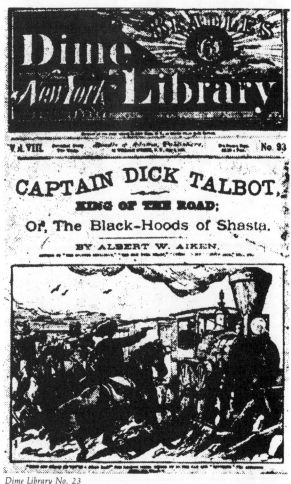

Dime Library No. 23
©1863 Eratus F. Beadle

If the comic book and the pulp magazine appeared to be closely linked to each other, it was due to the fact that the great-granddaddy of them both was *Beadle Dime Novel*, founded by Erastus F. Beadle in 1860 and published twice monthly for thirty years up to 1893. These 32-page booklets sold for ten cents and contained short story fiction with an early American background. The stories dwelled upon the country's growth from the landing of the first settlers to the taming of the Wild West frontier.

In the beginning, each booklet was titled after its story. The first issue, January 1860, was "Malaeska," an original pioneer-Indian classic drawn along the lines of James Fenimore Cooper's famous "The Last of the Mohicans." "Malaeska" and "The Last of the Mohicans" set the foundation for the much later literary trend of features in the "Daniel Boone" category, a popular subject for many character concepts in the adventure pulps of the 1930s and comic books of the 1940s.

During 1868, Beadle expanded the dime novel into two monthly publications. One was called *Beadle's Pocket Library* which stressed historical drama while the second, *Pluck and Luck*, popularized stories that became

known as "blood and thunder tales." One of *Pluck and Luck's* most famous authors was Mrs. Ann S. Stephans who wrote more than 200 blood and thunder tales of the Wild West. Mrs. Stephans not only introduced the heroic action adventure of the fast-drawing cowboy, but she conceived as well the first heroic legends of Buffalo Bill, Kit Carson, Wild Bill Hickok, frontier marshals like Wyatt Earp, and frontier bad men like Billy the Kid and Jesse James.

After Beadle's death in 1893, *Pluck and Luck* was continued by Frank Tousey, who lowered the price tag to five cents and increased publication to weekly circulation. Tousey also added two new titles, *Wild West Weekly* (which often contained reprints of Mrs. Stephans' stories) and *Secret Service*, both of which would spark the growth of the Wild West and detective pulp magazines. The quick-on-the-draw cowboy and the secret agent would later become two of the most popular adventure themes in comic books.

In addition, the new dime novel under Frank Tousey began to utilize hand-drawn illustrations that accompanied the text—a practice that would be adopted by pulp publishers of the 1920s and 1930s.

Pluck and Luck also featured a few "blood and thunder tales of science and invention" that would later, by 1926, satisfy Hugo Gernsbach's definition of science fiction as published in *Amazing Stories*. A good example is "Two Boys Trip to an Unknown Planet" by Richard Montgomery which appeared in *Pluck and Luck* October 2, 1901.

In this story, Montgomery described the use of a galleon ship supported by air-filled balloons which lifted it into the sky until it floated beyond the clouds and into space towards a small undetected planetoid that was much closer to Earth than the moon. Although Montgomery's description lacked scientific credibility, the story nevertheless introduced an intriguing suggestion that a small undetected planetoid just might exist somewhere in outer space. The suggestion was explored further in pulp science fiction of the 1930s and was often utilized in comic books of the 1940s. It was in 1942 that Captain Marvel discovered a small undetected planetoid just beyond the atmosphere when he was searching for Mr. Mind's headquarters.

In the wake of the growing competition from the higher quality "slick" magazines, Tousey's cheaper line of weekly dime novels, which was viewed by many literary critics as a hindrance to better reading, was eventually discontinued by 1912. Except for *Wild West Weekly* which was continued for a while by Street & Smith, Towsey's dime novels vanished from sight and were soon dismissed as having had no literary value. During the 1920s the first pulp magazines came into existence. Included were *Weird Tales* beginning in 1923 and then *Amazing Stories* beginning in 1926. Their precursor, the dime novel, suddenly came to light again almost thirty years later after its seeming demise at the New York World's Fair in 1939 when a few samples of the genre were displayed as part of an exhibit of rare books by American publishers.

During this exhibit, the staff of the New York Public Library, for the first time anywhere, appraised the dime novel as *A VALUABLE HISTORICAL RECORD* that portrayed the struggles, exploits, trials, hardships and dangers of the early American pioneers who settled this country. A nationwide search was conducted to uncover *any* dime novel specimens that might have been buried among old attic relics. Unfortunately, only a few hundred were found, and the outbreak of World War II brought an end to the search. The dime novels that were then to be found were turned over to junk dealers as part of the national paper drive, a lamentable graveyard for the grandfather of popular American literature as well as for its direct descendants, the famous pulp magazines and comic books of the then current day.

Pluck and Luck No. 174 (Oct. 1901)
©1901 Frank Tousey

Pluck and Luck No. 567 (April 1909)
©1909 Frank Tousey

A CHRONOLOGICAL SUMMARY OF THE DEVELOPMENT OF COMIC BOOK
LITERATURE—1895

1860: Erastus F. Beadle introduces the *Dime Novel* as the first ten-cent magazine of short story fiction.

1895: The *New York World* (May 5, 1895) introduces R. F. Outcault's "Circus in Hogan's Alley" as the first humor comic strip with a cast of regular characters.

1896: "Circus in Hogan's Alley" changes its title to "Hogan's Alley" in which Yellow Kid emerges as the strip's main character; and the strip's creator, R. F. Outcault, quits the *World* and joins W. R. Hearst's *New York Journal* to resume the comic strip as "Yellow Kid" which subsequently emerges as the first continuing character of the comic strip, but is discontinued two years later. Street & Smith introduces *Tip Top Weekly* with Burt L. Standish's "Frank Merriwell" series as the first continuing hero in dime novel short story fiction.

1897: The *New York Journal* (December 12, 1897) introduces Rudolph Dirk's "Katzenjammer Kids" which emerges as the first major comic strip feature to be syndicated in many different newspapers and becomes one of the first strips to be reprinted in comic book format during the 1930s.

1912: *All Story Magazine* introduces Edgar Rice Burroughs' "Tarzan of the Apes" which later emerges as a major adventure comic strip feature.

1917: Pat Sullivan's Felix, the Cat begins as the first continuing character of animated cartoon films and is later adapted to comic book format as a major feature in the animal fantasy category.

1922: Embee Distributing Company publishes eight black-and-white issues of *Comic Monthly* with reprints of daily newspaper strips, and the magazine serves as the forerunner to the color comic book that begins in the next decade.

1923: *Weird Tales* begins as the first pulp magazine of supernatural fantasy.

1926: *Amazing Stories* begins as the first pulp magazine of science fiction.

1927: Walt Disney introduces Mickey Mouse in animated cartoon form.

1928: Buck Rogers begins in *Amazing Stories*.

1929: Hollywood introduces sound movie serials; Universal Pictures adapts "Tarzan of the Apes" as its first movie serial in sound. United Feature Syndicate introduces "Tarzan of the Apes" as a comic strip for newspaper syndication; and John F. Dille Syndicate introduces "Buck Rogers" as a comic strip for newspaper syndication. *Weird Tales* introduces Robert E. Howard's "Shadow Kingdom" and the genre of sword-and-sorcery fantasy begins.

1930: Mickey Mouse begins as a newspaper comic strip.

1932: The Lone Ranger begins in radio drama as the first continuing hero in Wild West fiction. Buck Rogers is adapted to radio drama. King Features Syndicate introduces Alex Raymond's "Flash Gordon" series as a comic strip for newspaper syndication.

1933: Whitman Publishing Company introduces the *Big Little Book*. Eastern Color Printing Company introduces full color comic book premiums.

1934: Eastern Color Printing Company introduces *Famous Funnies* as the first monthly comic book in full color which features reprints of syndicated comic strips in the newspaper, and reprints of "Buck Rogers" begin in the third issue. Universal Pictures adapts Hal Forrest's "Tailspin Tommy" to the screen as Hollywood's first movie serial based on a comic strip feature. Donald Duck appears in the newspaper comic strip "Silly Symphonies."

1935: D-C Comics introduces *New Fun Comics*, the first comic book to feature original humor stories that never appeared as a comic strip in the newspapers. Leon Schlesinger Studios introduces Porky Pig in animated form as the first Warner Brothers' character.

1936: Universal Pictures adapts "Flash Gordon" to the screen as Hollywood's second movie serial based on a comic strip character which becomes a movie serial classic. King Features Syndicate introduces *King Comics* which features reprints of "Flash Gordon," "Mandrake," "Popeye," "King of the Royal Mounted," and other comic strips. United Feature Syndicate introduces *Tip Top Comics* featuring reprints of "Tarzan," "Captain and The (Katzenjammer) Kids," "Tailspin Tommy," and other comic strips.

1937: D-C Comics introduces *Detective Comics*, the first comic book to feature original short story detective fiction. Republic Pictures adapts three comic strip characters to the movie serial: "Dick Tracy," "Jungle Jim," and "Secret Agent X-9."

1938: D-C Comics introduces *Action Comics* featuring Jerry Siegel's and Joe Shuster's "Superman," and the era of superhero fantasy begins. Fiction House introduces *Jumbo Comics* featuring William Thomas' "Sheena." Bugs Bunny debuts in an animated cartoon about Porky Pig.

1939: Timely Publications introduces *Marvel Comics* featuring the origin of the Human Torch, and the origin of Sub-Mariner reprinted from *Motion Picture Funnies Weekly*. Batman begins in *Detective Comics*, and the Spectre begins in *More Fun Comics*. Universal Pictures adapts "Buck Rogers" to the movie serial, and Columbia Pictures adapts "Mandrake" to the movie serial.

1940: Dell Publishing Company adapts characters from animated cartoons and introduces *Walt Disney Comics* featuring Mickey Mouse and Donald Duck, and other comic books that feature Bugs Bunny, Porky Pig, Felix, Andy Panda, Woody Woodpecker, and others. Street & Smith introduces comic books based on their leading pulp heroes, The Shadow and Doc Savage. Fiction House introduces the single theme comic books with titles as *Jungle Comics, Wings Comics*, and *Planet Comics*. Invisible Scarlet O'Neil begins in *Famous Funnies*. The Justice Society of America is organized in *All Star Comics No. 3*. Eastern color Printing Company publishes the first full-length comic book edition of Buck Rogers. United Feature Syndicate publishes the first full-length comic book color edition of Tarzan. King Features Syndicate publishes the first full length comic book editions of Prince Valiant and Flash Gordon. Daredevil begins in *Silver Streak Comics*. Columbia Pictures adapts "The Shadow" and "Terry and the Pirates" for the movie serials; Universal Pictures adapts "The Green Hornet" for the movie serial; and Republic Pictures adapts "Red Ryder" and "King of the Royal Mounted" for the movie serial. Captain Thunder becomes Captain Marvel in *Whiz Comics*.

1941: The outbreak of World War II sparks a wave of patriotic themes in comic book literature. Tex Thomson becomes Mr. America in *Action Comics No. 33* as the nation's first patriotic hero in comic books. Timely Publications introduces Captain America, and Fawcett Publications publishes the first full-length comic book edition of Spy Smasher. Fawcett also publishes the origin of Captain Nazi in *Master Comics No. 21* as the first anti-American super villain in comic books and the origin of Captain Marvel Jr. in *Whiz Comics No. 25* whose chief opponent becomes Captain Nazi. Human Torch and Sub-Mariner team up for the first time in *Marvel Mystery Comics No. 17* to fight the Axis powers. Daredevil battles Hitler in the first full-length edition of *Daredevil Comics*. Eastern Color Printing Company introduces *Heroic Comics* featuring Hydroman and other superhero characters but which later adopts a new format to become the first magazine of illustrated military history. Hillman Periodicals introduces *Air Fighters Comics* with the origin of Airboy in the second issue and the origin of the Heap in the third issue. Quality Comics Group introduces *Military Comics* featuring Blackhawk and several patriotic characters. Quality also introduces *Police Comics* and its Plastic Man. Gilberton Company introduces the first series of Classic Comics. Fox Features introduces *Big-3 Comics* whose title unintentionally creates confusion on the newsstands and is terminated with the seventh issue. Max Fleischer Studios adapts Superman for animated cartoons. And Republic Pictures adapts Captain Marvel for the movie serial.

1942: Eastern Color Printing Company publishes its 100th Anniversary Issue of *Famous Funnies*. Wonder Woman starts in *Sensation Comics* and later becomes Secretary of the Justice Society of America in *All Star Comics*. Archie begins in *Pep Comics*. Captain Marvel discovers his twin sister, Mary Marvel, and battles an all-villain team led by Mr. Mind. Gleason Publications introduces *Crime Does Not Pay* and *Boy Comics* featuring Crimebuster versus Iron Jaw. Superman moves to radio drama and the adventures of Superboy begin in *More Fun Comics*. Republic Pictures adapts Spy Smasher for the movie serial which emerges as one of Hollywood's major patriotic films. Fawcett Publications introduces the first issue of *Captain Midnight Comics* which coincides with Columbia's release of the *Captain Midnight* movie serial.

1943: Columbia Pictures adapts D-C's Batman and King Features' Phantom for the movie serial.

1944: Republic Pictures adapts Captain America for the movie serial.

1945: The end of World War II causes demise of the patriotic and war themes in comic books. Spy Smasher becomes Crime Smasher, and Captain America as Steve Rogers becomes school teacher. Dell adapts Little Lulu to comic books. D-C Comics introduces *Real Screen Comics* featuring "The Fox and The Crow" animal fantasy series by James Davis.

1946: Big Chief Wahoo concludes his patriotic adventure in *Famous Funnies*.

1947: Fox Features introduces *Sunny, America's Sweetheart*, the first confession comic book with a romance theme. Imitations of *Crime Does Not Pay* begin to appear. Columbia Pictures adapts King Features' "Brick Bradford" and the "Vigilante" feature from *Action Comics* for the movie serial.

1948: Columbia Pictures adapts two more *Action Comics'* features for the movie serial, first "Superman" and then "Congo Bill."

1949: Columbia Pictures adapts Batman for a movie serial remake. Fox Features introduces a series of confession comic books as *My Great Love, My Intimate Affair, My Love Life* and others which establish a new trend in comic book literature. Quality Comics follows the trend with the first full-length edition of *Torchy*, and the Marvel Comics discontinues its superhero features and replaces them with romance titles. Fawcett Publications introduces *Exciting Romances, Cowboy Love Comics, Sweetheart Diary* and other similar confession comic books. D-C Comics introduces *Girl's Love Stories*, and Dell introduces the fourth issue of "Tillie the Toiler" in the "4-Color" series. Street & Smith discontinues its comic book line featuring Doc Savage and the Shadow, and also discontinues its pulp line to develop *Mademoiselle Magazine*.

1950: Publisher William M. Gaines introduces the "E-C Comics" series with the horror titles beginning in mid-1950. Columbia Pictures adapts Superman for another movie serial.

1951: Imitations of the "E-C" horror titles begin to appear as the changing trend in comic book literature stresses crime titles, horror titles, and romance titles with themes of sex and violence. The new trend creates widespread controversy and the crusade of critics begins against comic book publishers. D-C Comics enters lawsuit against Fawcett Publications for alleged copyright infringement on Superman.

1952: The impact of television as home entertainment begins to threaten the motion picture industry, the comic book industry, pulp magazines, radio drama, and the adventure comic strip in the newspaper. Columbia Pictures adapts Blackhawk as Hollywood's last movie serial based on a character from the comics.

1953: As a result of the lawsuit with D-C Comics, Fawcett Publications discontinues Captain Marvel and phases out its comic book line. Dr. Frederic Wertham's book, *Seduction of the Innocent* causes nationwide anti-comic book hysteria.

1954: Senate subcommittee hearings investigate the critics' charges that claim comic books are responsible for juvenile delinquency. New York City Judge Charles F. Murphy is appointed to head the newly formed Comics Code Authority (September 17, 1954). Mickey Mouse moves to television.

1955: Comics Code Authority's Seal of Approval appears on all approved comic books beginning in January. The era of the Golden Age of Comics comes to an end as most publishers discontinue their magazines and quit the business. The "E-C" comic books are terminated; Gleason terminates *Crime Does Not Pay, Daredevil, Boy Comics* and other titles; the Quality Comic Group ceases publication as does the Fiction House; and Eastern Color Printing Company discontinues *Famous Funnies* after twenty-one years of monthly publication. The Thomas Alva Edison Foundation is formed to give national recognition to comic books of outstanding literary quality—three Dell titles and two Gilberton titles win awards. *Mad Comics* becomes *Mad Magazine*.

1956: The Silver Age of Comics begins with D-C's publication of *Showcase Comics No. 4* featuring the revival of the Flash as a different character concept, followed by the revival of Green Lantern in *Showcase Comics No. 22* and the revival of the Atom in *Showcase Comics No. 34*.

1961: The Marvel Comics Group introduces *Fantastic Four* as the first new superhero feature of the Silver Age, and later issues of *Fantastic Four* begin to include the first appearances of several Marvel characters as Dr. Doom, the revival of Sub-Mariner, the Inhumans, the Silver Surfer, Black Panther, and others.

1962: Spider-Man begins in *Amazing Fantasy Comics No. 15*. The Marvel Comics Group also introduces The Hulk and Thor.

1963: Hanna-Barbera, established in television animation with such humor programs as "The Flintstones," "Huckleberry Hound," and "Yogi Bear," begin to introduce other animated features that utilize the adventure and superhero fantasy element. The latter included "The Herculoids," "Space Ghost," and the popular "Jonny Quest," plus many others. The changing trend toward adventure in television animation was developed further as the Marvel Comics Group adapts "Spiderman" and "Fantastic Four" for animated programs while D-C adapts "Superman" for live television. Similarly, several comic strip characters of King Features Syndicate are adapted for animated television over the next few years, including "Flash Gordon."

1965: James Warren introduces black-and-white photo illustrated magazines about the former science fiction and fright movies of the 1950s in such titles as *Creepy Magazine, Eerie Magazine,* and *Vampirella* which also include some black-and-white comic book art. Warren's magazines start the trend for the revival of "monster fantasy" and for adult-oriented illustrated publications that are similar to comic books but which lay beyond the jurisdiction of the Comics Code Authority.

1966: Batman becomes a television hit and sparks renewed interest in superhero fantasy from the Golden Age of Comics. A rare copy of *Action Comics No. 1* is found and sells for $2,000 as a valuable literary antique. The Green Hornet is adapted to television and introduces Bruce Lee in the role of "Kato" whose dynamic performance later becomes instrumental in influencing comic book adaptions of martial arts adventure and fantasy.

1967: Gold Key Comics introduces the comic book adaptation of "Star Trek" based on the popular television series.

1968: D-C Comics introduces *The Swamp Thing* as a revival of the Golden Age concept of the Heap. The Marvel Comics Group revives Captain America.

1970: Comic book literature features sword-and-sorcery fantasy with Marvel's introduction of *Conan, the Barbarian* adapted from Robert E. Howard's literary innovation that originated in the 1929 *Weird Tales* story, "Shadow Kingdom." Robert Overstreet introduces *The Comic Book Price Guide*, the first published attempt to identify and list discontinued and back-issue comic books for establishing their current market values as literary antiques.

1972: D-C adapts "Tarzan of the Apes" for a new comic book series with art by Joe Kubert.

1973: D-C Comics revives Captain Marvel as "Shazam" for a new comic book series with art by C. C. Beck, and then revives the Shadow. Marvel's "Black Panther," comicdom's first black superhero, begins his own comic book series.

1974: "Shazam" is adapted for live television; and D-C Comics introduces the "Famous First Edition" series featuring a limited number of oversize reprints of the Golden Age comic books that contained the first appearance of Superman, Batman, Wonder Woman, Captain Marvel, and the Flash. The Marvel Comics Group introduces the comic book adaptation of "Planet of the Apes" based on the popular movie and television series, and *Deadly Hands of Kung Fu*, the first magazine devoted to martial arts film reviews and original comic stories about martial arts heroes of the Orient featuring Chang-Chi.

1976: Tarzan and the Katzenjammer Kids are adapted for animated television, and Wonder Woman is adapted for live television. The Charlton Comics Group introduces the comic book adaptation of "Six Million Dollar Man" based on the popular television series, and the Marvel Comics Group introduces Howard, the Duck. Ultimate Publishing Company produces the 50th Year Anniversary Issue of *Amazing Stories*, the first magazine of science fiction. D-C Comics and the Marvel Comics Group collaborate to produce *Superman vs. The Amazing Spiderman*.

1977: Mickey Mouse becomes fifty-years old! Spider-Man is adapted for a live television special and also becomes the first superhero of recent times to be adapted from the comic book to newspaper syndication as a continuous adventure comic strip; and the Marvel Comics Group introduces Spider-Woman. Marvel also introduces the comic book adaptation of "Star Wars" based on the popular movie while D-C Comics introduces Black Lightning. Hollywood plans full-length movies on comic strip characters and enters film production for "Superman" and "Flash Gordon." Hollywood also enters film production for a new television series of "Buck Rogers." A rare copy of *Marvel Comics No. 1* sells for $7,000 as a valuable literary antique.

1978: Buck Rogers is revived for television. *All Rare Magazine* begins. The first issue features Phil Nowlan's original Buck Rogers' adventure ("Armageddon-2419") reprinted from the August 1928 edition of *Amazing Stories*, and the second issue features H.G. Wells' original "War of the Worlds" reprinted from the May 1897 edition of *Cosmopolitan* with art by Warwick Gable. Marvel Comics Group introduces a historical book of cover reproductions of the Golden Age titles of Timely Publications. D-C's *Action Comics* enters 40th year of publication.

Master Index

Index of Publishers' Titles

Specific comic book titles not mentioned in the Master Index will be found listed in alphabetical order at the end of each chapter: